Na Fianna Éireann and the Irish Revolution, 1909–23

Manchester University Press

Na Fianna Éireann and the Irish Revolution, 1909–23

Scouting for rebels

Marnie Hay

Manchester University Press

Copyright © Marnie Hay 2019

The right of Marnie Hay to be identified as the author of this work has been asserted by her in accordance with the Copyright, Designs and Patents Act 1988.

Published by Manchester University Press
Altrincham Street, Manchester M1 7JA, UK
www.manchesteruniversitypress.co.uk

British Library Cataloguing-in-Publication Data is available

ISBN 978 0 7190 9683 9 hardback
ISBN 978 1 5261 5612 9 paperback

First published by Manchester University Press in hardback 2019

This edition published 2021

The publisher has no responsibility for the persistence or accuracy of URLs for any external or third-party internet websites referred to in this book, and does not guarantee that any content on such websites is, or will remain, accurate or appropriate.

Typeset by TJ International Ltd, Padstow

For Ivar Will with love

Contents

List of figures	*page* viii
List of tables	ix
Acknowledgements	x
List of abbreviations	xii
1 Na Fianna Éireann in context	1
2 The countess and the Quaker	20
3 A handful of boys against the British Empire, 1909–16	37
4 Expansion and contraction, 1916–23	69
5 Who joined the Fianna?	101
6 The Fianna experience	130
7 Moulding minds and marketing martyrdom	161
8 Youth in arms	186
Conclusion	224
Appendices	229
Bibliography	256
Index	267

Figures

1	Countess Constance Markievicz.	25
2	Bulmer Hobson (seated) and Pádraic Ó Riain.	28
3	Dublin Fianna officers, c. 1913–14. Front row (left to right): Paddy Holohan, Michael Lonergan and Con Colbert. Back row: Garry Holohan and Pádraic Ó Riain.	47
4	Sean Heuston (1891–1916).	58
5	Na Fianna Éireann at their annual *ard-fheis* at the Mansion House in Dublin c. 1913.	106
6	Fianna Éireann scouts carrying out signalling training with flags.	135
7	Fianna Éireann scouts engaged in field medical training.	140
8	Members of the Fianna and the Irish Volunteers at the Howth gunrunning on 26 July 1914.	197

(All images are reproduced courtesy of the National Library of Ireland.)

Tables

1 Deaths of serving and former Fianna members in the MSPC sample, 1916–23.   210

2 Military ranks of service pension recipients in the MSPC sample of former Fianna members.   215

Acknowledgements

This monograph grew out of a chapter from my doctoral thesis on the Irish nationalist career of Bulmer Hobson and a subsequent postdoctoral research project on Irish nationalism and youth in the early twentieth century, both of which were funded by the former Irish Research Council for the Humanities and Social Sciences. I would like to take this opportunity to thank the institutions and individuals who helped me to bring this book to fruition. I am grateful to the directors, trustees and boards of the following libraries/archives for granting permission to cite manuscript material and to reproduce photographs from their collections: Irish Military Archives, the National Library of Ireland, UCD Archives and the National Archives, London. I am also grateful to Michael Laffan and Ivar McGrath for reading draft chapters of this book and providing feedback that was helpful and heartening. Any mistakes that remain in the text are, of course, my own.

I would also like to thank the following individuals who in their own various ways have helped me with this research project (in alphabetical order): Juliana Adelman, Tim Bowman, Marie Coleman, Catherine Cox, Clara Cullen, Lindsey Earner-Byrne, Tony Gaughan, James Kelly, Michael Kennedy, Sylvie Kleinman, Leeann Lane, Brendan Lynch, Robert Lynch, Ciaran MacGonigal, Ann Matthews, Richard McElligott, Christina McLoughlin, Deirdre McMahon, Aaron Mooney, Eve Morrison, William Mulligan, Eamon Murphy, Sharon Murphy, Will Murphy, Ríona Nic Congáil, Daithí Ó Corráin, Eunan O'Halpin, the late Margaret Ó hÓgartaigh, Peter Rigney, Susannah Riordan and Margaret Scanlon. Last but certainly not least, I would like to thank my husband Ivar and our son Ivar Will for their patience and support while I have been holed up in my study, working away on this book.

This project ended up being about boys in more ways than one. Around the time I began the Government of Ireland Postdoctoral

Fellowship at Trinity College Dublin, which enabled me to initiate research for this book, I discovered that I was expecting Ivar Will. His presence, both antenatal and postnatal, has been a constant joy and welcome distraction while researching and writing *Scouting for rebels*. Thus, it is dedicated to him with love.

Abbreviations

ACS	*An Claidheamh Soluis*
AOH	Ancient Order of Hibernians
APA	Army Pensions Acts
ASU	Active Service Unit
B na hÉ	*Bean na hÉireann*
BMH	Bureau of Military History
CD	Contemporary Documents
CIÉ	Coras Iompar Éireann
CO	Colonial Office
Coy	Company
CSB	Crime Special Branch
DIB	*Dictionary of Irish Biography*
DMP	Dublin Metropolitan Police
Ed.	Editor
Edn	Edition
FJ	*Freeman's Journal*
GAA	Gaelic Athletic Association
GHQ	General Headquarters
GPO	General Post Office
HQ	Headquarters
ICA	Irish Citizen Army
IF	*Irish Freedom*
IRA	Irish Republican Army
IRB	Irish Republican Brotherhood
IV	*Irish Volunteer*
MA	Military Archives, Dublin
MP	Member of Parliament
MSPA	Military Service Pensions Acts
MSPC	Military Service Pensions Collection
NAI	National Archives of Ireland

NCO	Non-commissioned officer
NLI	National Library of Ireland
O/C	Officer Commanding
RIC	Royal Irish Constabulary
RTÉ	Radio Teilifís Éireann
SF	*Sinn Féin*
TCD	Trinity College Dublin
TD	Teachta Dála (deputy/member of the Irish parliament)
TNA	The National Archives, London
UCD	University College Dublin
UCDA	University College Dublin Archives
UI	*United Irishman*
UVF	Ulster Volunteer Force
VAD	Voluntary Aid Detachment
WS	Witness Statement
YCV	Young Citizen Volunteers
YI	*Young Ireland*

1   Na Fianna Éireann in context

Small boys are natural radicals, and the boys, given a uniform and some semblance of a military organisation, needed no encouragement to declare themselves openly as revolutionaries who looked forward to the day when they might strike a blow in another fight for freedom. Of course, adults smiled tolerantly at this, not realising that the boy will soon be a man, and that the sentiments imbibed in his formative years are likely to remain with him in after life, to fructify as deeds when opportunity offers.[1]

That was how one Irish nationalist activist, Colonel Joseph V. Lawless, remembered the revolutionary boys of Na Fianna Éireann, or the Irish National Boy Scouts. The Fianna's founders, Countess Constance Markievicz and Bulmer Hobson, had two main aims when they established this youth organisation in Dublin in 1909. They wanted to provide an Irish nationalist alternative to British uniformed youth groups operating in Ireland and to prepare Irish boys for their future role in the Irish struggle for independence from Great Britain. They succeeded in both aims.

Irish historians have increasingly referred to a series of events that took place during the period *c.* 1913–23 as the 'Irish Revolution', though this term and the exact time frame involved remain contentious.[2] These events include the 1913 Dublin Lockout, the 1916 Easter Rising, the Irish War of Independence (or Anglo-Irish War, 1919–21) and the Irish Civil War (1922–23). Serving and former members of the Fianna participated in all of these events. By the end of the Irish Revolution, Ireland had been partitioned into two distinct political entities: the effectively independent twenty-six-county Irish Free State and the devolved government of six-county Northern Ireland, which remained in political union with Britain within the United Kingdom.

Na Fianna Éireann became the military trailblazers of the Irish nationalist movement in the early twentieth century. In 1914, Patrick Pearse proclaimed that 'if the Fianna had not been founded in 1909, the [Irish] Volunteers of 1913 would never have arisen'.[3] The Fianna were probably the first Irish nationalist group to begin military training in the twentieth century. This training enabled senior Fianna officers to serve as instructors when the Irish Volunteers were formed in November 1913. This adult paramilitary organisation, or citizens' militia, was established as a nationalist counterblast to the Ulster Volunteer Force (UVF), which had been founded in January 1913 to assert Ulster unionist opposition to home rule for Ireland.

Pearse's proclamation can be taken one step further. Without the foundation of the Fianna and the Irish Volunteers, the 1916 Easter Rising and the subsequent War of Independence would not have occurred, military personnel with the requisite training and militant mindset being essential for the execution of rebellions and guerrilla wars. The Fianna and the Irish Volunteers were designed to prepare Irish boys and men physically and mentally to engage in combat against British government forces in Ireland as part of the struggle for Irish independence. The Irish Volunteers may have been formed as a response to the UVF, but the Fianna began their military training four years prior to the establishment of both adult volunteer forces. Thus, the purpose of this book is to examine how what started as an Irish nationalist scouting organisation served not only as a conduit for the involvement of youth in the Irish Revolution but also as the military vanguard of this period of nationalist insurgency in Ireland.

NA FIANNA ÉIREANN IN IRISH HISTORIOGRAPHY

Until recently, Na Fianna Éireann tended to be mentioned only in passing, if at all, in studies of the Irish Revolution. It is only in the past decade or so that the history of the Fianna has been the subject of popular and scholarly studies. The exception is a doctoral thesis submitted in 1981, the year in which ten republican hunger strikers died in prison in Northern Ireland. John R. Watts's unpublished PhD thesis examined the Fianna as a case study of a political youth organisation, covering the group's history from its inception in 1909 up to 1981.[4] More recent publications began with J. Anthony Gaughan's 2006 study *Scouting in Ireland*, which considers the history of three Irish scouting movements: the Baden-Powell Boy Scouts, the Fianna and the Catholic Boy Scouts of Ireland.[5] To mark the 2009 centenary of the Fianna's foundation, Damien Lawlor published a narrative history entitled *Na Fianna Éireann and the Irish Revolution, 1909 to 1923*.[6] In 2014, Eamon Murphy began to document online the history of the Fianna in the period 1909–23 through illustrated blog entries on topics such as individual Fianna members, various troops and specific historical events.[7] I started to publish a series of scholarly articles on aspects of the Fianna's history in academic journals and edited collections from 2008 onwards, an undertaking that grew out of my doctoral research on Fianna co-founder Bulmer Hobson and has culminated in the present monograph.[8]

The recent growth in historiography on the Fianna has been fuelled by the greater availability of primary source material, beginning with the opening of the Bureau of Military History (BMH) collection in 2003, as well as public interest generated by the current decade of centenaries commemorating the events of Ireland's revolutionary era.[9] Increasing academic research into the history of Irish children and childhood has also played a role.[10] All three of these factors are evident in the Fianna's heightened profile in relation to the 1916 Rising. For instance, Fearghal McGarry included a chapter on the Fianna in *Rebels: Voices from the Easter Rising*, a book of edited extracts from BMH witness statements.[11] Two young men associated with the Fianna, Con Colbert and Sean Heuston, have been the subjects of biographies as part of the O'Brien Press's ongoing 16 Lives series to commemorate the lives of the sixteen men who were executed for their roles in relation to the Easter Rising.[12] Furthermore, RTÉ broadcaster Joe Duffy excavated the lives and deaths of three Fianna members, Sean Healy, James Fox and James Kelly, in *Children of the Rising*, a study of the forty children aged sixteen and under who died during the 1916 rebellion. *Children of the Rising* has emerged as one of the most popular books published so far during the decade of centenaries.[13]

The present monograph on Na Fianna Éireann aims to provide a scholarly yet accessible account of the nationalist youth organisation's early history and contribution to the Irish Revolution during the period 1909–23, situating it within the wider international context of uniformed youth groups in the late nineteenth and early twentieth centuries. The book not only builds upon the research of the authors noted previously but also revises and extends my own previously published articles on the subject. The remainder of this chapter and the ones that follow take a thematic approach to the Fianna's history during the revolutionary era by exploring in turn the organisation's broader international and national contexts, inception, development, membership, range of activities, print propaganda and military contribution to the Irish Revolution. It is my hope that this monograph will encourage other scholars to delve into the history of the Fianna to produce, for example, regional studies of the youth group or research on the organisation post 1923.

THE ADVENT OF UNIFORMED YOUTH GROUPS

Na Fianna Éireann were an Irish nationalist manifestation of the 'pseudo-military' youth groups that arose in Europe in the late nineteenth and early twentieth centuries. These organisations were part of the cult of discipline, training and manliness that grew out of the increasing anticipation of the coming war in Europe.[14] For instance, during the First World War, about 30,000 Galician men served in the Polish Legions or their Ukrainian counterpart, the United Sich Riflemen, both of which had grown out of scouting, sporting or paramilitary groups that had been formed in the previous decade.[15] Uniformed youth groups were also a reaction to a widely perceived *fin-de-siècle* 'decadence'.[16] In the early years of the twentieth century, many Germans worried that 'middle-class boys were effeminate' and 'the country lacked virile soldiers'.[17] Similarly, the British army's poor performance against a force of South African farmers during the Boer War (1899–1902) had provoked concern that Britain was in a state of decline. Fearing that they were losing their competitive edge in industrial and military affairs and that their populations were deteriorating both physically and morally, Western countries like Germany and Britain began to concern themselves with the health, education and moral welfare of the new generation.[18] Uniformed youth groups were one way of addressing this concern.

The best known of these youth groups was the international Boy Scout movement founded by Robert Baden-Powell in 1908. A British army officer who specialised in reconnaissance and scouting, Baden-Powell started this movement in response to the interest that boys had shown in his 1899 army training manual, *Aids to Scouting*. He was also inspired by the model of the Boys' Brigade, which was launched by William Alexander Smith in 1883 in Glasgow.[19] Smith was a businessman and an officer in the Volunteers, a British part-time military force that was later replaced by the Territorial Army.[20] He used military drill and discipline as a way of providing guidance to the boys who attended his Scottish Free Church Sunday School.[21] Smith's example also inspired the formation of the Church Lads' Brigade for Anglicans, the Jewish Lads' Brigade and the Catholic Boys' Brigade.[22] Baden-Powell, in contrast, put less overt emphasis on militarism. Instead, he focused on outdoor activities and personal development in order not only to train boys to be better citizens but to counter what he saw as the moral and physical decline of the upcoming generation.[23]

The impetus for the outdoor element of scouting came from the US-based naturalist Ernest Thompson Seton and his Woodcraft movement, which promoted outdoor life and the lore of Native American tribes. Baden-Powell and Seton met in 1906, sharing their respective ideas on youth groups. Seton co-founded the Boy Scouts of America, subsuming his own Woodcraft movement into the new group; however, he objected to the Scout movement's emphasis on patriotism and was forced out of the American organisation in 1915.[24] Whether Baden-Powell's main concern prior to 1920 was training citizens or future soldiers has sparked much scholarly debate.[25] Tensions within the early Scout movement, as exemplified by Seton and others, suggest that Baden-Powell initially sought to train both.

Girls took an early interest in the scouting movement with a large group attending the first big Scout rally at Crystal Palace in London in September 1909. Baden-Powell was opposed to including girls in his scouting organisation because he thought they would inhibit boys from joining. Instead, his sister Agnes formed the Girl Guides in 1910, initially attracting about 8,000 girls.[26] When the Girl Guides were first established, the organisation's primary goal was to create 'good wives and mothers for the British Empire', seeking to nurture femininity and domesticity in girls. Such a conservative goal may have contributed to the Girl Guides' failure in their early years to expand as quickly as the scouting movement for boys.[27] In response, Baden-Powell took over as chairman in 1915 and revamped the Girl Guides by developing a more efficient organisational structure and recruiting younger women into the movement, such as his wife Olave.[28]

Richard A. Voeltz has argued that the context of the First World War also played an important part in increasing the popularity of the Girl Guides in Britain: 'The new freedom associated with the war experience changed the common ways of thinking about what constituted appropriate behaviour outside the home for young women and girls, allowing the Guides to incorporate all the elements of the original scouting scheme ... without fear of bruising their femininity.'[29] As a result, Girl Guides could participate in signalling, drill and camping like their brothers, as well as contribute to the war effort through more traditional feminine activities such as fundraising, knitting socks for soldiers and volunteering in hospitals.[30]

UNIFORMED YOUTH GROUPS IN IRELAND

British uniformed youth groups soon established themselves in Ireland. Although the Boys' Brigade came to Ireland first, the Boy Scout movement spread more quickly. The first Irish companies of Smith's Boys' Brigade were founded in Belfast in 1888 and Dublin in 1891, followed by the establishment of a branch of the Catholic Boys' Brigade in Dublin in March 1894.[31] Boy Scout troops were in existence in Bray, County Wicklow, Dublin city and county, and Belfast from early 1908. Irish girls also joined in the female equivalent of scouting with the formation of Ireland's first official Girl Guide company in Harold's Cross in Dublin in 1911. Members of the Anglo-Irish aristocracy, such as the 12th Earl of Meath, supported the new youth movement from the beginning, often providing leadership and camping facilities on their estates.[32]

Not everyone in Ireland greeted this new British cultural import with such open arms, especially at a time when nationalists were actively engaged in combating cultural assimilation through the revival of aspects of traditional Irish culture, such as the Irish language and the sport of hurling. Some Irish nationalists, however, could see the value of Baden-Powell's vision of training male youth for their future roles as citizens and soldiers, but not in the service of Britain and its Empire. Among the advanced Irish nationalists who viewed British uniformed youth groups as a threat that could be turned into an opportunity was Arthur Griffith (1871–1922), founder of the Sinn Féin (ourselves) movement. In 1903, he condemned the Catholic Boys' Brigades as a recruiting ground for the British army, but recognised that if 'properly conducted', boys' brigades could be turned into 'a great national force', contributing to 'the intellectual and physical good of the young'.[33]

Two Protestant Irish nationalist activists, Countess Constance Markievicz (née Gore-Booth; 1868–1927) and John Bulmer Hobson (1883–1969), also shared this view. In August 1909, they founded Na Fianna Éireann in Dublin in order to counteract the growing popularity and influence of the Boy Scout movement and the Boys' Brigade in Ireland. Na Fianna Éireann offered its mainly male membership a combination of military training, outdoor pursuits and Irish cultural activities. The youth group later proved its value to the Irish Volunteers by providing the adult organisation with trained instructors, leaders and members. The Fianna would become the best known and most significant Irish nationalist manifestation of the uniformed 'pseudo-military' youth group in the early twentieth century.

Markievicz and Hobson were not the only Irish nationalists to recognise the value and appeal of uniformed youth groups during this period. In late 1911, the Ancient Order of Hibernians (AOH) established its own juvenile organisation, the Hibernian Boys' Brigade, which was aimed at 'all Catholic boys of Irish parentage, between the ages of 10 and 17'.[34] The AOH was a Catholic benevolent society that supported home rule for Ireland. It may have started the Hibernian Boys' Brigade as part of its efforts to expand its appeal beyond adult men and to ensure future members. From 1910, the AOH had provided women with the opportunity to join a Ladies' Auxiliary and, as Senia Pašeta has noted, 'by 1914 there were apparently several hundred branches of the Ladies' Auxiliary throughout Ireland'.[35] Every division of the AOH was encouraged to start the Boys' Brigade in its district if the population warranted it, in the hope that Brigade membership would give boys insight into the activities of the AOH and serve as a feeder for future members of the parent organisation. Members engaged in physical and military drill, participated in public processions, developed their Irish language skills, held concerts and played football in the Dublin Schools League, among other activities.[36] Michael F. Ryan, who joined the Waterford branch of the Hibernian Boys' Brigade when he was about nine years of age, recalled attending first aid lectures at the AOH Hall on O'Connell Street and participating in route marches.[37]

The year 1912 saw the formation of the Irish National Girl Scouts which changed their name to the Clann na Gael Girl Scouts in 1915 when the organisation became an auxiliary to the Hibernian Rifles. May Kelly (1901–64) and her sister Elizabeth initially started this uniformed youth group with the help of fellow Drumcondra resident Seamus McGowan (born 1887).[38] McGowan had previously been involved in organising Fianna troops on the north side of Dublin.[39] The Clann na Gael Girl Scouts catered for girls between the ages of eight and sixteen years. Like the Fianna, the organisation offered its members military training, camping trips and Irish cultural activities. The latter included Irish language lessons and the playing of camogie, the female equivalent of hurling. This girls' group mainly functioned in Dublin, but branches were later formed elsewhere, such as Cork, Tullamore, Athlone and Derry.[40]

Clann na Gael shared a meeting hall at 28 North Frederick Street in Dublin with the Hibernian Rifles. The latter organisation was the military wing of the Irish-American Alliance, the more radical, less sectarian section of the AOH.[41] *The Hibernian*, an AOH publication, 'declared it was as much the duty of Irish girls, "to learn the art of war, so as to be able to fight for your country as it is for boys"'.[42] The Clann na Gael Girl Scouts became more militant than the AOH's organisations for boys and women. In terms of both political motivation and exposure to physical danger, the courier duties performed during the 1916 Easter Rising by Clann na Gael member Mary McLoughlin were a far cry from the voluntary social work and contributions to the Great War effort on the home front undertaken by lady Hibernians.[43] When Clann na Gael spread to Cork in 1917, it was viewed as 'a junior auxiliary' of the nationalist women's organisation Cumann na mBan and 'on a par with the Fianna Boy Scouts'.[44] In later years, the Clann na Gael Girl Scouts were clearly aligned with republicanism and supported the anti-Treaty side during the Irish Civil War, a stance shared by Na Fianna Éireann as an organisation.[45]

Other political persuasions in Ireland, such as the trade union movement, also had their uniformed youth groups. The Irish Citizen Army (ICA), which was established in November 1913 to protect protesting workers during the Dublin Lockout, formed its own Scout Corps in June 1914 as part of a broader initiative to improve the efficiency of the army after the Lockout's failure. As John R. Watts has suggested, the decision to form a junior section of the ICA was likely influenced by the example of the role played by the Fianna within the advanced nationalist movement; the Scout Corps was viewed as a training ground for future ICA recruits and a way of including boys within the wider trade union family. Markievicz joined Seamus McGowan in taking a leading role in the establishment and subsequent organisation of the ICA Scout Corps, which attracted a core group of twenty boys who were trained in military drill, marksmanship and first aid. In contrast to the Fianna and despite being called 'scouts', the corps did not include woodcraft or camping as part of its training programme.[46] Like members of the Fianna and Clann na Gael, the ICA scouts accompanied their adult counterparts on marches, manoeuvres and parades.[47]

Irish youths who supported the continuance of the political union between Ireland and Great Britain tended to join British organisations, so there was less perceived need to establish specifically Irish unionist or loyalist uniformed youth groups. For instance, members of the Boys' Brigade and the Church Lads' Brigade demonstrated their commitment to unionism and opposition to the third home rule bill through their participation in public parades in County Armagh in 1912.[48] In Belfast, the Young Citizen Volunteers (YCV) were formed on 10 September 1912 to continue among older teens and young men the training and discipline provided by such youth groups. According to the YCV's inaugural president, Belfast Lord Mayor R. J. McMordie, MP, 'the young men of our country have been handicapped in the past in not having any general organisation capable of continuing the good work done by the Boys' Brigade, Church Lads' Brigade, and the Boys' Scouts Movement'.[49] The 1st Battalion of the YCV was later amalgamated into the UVF in 1914.[50] In rural Ulster, there were links between the Baden-Powell Boy Scouts and the UVF.[51]

British uniformed youth groups provided a template that was imitated and in some cases subverted by similar Irish groups. Despite their differing political loyalties, the Fianna, the Clann na Gael Girl Scouts, the ICA Scout Corps and the YCV all served as conduits into adult paramilitary organisations in Ireland. These Irish uniformed youth groups and their adult counterparts were manifestations of the spirit of popular militarism that took hold in Europe and beyond in the years leading up to the First World War.

THE PURPOSES OF UNIFORMED YOUTH GROUPS

Many of the youth groups formed in the late nineteenth and early twentieth centuries were designed to keep young working-class boys off the streets and provide them with a leisure-time activity that promoted middle-class values of order and discipline. The Boys' Brigade is a good example. Its founder, Smith, 'reasoned that a new uniformed organisation appealing to a boy's sense of patriotism and martial spirit would serve as a useful instrument for a primarily religious end'.[52] In this case, order and discipline included the practice of one's religion. One early Brigade member recognised the important function that the organisation served for his age cohort:

> When we reached thirteen most of us felt we were too big for the Sunday School, and there was a gap of a few years until we were able to join the YMCA [Young Men's Christian Association] at seventeen. To fill this gap period, many working-class boys ran wild, became hooligans and street-corner loafers. What else was there for them in those days, to do?[53]

Many teenage boys welcomed the advent of uniformed youth groups because they gave them something enjoyable and constructive to do with their free time. The 'uniformed' aspect of such youth groups chimed with the romantic view of the military prevalent in the years prior to the First World War.

In the British context, the establishment of uniformed youth groups revealed an underlying adult view of youth, particularly working-class youth, as a problem that required a solution. Influenced by his experience of the Boer War, Baden-Powell's decision to start the Boy Scouts reflected his fears of the moral and physical 'degeneration of the young and for the survival of the British Empire which they would have to maintain'.[54] One anonymous fan of the new movement argued that 'in the next generation there should be no overgrown lads standing idly and foolishly at the street corners, gaping after they know not what, smoking cigarettes ... there will be a new race of boys in England when the Scouts of today have little Scouts of their own'.[55]

Thus, uniformed youth groups were seen as an important tool in the renewal of British society. As John Springhall has noted, 'the development of "character" and "esprit de corps" found in the [British] public schools was to be extended to the "lower ranks" in society through the agencies of the various boys' brigades and, later, the Boy Scouts'.[56] Such youth groups would transmit middle-class values of order and discipline to working-class boys, values that would serve the state well during time of war.

Markievicz in particular recognised the value and appeal of the activities offered by the boys' brigades and the Boy Scouts but wanted to provide Irish boys with an Irish nationalist alternative to what she viewed as British imperialist bodies. In essence, she was less interested in keeping Irish boys off the streets than in keeping them out of the meeting halls of British youth groups operating in Ireland. Where Baden-Powell and other British youth leaders saw boys as a potential resource for the British army and for the maintenance of the British Empire, Markievicz and Hobson saw them as a potential resource for the Irish nationalist movement. The Fianna would provide members with the military training and nationalist nurturing to enable them to play an important role in the struggle for Irish independence. The organisation proffered a combination of political indoctrination and youth empowerment. The Fianna served not only as a focus for the spare time and energy of nationalist youth but also as a recruiting ground for the future soldiers of the Irish Revolution and community leaders of an independent Ireland. The youth group enabled its members to gain skills in organisation and governance in much the same way that older Irish nationalists were acquiring experience through their involvement in local government.

While so many of the British youth groups of the period were divided by religious denomination, the Fianna tried to promote unity among

Irish boys by welcoming members of all creeds. In light of Ireland's long history of religious division, it is not surprising that the Fianna eschewed the Bible study of the Boys' Brigade and the non-denominational, nature-loving Christian spirituality of the Baden-Powell movement.[57] The Irish youth group emphasised the importance of morality, but rarely made specific reference to religion, though most of its members were Roman Catholic.

Not all Irish nationalists could see the value of the Fianna, however. Liam Mellows, who travelled around Ireland in 1913 to organise new Fianna troops, recalled that some of the 'would-be Nationalists' that he 'appealed to for help, spoke of the movement with sarcasm and pointed out how, in *their* worldly wisdom, it was doomed to failure'. 'What can a handful of boys do against the great British Empire?' some shrugged. Others feared that the Fianna would give boys a taste for military life that would inspire them to join the British army. Still others found the youth group's advanced nationalist principles too extreme.[58] Rosamond Jacob, who became honorary president of a short-lived troop of Fianna girls in Waterford, had concerns about the nature of Markievicz's leadership and its impact on members: 'Madame is a bloodthirsty woman … and the [Fianna] boys seem the same in theory.'[59]

As these observations suggest, uniformed youth groups like the Fianna did not just instil order, discipline and specific skills in their members, they could also be training grounds for nationalist fundamentalism. In Germany, the years of the First World War saw the expansion of military youth companies. Andrew Donson has argued that these groups not only 'reinforced the idea that … aggressiveness and a willingness to sacrifice life for nation were positive traits' but also helped to mould future Nazis.[60] The Fianna proved to be a training ground for Irish republican fundamentalism, with many members participating in the struggle for Irish independence during the period 1913–23. The participation of serving and former members of the Fianna in the events of the Irish Revolution will be discussed in the chapters that follow.

Members of other Irish nationalist youth groups also participated in these events. For example, thirteen members of the ICA Scout Corps mobilised during the 1916 Rising, including fifteen-year-old Roddy Connolly. He was the son of James Connolly, one of the rebellion's leaders.[61] Another member of the same age, draper's assistant Charles Darcy, was killed in action on Easter Monday 1916 when he was shot while serving as a sniper on the roof of the Henry and James clothing store on the corner of Parliament Street across from City Hall and Dublin Castle.[62] After the surrender, the surviving ICA scouts were rounded up by the authorities, given a lecture and sent home. This apparently marked the end of the ICA's junior section. When the ICA reorganised in the summer after the rebellion, about two-thirds of the boys joined the adult organisation. Some, such as Joe Keeley and Fredrick Norgrove, went on to play a role in the War of Independence and the Civil War.[63]

Members of the Clann na Gael Girl Scouts also engaged in nationalist activism before and after the 1916 Rising. At least four members, May Kelly, Cecilia Conroy, Margaret (Maggie) Fagan and Mary McLoughlin, participated in the rebellion. McLoughlin, then aged fifteen, served as a courier, delivering messages and ammunition between garrisons.[64] After the Rising, Clann na Gael Girl Scouts are reported to have participated in republican parades and sold lapel flags as part of the anti-conscription campaign in 1918. They also carried messages for the Irish Republican Army (IRA), as the Irish Volunteers were later known, during the War of Independence and held vigils at the gates of Mountjoy prison while republican prisoners were on hunger strike in 1920. After the outbreak of the Civil War in 1922, Clann na Gael helped those IRA members who were opposed to the Anglo-Irish Treaty when their garrison in Dublin's Four Courts was being shelled by the forces of the pro-Treaty provisional Irish government.[65]

Clann na Gael members faced arrest and imprisonment as a result of their activities. In the summer of 1916, May Kelly (also known as O'Kelly), Eileen Conroy and Maggie Fagan were arrested for carrying an American flag as part of a wreath-laying ceremony at the grave of veteran Fenian Jeremiah O'Donovan Rossa in Glasnevin Cemetery. They were detained in custody for three to four days before the military authorities ordered their release.[66] Research undertaken by Ann Matthews indicates that Clann na Gael members were among the women interned by the Irish Free State government during the Civil War.[67] For example, in March 1923, Christina (Chrissie) Behan was arrested for being a member of the Clann na Gael Girl Scouts, which had supported the anti-Treaty side in opposition to the Irish government.[68] Behan served 130 days in prison between 16 March and 24 July 1923, during which time she spent eleven days on hunger strike.[69] May Kelly was also interned for ninety-five days between 31 March and 4 July 1923.[70]

As the examples in this chapter show, the Fianna were not the only uniformed youth group in Ireland to instil nationalist fundamentalism in its members during the revolutionary era. Na Fianna Éireann were, however, the era's most significant Irish nationalist youth group in terms of size and impact on the Irish struggle for independence. The organisation also generated the largest body of primary sources on which to base a study of its contribution to the Irish Revolution.

NOTES

1. Colonel Joseph V. Lawless, witness statement, 9 Dec. 1954 (MA, BMH, WS 1,043).
2. Joost Augusteijn (ed.), *The Irish Revolution, 1913–1923* (Basingstoke: Palgrave, 2002), p. viii. Readers who require a primer on the Irish Revolution are directed to the following concise and highly readable introduction: Marie Coleman, *The Irish Revolution, 1916–1923* (London: Routledge, 2014).
3. Patrick Pearse, 'To the boys of Ireland', *IF*, Feb. 1914, p. 6.
4. John R. Watts, 'Na Fianna Éireann: A case study of a political youth organisation' (PhD thesis, University of Glasgow, 1981).
5. For a discussion of the Fianna, see J. Anthony Gaughan, *Scouting in Ireland* (Dublin: Kingdom Books, 2006), pp. 33–77.
6. Damian Lawlor, *Na Fianna Éireann and the Irish Revolution, 1909 to 1923* (Rhode, Co. Offaly: Caoillte Books, 2009). This book, which appears to be privately published, is not widely available.
7. See https://fiannaeireannhistory.wordpress.com. Murphy is a relative of Fianna officer Eamon Martin.
8. Marnie Hay, 'Na Fianna Éireann' in John Crowley *et al.* (eds), *Atlas of the Irish Revolution* (Cork: Cork University Press, 2017), pp. 173–6; Marnie Hay, 'Scouting for rebels: Na Fianna Éireann and preparation for the coming war, 1909–1918' in Lissa Paul *et al.* (eds), *Children's Literature and Culture of the First World War* (London and New York: Routledge, 2016), pp. 268–82; Marnie Hay, 'An Irish nationalist adolescence: Na Fianna Éireann, 1909–1923' in Catherine Cox and Susannah Riordan (eds), *Adolescence in Modern Irish History* (Basingstoke: Palgrave Macmillan, 2015), pp. 103–28; Marnie Hay, 'The propaganda of Na Fianna Éireann, 1909–26' in Mary Shine Thompson (ed.), *Young Irelands: Studies in Children's Literature* (Dublin: Four Courts Press, 2011), pp. 47–56; Marnie Hay, 'The foundation and development of Na Fianna Éireann, 1909–16', *Irish Historical Studies*, 36:141 (May 2008), pp. 53–71. For a discussion of Hobson and the Fianna, see chapter 6 of Marnie Hay, 'Bulmer Hobson: The rise and fall of an Irish nationalist, 1900–16' (PhD thesis, University College Dublin, 2004). When I revised

this thesis for publication as a monograph, I chose not to include a specific chapter on the Fianna and instead published my doctoral research on the youth group as the article in *Irish Historical Studies* noted previously. See Marnie Hay, *Bulmer Hobson and the Nationalist Movement in Twentieth-Century Ireland* (Manchester: Manchester University Press, 2009).

9 Further information about the BMH is included in chapter 5 of this book. Witness statements made to the BMH are available online at http://www.militaryarchives.ie/collections/online-collections/bureau-of-military-history-1913-1921.

10 In recent years, three collections of essays and two special issues of journals have examined youth as a category of Irish historical research. These publications arose from conferences and workshops. See Mary Hatfield, Jutta Kruse and Ríona Nic Congáil (eds), *Historical Perspectives on Parenthood and Childhood in Ireland* (Dublin: Arlen House, 2017); the special issue on children and childhood in Ireland, edited by Sarah-Anne Buckley, Marnie Hay and Ríona Nic Congáil, *The Journal of the History of Childhood and Youth*, 9:2 (2016); Cox and Riordan (eds), *Adolescence in Modern Irish History*; Maria Luddy and James M. Smith (eds), *Children, Childhood and Irish Society: 1500 to the Present* (Dublin: Four Courts Press, 2014); 'Children, childhood and Irish society', special issue edited by Maria Luddy and James M. Smith, *Éire-Ireland*, 44:1 and 2 (2009).

11 See chapter 3 of Fearghal McGarry, *Rebels: Voices from the Easter Rising* (Dublin: Penguin Ireland, 2011).

12 John O'Callaghan, *Con Colbert* (Dublin: O'Brien Press, 2015); John Gibney, *Sean Heuston* (Dublin: O'Brien Press, 2013).

13 Joe Duffy, *Children of the Rising* (Dublin: Hachette Books Ireland, 2015).

14 David Fitzpatrick, 'Militarism in Ireland, 1900–1922' in Thomas Bartlett and Keith Jeffrey (eds), *A Military History of Ireland* (Cambridge: Cambridge University Press, 1996), pp. 382–3.

15 Norman Davies, *Vanished Kingdoms: The History of Half-forgotten Europe* (London: Penguin Books, 2012), p. 473. Formed by Józef Piłsudski, the Polish Legions 'belonged to the anti-nationalist branch of Polish patriotic opinion, upholding the country's multi-religious and multi-cultural traditions'. The Sich Riflemen were equally as keen as their Polish counterparts to fight Russia during the war, but less clear about their fundamental political goals (pp. 473–4).

16 See Walter Laqueur, 'Fin-de-siècle: Once more with feeling', *Journal of Contemporary History*, 31:1 (Jan. 1996), pp. 5–47.

17 Andrew Donson, *Youth in the Fatherless Land: War Pedagogy, Nationalism and Authority in Germany, 1914–1918* (Cambridge, MA: Harvard University Press, 2010), p. 49.
18 Colin Heywood, *A History of Childhood* (Cambridge: Polity Press, 2005), pp. 29–30.
19 Richard A. Smith, 'Robert Baden-Powell', 'Boy Scouts' and 'Boys' Brigade' in John Cannon (ed.), *The Oxford Companion to British History* (Oxford: Oxford University Press, 1997), pp. 72, 119.
20 John Springhall, *Coming of Age: Adolescence in Britain, 1860–1960* (Dublin: Gill and Macmillan, 1986), p. 39.
21 Smith, 'Boys' Brigade', p. 119.
22 Paul Wilkinson, 'English youth movements, 1908–30', *Journal of Contemporary History*, 4:2 (Apr. 1969), p. 6; Richard McElligott, '"A youth tainted with the deadly poison of Anglicism"? Sport and childhood in the Irish independence period' in Ciara Boylan and Ciara Gallagher (eds), *Constructions of the Irish Child in the Independence Period* (Basingstoke: Palgrave Macmillan, 2018), p. 291. Also see Richard A. Voeltz, '"…A good Jew and a good Englishman": The Jewish Lads' Brigade, 1894–1922', *Journal of Contemporary History*, 23:1 (Jan. 1988), pp. 119–27.
23 Smith, 'Boy Scouts', p. 119; Henry Collis *et al.*, *B.-P.'s Scouts: An Official History of the Boy Scouts Association* (London: Collins, 1961), pp. 48, 55.
24 Brian Morris, 'Ernest Thompson Seton and the origin of the Woodcraft movement', *Journal of Contemporary History*, 5:2 (Apr. 1970), pp. 185, 187–8.
25 See Michael Rosenthal, 'Knights and retainers: The earliest version of Baden-Powell's Boy Scout scheme', *Journal of Contemporary History*, 15:4 (Oct. 1980), pp. 603–17; Allen Warren, 'Sir Robert Baden-Powell, the Scout movement and citizen training in Great Britain, 1900–1920', *English Historical Review*, 101:399 (Apr. 1986), pp. 376–98; John Springhall, 'Baden-Powell and the Scout movement before 1920: Citizen training or soldiers of the future?', *English Historical Review*, 102:405 (Oct. 1987), pp. 934–42; Anne Summers, 'Scouts, Guides and VADs: A note in reply to Allen Warren', *English Historical Review*, 102:405 (Oct. 1987), pp. 943–7; Allen Warren, 'Baden-Powell: A final comment', *English Historical Review*, 102:405 (Oct. 1987), pp. 948–50.
26 Richard A. Smith, 'Girl Guides' in Cannon (ed.), *Oxford Companion*, p. 417.
27 Richard A. Voeltz, 'The antidote to "Khaki Fever"? The expansion of the British Girl Guides during the First World War', *Journal of Contemporary History*, 27:4 (Oct. 1992), p. 627.

28 Smith, 'Girl Guides', p. 417; Voeltz, 'The antidote to "Khaki Fever"?', p. 627.
29 Voeltz, 'The antidote to "Khaki Fever"?', p. 629.
30 *Ibid.*, pp. 629–30.
31 Donald M. McFarlan, *First for Boys: The Story of the Boys' Brigade, 1883–1983*, pp. 14, 19–20, available at www.boys-brigade.org.uk/first-for-boys.htm (accessed 15 May 2014); Gaughan, *Scouting in Ireland*, p. 81.
32 Gaughan, *Scouting in Ireland*, pp. 5–8; Irish Girl Guides, 'History of Irish Girl Guides', 2009, available at www.irishgirlguides.ie/index.php/history-of-irish-girl-guides (accessed 14 May 1914).
33 *UI*, 24 Jan. 1903, p. 1. The Catholic Boys' Brigade formed in Dublin in 1894 met at premises in Church Street and had over 700 members after its first four years in existence (Gaughan, *Scouting in Ireland*, p. 81).
34 'Physical training for boys', *FJ*, 14 Dec. 1911, p. 10.
35 Senia Pašeta, *Irish Nationalist Women, 1900–1918* (Cambridge: Cambridge University Press, 2013), p. 64.
36 'Physical training for boys', *FJ*, 14 Dec. 1911, p.10; 'Hibernian Notes', *Connacht Tribune*, 16 Oct. 1915, p. 3. I have found references to companies existing in Dublin city centre and the suburbs of Glasnevin and Dún Laoghaire, the cities of Belfast, Waterford and Cork, in towns such as Bray, County Wicklow, Kells and Bailieboro, County Meath, New Ross, County Wexford, Carrickmacross, County Monaghan and in County Roscommon, as well as in Glasgow in Scotland. See 'Hibernian Boys' Brigade visit to Connor's Grand Circus', *FJ*, 5 Feb. 1915, p. 2; 'Hibernian Boys' Brigade (Glasnevin Co.)', *FJ*, 3 Sept. 1912, p. 2; 'Hibernian Boys' Brigade', *Irish Independent*, 11 Dec. 1914, p. 6; 'Hibernian Notes', *Connacht Tribune*, 16 Oct. 1915, p. 3; Waterford County Inspector's Report, April 1914 (TNA, CO 904/93); *Guy's 1921 City and County Almanac and Directory* (Cork: Guy, 1921), p. 113; *FJ*, 28 May 1914, p. 6; 'Local snapshots', *Meath Chronicle*, 19 Sept. 1914; Wexford County Inspector's Report, May 1912 (TNA, CO 904/87); Monaghan County Inspector's Report, Mar. 1913 (TNA, CO 904/89); and Roscommon County Inspector's Report, Jan. 1917 (TNA, CO 904/102).
37 Michael F. Ryan, witness statement, 9 Dec. 1957 (MA, BMH, WS 1,709).
38 Mary (May) Chadwick (née Kelly), pension file (MA, MSPC, MSP34REF20098). In some contemporary documents, the organisation's name is spelled Clan na Gael and its members called Girl Guides. According to the 1911 Irish census, May and Elizabeth Kelly were scholars aged twelve and fourteen, respectively. Originally from County Cork, the Kelly family resided at 40 Elizabeth Street in Drumcondra, Dublin. Their father Thomas was listed as an unemployed carpenter. See www.

census.nationalarchives.ie/pages/1911/Dublin/Drumcondra/Elizabeth_Street/249321/ (accessed 28 May 2014). Although Joseph E. A. Connell, Jr, states that Markievicz joined the Kelly sisters in forming the Clann na Gael Girl Scouts, I have found no contemporary reference to Markievicz's involvement with the endeavour. See 'Inghinidhe na hÉireann/Daughters of Ireland, Clan na nGaedheal/Girl Scouts of Ireland', *History Ireland*, 19:5 (Sept./Oct. 2011), p. 66.

39 Seamus Kavanagh, witness statement, 9 Sept. 1957 (MA, BMH, WS 1,670); Seamus McGowan, pension file (MA, MSPC, MSP34 REF4289).

40 Mary McLoughlin, witness statement, c. Feb. 1954 (MA, BMH, WS 934); Mary (May) Chadwick (née Kelly), pension file (MA, MSPC, MSP34REF20098); McElligott, '"A youth tainted with the deadly poison of Anglicism"?', p. 293; Francis McKay, 'Clann na nGaedheal Girl Scouts', *Irish Press*, 3 May 1966, p. 11; Ann Matthews, *Renegades: Irish Republican Women, 1900–22* (Cork: Mercier Press, 2010), p. 109; Pádraig Óg Ó Ruairc, 'A short history of the Hibernian Rifles, 1912–1916', 31 Mar. 2013, available at www.theirishstory.com/2013/03/31/a-short-history-of-the-hibernian-rifles-1912–1916/#.UjHVCNKOSuI (accessed 14 Aug. 2013).

41 Ó Ruairc, 'A short history of the Hibernian Rifles'.

42 *The Hibernian*, 17 July 1915, quoted in McElligott, '"A youth tainted with the deadly poison of Anglicism"?', p. 293.

43 Mary McLoughlin, witness statement, c. Feb. 1954 (MA, BMH, WS 934); Pašeta, *Irish Nationalist Women, 1900–1918*, pp. 64–5. Mary's witness statement was transcribed in 1954 by her friend Ina Connolly Heron, a former Fianna member, but remained unsigned by Mary who was gravely ill with cancer and nearing death at the time (email from Christina McLoughlin [Mary's niece] to Marnie Hay, 18 May 2016).

44 Peg Duggan, witness statement, 14 Feb. 1957 (MA, BMH, WS 1,576).

45 McKay, 'Clann na nGaedheal Girl Scouts', p. 11.

46 For a discussion of the Irish Citizen Army Scouts, see Appendix III of Watts, 'Na Fianna Éireann: A case study of a political youth organisation', pp. 398–404.

47 Ann Matthews, *The Irish Citizen Army* (Cork: Mercier Press, 2014), pp. 59, 63, 71.

48 Alvin Jackson, 'Unionist politics and Protestant society in Edwardian Ireland', *Historical Journal*, 33:4 (Dec. 1990), p. 860.

49 Quoted in Timothy Bowman, *Carson's Army: The Ulster Volunteer Force, 1910–22* (Manchester: Manchester University Press, 2012), p. 26; Gareth Mulvenna, *Tartan Gangs and Paramilitaries: The Loyalist Backlash* (Liverpool: Liverpool University Press, 2016), p. 15.

50 Bowman, *Carson's Army*, pp. 30–1.
51 Brendan Power, 'The Boy Scouts in Ireland: Urbanisation, health, education and adolescence, 1908–1914' in Boylan and Gallagher (eds), *Constructions of the Irish Child in the Independence Period*, p. 259.
52 John Springhall, *Youth, Empire and Society* (London: Croom Helm, 1977), p. 24.
53 William Wylie quoted in Springhall, *Youth, Empire and Society*, p. 24.
54 Springhall, *Youth, Empire and Society*, p. 56.
55 M. W. quoted in Springhall, *Youth, Empire and Society*, p. 56.
56 Springhall, *Coming of Age*, p. 64.
57 For a discussion of the spiritual aspects of the Boy Scout movement, see Warren, 'Sir Robert Baden-Powell, the Scout movement and citizen training', pp. 388–91.
58 Liam Mellows, 'The Irish Boy Scouts by an Irish Volunteer officer, Chapter IV', 1917 (MA, BMH, Colonel Dan Bryan Collection, CD 129/1).
59 Leeann Lane, *Rosamond Jacob: Third Person Singular* (Dublin: UCD Press, 2010), p. 64.
60 Andrew Donson, 'Why did German youth become fascists? Nationalist males born 1900 to 1908 in war and revolution', *Social History*, 31:3 (2006), p. 353.
61 A list of the members who mobilised in 1916 is included in Matthews, *Irish Citizen Army*, p. 212.
62 Matthews, *Irish Citizen Army*, pp. 110, 212; Duffy, *Children of the Rising*, pp. 183, 223.
63 Watts, 'Na Fianna Éireann: A case study of a political youth organisation', p. 404; Matthews, *Irish Citizen Army*, pp. 220–1.
64 Mary (May) Chadwick (née Kelly), pension file (MA, MSPC, MSP34REF20098); Cecilia O'Neill (née Conroy), pension file (MA, MSPC, MSP34REF22268); Margaret Mary MacSherry (née Fagan), pension file (MA, MSPC, MSP34REF54707); Mary McLoughlin, witness statement, c. Feb. 1954 (MA, BMH, WS 934).
65 McKay, 'Clann na nGaedheal Girl Scouts', p. 11.
66 'Is the United States flag illegal?', *FJ*, 11 Aug. 1916, p. 2; 'Dublin girls released', *Southern Star*, 12 Aug. 1916, p. 1.
67 Ann Matthews, *Dissidents: Irish Republican Women, 1923–1941* (Cork: Mercier Press, 2012), p. 53.
68 *Ibid.*, p. 62.
69 *Ibid.*, pp. 258, 292. Behan was one of four women who went on hunger strike in July 1923 to protest against their continued detention in the North Dublin Union even though the Civil War had ended the previous

April. The slow release of prisoners had led to restlessness and frustration among internees (pp. 102–3).

70　*Ibid.*, p. 281. Matthews' list of internees also includes a Maggie Fagan, who resided at 8 Mercer St. in Dublin (p. 265). It is unclear whether this was the same Maggie Fagan who had been arrested with May Kelly in 1916 for carrying an American flag as part of a Clann na Gael wreath-laying ceremony.

2 The countess and the Quaker[1]

> [A] meeting will be held on Monday next at 8 pm at 34 Camden Street, Dublin, to start a National Boys' Brigade, to be managed by the boys themselves on national, not party lines. Boys interested are invited to attend.[2]

Michael Lonergan was about fifteen years of age when he attended a meeting 'held in a dingy hall at the rear of 34 Lower Camden Street' in Dublin on 16 August 1909.[3] It was the first public organisational meeting of a proposed nationalist youth group called Na Fianna Éireann, or the Irish National Boy Scouts. He recalled that 'there were fifty or sixty boys present, mostly adventurers from the Coombe and the neighbourhood, and I found myself seated beside a lad whom I judged was not from Dublin at all by reason of his accent'. The lad was Con Colbert, who would be executed seven years later as a result of his role in the 1916 Easter Rising. In Lonergan's retrospective view, this 'dingy' theatrical hall should be 'designated some kind of a national shrine' because it was there that the events leading to Easter Week began. It was there that military training in preparation for a rebellion started in earnest.[4]

THE ORIGINS OF NA FIANNA ÉIREANN

Bulmer Hobson founded two nationalist organisations called Na Fianna Éireann. They were named after the Fianna, the band of warriors led by the mythical Irish hero Fionn Mac Cumhaill. The first was a boys' hurling and cultural club, which Hobson launched in Belfast in 1902.[5] The second, more successful and enduring organisation was established in Dublin in 1909 when Countess Constance Markievicz, a relatively recent convert to Irish nationalism, teamed up with Hobson to establish a nationalist youth group designed to counteract the pro-British Boy Scout movement founded by Robert Baden-Powell in the previous year.

The two founders of the Fianna met in Dublin in 1908. Not only were both Markievicz and Hobson the descendants of seventeenth-century planters on the paternal sides of their families, but they also had English mothers. The daughter of landowner and philanthropist Sir Henry Gore-Booth of Lissadell, County Sligo, and his wife Georgina Mary Hill of Tickhill Castle, Yorkshire, Markievicz was born into a life of Anglo-Irish privilege. Educated at home on her father's estate, Markievicz gained an appreciation of the arts and enjoyed riding and hunting. Her education was capped by a grand tour of continental Europe and her presentation to Queen Victoria at Buckingham Palace. As an adult, she supported the cause of women's suffrage and studied art in London and Paris. While at art school in the latter city, she met her future husband Count Casimir Dunin-Markievicz of a Polish landowning family, whom she married in 1900. A year later they had a daughter, Maeve, who was mainly raised by her Gore-Booth grandparents. The Markieviczes moved to Dublin where they enlivened the cultural scene through their painting and theatrical productions.[6]

Hobson, in contrast, was the product of a middle-class north Belfast Quaker family. His father, Benjamin Hobson Jr, was a commercial traveller and a Gladstonian home ruler, while his mother Mary Ann Bulmer was a women's rights activist and amateur archaeologist from Darlington, County Durham. It was through his mother that Hobson met the poets Alice Milligan and Ethna Carbery (the pseudonym of Anna Johnston) who helped to spark his interest in Irish nationalism. Milligan lent the adolescent Standish O'Grady's retellings of Irish sagas and Carbery encouraged him to join the Gaelic League, an Irish-language organisation founded in 1893. While a student at a Quaker boarding school in Lisburn, he subscribed to the *Shan Van Vocht*, the nationalist paper edited by the two women. After he left the Friends' School, Hobson became an apprentice printer. In his spare time, he participated in such organisations as the Gaelic League, the Gaelic Athletic Association (GAA), Sinn Féin and the Irish Republican Brotherhood (IRB). The latter was a secret society dedicated to the foundation of an independent Irish republic through the use of physical force if necessary. An active propagandist from his late teens onwards, Hobson contributed articles and poetry to advanced nationalist newspapers and set up a few new nationalist groups of his own, including the first version of Na Fianna Éireann.[7]

Hobson founded this boys' hurling club after the Belfast County Board of the GAA showed no interest in holding competitions for the junior clubs. Hobson had attended the first meeting of the Belfast

Hurling Committee in August 1901, which consisted of two representatives from each of the city's seven hurling clubs. Representing the hurling club linked to the Gaelic League's Tír na nÓg (Land of Youth) branch, he became secretary of the new organisation.[8] In the following month, the committee decided to affiliate with the GAA as soon as possible and began calling itself the Belfast County Board of the GAA. It later became the first Antrim County Board of the GAA.[9] Although there had been hurling clubs in Antrim previously, not enough clubs had existed to form a county committee.[10] The committee intended to spare no effort to revive hurling in the North: 'All that can be done to start hurling clubs in Ulster, will be done, and it will not be long now till the old game will be a potent factor in making Belfast as Irish as in the past it has been English.'[11]

Hobson, who was eighteen years of age at the time, wanted the board to promote hurling among the youth. Unlike adults who took up hurling, young boys 'had grace and acquired skill very rapidly'. He thought that if Antrim were ever to have hurling teams that could compete with those in other counties, they 'should concentrate on training the young boys and making first-class hurlers out of them'.[12] Hobson proposed that the county board of the GAA should hold competitions for the junior clubs. The other board members had no interest in this proposal, so Hobson resigned from his position as secretary in September 1901.[13]

On 22 June 1902, at the beginning of the hurling season, he called a mass meeting in the Catholic Boys' Hall on the Falls Road, which was attended by nearly 300 boys.[14] At this meeting, he proposed the formation of Na Fianna Éireann, suggesting that the organisation would help to revive 'this old Irish sport' and teach the boys 'to speak their own native tongue', which would enable them to do 'noble, and exhalted [sic] work for Ireland'.[15] In keeping with the organisation's name, each club was named after one of the warriors in Fionn Mac Cumhaill's old Fianna, such as Conan Maol or Goll Mac Morna, and the playing field's name was changed from Klondyke to Cnoc Aluinn, the legendary home of the Fianna.[16] By July 1902, twelve hurling clubs belonged to Na Fianna Éireann.[17]

The tremendous excitement of the Fianna's inaugural meeting convinced Hobson that the fledgling organisation was something that could be moulded 'into a strong force to help in the liberation of Ireland'.[18] Arthur Griffith's paper, *United Irishman*, saw the organisation as an antidote to the Catholic Boys' Brigades that had turned into recruiting grounds for the British army: 'Twenty thousand Irish boys enrolled in national brigades North and South to-day would mean twenty thousand thinking and disciplined men to-morrow, and twenty thousand thinking, disciplined men, filled with one purpose – what might they not accomplish in a land like ours!'[19]

The Belfast Fianna developed into a sporting and cultural club. It held inter-club hurling competitions and classes on Irish language and history. Later it expanded to include Gaelic football and theatre. At a meeting of the executive of the Belfast Fianna on 17 October 1902, Hobson announced that 'he intended to form a dramatic section from the various clubs' and asked each club representative to provide him with a list of suitable members from each club. A meeting of boys who qualified for the dramatic section was to be held on 4 November 1902.[20] A former member of the first Belfast Fianna, Seamus Robinson, recalled an attempt to produce a play by Hobson, but did not know whether this play about United Irishman Theobald Wolfe Tone was ever staged.[21]

Although this initial version of the Fianna got off to a successful start in Belfast, the organisation later ran into difficulties due to lack of money and Hobson's increasing commitments to other advanced nationalist activities. Despite the problems of sustainable finance and leadership, Hobson believed 'it accomplished quite a lot for the national movement in Belfast'.[22] The organisation 'continued to exist for many years with various efforts from time to time to infuse new life into it'.[23] On 28 January 1907, two members of the Royal Irish Constabulary (RIC) apparently deemed the activities of the Fianna suspicious enough to warrant entering its hall at Willowbank through a window in order to interrogate two sixteen-year-old members about the organisation and several Belfast nationalists.[24] Remnants of Hobson's original Fianna were still in existence in 1909 when he joined Markievicz in establishing a new version of the Fianna as a nationalist youth organisation in Dublin.[25]

Hobson was in his mid-twenties when he served as one of Markievicz's first mentors in the Sinn Féin movement. The countess, who was in her early forties, had been converted to Irish nationalism after stumbling across a bundle of back issues of the advanced nationalist newspapers *The Peasant* and *Sinn Féin*. She initially approached Griffith about getting involved in the movement, but her Anglo-Irish credentials roused his suspicions that she was a British spy. She then met Hobson who was, as she later put it, 'leader of the opposition' against Griffith on the Sinn Féin executive. The all-embracing Hobson took her in hand and launched her into the advanced nationalist world.

He arranged for her to join the Drumcondra branch of Sinn Féin and introduced her to his friend Helena Molony, who brought her into the fold of the nationalist women's organisation Inghinidhe na hÉireann (Daughters of Erin). Years later, after their friendship had soured due to political differences, the countess insisted that Hobson only patronised her in order to gain another ally in his power struggle with Griffith.[26]

After reading an *Irish Times* account of the Lord Lieutenant Lord Aberdeen's interest in a number of Boys' Brigades and Boy Scout troops in the spring of 1909, Markievicz was haunted by the image of these Irish boys, as she put it, 'saluting the flag that flew in triumph over every defeat their nation has known'.[27] This sparked her decision to administer a nationalist antidote.[28] Over the next two months, she raised the issue of starting a nationalist boy scout troop at Sinn Féin meetings, but got little response.[29] She also approached Griffith directly about gaining support for her plan from Sinn Féin, but was turned down – no doubt due to her vision of a physical force troop and her existing connection with Hobson.[30] Ironically, Griffith had been in favour of the formation of a nationalist boys' brigade organisation when Hobson, who was not yet a threat, had established the first incarnation of the Fianna in 1902.[31]

Prior to teaming up with Hobson, Markievicz had experienced ongoing difficulties in her own attempts to start a nationalist boy scout troop. Her first step had been to enlist the assistance of a schoolmaster with nationalist sympathies to help her attract boy recruits. A unionist schoolmaster friend recommended William O'Neill who taught at St Andrew's National School on Brunswick Street (now Pearse Street).[32] During a visit to IRB leader Tom Clarke's shop, the countess mentioned her plan to approach O'Neill about recruiting some boys to start a nationalist boy scout troop. Clarke 'thought it a good idea but pointed out to her that as she was a non-Catholic O'Neill might look upon her with suspicion. In fact … he might suspect proselytism.' At Clarke's suggestion, she asked Sean McGarry, a future president of the IRB Supreme Council, to accompany her. Once they had convinced O'Neill that Markievicz was not 'an emissary' from the Lord Lieutenant's wife Lady Aberdeen,[33] he introduced them to eight or nine boys, who helped to form the nucleus of what would later become the new Fianna.[34]

The countess invited these boys to her home on Frankfort Avenue in the well-heeled south Dublin suburb of Rathgar, and dubbed them 'The Red Branch Knights'. With the help of Molony, McGarry and another IRB member, Patrick McCartan, she tried – unsuccessfully – to instruct them in signalling, drill and scouting, while they – successfully – raided

Figure 1 Countess Constance Markievicz.

her husband's whiskey supply.[35] Markievicz later admitted that 'none of us elders understood boys in the least, and no one knew anything about the subjects we set out to teach'.[36]

This was certainly the case when Markievicz and Molony blithely took six of the boys on a camping trip to a picturesque 'little valley away up on the side of Three Rock Mountain', south of Dublin. After long hours hauling their equipment, provisions and poetry books uphill with the assistance of a pony and cart, they reached their destination where they struggled to pitch their tents in the dark. The next morning the countess awoke to find her towel and soap 'a brown dripping rag, wrapped round a sticky mess', the boys having used the cloth to polish their boots. While the boys attended mass, the women settled themselves down to read, but the appearance of a sudden rainstorm sent them scurrying for cover. It had not occurred to them to dig a ditch around their tent, which they had pitched on the side of a hill, so all the blankets and cushions were soon soaked. Thanks to the reappearance of sunshine and the heat of a primus stove, these items were dry by bedtime. The following day saw the end of their outdoor adventure, though the repeated refusal of the pony to be caught and harnessed delayed their departure for home.[37]

After such a chaotic camping trip, Markievicz decided that the only way for her experiment to work was to organise the boy scout project on a more official footing with the help of Hobson, who, she was told, not only 'liked and understood boys' but also had previous experience running a boys' organisation.[38] He pointed out to her that the biggest obstacle to starting a nationalist youth organisation was funding. Money, however, was a mere bagatelle for the countess.[39] Thus, in August 1909, she secured Hobson's assistance and rented a hall at 34 Lower Camden Street in Dublin. At Hobson's request, the Red Branch Knights became Na Fianna Éireann in homage to his previous Belfast group.[40]

THE 1909 INAUGURAL MEETING OF THE FIANNA AND ITS AFTERMATH

On Monday, 16 August 1909, Hobson chaired a meeting in the Camden Street hall 'to form a National Boys' Organisation to be managed by the boys themselves on national non-party lines'.[41] Estimates suggest that between thirty and one hundred boys turned up for this meeting to form what became known as Na Fianna Éireann.[42] Markievicz, Molony and a few other adults were also in attendance. In his address, Hobson explained that the organisation would be run on a semi-military basis along the lines of Baden-Powell's Boy Scout movement. In fact, it was one of the immediate objectives of this new group to counteract the influence in Ireland of that pro-British body.[43]

Patrick Ward, who attended the meeting with his friend Eamon Martin, reported that Markievicz, Hobson and the young Gaelic Leaguer Pádraic Ó Riain acted as the initial organising committee. He recalled:

> Madame Markievicz was very intense. She was the first person who captured your notice; then Bulmer Hobson, very quiet and affable and very competent to deal with any question you would like to

put, was next, apparently, in our mind in importance … There was also Pádraig Ó Riain, a good, efficient secretary.

Soon afterwards, Ward came to reverse his assessment of the relative importance of these three individuals, instead considering Ó Riain 'as by far the most significant member of that small committee at the time'. Ward regarded Ó Riain's 'intellectual and studious development' as ten years in advance of his age, adding that he possessed 'a quiet sense of humour and perfect sense of justice'.[44]

Eamon Martin and Hobson agreed with this assessment of Ó Riain.[45] Martin recalled that though Ó Riain appeared to be only sixteen or seventeen (he was actually about eighteen), 'it was quite obvious that he was well used to meetings and their procedure' and that he had a 'capacity for orderly organisation'.[46] Hobson also praised Ó Riain, citing him as the 'dominating personality in the Fianna' during the period 1909–16. Hard-working and a natural leader, Ó Riain was responsible, in his view, for the success of the Fianna in these critical early years.[47]

Accounts of this first Fianna meeting provide differing details regarding the election of officers and a provisional committee.[48] All accounts agree that Hobson was elected president. Some refer to the election of Markievicz and Ó Riain as joint secretaries, while others suggest that Markievicz became vice-president and Ó Riain secretary. This discrepancy may have arisen because a number of organisational meetings were held at the time.[49] Markievicz reported that she served as secretary at the inaugural meeting on 16 August 1909, with Ó Riain replacing her in this role at subsequent meetings.[50]

The countess's election – let alone the mere presence of women at the meeting – sparked controversy. Markievicz was taken aback when 'one of the bigger lads' – probably fifteen-year-old Robert (Bob) Harding – stood up and called for Molony and herself to be 'put out' of the hall.[51] Many boys were reluctant to accept a woman in office because they felt there was no place for a female in a physical force association.[52] Ironically, she was the best qualified person in the room to teach them how to handle firearms.[53] According to Hobson, he often had to point out discreetly that the boys could not take her money and at the same time deny her membership or office. In his view, 'this feeling against the presence of a woman in the organisation continued in varying degrees of intensity for many years and probably never completely disappeared'.[54]

An Chéad Sluagh (The First Troop) was born out of this inaugural meeting in August 1909.[55] Its members met regularly in the Camden Street

Figure 2 Bulmer Hobson (seated) and Pádraic Ó Riain.

hall, adopting a dark green jersey and kilt as their uniform.[56] With the future expansion of the organisation, other Fianna members chose to wear dark breeches and an olive green tunic with brass buttons.[57] A month after its formation, it was reported that officers and a committee had been elected at a general meeting of the *sluagh*. The officers included B. Hobson (president); Patrick Walsh, C. de Markievicz, J. Robinson and J. Dundon (honorary secretaries); and P. Ó Riain (treasurer of the camping fund), while the committee consisted of S. Mac Caisin, C. Colbert, G. Harvey, R. Harding, G. Sherry, S. McGarry and H. Molony.[58]

By September 1909, a growing number of boys were meeting at the hall every Tuesday and Thursday evening for military drill.⁵⁹ Con Colbert was the first instructor in elementary drill formations. Eamon Martin reported: '[Colbert] was no great expert at this time. By intense swotting, however, he improved as the weeks went on, and, consequently, so did the *sluagh*.' Later on, certain members of the *sluagh*, such as the dapper Michael Lonergan, emerged as natural instructors.⁶⁰ The troop also received drill instruction from Sean Kavanagh, an ex-member of the British army, to whom Seamus Mac Caisin attributed not only the discipline of the Fianna but also the later Irish Volunteers.⁶¹

The activities of the Fianna soon expanded. In October 1909, the newspaper *Bean na hÉireann* reported that 'the hall at 34 Lr. Camden St. is open almost every night in the week. On Monday it is drill, on Tuesday games, on Wednesday language and history classes, on the Thursday the leaders of sections drill, and on Friday the room is open for games and drill.'⁶² Route marches, scouting, camping and a lecture series on inspirational topics such as the 'boy heroes' of the 1798 rebellion were also on offer.⁶³ The range of activities available continued to expand so that through their involvement with the Fianna the boys had the opportunity to learn elementary drill, signalling, first aid, route marching and scouting skills such as map reading, path-finding and elementary astronomy. They also studied Irish language and history, particularly that of battles and insurrections. As Eamon Martin explained, 'in this way the boys were being given a reason for their own military training'.⁶⁴

The Fianna initially faced 'opposition, ridicule and indifference', even from fellow nationalists.⁶⁵ For instance, a correspondent to Griffith's *Sinn Féin* newspaper was keen to dissociate the local branches of Sinn Féin and the Gaelic League from the new boys' group.⁶⁶ Alternatively, some Sinn Féin branches, such as the one in Drumcondra with which Markievicz was affiliated, later encouraged the formation of new Fianna *sluaighte* by allowing the boys to use their meeting rooms.⁶⁷

Inghinidhe na hÉireann's paper *Bean na hÉireann* (Woman of Ireland), which Molony edited, was supportive from the start and provided coverage of early Fianna activities. For example, in September 1909, the paper asserted: 'Some Nationalists think that the boys don't count in the nation, but the founders of Na Fianna Éireann rightly consider them of supreme importance. They are the recruits for the future armies of Ireland, and on them the future of Ireland must depend.'⁶⁸ Inghinidhe na hÉireann had long recognised the value of youth to the nationalist movement. Shortly after its inception in 1900, this women's nationalist organisation established free classes in Irish language, literature, history and music for children over the age of nine, mainly in Dublin and Cork, but ended up abandoning 'its boys' classes because they were too hard to manage'.[69] The foundation of the Fianna helped to fill this gap. Publications associated with Hobson, such as the IRB-backed newspaper *Irish Freedom* and the eponymous Irish Volunteer organ, also published regular reports of Fianna activities.[70]

Around the same time that Markievicz and Hobson started Na Fianna Éireann, the pair also hatched a scheme to establish an agricultural commune. Hobson had come up with the idea of living on a small farm, possibly in an agricultural colony, so that he could spend half his time farming and the other half reading and writing.[71] However, he lacked the money to undertake the plan which had been inspired by E. T. Craig's book *A History of Ralahine*. This book outlined the fortunes of a short-lived co-operative colony established by County Clare landlord John Scott Vandeleur on his Ralahine estate. Vandeleur had been inspired by a series of lectures given by Robert Owen, the originator of the co-operative movement, in the Rotunda in Dublin in 1823. He invited Owen's follower Craig to organise the experiment among the tenants on his estate. Hobson saw it as 'the first ... attempt to establish a national social order' in Ireland.[72] The Ralahine project worked for a while but was later scuttled by a combination of Vandeleur's gambling debts and the fact that there was no legal recognition of the collective ownership of the property.[73]

Hobson lent Craig's book to Markievicz. She was not only charmed by the idea of an agricultural commune but also possessed the financial means to put his idea into action. Fired with enthusiasm, Markievicz and Hobson, with their friend Molony in tow, decided to resurrect the commune in what is now the north Dublin suburb of Finglas. Markievicz rented Belcamp Park, 'a fine, big, roughcast-limestone house about six miles north of Dublin off the Malahide Road'. For a rent of about £100 per year, they got the house, which had about twenty rooms, seven and a half acres of land, stables and a walled garden – all in a state of disrepair.[74] They moved into the house at the end of the summer of 1909. The commune mainly consisted of Markievicz, Hobson, Molony and Donnchadh O'Hannigan, a graduate of Glasnevin Agricultural College.[75] It was soon inundated by Fianna boys, who came for camping trips and shooting practice. Perhaps unsurprisingly, the countess and Molony were stuck cooking and washing up from eight in the morning to eight in the evening while Hobson commuted to Dublin on a daily basis to deal with his political and journalistic commitments. Only O'Hannigan was free to engage in any market gardening.[76]

The countess's biographer Sean O'Faolain offers a vivid account of various reactions to the commune. Apparently, Casimir Markievicz returned to Ireland to discover that his wife was the laughing stock of Dublin.[77] Even their friend Sean McGarry had branded the trio of Hobson, Molony and the countess 'idiots' for starting the commune.[78] Not surprisingly, the project gave rise to a medley of rumours. Some gossips claimed that Count Markievicz was threatening to fight a duel with Hobson while others discussed the alleged fears of Denis McCullough, Hobson's Belfast partner in nationalism, that this married lady would destroy the young man's political career in the same way that Charles Stewart Parnell's relationship with Katharine O'Shea had destroyed his.[79] Less whimsical rumours linked Hobson and Molony romantically.[80]

In a bid to end the commune through harassment, the count gleefully fed the rumour mill by spreading unscrupulous stories about his wife, Hobson and Molony. When this tactic did not work, he turned dinners at Belcamp Park into board meetings at which he bombarded the would-be 'communists' with economic figures that deflated their enthusiasm for the scheme. O'Faolain estimated that the experiment, which lasted about two months (probably September and October 1909), accumulated a net loss of £250. The countess and Molony remained at the house until they could get out of the five-year lease.[81] Molony recalled the episode in a more positive light than O'Faolain: 'Financially it was not a success, but the Fianna enjoyed it thoroughly and put a lot of work into developing the grounds. When we decided to wind up the experiment we succeeded in getting a buyer, and the losses which we shared were not very great.'[82]

Meanwhile, unemployment forced Hobson back home to Belfast in early November 1909, leaving behind rumours that a romance between himself and Molony had failed along with the commune.[83] In Hobson's absence, the countess was elected president of the Fianna, a position that she retained even after Hobson moved back to Dublin in 1911. Upon his return, he resumed his active involvement with the Fianna nationally, serving as vice-president until the Fianna's reorganisation in mid-1915 and a member of the *ard-choisde* (central council) until the 1916 Easter Rising.[84] Hobson's opposition to the Rising effectively ended his involvement with the Fianna, but the countess maintained her connection to the organisation until her death in 1927.

A former Fianna member, Fr Thomas O'Donoghue, once described Hobson as the 'head' of the nationalist youth group and Markievicz the 'heart'.[85] To make his dream of creating 'a strong force to help in the liberation of Ireland' come true, Hobson needed Markievicz's energy, enthusiasm, initial injection of money and, due to her gender and social position, ability to inspire the trust and confidence of the parents of the younger boys.[86] Without her impetus, he probably would not have attempted to resurrect the Fianna. To make her dream come true, she needed his organisational experience, the template of his previous boys' group, and though she may not have been aware of it, his connection to the IRB. Although the united front of the countess and the Quaker later disintegrated due to political differences, their brainchild survived.

NOTES

1. An earlier draft of this chapter and the one that follows were published as Marnie Hay, 'The foundation and development of Na Fianna Éireann, 1909–16', *Irish Historical Studies*, 36:141 (May 2008), pp. 53–71.
2. 'A Boys' Brigade', *SF*, 14 Aug. 1909, p. 4.
3. The building that housed the first Fianna hall was demolished in 2012.
4. Michael Lonergan, witness statement, 1 Aug. 1948 (MA, BMH, WS 140).
5. Marnie Hay, *Bulmer Hobson and the Nationalist Movement in Twentieth-Century Ireland* (Manchester: Manchester University Press, 2009), pp. 28–9.
6. Senia Pašeta, 'Markievicz, Constance Georgine' in James McGuire and James Quinn (eds), *Dictionary of Irish Biography* (Cambridge: Cambridge University Press, 2009), available from http://dib.cambridge.org.
7. For more detail on Hobson's nationalist career, see Hay, *Bulmer Hobson and the Nationalist Movement in Twentieth-Century Ireland*.
8. *UI*, 17 Aug. 1901, p. 5; *UI*, 24 Aug. 1901, p. 5.
9. *UI*, 14 Sept. 1901, p. 5.
10. Marcus de Búrca, *The GAA: A History* (Dublin: Cumann Lúthchleas Gael, 1980), p. 58.
11. *UI*, 28 Sept. 1901, p. 5.
12. Bulmer Hobson, *Ireland Yesterday and Tomorrow* (Tralee: Anvil Books, 1968), p. 15.
13. *Irish News*, 18 Sept. 1901, p. 8.
14. Na Fianna Éireann minute book, 1902 (NLI, Bulmer Hobson Papers, MS 12,176).
15. *Ibid.*

16 Bulmer Hobson, 'The IRB and the Fianna' in F. X. Martin (ed.), *The Irish Volunteers 1913–1915: Recollections and Documents* (Dublin: James Duffy, 1963), p. 18; *UI*, 24 Jan. 1903, p. 1.
17 'Belfast notes', *ACS*, 5 July 1902, p. 293.
18 Hobson, *Ireland*, p. 15.
19 *UI*, 24 Jan. 1903, p. 1.
20 Fianna minute book (NLI, Hobson Papers, MS 12,176).
21 Seamus Robinson, witness statement, 26 Oct. 1948 (MA, BMH, WS 156). His elder brother Joseph was also a member of Hobson's original Belfast Fianna. The Robinson family moved to Glasgow in 1903 where the brothers continued their involvement in Irish nationalist activities. See Máirtín Ó Catháin, *Irish Republicanism in Scotland, 1858–1816* (Dublin: Irish Academic Press, 2007), pp. 228–9.
22 Hobson, *Ireland*, p. 16.
23 Hobson, 'IRB and Fianna', p. 18.
24 'A warning to the autocrats', *The Republic*, 7 Feb. 1907, p. 1.
25 Hobson, 'IRB and Fianna', p. 18.
26 Constance de Markievicz, 'Memories', *Éire*, 18 Aug. 1923, p. 5.
27 Constance de Markievicz, 'How the Fianna was started', *Nodlaig na bhFiann*, Dec. 1914, p. 2.
28 *Ibid.*; Anne Marreco, *The Rebel Countess* (London: Weidenfeld and Nicolson, 1967), p. 112; Jacqueline Van Voris, *Constance de Markievicz in the Cause of Ireland* (Amherst, MA: University of Massachusetts Press, 1967), p. 67.
29 Markievicz, 'How the Fianna was started', p. 2.
30 Marreco, *Rebel Countess*, pp. 113–14.
31 *UI*, 24 Jan. 1903, p. 1.
32 Marreco, *Rebel Countess*, p. 114.
33 Markievicz, 'How the Fianna was started', p. 2.
34 Sean McGarry, witness statement, 15 Apr. 1950 (MA, BMH, WS 368).
35 Marreco, *Rebel Countess*, p. 115.
36 Markievicz, 'How the Fianna was started', p. 2.
37 *Ibid.*, pp. 2–3.
38 *Ibid.*, p. 3.
39 Hobson, 'IRB and Fianna', pp. 18–19; Sean O'Faolain, *Constance Markievicz* (2nd edn, London: Hutchinson, 1987), p. 85; Van Voris, *Constance de Markievicz*, pp. 69–70.
40 Marreco, *Rebel Countess*, p. 117.
41 Hobson, 'IRB and Fianna', pp. 18–19.
42 Michael Lonergan, witness statement, 1 Aug. 1948 (MA, BMH, WS 140); Seamus Mac Caisin, witness statement, 8 June 1947 (MA, BMH, WS 8).

43 Eamon Martin, witness statement, 1 Oct. 1951 (MA, BMH, WS 591).
44 Patrick Ward, witness statement, 30 Mar. 1955 (MA, BMH, WS 1,140).
45 Cathleen McCarthy (née Ryan), witness statement, 31 Mar. 1954 (MA, BMH, WS 937); Seamus Mac Caisin, witness statement, 8 June 1947 (MA, BMH, WS 8).
46 Eamon Martin, witness statement, 1 Oct. 1951 (MA, BMH, WS 591). Ó Riain was listed in the 1911 census as a twenty-year-old bilingual clerk residing with his family at 41 Rutland Square in Dublin; available at www.census.nationalarchives.ie/pages/1911/Dublin/Rotunda/Rutland_Square__West/37530/ (accessed 21 July 2018). This would make him about eighteen when the Fianna was formed in 1909.
47 Hobson, 'IRB and Fianna', p. 23.
48 *An Claidheamh Soluis* (Sword of Light) reported that officers and a provisional committee were appointed at the inaugural meeting, but did not list any names ('Fianna Éireann', *ACS*, 21 Aug. 1909, p. 10).
49 Eamon Martin, witness statement, 1 Oct. 1951 (MA, BMH, WS 591); Patrick Ward, witness statement, 30 Mar. 1955 (MA, BMH, WS 1,140); Hobson, *Ireland*, p. 16; Marreco, *Rebel Countess*, p. 117; Van Voris, *Constance de Markievicz*, p. 78.
50 Markievicz, 'How the Fianna was started', p. 3.
51 *Ibid*. Seamus Mac Caisin identified this boy as Harding, who was a member of the Michael Dwyer hurling club (MA, BMH, WS 8). In the 1911 census, Harding was listed as a seventeen-year-old painter's messenger who lived on Redmond's Hill, which was down the road from the Fianna hall on Camden Street; available at www.census.nationalarchives.ie/pages/1911/Dublin/Mansion_House/Redmond_s_Hill__West_Side/74721/ (accessed 21 July 2018).
52 Seamus Mac Caisin, witness statement, 8 June 1947 (MA, BMH, WS 8); Marreco, *Rebel Countess*, p. 117; Van Voris, *Constance de Markievicz*, p. 70.
53 Marreco, *Rebel Countess*, p. 118.
54 Hobson, 'IRB and Fianna', pp. 18–19.
55 I have chosen to use the Irish language spellings of Fianna terminology that were utilised in the early twentieth century rather than the modern versions. Thus, I use *sluagh* rather than the modern *slua*.
56 Garry Holohan, witness statement, 7 Dec. 1949 (MA, BMH, WS 328).
57 Pádraic Ó Riain (ed.), *Fianna Handbook* (Dublin: Central Council of Na Fianna Éireann, 1914), pp. 21–2.
58 *B na hÉ*, Sept. 1909, p. 9.
59 One of the Fianna, 'Na Fianna Éireann (National Boys' Brigade)', *B na hÉ*, Sept. 1909, pp. 8–9.

60 Eamon Martin, witness statement, 1 Oct. 1951 (MA, BMH, WS 591).
61 Seamus Mac Caisin, witness statement, 8 June 1947 (MA, BMH, WS 8).
62 One of the Fianna, 'Na Fianna Éireann (National Boys' Brigade)', *B na hÉ*, Oct. 1909, p. 8.
63 *B na hÉ*, Sept. 1909, p. 9; One of the Fianna, 'Na Fianna Éireann (National Boys' Brigade)', *B na hÉ*, Oct. 1909, p. 8.
64 Eamon Martin, witness statement, 1 Oct. 1951 (MA, BMH, WS 591).
65 Oscar, 'Na Fianna Éireann', *IF*, Sept. 1911, p. 7.
66 'National Boys' Brigade', *SF*, 21 Aug. 1909, p. 4.
67 One of the Fianna, 'Na Fianna Éireann (National Boys' Brigade)', *B na hÉ*, Oct. 1909, p. 8.
68 One of the Fianna, 'Na Fianna Éireann (National Boys' Brigade)', *B na hÉ*, Sept. 1909, p. 8.
69 Helena Molony, witness statement, 19 May 1950 (MA, BMH, WS 391). For more on Inghinidhe na nÉireann's work with children, see Marnie Hay, 'What did advanced nationalists tell Irish children in the early twentieth century?' in Ciara Ní Bhroin and Patricia Kennon (eds), *What Do We Tell the Children? Critical Essays on Children's Literature* (Cambridge: Cambridge Scholars Press, 2012), pp. 148–62.
70 Hobson was one of the editors of *Irish Freedom* until June 1914 and served as the business manager and unofficial editor of *Irish Volunteer* from December 1914 onwards.
71 León Ó Broin, *Protestant Nationalism in Revolutionary Ireland* (Dublin: Gill and Macmillan, 1985), p. 37.
72 'A history of Ralahine', *IF*, Oct. 1912, p. 2.
73 O'Faolain, *Constance Markievicz*, pp. 88–9.
74 *Ibid.*, p. 89.
75 *Ibid.*, p. 91; Marreco, *Rebel Countess*, p. 133. The Glasnevin graduate has sometimes been referred to as Donald Hannigan. I have chosen to use the form of his name used by his younger brother Dónal, who lived at Belcamp Park and joined the Fianna and later the Irish Volunteers. See Dónal O'Hannigan, witness statement, 2 Dec. 1948 (MA, BMH, WS 161).
76 O'Faolain, *Constance Markievicz*, p. 91.
77 *Ibid.*, pp. 89–91.
78 Helena Molony, witness statement, 19 May 1950 (NAI, BMH, WS 391).
79 Ó Broin, *Protestant Nationalism*, p. 37.
80 Nell Regan, 'Helena Molony' in Mary Cullen and Maria Luddy (eds), *Female Activists: Irish Women and Change, 1900–1960* (Dublin: Woodfield Press, 2001), p. 144; Nell Regan, *Helena Molony: A Radical Life, 1883–1967* (Dublin: Arlen House, 2017), pp. 69–70, 201.
81 O'Faolain, *Constance Markievicz*, pp. 93–4.

82 Helena Molony, witness statement, 19 May 1950 (MA, BMH, WS 391).
83 Regan, 'Helena Molony', p. 144. Molony apparently told Louie Coghlan-O'Brien in the 1930s that Hobson had reneged on a promise to marry her and thus broken her heart (Regan, *Helena Molony*, pp. 69, 201).
84 Hobson, 'IRB and Fianna', p. 21; Hobson, *Ireland*, p. 17. At the fourth annual Fianna congress held on 13 July 1913 in the Oak Room of the Mansion House in Dublin, Hobson and Joseph Robinson were elected co-vice-presidents ('Na Fianna Éireann', *IF*, Aug. 1913, p. 7).
85 Thomas O'Donoghue, witness statement, n.d. (MA, BMH, WS 1,666). Fr O'Donoghue died before he could sign his witness statement.
86 Hobson, *Ireland*, p. 15; Helena Molony, witness statement, 19 May 1950 (MA, BMH, WS 391).

3 A handful of boys against the British Empire, 1909–16

> The interest taken in the Fianna by young and old is gradually, if slowly, increasing as they increase in numbers. There are those who think the organisation of little importance because it is made up of boys, but such people forget that though one may be too young to be the possessor of that powerful weapon called a vote, nobody is too young to serve his country, and, if necessary, fight for his country.[1]

In 1913, Liam Mellows, the newly appointed Fianna organiser, took to the open road on his bicycle to accelerate the expansion of the nationalist youth group around the country. In a published report, he described slogging through wet weather and muddy roads in counties Wexford, Waterford, Kilkenny and Tipperary in order to liaise with local contacts and hold meetings to form new *sluaighte* (troops). Very few people appeared to realise 'what an asset to Ireland the boys were'. According to Mellows, some of the 'would-be Nationalists' that he 'appealed to for help, spoke of the movement with sarcasm and pointed out how, in *their* worldly wisdom, it was doomed to failure. "What can a handful of boys do against the great British Empire?"' they shrugged. Others worried that the military training provided by the Fianna would inspire boys to join the British army. Still others found the youth group too extremist in its commitment to Irish nationalism.[2]

Despite being faced with such negative attitudes, Na Fianna Éireann soldiered on, preparing boys (and some girls) for their future roles in the struggle for Irish independence. Between its establishment in 1909 and the end of the Irish Civil War in 1923, the youth organisation developed in terms of structure, purpose, policies, membership figures and geographical spread. Changes in the organisation's development were often linked to political events and trends within the wider nationalist movement. This chapter will take a chronological look at the Fianna's organisational development up to the 1916 Easter Rising, with the following chapter covering the period 1916–23.

BRANCHING OUT

Na Fianna Éireann soon grew beyond *An Chéad Sluagh*. On 29 September 1909, Hobson presided over a meeting held in the rooms of the Drumcondra Branch of Sinn Féin on St Joseph's Avenue to form a second branch of the Fianna that would cater to boys on the north side of Dublin.[3] A third branch of the Fianna was then established by Micheál O'Neill in Waterford *c*. October 1909, though it is unclear how long it initially survived.[4] In the pages of *Bean na hÉireann*, the adult nationalist organisations were exhorted to do their duty so that no town within Ireland would be without a branch of the Fianna.[5]

In the northeast of Ireland, the Fianna first spread to Belfast. Although plans for the formation of a Belfast branch were underway in December 1909, it appears that the *sluagh* was not officially established until a meeting held in the Dungannon Club on 7 March 1910.[6] Joseph Robinson, a member of Hobson's original Belfast Fianna, and William Woods recruited Belfast boys through the Peter O'Neill Gaelic Football Club and the O'Neill's Pipe Band. One of those boys was David McGuinness who recalled that seventy boys had joined within three months. The Belfast Fianna initially met in the band's room above a tobacconist's shop on Mill Street, but as numbers grew they moved their premises to the huts at Willowbank which had been used by a British cavalry unit.[7]

Growth of the organisation continued in 1910. Under the auspices of the North Dock branch of Sinn Féin, a new Fianna *sluagh* was formed at 10 Beresford Place in Dublin early in the year.[8] In the summer of 1910, *Bean na hÉireann* reported the creation of four new *sluaighte*, three in Dublin and one in Glasgow. The new Dublin *sluaighte* were based in John Street (May 1910), James's Street (June 1910) and Sandwith Street (July 1910). Joseph Robinson, who was also involved with the Belfast Fianna, was the president of the Glasgow branch, which was formed in April 1910 and soon attracted about fifty members.[9]

As a result of the growing number of *sluaighte*, the Fianna leadership recognised that the youth organisation required clear rules and a formal structure. As early as the autumn of 1909, a joint committee of the section leaders of the Dublin Fianna was formed to meet on a monthly basis to revise the rules in order to make them uniform throughout the city.¹⁰ The structure of the organisation was further solidified by the first annual Fianna conference, which was held in the Mansion House in Dublin on 21 August 1910. At this event, a national executive was elected that included: Countess Markievicz (president), Councillor Paul Gregan and Bulmer Hobson (vice-presidents), Pádraic Ó Riain (honorary secretary), Michael Lonergan (honorary assistant secretary) and James Gregan (treasurer).¹¹ In addition to its executive, the Fianna consisted of an *ard-fheis* (congress), an *ard-choisde* (central council), district councils and *sluaighte*. The *ard-fheis*, which met annually, was the 'supreme governing and legislative body of the Fianna'. It comprised the *ard-choisde* and delegates from the various *sluaighte* and district councils, which were formed in 1911 in Dublin and Belfast, where there were three or more *sluaighte*. The *ard-choisde* was responsible for the general direction of Na Fianna Éireann and served as the governing body of the organisation when the *ard-fheis* was not sitting.¹²

At the Fianna's first *ard-fheis*, Ó Riain reported that seven *sluaighte* were officially affiliated to the national organisation, five in Dublin, one in Waterford and one in Glasgow, with each *sluagh* consisting of twenty to sixty members.¹³ It is unclear whether the Belfast *sluagh* and one of the Dublin branches previously mentioned had ceased to exist or they were not officially affiliated to the national organisation. In any case, October 1910 saw the inauguration of a *sluagh* in Belfast with plans for the formation of another one there. Elsewhere in the country, a Fianna branch had been established in Clonmel, County Tipperary, while plans were underway to form a troop in Cork.¹⁴

In November 1910, a branch of the Fianna was started at St Enda's School for boys, which Patrick Pearse had founded in 1908 in order to combine a more progressive, child-centred way of teaching with a curriculum that was truly Irish. He not only fostered bilingualism in Irish and English at the school but also ensured that Gaelic games, musical evenings and the production of Irish plays and pageants were an important part of school life. On 24 November 1910, the day after Con Colbert had given the students their 'first lesson in military foot drill', Pearse announced his plan to form 'a body of the Fianna in the School, with the object of encouraging moral, mental, and physical "fitness"'. The new branch was 'duly organised' on 28 November with members being 'divided into eight *buidheanta* or companies', each under the leadership of a Taoiseach or Captain. The companies were then 'grouped into two *catha* or battalions' under the leadership of a Mór-Thaoiseach or Colonel. Pearse served as the branch's commander-in-chief or Ard-Taoiseach'. The branch's activities included 'drill, gymnastics, shooting, fencing, boxing, wrestling, swimming, ambulance work, mountain marches, camping out, and scouting'.[15]

In January 1911, it was reported that the Fianna were 'making splendid headway in Belfast' with close to 150 boys enrolled in the city's first *sluagh*, entitled Clann Rudhraighe. Not only was a second Belfast troop called Sluagh Willie Nelson 'doing well', but plans were afoot to form a third *sluagh* in the northern city.[16] Within two months Eithne Ní Baoghaoil (Annie O'Boyle) had organised a girls' troop in Belfast that consisted of '25 most enthusiastic young girls all striving to follow in the footsteps of the Irish women of the past'.[17] O'Boyle was one of the women associated with the Belfast Dungannon Club, which had been co-founded by Hobson and had a women's division called Cumann na Cailíní.[18] Although *Irish Freedom* initially reported that the girls' *sluagh* was named in honour of the late Belfast poet Ethna Carbery (the pseudonym of Anna Johnston McManus), it actually became known as the Betsy Gray *sluagh*, honouring a heroine of the 1798 rebellion.[19] The girls' troop had its own version of the Fianna uniform: the girls wore 'green linen shirts' while the boys' shirts were made of 'hopsack'.[20]

The establishment of this girls' troop may have been a nationalist reaction to the formation in Belfast in 1910 of what was one of the few pre-war Girl Guide companies in Ireland.[21] Alternatively, O'Boyle may have wanted to extend the Fianna's activities to nationalist girls. In any case, reaction to the new troop was mixed. David McGuinness recalled that the girls' *sluagh* 'met with considerable opposition from many of the Fianna boys'.[22] Historian Sinéad McCoole notes that it faced 'endless opposition' before it became affiliated with the Belfast District Council.[23] Yet when Markievicz gave the oration at the annual Manchester Martyrs commemoration in November 1911 in Belfast, this girls' *sluagh* presented an exhibition of drill that apparently 'received general approbation'.[24]

Among the members of the Betsy Gray *sluagh* were two daughters of labour leader and future 1916 insurrectionist James Connolly. They joined the troop shortly after their family returned from the United States. Nora became the chief officer of the *sluagh*, though she did not remember being called captain, while Ina served as secretary.[25] Their younger brother Roddy also joined the Fianna in Belfast, but unlike his sisters was not a prominent member there.[26]

At the second annual Fianna *ard-fheis* held in the summer of 1911, fifteen *sluaighte* were affiliated, including seven in Dublin and six in Belfast.²⁷ However, many of these troops were 'in a very disorganised condition' and three of them soon collapsed.²⁸ The situation improved over the ensuing year – at least in some places. In July 1912, Ó Riain recorded the existence of twenty-two branches, 'all in a very healthy condition'.²⁹ Between the summers of 1911 and 1912 three new troops had been established in County Dublin, one in the city and two in Ballybrack and Lusk.³⁰ Troops also existed in Derry, Athlone, Moate, Portlaoise, Enniscorthy and Rathkeale.³¹ The Limerick *sluagh*, which boasted 250 members, even opened the first purpose-built Fianna hall in the country in December 1912.³² The Belfast branches of the Fianna, however, had faced 'serious difficulties' for reasons that Ó Riain did not elucidate. He reported that 'one *sluagh* had to be suspended, and three others ceased to exist as *sluaighte* of the Fianna'. The Belfast District Council, however, had established new troops to replace the ones lost.³³

The Fianna soon spread to other places in Ulster. Around 1912, Paddy Rankin started a Fianna troop in Newry, which Edward Fullerton joined in 1914. He recalled that the officers were Malachy Quinn and Peter O'Hare and that between twenty-five and thirty boys belonged to the troop prior to the 1916 Rising.³⁴ By September 1912, there was also a Fianna troop in Derry.³⁵ Although the Royal Irish Constabulary's county inspector recorded that efforts were underway to form a Fianna troop in Armagh around December 1911 and January 1912, he later noted in December 1913 that this attempt was unsuccessful.³⁶

A Fianna *sluagh* was started in Cork city *c*. 1910–11 by a group of men associated with various nationalist organisations, particularly the Gaelic League. The Cork *sluagh*'s initial headquarters was in An Dún on Queen Street. Markievicz and Hobson visited the fledging troop to offer encouragement.³⁷ The Cork *sluagh* soon consisted of about thirty to forty boys between the ages of eleven and seventeen. Numbers apparently rose to nearly 100 by 1916.³⁸ Until the formation of the Irish Volunteers, Cork Fianna activities were supervised by a committee of five men: Tomás MacCurtain, Sean O'Sullivan, Martin Donovan, Paddy Corkery and Donncadh O'Donoghue. Once they became too busy with their Volunteer duties, the committee shifted responsibility for the *sluagh* to Tadg Barry and George Osborne in 1914.³⁹ The committee continued to appoint the troop's scoutmaster until the Munster Convention of Fianna held in Limerick in 1915 when the scoutmaster became known as the captain of the *sluagh*.⁴⁰

UNSTEADY GROWTH

Between 1909 and 1913 the growth of the Fianna was often unsteady, especially outside of the city of Dublin. According to the monthly police reports of the Inspector General for 1912–13, the only place outside of Dublin where the Fianna were making significant headway was in the city of Limerick. There the boys were under the patronage of former Fenian convict John Daly who provided them with a parade ground at the rear of his Barrington Street home, which became the location of the first purpose-built Fianna hall. In February 1913, the Inspector General reported that 'elsewhere it [the Fianna] is discouraged by the [Roman Catholic] clergy'.[41] This tallies with Mellows' assertion that 'very few of the clergy gave the movement any support, and those who did were nearly all what Canon Sheehan described as "the young bicycle riding curates" who had been influenced in Maynooth by the Gaelic League'.[42] It must be noted, however, that county inspectors' monthly reports did not mention all of the Fianna *sluaighte* covered in the advanced nationalist press of the time, possibly because some troops operated below the radar of the local police or an organisation of mere boys was not deemed worthy of notice.[43] Conversely, many of the troops noted in the police reports were not mentioned in the press.

Even the Fianna branch at St Enda's School appears to have collapsed at some point in the years 1911–12; had the branch survived, it is unlikely that a new initiative would have been launched in 1913. During that year, Eamonn Bulfin and Desmond Ryan, who had been captains in the school's former Fianna branch, organised the students 'into a little club on the model of the Fianna Éireann', which they called 'An Chraobh Ruadh' (The Red Branch), in order to teach the boys 'rifle-shooting, boxing, signalling, marching, camping, first aid, etc.'[44]

Growth of the Fianna organisation was often stunted for a variety of reasons, including absence of sustained interest, local opposition or rivalry and insufficient funding. For instance, in August 1912 the county inspector recorded that 'a branch of the Irish National Boy Scouts was established in Listowel [County Kerry] in July last but has since disbanded'.[45] Other *sluaighte* may not have died such an early death but appeared to be in need of rebirth. For example, the county inspector's reports for County Laois in 1912–13 generally referred to the troop in Maryborough (Portlaoise) as 'nearly dead' or 'inactive'.[46] Rivalry between different nationalist organisations also had an impact on the Fianna. In the summer of 1912, Pádraic Ó Riain reported that local members of the Ancient Order of Hibernians (AOH) had broken up a Fianna *sluagh* in Newcastle-West, County Limerick.[47] Relations between the two nationalist organisations were further strained in Limerick after the AOH and the Fianna accused one another of having orchestrated window breaking during riots in the city on 10–11 October 1912.[48] Elsewhere, the Hibernians started their own Boys' Brigades in places such as New Ross, County Wexford, Carrickmacross, County Monaghan and the city of Waterford.[49]

Limited funding curtailed the *ard-choisde*'s ability to engage in systematic organisation around the country and postponed the publication of a planned Fianna instruction handbook until 1914. While Markievicz provided an initial injection of money to start the organisation, in actual fact the Fianna's ongoing funding came from the boys' own subscriptions of one penny a week and fundraising events such as concerts. In addition, humanitarian and diplomat Roger Casement provided gifts of money while Hobson engaged in various fundraising activities. The Irish Republican Brotherhood (IRB) also contributed funding 'in a small way' through the conduit of Hobson.[50] For instance, between July 1911 and June 1912 Hobson's efforts brought in £10, almost one third of the Fianna's annual income for that year. Aside from affiliation fees, which amounted to £4 10s., most of the Fianna's annual income for the year 1911–12 (£33 13s. 1d.) came from Dublin.[51] It was believed that 'great work could be done' in County Wexford, where public opinion was apparently favourable to the Fianna, if only the *ard-choisde* could afford to send an organiser there.[52] Despite such setbacks, however, by 1913 the organisation had spread beyond the Dublin region to Belfast, Cork, Limerick, Derry, Waterford, Clonmel, Dundalk, Newry, Listowel and Glasgow.[53]

SPLITS AND RIVALRIES

In May 1912, *Irish Freedom* reported that alongside the Fianna a number of similar boys' associations had sprung up and an alliance of these groups in Dublin was proposed. Rather than interfere with the working of these different bodies, the proposed alliance would facilitate the arrangement of 'friendly scouting contests, displays, parades, etc.' According to the report, such an alliance would not only 'stimulate and encourage the spirit of friendly rivalry' but would also 'discourage, and to a very large extent, be able to prevent any ill-feeling or jealousy arising between the boys of the different organisations at present in existence'. In addition, it would serve 'to consolidate the forces of national boys if occasion required'.[54]

The proposed alliance may have been partly a response to a split in the Fianna that occurred c. 1912, leading to the establishment of a new organisation called the Irish National Guards. Accounts vary regarding the true cause of the split. Sean Kennedy and Seamus Bevan recalled that it was due to a dispute over the hat to be worn by Fianna members. Although most of the Fianna uniform was made in Ireland of Irish materials, the hat had to be imported from England, which caused 'dissatisfaction' and a decision to breakaway and form a new organisation.[55] Thomas O'Donoghue, however, suggested that the split resulted from something more fundamental than hats, asserting that the idea behind the National Guards was to train youths rather than boys in the use of arms. 'We did not mean to be in opposition to the Fianna', he explained. 'We only wanted youths – not boys.'[56] He did not indicate, however, at what age a boy became a youth.[57]

The Irish National Guards initially had rooms in Blackhall Place, but later moved to York Street and later North Great George's Street in Dublin. Members were 'well drilled in the use of firearms and side arms', learned signalling and held lectures and debates.[58] O'Donoghue noted that the breakaway organisation had IRB support and consisted of branches in Dublin and Galway and maybe one in Cork.[59] Bevan estimated that the National Guards only had about forty members, though he may have been referring to a single troop.[60] John Kenny recalled the involvement of girls in activities associated with the National Guards, mentioning, among others, May and Kathleen Kelly of the Clann na Gael Girl Scouts.[61]

The Bureau of Military History (BMH) witness statements suggest that the National Guards may have been known by two other names, the Dublin Guards and Na Curaigh Gaeilge (The Gaelic Warriors). For example, Sean Kennedy reported that he was among those who left the Fianna in 1912 to join 'the militant body then known as the Dublin Guards'.[62] In Loughrea, County Galway, Martin O'Regan was an officer in Na Curaidh Gaeilge, which he thought was an off-shoot of the Fianna that had fallen out with the latter organisation over hats. During Easter Week 1916, O'Regan was taking a scholarship exam in Galway when he was arrested and questioned about his involvement with Na Curaidh Gaeilge.[63] Members of the Fianna and the National Guards participated in the Easter Rising. For instance, Sean Howard, who was killed in action during the Rising, was one of the Fianna members who had shifted his membership to the National Guards.[64]

It is unclear whether a reported split in a north Dublin Fianna troop was part of the wider division that led to the formation of the National

Guards. Garry Holohan recalled that in 1913 some members of Sluagh Emmet, which met in Beresford Place, broke away from the Fianna, taking a tent with them. While the breakaway boys were camping, their erstwhile colleagues from Sluagh Emmet stole it back. As a result of this tit-for-tat tent stealing, beatings ensued.[65]

A REVOLUTIONARY *ARD-FHEIS*

At the third annual *ard-fheis* in July 1912, the constitution was amended to assert that the object of the Fianna was to re-establish the independence of Ireland and that this object was to be achieved through 'the training of the youth of Ireland, mentally and physically … by teaching scouting and military exercises, Irish history, and the Irish language'. Members also promised 'to work for the Independence of Ireland, never to join England's armed forces, and to obey [their] superior officers'.[66]

It was no coincidence that 1912 was the year that Hobson started a special Fianna circle of the IRB after his election as the Dublin Centre of that secret society. This new Fianna circle was known as the John Mitchel Literary and Debating Society with Con Colbert as head. The membership included Pádraic Ó Riain, Eamon Martin, Michael Lonergan, Garry Holohan, Sean Heuston, Desmond Ryan and the Mellows brothers, Liam and Barney.[67]

The 1912 annual congress had been revolutionary in another way. Resolutions were carried by small majorities to admit girls to the organisation and to instruct district councils to establish girls' *sluaighte*. The Betsy Gray *sluagh* formed in 1911 was represented at this *ard-fheis* by three elected delegates: Ina Connolly, Kate O'Kane and Rose Leckey.[68] These resolutions generated a great deal of discussion with emotions running high. Boys who were against the admission of the opposite sex argued that there should be a separate organisation founded for girls. In the end, the resolution to admit girls was carried by only one vote.[69] Even though she was reputed not to like girls, the countess was the one who managed to carry the proposal to open the Fianna to her own gender. The suffragist newspaper *Irish Citizen* reported that this feminist advance was later flouted by 'the newly-elected committee of the Fianna, which [endeavoured], by delay and obstruction, to thwart the expressed wishes of the congress which elected it'.[70]

Implying that the *ard-fheis*'s decision to open the Fianna to girls was invalid because some troops were not represented at the annual congress, the *ard-choisde* held a plebiscite among the *sluaighte* in which a majority (twelve to five) voted in favour of changing the constitution back to its original 'boys only' condition. Six of the twelve branches that voted against the inclusion of girls in the organisation were based in the Dublin area. Of the five *sluaighte* who supported female membership, three were listed as being based in Belfast, while the two others had names associated with Ulster.[71]

Ernest Blythe, a Belfast member of the IRB and future Free State finance minister, later contested the evidence provided by the results of the 1912 plebiscite, in which the Betsy Gray *sluagh* was among the Belfast troops that voted in favour of female membership. He contended that 'the Belfast boys tried to get rid of the girls' branch every year at the organisation's *ard-fheis*, and [that] it survived only because of the support of the other groups "who had no girls to annoy them"'.[72] Although the Belfast girls' *sluagh* was barred from affiliating with the *ard-choisde*, representatives, such as the Connolly sisters, continued to attend the annual *ard-fheis*.[73] Belfast girls remained involved in the Fianna even if they had no official representation at the national level.[74]

Despite calls for a separate girls' organisation to be established nationally, neither Markievicz nor Hobson undertook the task.[75] Envious of her three brothers' involvement in the Dublin Fianna, Molly Reynolds asked Hobson in early 1913 'if they would start a girls section in the Fianna and he replied that if I started it, they would give me all the assistance I needed'. By her own admission, however, she lacked 'the self confidence and initiative' to take up the task, 'and so the matter was dropped'.[76]

INCREASING MILITANCY AND MOMENTUM

The year 1913 saw a further expansion of the Fianna around the country after Liam Mellows was sent on the road between April and November as the Fianna's new full-time organiser and instructor. Although a special fund was set up for his maintenance, his expenses were few because he travelled around the country on his own Irish-built bicycle and stayed with people connected to the IRB.[77] Eamon Martin credited the increasing growth of the Fianna from 1913 onwards as a 'testimony' to Mellows' work in establishing new branches and giving existing troops a boost.[78] For instance, new *sluaighte* were established in Wexford and Tullamore in 1913. The Tuam and Liverpool branches may have been formed around this time as well.

The fourth annual *ard-fheis* in July 1913 may not have been controversial on the surface, but behind the scenes Fianna officers who were also members of the IRB had gained control of the organisation and were to hold sway until 1923. From 1913 onwards, it became the practice that the night before the *ard-fheis* all Fianna officers who were IRB members attended a meeting of the Fianna circle at which 'all matters of policy were decided'. Eamon Martin recalled that 'certain resolutions of no great importance were left open for free voting but apart from the discussion arising out of these the rest was all so much eye-wash'. Although these young men – they were hardly boys anymore – found it expedient to retain the countess as president, Martin revealed that 'she really had no voice in shaping policy and was overruled or out voted whenever her ideas ran counter to the decisions of this group'.[79] While Martin believed that Markievicz was oblivious to the take-over by IRB members, her biographer Jacqueline Van Voris claimed that the countess 'was aware of it almost at once' and often expressed her disapproval of secret societies.[80] Markievicz had her own cadre within the Fianna, who were known as 'Madame's boys' or the 'Surrey House clique'. This was a reference to her home on Leinster Road in Rathmines where they gathered. These boys included Seamus Pounch, Patsy O'Connor, Harry Walpole, Jack Shallow, Eddie Murray and Andy Dunne.[81]

Figure 3 Dublin Fianna officers, *c.* 1913–14. Front row (left to right): Paddy Holohan, Michael Lonergan and Con Colbert. Back row: Garry Holohan and Pádraic Ó Riain.

The Fianna's military training programme began to prove its value to the advanced nationalist movement when adult paramilitary organisations were formed in Ireland in 1913. The year began with the official establishment of the Unionist Ulster Volunteer Force to oppose the impending implementation of home rule in Ireland. At the behest of Hobson, senior Fianna officers began to drill Dublin members of the IRB in the summer, in anticipation of the formation of a nationalist counterblast to the Ulster Volunteers. In November 1913, when Hobson helped to form the Irish Volunteers, later known as the IRA, he recruited five senior Fianna officers to the provisional committee of the new body: Pádraic Ó Riain, Con Colbert, Eamon Martin, Michael Lonergan and Liam Mellows. These young men visited various halls in the evenings, instructing the Volunteer officers and directing the course of training.[82] As Mellows asserted, 'in Dublin the Fianna proved a great asset to the Volunteer movement by providing capable instructors and energetic workers for the new movement'.[83] In December 1913, Ó Riain wryly commented that people who had laughed at the Fianna learning drill were now advocates of the Volunteers.[84]

In addition to providing officers and instructors to the new body, the Fianna contributed numerous rank-and-file Volunteers. The Fianna introduced a new rule in which members who had reached the age of eighteen but had not achieved the rank of lieutenant were automatically transferred to the Volunteers.[85] For instance, Patrick Ward was instructed to leave the Fianna and join the Volunteers shortly after the establishment of the latter body.[86]

Although the formation of the Irish Volunteers generated enthusiasm within the nationalist community in Belfast, some Fianna members felt slightly uneasy, especially when many supporters of the Irish Parliamentary Party joined the new citizens' militia. David McGuinness added: 'We in the Fianna felt that our organisation was in danger of losing its Fianna identity in the larger organisation of the Volunteers. This fear prompted us to join up in two companies, C and F, which would be mainly composed of Fianna members.'[87] During this period, Fianna members encouraged Irishmen not to join the British forces by posting anti-recruitment bills around the city.

Members of the Betsy Gray *sluagh* were recruited into Cumann na mBan (The League of Women), the women's auxiliary of the Irish Volunteers, when a branch was formed in Belfast in 1914. Ina Connolly had attended the inaugural meeting of Cumann na mBan in Dublin with Countess Markievicz.[88] 'I sent a letter to all the nationalist newspapers, and had a meeting, and got Cumann na mBan started in Belfast', her sister Nora recalled, adding that 'there was only a small body to call on' because of the overlapping membership of nationalist organisations in the northern city.[89] Nora's influence and Fianna training also helped to ensure that the Belfast members were often the best shots in Cumann na mBan in its early days.[90] The creation of the women's organisation appears to have spelled the end of the girls' Fianna troop in Belfast.

Fianna members whose dominant loyalty was to the labour movement chose to gravitate to the Irish Citizen Army (ICA) instead of the Irish Volunteers. The ICA had also been formed in November 1913, but with the purpose of protecting striking workers during the Dublin Lockout. Andy Dunne, Thomas O'Donoghue and Joe Connolly are examples of Fianna members who joined the ICA and later served with Markievicz as part of the St Stephen's Green garrison during the Easter Rising.[91]

In late 1914, James Connolly, Walter Carpenter and Seamus McGowan established two youth groups for the 'boys and girls' who had been 'hanging around' Liberty Hall: the ICA Boy Scout Corps and the Girls' Ambulance Corps.[92] Perhaps the involvement of his children Nora, Ina and Roddy in the Belfast Fianna had convinced Connolly of the value of such groups. It was through their membership in the Fianna that Connolly had met such impressive Fianna officers as Liam Mellows, Sean Heuston and Con Colbert.[93] Roddy Connolly joined the ICA Boy Scout Corps.[94]

The Fianna's momentum continued into 1914. Between January and October of that year, eleven new *sluaighte* were formed in Gorey, Ballybunion, Cashel, Tipperary, Carrick-on-Suir, Mitchelstown, Athy, Sandyford, Clontarf, Chapelizod and Tallaght.[95] By August 1914, the Dublin Battalion of the Fianna consisted of over 350 members.[96] The Limerick branch, in contrast, had decreased from a high of 250 boys down to about 160 by May 1914.[97] The increasing growth of the organisation at this time was connected to the establishment of the Volunteer movement, as many sons of Volunteers joined the Fianna.[98]

The year 1914 also saw the opening of a Fianna Headquarters at 12 D'Olier Street and the launch of two Fianna publications.[99] In that year, the *ard-choisde* finally issued the first *Fianna Handbook*, which was designed to instruct and guide members of the Fianna. A one-off Fianna Christmas publication also appeared in 1914. *Nodlaig na bhFiann*, which was edited by Fianna members Patsy O'Connor and Percy Reynolds, was not published by *Fianna* Headquarters but did have official sanc-tion. Buoyed by its financial success, the pair established an unofficial monthly paper entitled *Fianna* in February 1915.[100] These publications will be discussed in greater detail in a later chapter on Fianna print propaganda.

A SPLIT IN THE IRISH VOLUNTEER MOVEMENT

In June 1914, Hobson's role within the IRB diminished after he defied IRB orders and supported for strategic reasons the acceptance of Irish Parliamentary Party leader John Redmond's nominees to the provisional committee of the Irish Volunteers. Redmond, alarmed by the growing popularity of the Volunteers, had threatened to split the movement if twenty-five of his nominees were not co-opted to this governing committee. In Hobson's view, the Volunteer movement was not yet strong enough to withstand a split. Convinced that a strong minority group could secretly control the committee, Hobson not only voted in favour of the co-option of the nominees but influenced others to vote likewise, ensuring the acceptance of the nominees. Although his actions succeeded in postponing a split in the movement until after the outbreak of the First World War, they earned him the wrath of Tom Clarke and Sean MacDermott, the most powerful members of the IRB executive.

Hobson's falling-out with Clarke and MacDermott does not appear to have affected his role within the Fianna nor diminished the position of the Fianna officers within the IRB, with the possible exception of his close friend Pádraic Ó Riain. In October 1914, Hobson was re-elected vice president at the fifth annual Fianna *ard-fheis*.[101] According to Garry Holohan, 'the Fianna officers with, I should think, the exception of Con Colbert, still had implicit faith in Bulmer Hobson, while at the same time we enjoyed the full confidence and friendship of Tom Clarke and Sean McDermott'.[102] Eamon Martin suggested that Hobson's role in the Fianna was not affected by his bitter conflict with Clarke and MacDermott because his 'counsel and guidance' had 'so impressed and influenced the young men of the [Fianna], all of whom held him in high esteem'. Martin – who voted against the acceptance of Redmond's nominees – and Holohan ultimately agreed that Hobson's actions were justified. In Holohan's opinion, Hobson, Clarke and MacDermott 'were all equally sincere in their efforts to advance the movement as they thought best'.[103]

The split in the Irish Volunteers that finally came in September 1914 impacted on membership numbers in the Fianna, both positively and negatively. The split occurred after Redmond, without consultation, urged the Volunteers to fight in the First World War. While a majority followed Redmond under the new name, National Volunteers, and joined the British army, a minority adhered to the force's original aims and name. After the split, Redmond's supporters in the Irish Parliamentary Party denounced the Irish Volunteers and the Fianna, particularly for their stance against recruitment into the British military. Ó Riain commented:

> Not being satisfied with their efforts to disrupt the adult Volunteer organisation, many of the party politicians who pollute the public life of our country showed unusual zeal in attributing Sinn Féin tendencies to the Fianna. A self-governing boys' organisation is inconceivable to the mentality of the machine politician.[104]

For instance, the mayor of Kilkenny allegedly urged 'boys not to sign the Fianna declaration' and to secede from the organisation, while in Belfast 'an ignorant section' of the AOH apparently pursued 'the same sort of tactics'.[105]

Ó Riain noted that such publicity attracted 'hundreds of recruits' in places like Dublin, where the Fianna organisation was strong.[106] By November 1914, the Dublin Battalion boasted 500 members.[107] Fianna members also proudly claimed that the Volunteer split did not affect numbers in Cork.[108] However, while Waterford 'weathered the storm that … wrecked more than one of our country *sluaighte*', other places were not so resilient.[109] For example, membership in the Limerick *sluagh* was down to sixty boys in March 1915 and only three Belfast troops were described as 'hard at work' in June of that year.[110]

THE WAR IN EUROPE

After the outbreak of the Great War in August 1914, it appears that an attempt was made to use the Belfast Fianna as a recruiting ground for the British army. An unnamed Fianna instructor, who had served in the army, approached some of the boys about enlisting. Having given him a noncommittal answer, the boys reported the incident to some senior Fianna members who took action. They eschewed a formal court martial for fear that the instructor might seek outside aid and instead staged a showdown at a forthcoming céilí. According to Ina Connolly, they decided 'that at a given hour we would all take part in a sixteen hand reel and when the music was about to stop we would all encircle this instructor and give him a time limit to leave the city and on no circumstance to enter the Fianna premises'. The individual initially refused to consent, demanding a court martial, but faced with the determination of his former pupils, gave in and disappeared from the Fianna scene.[111]

In contrast to this incident, some Fianna members did choose to serve in the British army during the war, breaking their Fianna pledge not to do so. David McGuinness estimated that about twenty Belfast Fianna members out of a total of about 300 joined the British forces.[112] Several older Cork members also joined up, including Christy Moynihan, the Cork *sluagh*'s second scoutmaster (or captain) who had previously transferred from the Baden-Powell scouts to the Fianna.[113]

Another example was Waterford Fianna officer Thomas Barr.[114] According to his Fianna colleague Patrick Hearne, Barr became a second lieutenant in the British army: 'One could secure this position in the British Forces easily at that time; the only qualification necessary was to ride a motor bicycle and you were automatically a dispatch carrier with 2nd Lieutenant rank.'[115] Michael F. Ryan appears to be alluding to Barr when he recalled 'how critical some of us were of the action of a fairly prominent officer of the Fianna who joined up'. Ryan noted that 'many young Waterford men attracted by the glamour of the despatch riders joined up' after the Signals detachment of the Royal Engineers began to provide training in 'cycle and motor cycle despatch carrying and flag and lamp signalling' in the city shortly after the war broke out.[116]

Fianna members who served during the First World War may have been supporters of home rule, heeding Redmond's call for Irishmen to support the war effort. Perhaps in different circumstances they would not have joined the British army. Alternatively, Fianna members who joined the British forces may have been attracted to the perceived glamour of certain military roles in wartime, such as delivering dispatches by motorcycle.

The conflicting responses to the war effort demonstrated by individual Fianna members mirrored disputes among adults espousing differing degrees of nationalism. For instance, in some areas of Ireland, support for the British war effort had a negative impact on the advanced nationalist movement. 'Encouraged by a recruiting campaign launched by the Irish Parliamentary Party on behalf of the British Army, enemies emerged from everywhere', recalled Liam Langley, a Fianna leader in Tuam, County Galway. 'Pastors, parents, merchants and employers were approached and pressed to withdraw support from the national organisations. Cases were reported where they went even further, a

Fianna uniform ... having been burnt to ashes by the employer of the Fianna boy concerned.'[117]

Despite such opposition and a dip in membership, Pádraic Ó Riain reported in April 1915 that the first five years of the Fianna's existence had placed the organisation on a sound basis. But there was still much more work to be done because 'only a small fraction of the boys of Ireland' had pledged themselves to the Fianna. Ó Riain warned members that they could not 'afford to go plodding along slowly' as they had previously. Alluding to the possibility that Britain's weakness during the war in Europe might be Ireland's opportunity, he predicted that 'great changes' in the country's national life were ahead. He advised the Fianna to 'be organised and strong' in order to prevent their movement from 'being submerged by coming crises'.[118]

REORGANISATION ALONG MILITARY LINES

The Dublin Fianna were the first to shift from the *sluaighte* system to a more formal military structure. By February 1914, the Dublin *sluaighte* had formed a battalion consisting of two companies (A-B), possibly to bring themselves in line with the emerging organisational structure of the Irish Volunteers.[119] In July 1914, the Fianna's Dublin Battalion again reorganised, dividing itself into three companies.[120] The Dublin district council later expanded its battalion into nine companies in 1915.[121]

Changes in the Fianna were afoot elsewhere in the country. According to former members, the Cork Fianna was 'purely a scout movement' up until 1915. 'After that it became more of a military body and a training ground for the Volunteers', recalled Sean Healy and Liam O'Callaghan.[122] The turning point appears to have been the Munster Convention of the Fianna held in Limerick on Whit Monday 1915, at which Hobson 'pointed out how the future of the Volunteer movement would depend on the training and spirit of the boys of to-day' and 'urged Volunteer officers to set about at once the formation of boy scout corps in connection with their companies'.[123] Prior to this convention the leader of the Cork Fianna *sluagh* had been known as the scoutmaster, but after it he was referred to as captain. In the past, the adult supervisory committee of the *sluagh* would appoint the scoutmaster, but under a new policy Sean Healy became captain in 1915 after achieving the highest marks in an exam. Healy remained in this role until 1918 when he joined the Volunteers.[124]

At a national level, the Fianna reorganised its governing body at the sixth annual *ard-fheis* in July 1915. Captain Eamon Martin proposed resolutions that provoked a lengthy discussion that had probably been rehearsed at an IRB meeting beforehand. He suggested that the presidency of the Fianna should be abolished and replaced with a Fianna Chief who would be appointed to hold military command of the entire organisation and that the *ard-choisde* should be replaced by a 'competent' Headquarters' Staff, which would help the Fianna Chief run the organisation. Martin asserted 'that the anomaly of having a president instead of a military chief at the head of their organisation was ludicrous' in a movement that over the years had become 'essentially a military one'. He added that over the past six months, the general secretary, rather than the *ard-choisde*, had been doing most of the work at its D'Olier Street headquarters in Dublin. Due to the growth of the Fianna, the workload was now too great to be done efficiently by one or two boys.[125]

Hobson opposed the resolutions, pointing out that if they were passed, the *ard-fheis* would be handing over 'the government of the Fianna to a half-dozen Fianna officers'. He argued that 'there was a civil side in the Fianna which was of even greater importance than the military one'.[126] Hobson may have been 'scripted' at the IRB meeting prior to the *ard-fheis* to play the part of devil's advocate. Alternatively, he may have feared that the IRB would draw the Fianna into a premature insurrection. Clarke and MacDermott were keeping Hobson, whom they no longer trusted, in the dark about their precise plans for a rebellion, but he had been informed of the decision to stage an insurrection before the end of the war.[127]

Through discussion, the proposed changes were eventually crafted into a compromise. The *ard-fheis* decided to retain Markievicz's position as president and elect an *ard-choisde* of twelve members, which was instructed to appoint an *ard fhéinne* (Fianna Chief) and Headquarters' Staff at their first meeting.[128] The subsequent appointments of Pádraic Ó Riain as *ard fhéinne* and Bulmer Hobson as chief of staff hint at the deterioration in relations between Markievicz and Hobson.

When the Fianna were established in 1909, Hobson and Markievicz were close nationalist associates. Over time, however, their relationship suffered due to political differences. Markievicz and Helena Molony resented the control that the IRB had over their republican men friends. They were incensed in July 1911 when these young men, on IRB orders, journeyed to the grave of United Irish leader Theobald Wolfe Tone in Bodenstown, County Kildare, to commemorate the anniversary of his death instead of staying in Dublin to participate in street protests against the royal visit.[129] They assumed that they had convinced

Hobson to join them on the streets, and so felt doubly betrayed when he too accompanied the Bodenstown crowd. Markievicz later accused her one-time mentor of being 'one of those who preferred the limelight and laurels to be won by a fierce speech at a rebel's graveside to the possibility of getting a hammering from the police or being arrested'.[130] Hobson's opposition to active IRB support for the workers during the 1913 Dublin Lockout and his acceptance of Redmond's nominees onto the provisional committee of the Irish Volunteers also had an adverse effect on his relationship with the countess.[131]

Thus, the seemingly incongruous appointments of Ó Riain, a natural organiser, to a role that was 'really no more than an honour' and of father figure Hobson to a managerial position were designed to appease Markievicz. Eamon Martin explained:

> [W]hile Madame [Markievicz] might feel hurt because she herself was not given the title of *ard fhéinne* she would tolerate it going to Pádraig, but by this time she would never have stood for it going to Bulmer. Therefore, these two positions were filled in this way because it was still considered expedient that Madame should not be too openly antagonised.

In actual fact, Hobson became only nominal chief of staff. Instead, Ó Riain directed and coordinated the work of the various departments. In addition, Markievicz's re-election to the position of president had been arranged behind the scenes in order to ensure that she was not eligible for appointment to Headquarters' Staff.[132]

Under their new organisational structure, the Fianna continued to extend and intensify their military training programme. In the period from the summer of 1915 to the spring of 1916, many members felt that the Fianna, along with their republican colleagues in the IRB and the Irish Volunteers, were 'moving rapidly towards a climax'.[133] This climax was the Easter Rising.

THE 1916 EASTER RISING

Eamon Martin was one of the first Fianna officers to get any 'definite information' about the planned insurrection. He heard about it on the Sunday prior to Easter 1916.[134] That same night, Hobson gave an impromptu speech at a concert organised by Cumann na mBan. In 'guarded language', he 'warned' the Volunteers in the audience 'of the extreme danger of being drawn into precipitate action', which he believed 'could only have the effect of bringing the Volunteer movement to an end'. He added that 'no man had a right to risk the fortunes of the country in order to create for himself a niche in history'.[135] Hobson was only in favour of insurrection if Germany provided enough assistance to guarantee military success or if Britain attempted to suppress the Volunteers. Instead, he favoured a campaign of guerrilla warfare.

Martin did not hear about Hobson's guerrilla warfare plan until after the Easter Rising. Even though he viewed this plan as 'sound and practicable', Martin maintained that he would still have supported an insurrection, explaining that Patrick Pearse's doctrine of the blood sacrifice 'had a greater appeal for those who had become tired of waiting for favourable opportunities'. Martin, like others, felt it would be 'shameful and disastrous' if the war ended before any attempt was made to take advantage of Britain's difficulty. Thus, 'even a glorious failure would be better than no attempt at all'.[136]

Hobson did not share this enthusiasm for a blood sacrifice and the triumph of failure. He has the dubious distinction of having been held against his will by members of the IRB from the afternoon of Good Friday, 21 April 1916, until the evening of Easter Monday, 24 April 1916, the day the Rising began. The Military Council of the IRB decided to detain him because its members recognised that Hobson, as quartermaster general and secretary of the Irish Volunteers and chairman of the Dublin Centres Board of the IRB, was the one man who possessed the influence and knowledge to scuttle their plans for a rebellion. Even after he was released, Hobson chose not to participate in the Rising because he 'was convinced the thing was wrong, that it was a blunder which I had honestly attempted to prevent, and to join up and add to the victims I felt would be a mistake'.[137] Perhaps he thought he would be in a position to pick up the pieces after the insurrection failed. In any case, he refused 'to be driven against [his] judgement by being faced with a *fait accompli*'.[138] He was determined that his erstwhile associates Pearse, Clarke and MacDermott would not force him into doing something with which he so vehemently disagreed.

In contrast to Hobson, Markievicz and many former and serving members of the Fianna did participate in the Easter Rising as commanders, fighters, dispatch carriers, couriers and scouts. Eamon Martin asserted that 'there was not a single fighting post in the city or country which had not its quota of the Fianna'.[139] The rebellion enabled serving and former members of the Fianna to put their training into action and thus showcased the youth group's military value to the struggle for Irish independence.

For instance, the attack on the Magazine Fort in Phoenix Park that was to signal the start of the rebellion was meant 'to be an all-Fianna operation'. However, due to the confusion arising from Volunteer leader Eoin MacNeill's countermanding order cancelling 'manoeuvres' on Easter Sunday, the Fianna officers in charge 'had to borrow men from the Volunteers'. MacNeill's countermanding order was a symptom of the division within the Volunteer leadership between those who supported the IRB Military Council's plans to stage a rebellion and those like MacNeill and Hobson who only supported military action if the British government attempted to disarm the Volunteers or pursue a policy of conscription in Ireland. The countermanding order resulted in the postponement of the rebellion's start until Easter Monday and the mobilisation of less military personnel than expected. Despite the last minute changes in personnel, the majority of those involved in the Magazine Fort operation were from the Fianna.[140]

Among the garrisons most strongly associated with the Fianna was the Mendicity Institute where Sean Heuston commanded members of the Fianna and the Irish Volunteers. Acting on orders from James Connolly, about two dozen rebels seized this strategic building on the south quays of the River Liffey at Usher's Island at midday on Easter Monday. From this vantage point, they hindered the advance of British troops from Kingsbridge train station to the city centre and protected the Four Courts garrison across the river. Under fire from almost 400 government forces, they held out until Wednesday of Easter Week when Heuston decided that their only option was to surrender. They were the first garrison to capitulate during the Easter Rising. The nearby train station was later renamed in Heuston's honour.[141]

Seven Fianna members were killed during the Rising, some in action.[142] For instance, James Fox, aged sixteen, and James Kelly, aged fifteen, both died of fatal gunshot wounds sustained on 25 April 1916, the second day of the rebellion. Fox served with the garrison at St Stephen's Green, whereas surviving evidence suggests that Kelly did not join the Rising, but was merely going about the daily business of a Dublin adolescent when he was killed. Kelly's mother burned his Fianna uniform and wisely remained silent about his membership in the youth group in her claim for compensation after his death.[143]

Among the sixteen leaders executed for their part in the Rising were two young men connected with the Fianna. Sean Heuston, who had led the garrison at the Mendicity Institute, was director of training at Fianna Headquarters and vice-commandant of the Dublin battalion.

Figure 4   Sean Heuston (1891–1916).

Con Colbert, who was second in command at Marrowbone Lane Distillery and took command at the surrender, had devoted less of his energy to the Fianna after he joined the Volunteers in 1913, but still maintained a connection to the youth group. Heuston and Colbert were executed on 8 May 1916.[144] They were aged twenty-five and twenty-seven, respectively. Markievicz, who had been one of the commanders at St Stephen's Green and the Royal College of Surgeons, was saved from their fate because of her gender.

The Irish state later recognised the Fianna's contribution to the Easter Rising in the form of medals, military service pensions and allowances for the dependants of those who died while on active service.

A sample of former Fianna members derived from the Military Service Pensions Collection includes fifty-nine males who served during the Rising. This figure does not include individuals who were unable to prove their claims for service during the rebellion. An additional five males who were not part of this sample were also awarded the 1916 Medal. Of the former Fianna members who were military service pension recipients, 81% had participated in the Rising. The vast majority of these served in Dublin where most of the fighting took place. Four pension recipients participated in the rebellion outside of the capital, one in County Galway where Liam Mellows was in command, and three others in Enniscorthy, County Wexford.[145]

Some members of the Fianna were imprisoned after the Rising while others managed to go free. The Fianna officers who participated in the attack on the Magazine Fort in Phoenix Park had spent the remainder of the Rising involved in operations in the Four Courts area. In the aftermath of the rebellion, the Holohan brothers, Garry and Paddy, were imprisoned in Knutsford Jail, and Patrick (Paddy) O'Daly in Frongoch. Both O'Daly and Eamon Martin were wounded during the Rising. In contrast, Seamus Pounch, who served at Jacob's Biscuit Factory, was able to evade arrest after the surrender: 'We were told if we liked we could make a break, so I took advantage of this and got as far as Camden Street.' Luckily, a local Fianna member took Pounch into his home before British troops spotted the young rebel in his incriminating uniform.[146]

Some members of the Fianna, including Eoin MacNeill's son Niall, were later court-martialled by the organisation for not taking part in the Rising. Markievicz, Barney Mellows and a third (unnamed) Fianna officer exonerated Niall MacNeill on the grounds that he had been under his father's influence. MacNeill saw such courts martial as a 'face-saving' device to keep certain useful people in the Fianna after the rebellion.[147] Having demonstrated its value to the independence movement during Easter Week, the youth group was keen to play its part in the next phase of the Irish Revolution.

NOTES

1 Art, 'Na Fianna Éireann', *IF*, Dec. 1910, p. 3.
2 Liam Mellows, 'The Irish Boy Scouts by an Irish Volunteer officer – Chapter IV' (MA, BMH, Colonel Dan Bryan Collection, CD 129/1). This series of articles was originally published in the *Gaelic American* newspaper.

3 One of the Fianna, 'Na Fianna Éireann (National Boys' Brigade)', *B na hÉ*, Oct. 1909, pp. 8–9.
4 One of the Fianna, 'Na Fianna Éireann (National Boys' Brigade)', *B na hÉ*, Nov. 1909, p. 8. It is unclear how long this branch lasted as the county inspector's report for Apr. 1914 noted that a Fianna troop had just been formed in the city of Waterford in the past month (TNA, CO 904/93).
5 One of the Fianna, 'Na Fianna Éireann (National Boys' Brigade)', *B na hÉ*, Nov. 1909, p. 8.
6 One of the Fianna, 'Na Fianna Éireann (National Boys' Brigade)', *B na hÉ*, Dec. 1909, p. 8; C. Ua S. [probably Cathal O'Shannon], 'Volunteers' Branch', *B na hÉ*, Mar. 1910, p. 8.
7 David McGuinness, witness statement, 25 July 1950 (MA, BMH, WS 417).
8 'Fianna na h-Éireann', *B na hÉ*, Feb. 1910, p. 6.
9 'Na Fianna Éireann', *B na hÉ*, (July or Aug.?) 1910, p. 10; Máirtín Ó Catháin, 'A land beyond the sea: Irish and Scottish republicans in Dublin, 1916' in Ruán O'Donnell (ed.), *The Impact of the 1916 Rising: Among the Nations* (Dublin: Irish Academic Press, 2008), pp. 40–1. For a brief discussion of Joseph Robinson and the Glasgow Fianna, see Máirtín Ó Catháin, *Irish Republicanism in Scotland, 1858–1816* (Dublin: Irish Academic Press, 2007), pp. 228–9.
10 One of the Fianna, 'Na Fianna Éireann (National Boys' Brigade)', *B na hÉ*, Nov. 1909, p. 8.
11 'Na Fianna Éireann', *B na hÉ*, Sept. 1910, p. 11.
12 Na Fianna Éireann, *The Constitution of Na Fianna Éreann as Amended by the Ard-fheis, 1912* (Dublin: Na Fianna Éireann, 1912), p. 2; Pádraic Ó Riain (ed.), *Fianna Handbook* (Dublin: Central Council of Na Fianna Éireann 1914), p. 15.
13 'Na Fianna Éireann', *B na hÉ*, Sept. 1910, p. 11.
14 'Na Fianna Éireann', *B na hÉ*, Nov. 1910, p. 11.
15 D. Ó R. and P. Mac P. [presumably Desmond Ryan and Patrick Pearse], 'Annála Sgoil Éanna, Foghmhar go Nodlaig, 1910', *An Macaomh*, 2:3 (Christmas 1910), pp. 78–9. Mr O'Toole and Mr McLoughlin were named as the colonels of the two battalions while the company captains were Eamonn Bulfin, Vincent O'Doherty, Frank Connolly, Donal O'Connor, Patrick Delany, Willie Bradley, Desmond O'Ryan and John Dowling.
16 Ruaidhri, 'Na Fianna Éireann', *B na hÉ*, Jan. 1911, p. 13.
17 'Fianna na hÉireann', *B na hÉ*, Mar. 1911, p. 7.
18 Pádraig Mac Fhloinn, 'The history and tradition of Fianna Éireann' in *Fianna Éireann Handbook* (Dublin: Fianna Éireann, 1988), p. 9;

Cathal O'Shannon, 'Memories of 50 years ago', *Irish Press*, 20 July 1956 (UCDA, Denis McCullough Papers, P120/37 (15)). The Cumann na Cailíní associated with the Dungannon Clubs should not be confused with Cumann na gCailíní, the republican girl scout organisation formed by Cumann na mBan in the early 1930s.

19 Pádraic Ó Riain, 'Na Fianna Éireann', *IF*, Dec. 1911, p. 6 (edition edited by Patrick McCartan); 'Na Fianna Éireann', *IF*, Sept. 1912, p. 6.
20 Nora Connolly O'Brien, witness statement, 21 July 1949 (MA, BMH, WS 286).
21 David Fitzpatrick, 'Militarism in Ireland, 1900–1922' in Thomas Bartlett and Keith Jeffery (eds), *A Military History of Ireland* (Cambridge: Cambridge University Press, 1996), p. 383. Richard A. Voeltz has argued that the social conditions generated by the First World War contributed to the rapid expansion of the Girl Guide movement in Britain from 1916 onwards. See Voeltz, 'The antidote to "Khaki Fever"? The expansion of the British Girl Guides during the First World War', *Journal of Contemporary History*, 27:4 (Oct. 1992), pp. 627–38.
22 David McGuinness, witness statement, 28 July 1950 (MA, BMH, WS 417).
23 Sinéad McCoole, *No Ordinary Women: Irish Feminist Activists in the Revolutionary Years, 1900–1923* (Dublin: O'Brien Press, 2003), p. 26.
24 Ó Riain, 'Na Fianna Éireann', *IF*, Dec. 1911, p. 6.
25 Nora Connolly O'Brien, witness statement, 21 July 1949 (MA, BMH, WS 286); Ina Connolly Heron, witness statement, 25 Jan. 1954 (MA, BMH, WS 919); McCoole, *No Ordinary Women*, p. 26.
26 Charlie McGuire, *Roddy Connolly and the Struggle for Socialism in Ireland* (Cork: Cork University Press, 2008), pp. 10–11.
27 Oscar, 'Na Fianna Éireann', *IF*, Sept. 1911, p. 7.
28 Pádraig Ó Riain, Honorary General Secretary's report, 1912. A copy of this report can be found in a folder of Sinn Féin pamphlets in the NLI (IR 94109 S13).
29 Ó Riain, Honorary General Secretary's report, 1912 (NLI, IR 94109 S13).
30 *Ibid.*
31 Ó Riain, 'Na Fianna Éireann', *IF*, Dec. 1911, p. 6; 'Na Fianna Éireann', *IF*, Sept. 1912, p. 6; Ó Riain, Honorary General Secretary's report, 1912 (NLI, IR 94109 S13).
32 'Na Fianna Éireann', *IF*, Jan. 1913, p. 6.
33 Ó Riain, Honorary General Secretary's report, 1912 (NLI, IR 94109 S13).
34 Peadar McCann (Mac Cana), witness statement, 25 Oct. 1948 (MA, BMH, WS 171); John Southwell, witness statement, 15 Oct. 1948 (MA, BMH, WS 230); Edward Fullerton, witness statement, 16 Sept. 1953 (MA, BMH, WS 890).

35 'Na Fianna Éireann', *IF*, Sept. 1912, p. 6. Derry is mentioned as voting on whether girls should be allowed in the Fianna.
36 Inspector General's and County Inspectors' Monthly Confidential Reports, Dec. 1911, Jan. 1912, Dec. 1913 (TNA, CO 904/85–6, 91).
37 Joseph O'Shea, witness statement, n.d. (MA, BMH, WS 21).
38 Sean Healy and Liam O'Callaghan, joint witness statement, 4 Oct. 1947 (MA, BMH, WS 47).
39 Joseph O'Shea, witness statement, n.d. (MA, BMH, WS 21).
40 Sean Healy and Liam O'Callaghan, joint witness statement, 4 Oct. 1947 (MA, BMH, WS 47).
41 Inspector General's report, Feb. 1913 (TNA, CO 904/89).
42 Liam Mellows, 'The Irish Boy Scouts by an Irish Volunteer officer – Chapter IV' (MA, BMH, Colonel Dan Bryan Collection, CD 129/1).
43 County Inspectors' Reports for the period 1911–14 note the existence of Fianna troops in: Athlone, Moate and Castlepollard, County Westmeath; Armagh City, County Armagh; an unnamed location in County Galway East Riding; Tuam and Galway City, County Galway West Riding; Rathkeale, Limerick, Newcastle, Adare and Foynes, County Limerick; Clonmel and Tipperary Town, County Tipperary; Maryborough (Portlaoise), County Laois; Malahide, Ballybrack and Lusk, County Dublin; Kilkenny, County Kilkenny; Wexford Town, Enniscorthy, Newtownbarry and Courtown, County Wexford; Listowel and Tralee, County Kerry; two branches in unnamed locations in County Mayo; three branches in unnamed locations in County Cork East Riding; Tullamore, County Offaly; Waterford City, County Waterford. See Inspector General's and County Inspectors' Reports (TNA, CO 904/85–93).
44 [Anon.], 'A chronicle… of regiment of health', *An Macaomh*, 2:2 (May 1913), p. 49.
45 County Inspector's Report, Aug. 1912 (TNA, CO 904/87).
46 County Inspector's Reports, Apr.–May 1912 (TNA, CO 904/86–87).
47 Ó Riain, Honorary General Secretary's report, 1912 (NLI, IR 94109 S13).
48 County Inspector's Report, Nov. 1912 (TNA, CO 904/88).
49 County Inspector's Report, May 1912 (TNA, CO 904/87); County Inspector's Report, Mar. 1913 (TNA, CO 904/89); County Inspector's Report, Apr. 1914 (TNA, CO 904/93).
50 Bulmer Hobson, *Ireland Yesterday and Tomorrow* (Tralee: Anvil Books, 1968), p. 17.
51 'Na Fianna Éireann', *IF*, Aug. 1912, p. 6.
52 Ó Riain, Honorary General Secretary's report, 1912 (NLI, IR 94109 S13).
53 Eamon Martin, witness statement, 1 Oct. 1951 (MA, BMH, WS 591); Jacqueline Van Voris, *Constance de Markievicz in the Cause of Ireland*

(Amherst, MA: University of Massachusetts Press, 1967), pp. 72–3; Oscar, 'Na Fianna Éireann', *IF*, Sept. 1911, p. 7.
54 'Na Fianna Éireann – a suggestion for Dublin', *IF*, May 1912, p. 6.
55 Seamus Bevan, witness statement, 7 Jan. 1955 (MA, BMH, WS 1,058); Sean Kennedy, witness statement, 1 May 1953 (MA, BMH, WS 842).
56 Thomas O'Donoghue, witness statement, n.d. (MA, BMH, WS 1,666).
57 *Ibid*.
58 John Kenny, witness statement, 6 Nov. 1957 (MA, BMH, WS 1,693). Kenny (1897–1978) joined the Irish National Guards with his brother Michael in early 1912. He stated that this 'off-shoot of the Fianna' was led by a man called Finlay. He listed the following members: Bob, George and Bill Oman, Tom and Eddie Donohoe (elsewhere known as O'Donoghue), Joe and Mattie Gahan, Jack Bannon, Jack Murphy, Dick Gibson, John Conway, Jim and Dick Seville, Paddy Lalor, Alex Thompson, Frank Bolster, Sean Howard, Tommy Bryan, Hugh Early, Paddy Houlihan, Sean Kennedy, the Mason brothers, Walter Williams, Ted Tuite, Sean (Gurra) Byrne and Mattie Kelly (a brother of Sean T. O'Kelly).
59 Thomas O'Donoghue, witness statement, n.d. (MA, BMH, WS 1,666).
60 Seamus Bevan, witness statement, 7 Jan. 1955 (MA, BMH, WS 1,058).
61 John Kenny, witness statement, 6 Nov. 1957 (MA, BMH, WS 1,693). He also mentioned that the following girls were associated with the Irish National Guards: Alice and Katy Byrne, May Murray, May Gahan, May Crimmins, Mary and Nellie Walker, Nellie Belton, Eileen Dempsey and Bridie and Rita McMahon.
62 Sean Kennedy, witness statement, 1 May 1953 (MA, BMH, WS 842).
63 Martin O'Regan, witness statement, 29 June 1955 (MA, BMH, WS 1,202).
64 Seamus Bevan, witness statement, 7 Jan. 1955 (MA, BMH, WS 1,058); John Kenny, witness statement, 6 Nov. 1957 (MA, BMH, WS 1,693).
65 Garry Holohan, witness statement, 7 Dec. 1949 (MA, BMH, WS 328).
66 'Na Fianna Éireann', *IF*, Sept. 1912, p. 6. Hobson stated that this amendment took place in 1913, but contemporary newspaper reports indicate that the change took place in 1912. See Bulmer Hobson, 'The IRB and the Fianna' in F. X. Martin (ed.), *The Irish Volunteers 1913–1915: Recollections and Documents* (Dublin: James Duffy, 1963), p. 20.
67 Hobson, 'IRB and Fianna', p. 21.
68 David McGuinness, witness statement, 28 July 1950 (MA, BMH, WS 417).
69 'Na Fianna Éireann', *IF*, Aug. 1912, p. 6.
70 Helena Molony, witness statement, 19 May 1950 (MA, BMH, WS 391); 'Girl Scouts', *Irish Citizen*, 10 Aug. 1912, p. 90.

71 'Na Fianna Éireann', *IF*, Sept. 1912, p. 6. The *sluaighte* that were against the inclusion of girls: An Chéad Sluagh (1st Dublin Co.), Sluagh Emmet (3rd Dublin Co.), Sluagh Wolfe Tone (5th Dublin Co.), Sluagh Patrick Sarsfield (6th Dublin Co.), Sluagh Fiach Mac Aodha (Baile Breach), Sluagh Finegal (Lusk), Sluagh Lord Edward (Limerick), An Chéad Sluagh Corcaighe, Sluagh Leo Cathasaigh (Athlone), Sluagh Wolfe Tone (1st Kerry Co., Listowel), Sluagh Vinegar Hill (Enniscorthy) and Sluagh John Mitchel (Derry). The *sluaighte* that were in favour: Sluagh Willie Nelson (Belfast), Sluagh Henry Munroe (Belfast), Sluagh Betsy Gray (Belfast), Sluagh H. J. McCracken and Sluagh Seáin Uí Néill.

72 Ernest Blythe, *Trasna na Bóinne* (Dublin: Sairséal and Dill, 1957), pp. 177–8; quoted in Aodán Mac Póilin, 'Irish language writing in Belfast after 1900' in Nicholas Allen and Aaron Kelly (eds), *The Cities of Belfast* (Dublin: Four Courts Press, 2003), p. 136.

73 Nora Connolly O'Brien, *James Connolly: Portrait of a Rebel Father* (Dublin: Four Masters, 1975), p. 177.

74 See chapter 5 for further discussion of the issue of girls in the Fianna.

75 Helena Molony, witness statement, 19 May 1950 (MA, BMH, WS 391).

76 Molly Reynolds, witness statement, 3 Feb. 1949 (MA, BMH, WS 195). Her father was John Richard Reynolds, a bookkeeper who shared an office at 12 D'Olier Street with Hobson in 1913–14 and served as auditor of the Irish Volunteers. A 'John Reynolds' was one of the auditors of the Fianna's accounts for 1911–12 ('Na Fianna Éireann', *IF*, Aug. 1912, p. 6).

77 C. Desmond Greaves, *Liam Mellows and the Irish Revolution* (London: Lawrence and Wishart, 1988), pp. 48, 53.

78 Eamon Martin, witness statement, 1 Oct. 1951 (MA, BMH, WS 591).

79 *Ibid.*

80 Van Voris, *Constance de Markievicz*, pp. 89–90.

81 Seamus Pounch, witness statement, 15 June 1949 (MA, BMH, WS 267).

82 Eamon Martin, witness statement, 1 Oct. 1951 (MA, BMH, WS 591).

83 Liam Ó Maoil Íosa [Liam Mellows], 'Boy Scouts organising notes', *IV*, 7 Feb. 1914, p. 14.

84 Pádraic Ó Riain, 'Na Fianna Éireann', *IF*, Dec. 1913, p. 6.

85 Eamon Martin, witness statement, 1 Oct. 1951 (MA, BMH, WS 591).

86 Patrick Ward, witness statement, 30 Mar. 1955 (MA, BMH, WS 1,140).

87 David McGuinness, witness statement, 28 July 1950 (MA, BMH, WS 417).

88 Nora Connolly O'Brien, witness statement, 21 July 1949 (MA, BMH, WS 286); Denis McCullough, witness statement, 11 Dec. 1953 (MA, BMH, WS 915).

89 Nora Connolly O'Brien, witness statement, 21 July 1949 (MA, BMH, 286); Ina Connolly Heron, witness statement, 25 Jan. 1954 (MA, BMH, WS 919).

90 Denis McCullough, witness statement, 11 Dec. 1953 (MA, BMH, WS 915); Margaret Ward, *Unmanageable Revolutionaries* (London: Pluto Press, 1995), p. 104.
91 Seamus Kavanagh, witness statement, 9 Sept. 1957 (MA, BMH, WS 1,670).
92 Ann Matthews, *The Irish Citizen Army* (Cork: Mercier Press, 2014), p. 48.
93 Ina Connolly Heron, witness statement, 25 Jan. 1954 (MA, BMH, WS 919).
94 McGuire, *Roddy Connolly*, p. 11.
95 BMH Chronology, Part I, 1913–21 (UCDA, McCullough Papers, P120/24/13); Liam Ó Maoil Íosa, 'Boy Scouts organising notes', *IV*, 7 Feb. 1914, p. 14.
96 'Boy Scouts', *IV*, 22 Aug. 1914, p. 3.
97 'Boy Scouts', *IV*, 30 May 1914, p. 13.
98 Robert Holland, *A Short History of Fianna Éireann*, 14 Aug. 1949, p. 19 (NLI, MS 35,455/3/12A).
99 Pádraic Ó Riain, 'Na Fianna Éireann', *IF*, June 1914, p. 5.
100 Liam Mellows, 'Boy Scouts organising notes', *IV*, 21 Nov. 1914, p. 15; Willie Nelson [Pádraic Ó Riain], 'Na Fianna Éireann', *IV*, 9 Jan. 1915, p. 8. For a discussion of these three Fianna publications, see Marnie Hay, 'This treasured island: Irish nationalist propaganda aimed at children and youth, 1910–16' in Celia Keenan and Mary Shine Thompson (eds), *Treasure Islands in Children's Literature* (Dublin: Four Courts Press, 2006), pp. 33–42.
101 'National Boy Scout Convention', *IV*, 17 Oct. 1914, p. 16.
102 Garry Holohan, witness statement, 7 Dec. 1949 (MA, BMH, WS 328).
103 Eamon Martin, witness statement, 1 Oct. 1951 (MA, BMH, WS 591); Garry Holohan, witness statement, 7 Dec. 1949 (MA, BMH, WS 328).
104 Willie Nelson, 'Na Fianna Éireann', *IV*, 13 Feb. 1915, p. 8.
105 'National Boy Scouts', *IV*, 14 Nov. 1914, p. 16.
106 *Ibid*.
107 'National Boy Scouts', *IV*, 28 Nov. 1914, p. 15.
108 Sean Healy and Liam O'Callaghan, joint witness statement, 4 Oct, 1947 (MA, BMH, WS 47).
109 Willie Nelson, 'Na Fianna Éireann', *IV*, 13 Feb. 1915, p. 8.
110 Willie Nelson, 'Na Fianna Éireann', *IV*, 13 Mar. 1915, p. 8; 'Na Fianna Éireann', *IV*, 12 June 1915, p. 8.
111 Ina Connolly Heron, witness statement, 25 Jan. 1954 (MA, BMH, WS 919).
112 David McGuinness, witness statement, 28 July 1950 (MA, BMH, WS 417).
113 Joseph O'Shea, witness statement, n.d. (MA, BMH, WS 21). The 1911 census lists a nineteen-year-old shoemaker named Christopher Moynihan living with his family at 7 Commons Road in Cork. He may be the young man in question. See www.census.nationalarchives.ie/pages/1911/Cork/

Cork_No__4_Urban__part_of_/Commons_Road/387853/ (accessed 21 July 2018).
114 The 1911 census lists a thirteen-year-old student named Thomas Barr living with his family at 17 Mayors Walk in Waterford. He is probably the young man in question. See www.census.nationalarchives.ie/pages/1911/Waterford/No__1_Urban/Mayors_Walk/672131/ (accessed 21 July 2018).
115 Patrick Hearne, witness statement, 18 Aug. 1958 (MA, BMH, WS 1,742).
116 Michael F. Ryan, witness statement, 9 Dec. 1957 (MA, BMH, WS 1,709).
117 Liam Langley, witness statement, 19 Mar. 1953 (MA, BMH, WS 816).
118 Willie Nelson, 'Na Fianna Éireann', *IV*, 17 Apr. 1915, p. 8.
119 'Boy Scouts organising notes', *IV*, 14 Feb. 1914, p. 16.
120 After the July 1914 reorganisation of the Dublin battalion, a company consisted of three officers (one captain and two lieutenants), four leaders, eight corporals and sixty-four scouts. A company was divided into four sections. A section consisted of one leader, two corporals and sixteen scouts. Two sections formed a half company under a lieutenant. A military council supervised training and issued orders ('National Boy Scouts', *IV*, 25 July 1914, p. 11).
121 Joseph Reynolds, witness statement, 31 Jan. 1949 (MA, BMH, WS 191); Eamon Martin, witness statement, 1 Oct. 1951 (MA, BMH, WS 591); *IV*, 29 May 1915.
122 Sean Healy and Liam O'Callaghan, joint witness statement, 4 Oct. 1947 (MA, BMH, WS 47).
123 For a report on this Munster conference, see 'Na Fianna Éireann', *IV*, 5 June 1915, p. 8.
124 Sean Healy and Liam O'Callaghan, joint witness statement, 4 Oct. 1947 (MA, BMH, WS 47). The following served as the Cork scoutmaster or captain: Walter Furlong (first few months); Christy Moynihan (1912–13); Liam O'Callaghan (1913–14); Seamus Courtney (1914–15); Sean Healy (1915–18); Tadhg O'Sullivan (*c.* 1918–19). Frank McMahon served as Officer Commanding of the Cork brigade (*c.* 1919–22). Also see George Hurley, witness statement, 7 June 1957 (MA, BMH, WS 1,630).
125 Eamon Martin, witness statement, 1 Oct. 1951 (MA, BMH, WS 591); 'Fianna Congress, honorary officers abolished, headquarters' staff appointed', *Fianna*, Aug. 1915, pp. 6–7.
126 *Ibid*.
127 Denis McCullough, witness statement, 13 Apr. 1948 (MA, BMH, WS 111); Denis McCullough to Pádraig Ó Maidín, n.d. (UCDA, McCullough Papers, P120/23/20).

128 'Fianna Congress', *Fianna*, Aug. 1915, pp. 6–7. In addition to the president Markievicz, the following were elected to the *ard-choisde*: Bulmer Hobson, Pádraic Ó Riain, Eamon Martin, J. A. Dalton, Con Colbert, Sean Heuston, Leo Henderson, Pádraig O'Daly, Garry Holohan, Barney Mellows, Percy Reynolds and Niall MacNeill.
129 Helena Molony, witness statement, 19 May 1950 (MA, BMH, WS 391); Anne Marreco, *The Rebel Countess* (London: Weidenfeld and Nicolson, 1967), p. 142.
130 Quoted in Marreco, *Rebel Countess*, p. 142.
131 Members of the Fianna joined Markievicz in supporting the workers during the Dublin Lockout of 1913. One member, Patsy O'Connor, was administering first aid to an injured worker during a police baton charge when he too was attacked and sustained a head injury, which eventually resulted in his death (Willie Nelson, 'Na Fianna Éireann', *IV*, 26 June 1915, p. 8). Some Fianna members discussed the Lockout in their BMH witness statements. See Alex Klemm, 'Witnessing the lockout: Statements gathered by the Bureau of Military History' in Mary Muldowney and Ida Milne (eds), *100 Years Later: The Legacy of the 1913 Lockout* (Dublin: Seven Towers, 2013), pp. 18–37.
132 Eamon Martin, witness statement, 1 Oct. 1951 (MA, BMH, WS 591). The other appointments to Headquarters' Staff were: Adjutant – Percy Reynolds; Director of Training – Sean Heuston; Director of Organisation and Recruiting – Eamon Martin; Director of Equipment – Leo Henderson; Director of Finance – Barney Mellows ('Irish National Boy Scouts', *IV*, 24 July 1915, p. 3).
133 Eamon Martin, witness statement, 1 Oct. 1951 (MA, BMH, WS 591).
134 *Ibid*.
135 Hobson, *Ireland*, pp. 74–5.
136 Eamon Martin, witness statement, 1 Oct. 1951 (MA, BMH, WS 591).
137 Bulmer Hobson, statement to Joseph McGarrity, Apr. 1933 (NLI, Joseph McGarrity Papers, MS 17,453).
138 Bulmer Hobson, statement to McGarrity, 1934 (NLI, McGarrity Papers, MS 13,171).
139 Eamon Martin, witness statement, 1 Oct. 1951 (MA, BMH, WS 591).
140 *Ibid*.
141 Shane Hegarty and Fintan O'Toole, *The Irish Times Book of the 1916 Rising* (Dublin: Gill and Macmillan, 2006), pp. 85–7; Michael Foy and Brian Bartin, *The Easter Rising* (Stroud: Sutton Publishing, 2004), pp. 171–2, 177–8. For a detailed discussion of Heuston's contribution to the Rising and his subsequent execution, see chapters 5–9 of John Gibney's *Sean Heuston* (Dublin: O'Brien Press, 2013).

142 The following serving or former Fianna members were killed during Easter Week: Brendan Donelan, 24 Apr. 1916; Sean Healy, 24 Apr. 1916; James Fox, 25 Apr. 1916; James Kelly, 25 Apr. 1916; Gerald Keogh, 27 Apr. 1916; Sean Howard, 27 Apr. 1916; Frederick Ryan, 27 Apr. 1916. Donelan is listed as being from Galway, while the others were based in Dublin ('Fianna roll of honour' in Holland, *A Short History*, p. 25 (NLI, MS 35,455/3/12A)).

143 Joe Duffy, *Children of the Rising* (Dublin: Hachette Books Ireland, 2015), pp. 196–8, 213.

144 Joseph Reynolds, witness statement, 31 Jan. 1949 (MA, BMH, WS 191). For a discussion of their roles in the Easter Rising and subsequent executions, see Gibney, *Sean Heuston* and John O'Callaghan, *Con Colbert* (Dublin: O'Brien Press, 2015).

145 See Appendix III for a list of former Fianna members in this sample from the Military Service Pensions Collection, which is discussed in chapters 5 and 8. The following individuals participated in the Rising outside of Dublin: Michael Mulkerrins, pension file (MA, MSPC, 24SP906); Micheál S. Mac Eochaidh (Michael J. Kehoe), pension file (MA, MSPC, MSP34REF23991); James O'Brien, pension file (MA, MSPC, MSP34REF4836); Pádraic Toibin, pension file (MA, MSPC, MSP34REF21379).

146 Seamus Pounch, witness statement, 15 June 1949 (MA, BMH, WS 267).

147 Colonel Niall MacNeill, witness statement, 7 Jan. 1948 (MA, BMH, WS 69).

4 Expansion and contraction, 1916–23

> Work of the type necessary for training had to be intensified during 1918, because of the conscription threat, and many young lads and girls joined various organisations to fight against it .... But, needless to relate, when the danger passed on so did most of those members.[1]

This assertion from Fianna officer Patrick Hearne that membership in Irish nationalist organisations in his native Waterford waxed and waned depending on the public's perception of British threat illustrates why Na Fianna Éireann expanded and contracted in the years after the Easter Rising. Boys often joined the Fianna when they or their families wanted to take a strong stance against British policies in Ireland, but then drifted away either when the immediate threat receded or when involvement in the youth group was viewed as too dangerous.

Garry Holohan, a Dublin-based Fianna officer, noticed 'a tremendous change' in the advanced nationalist movement before and after the 1916 Rising. 'The movement changed from a small party of idealists, who were ready to do and die in face of all adversity, to a huge political movement embracing all classes and types',[2] he recorded. During the years from the outbreak of the Rising to that of the Civil War, the Fianna as an organisation went from being 'a small party of idealists' to embracing a greater number and range of members around the country and then returning to its original state. This chapter charts this trajectory, covering the Fianna's organisational development between the 1916 Easter Rising and the end of the Irish Civil War in 1923.

AFTER THE RISING

Na Fianna Éireann 'was probably the first of the military bodies to gather the threads of its organisation together' after the 1916 Easter

Rising, according to former member Hugo (Aodh) McNeill.³ The relative youth of the Fianna's officers meant that they were less likely than their counterparts in adult organisations to be arrested and imprisoned in the aftermath of the rebellion and thus in a better position to regroup in Dublin at an early stage. In early May 1916, a meeting was held at the Camden Street hall that was attended by all of the available officers who had served in the Rising and were still at liberty. They decided 'to hold together at least a skeleton organisation' by forming a Provisional Committee of Control, which would act on both an all-Ireland and a Dublin basis. There were eight *sluaighte* in existence in Dublin at the time.⁴ Under the nominal chairmanship of Eamon Martin, who had been severely wounded during the Rising, the committee consisted of Liam Staines, Seamus Pounch, Theo Fitzgerald and Joseph Reynolds. The committee not only covered the roles of the Dublin Battalion staff but also supervised the work of the *sluaighte* around the country. It served until January 1917 when it handed over control to the senior Fianna officers who had been released from internment the previous Christmas.⁵

The immediate impact of the Rising was largely negative for Fianna troops outside of Dublin. In some parts of Ireland, such as County Kerry, troops collapsed in the aftermath of the rebellion, but began to revive in the following year.⁶ Patrick Hearne recalled that in Waterford 'we lost quite a few members but we counteracted this by spreading out from the city and making initial contacts in other districts with a view to establishing branches there'.⁷ Although the Newry troop kept itself going after the Rising, with about twenty members later transferring to the Irish Volunteers in 1918,⁸ membership in the Derry *sluagh* of the Fianna 'greatly decreased' because 'the boys' parents refused to let them attend after the news of the Rising'.⁹ Thus, it is not surprising that girls were no longer admitted to the Belfast Fianna after the rebellion.¹⁰

The Provisional Committee of Control operated without the assistance and counsel of the Fianna's co-founders, as Countess Markievicz was in prison and Bulmer Hobson was on the run. When asking her sister Eva Gore-Booth to sort out her household and financial affairs while she was incarcerated in Dublin's Mountjoy Prison in May 1916, Markievicz included the payment of the rent for the Camden Street hall in her instructions.¹¹ She was later moved to Aylesbury Prison in Buckinghamshire in England where she remained until June 1917. In her prison letters from this period, she expressed interest in the Fianna as a group as well as in individual former members, such as Andy Dunne and Ina Connolly. She encouraged Dunne's singing and described Connolly as 'a splendid girl'.¹²

Even though Hobson had not participated in the rebellion, the Dublin Metropolitan Police (DMP) sought his apprehension in its aftermath.[13] He went on the run, hiding first in suburban south Dublin before fleeing to his parents' home in Holywood, County Down, a few weeks after his secret marriage to Claire Gregan in June 1916.[14] Scurrilous tales about his alleged treachery and cowardice abounded after the Rising. By late May 1916, his disappearance was fuelling suggestions that he had betrayed the republican cause.[15] In August 1916, the commander-in-chief of the British forces sent to Ireland to put down the Rising, General Sir John Maxwell, reported to Prime Minister Herbert Asquith 'an unconfirmed rumour' that the IRB had shot Hobson as a traitor during Easter Week.[16] When Hobson emerged from hiding after the June 1917 amnesty for individuals connected to the rebellion who had escaped arrest or were still serving time in prison, he found that many of his former colleagues in the nationalist movement ostracised him, due to a misinterpretation of his actions and a determination to punish him for his decision not to support the Rising.[17] His ultimate response to this ostracism was to shift his energies from the nationalist movement to his professional career. Thus, Hobson, through a combination of exclusion and choice, did not participate in the nationalist organisations to which he had belonged prior to the rebellion.

When Hobson returned to Dublin, he found employment first in book publishing before becoming a civil servant after the establishment of the Irish Free State.[18] He seems to have remained on friendly terms with some, but not all, of his Fianna protégés. Sean McLoughlin was a member of the Fianna and the Irish Volunteers who served with distinction during the Easter Rising. He recalled that around 1917 Barney Mellows and Eamon Martin took him to a house in Fairview in north Dublin where he 'met Bulmer Hobson who was anxious to justify his conduct prior to the Rising'. 'I refused to have anything to do with him and somewhat strained relations ensued between the Fianna and myself as a result', reported McLoughlin.[19]

Another notable absentee from the Fianna leadership after the 1916 Rising was Pádraic Ó Riain, who had been such a driving force in the years between the organisation's foundation and the rebellion. The leaders of the Rising had sent him to Omagh, County Tyrone, with Eimar O'Duffy and Liam Boyd just before the launch of the insurrection.[20] In its aftermath, Ó Riain remained in the north, using a false name, James 'Jimmy' Toal, while on the run from the authorities. He found employment with a bookmaker's firm and settled first in Belfast and then in Bangor, County Down, having met and married a northern

Protestant.²¹ After 1916, Hobson and Ó Riain both shifted their focus to their respective careers and personal relationships.

The Fianna reorganised twice in 1917, first in January at the national and Dublin levels and then again in June in the Dublin area. In January 1917, a new Headquarters' Staff took over. Eamon Martin served as not only Chief of Staff but also Acting Chief of the Fianna, replacing Markievicz who was still in jail. Barney Mellows became Adjutant General, but was soon rearrested, so Assistant Adjutant General P. J. Stephenson had to cover his duties. Garry Holohan and Alf White served as Quartermaster General and Assistant Quartermaster General, respectively. Director of Training Sean McLoughlin acted as Chief of Staff while Martin was away in the United States.²² Tensions between McLoughlin and his colleagues, as noted previously, may have contributed to his replacement as Director of Training by Eamon Martin later in the year. Battalions were also reorganised in Dublin, Belfast and Cork. In Dublin, a *sluagh* was revised and re-organised in Rathfarnham with Niall MacNeill, rehabilitated after his post-Rising court martial, appointed as Officer Commanding.²³

At the *ard-fheis* in August 1917, which was held at 41 York Street in Dublin, Countess Markievicz proposed Eamon de Valera as Chief of the Fianna. De Valera, the only male leader of the rebellion who had not been executed, was unanimously elected to this nominal position. It was a short-lived honour. The following year Markievicz was elected Chief of the Fianna at St Enda's School, Rathfarnham, and she was re-elected to the position at each subsequent *ard-fheis* until her death in 1927.²⁴ Despite her resumption of the position of Chief of the Fianna, Markievicz's influence on the youth group in the period 1917–23 was mainly symbolic because she spent most of this time in jail, on the run or, in the case of 1922, on an American tour.

GROWTH IN MEMBERSHIP

As the initial shock of the Easter Rising receded, the Fianna began to attract a growing number of members as a result of increasing public support for the advanced nationalist cause sparked by sympathy for the executed leaders of the Rising and frustration at the still distant prospect of home rule. The new staffs of Fianna Headquarters and the Dublin Battalion proceeded to undertake 'an intensive re-organising and recruiting drive' both in the Dublin area and around the country with what Joseph Reynolds called 'tremendous success'. The large number of new recruits led to the formation of new *sluaighte*.²⁵

The Fianna later boasted that the organisation had attracted an all-time high of over 30,000 members by June 1917, but police intelligence reports, though flawed, recorded only 359 members outside of Dublin city in that month, suggesting that the Fianna's figure may be inflated.[26] The Royal Irish Constabulary (RIC), however, may not have been aware of some *sluaighte* or in certain counties did not deem the youth group worthy of attention. For instance, the intelligence reports do not mention the Fianna troops in Belfast, although the November 1917 report records the arrest in Belfast of two Glasgow Fianna members, who had been caught conveying a box containing fifty pounds of explosives to Dublin. The boys, Michael O'Carroll and John Nelson, were acting on the request of Joseph Robinson, a Glasgow-based republican activist who had been a member of Hobson's original Belfast Fianna.[27]

In any case, the Fianna's growth spurt was certainly evident in the Dublin area. The numbers in the Dublin Battalion increased so much that a Dublin Brigade divided into two battalions had to be created in June 1917, each with its own staff. The 1st (South Dublin) Battalion consisted of eight companies (A-H) while the 2nd (North Dublin) included five (A-E).[28] The River Liffey was the dividing line between the two battalions. Garry Holohan and P. J. Stephenson served as the new Dublin Brigade's commandant and adjutant, respectively, while Joseph Reynolds became quartermaster.[29]

In Cork in the months following the 1916 Rising, the growing number of Fianna members necessitated a division into two *sluaighte*, one covering the area north of the River Lee from Mayfield to Clogheen and the other covering the area south of the river from Blackrock to Dennehy's Cross.[30] Membership figures soon rose from sixty to one hundred.[31] As a result of a continuing increase in numbers, the Cork Fianna split into three *sluaighte* in early 1919, covering the north, centre and south parts of the city. About thirty to forty boys belonged to each *sluagh*.[32] The new Centre *Sluagh* included the centre of the city from Mardyke in the west to the Custom House in the east.[33]

Revival and expansion were also evident elsewhere in the province of Munster. In County Kerry, Fianna troops began to revive after Austin Stack asked Michael O'Leary to reorganise the Fianna there around late 1917 and early 1918. The Listowel troop appears to have been reinvigorated in 1917 while the Tralee *sluagh* was resuscitated in early 1918.[34] In Waterford, the Fianna's strategy to expand beyond the city was paying off by 1918. New troops had been started in nearby areas such as Ferrybank, Dunkett, Ballyduff, Portlaw, Dunhill and Carrick-on-Suir.[35]

The general trend toward revival and expansion continued in certain parts of Ulster. For example, efforts were made in Derry to revitalise the Fianna after the collapse in membership in the aftermath of the 1916 Rising. Liam A. Brady, Phil McLaughlin and Hugh Deery began recruiting boys for a boxing club, which met in the same premises as the Fianna, using it as a conduit for bringing boys into the Fianna. Numbers began to increase again, with thirty-five members in the *sluagh* by the end of 1917.[36]

Furthermore, throughout 1917, the RIC county inspector's reports recorded the existence in County Down of five branches of the 'Irish National Boy Scouts', consisting of about 142–4 members.[37] It is not clear however, whether these were actually Fianna troops. The County Down report for March 1918 noted that the branch of the 'National Boy Scouts' in Newry had been 'dissolved' and its members had joined a company of 'Fianna' boy scouts under Sinn Féin's control, which had been formed in Newry on 5 March 1918 'with a membership of 70'.[38]

By October 1918, there were three *sluaighte* active in Belfast with efforts underway to start a fourth. They were named after Cúchullain, the hero of the Ulster cycle of tales, and Con Colbert and James Connolly, both of whom not only had associations with the Fianna but had been executed for their roles in the Easter Rising. In the end the fourth *sluagh*, which was named in honour of Sean MacDermott, was not affiliated to the Belfast District Council because the troop had abandoned its work. A total of 212 boys belonged to the Belfast Fianna in February 1919, but on average only 120 attended meetings regularly. In April 1919, Fianna Headquarters in Dublin gave the Belfast council the authority to organise the Fianna in Ulster where contacts had already been made in Armagh and Lurgan. By August 1919 two additional *sluaighte*, which were named after William Orr and Patrick Pearse, had been formed in Belfast. The Belfast District Council was responsible for coordinating the administration, finances and instruction of the local *sluaighte* as well as maintaining discipline. This could involve such tasks as keeping records, ordering badges and handbooks, organising training sessions, camping trips and fundraising events and holding courts martial.[39]

Gender continued to be an issue during the post-1916 period. In Waterford, girls under the age of eighteen began to join the Fianna in late 1916. There the Fianna shared premises with Cumann na mBan. Dislike for a bossy Cumann na mBan leader appears to have motivated the Waterford girls to defect to the Fianna. When a Mrs Roche had established the Cumann na mBan branch in July 1916, novelist and nationalist activist Rosamond Jacob had predicted that she would 'boss the girls like a mother' and it appears she did just that, much to the girls' annoyance.[40] In October 1916, Jacob reported that 'all the little girls had resigned [from Cumann na mBan] and decided to join the Fianna instead – thinking I suppose that they'd get dancing and drill every night with no work and no Mrs Roche to order them about'.[41] Jacob became the chairperson of the girls' troop. In early 1918, Fianna Headquarters in Dublin informed the Waterford girls that they should join the Clann na Gael Girl Scouts instead.[42]

OTHER NATIONALIST YOUTH GROUPS

The Fianna were not the only nationalist youth group to reorganise and expand in this period. Another example is the Irish National Guards. After his release from prison after the Easter Rising, John Kenny was elected chairman of this organisation, which began to regroup and enrol new members.[43] It spread to Waterford *c.* 1917–18 after a man named McEnri (also referred to as McHenry and McFinlay) applied to join the Fianna in Waterford, having moved from Dublin to work at a hotel. Once in, he apparently used his growing popularity to challenge the existing leadership and then started a branch of the National Guards, bringing about a dozen older Fianna members with him.[44] 'There were about 40 members of this organisation in Waterford city, comprising mostly Fianna lads who considered the Fianna too juvenile and who were not considered old enough to join one of the local Irish Volunteer companies', recalled Moses Roche. He was one of the Fianna members who had switched to the National Guards, but only remained 'for about eight or ten months' before he returned to his Fianna company.[45] Patrick Hearne reported that this unit of the National Guards only lasted for about nine months before most of its former Fianna members joined the Irish Volunteers and their leader left Waterford.[46]

The Clann na Gael Girl Scouts are another example. May Kelly reorganised this youth group after the Easter Rising, starting branches in Cork, Tullamore and Athlone *c.* 1917–19. In Cork, Annie Duggan 'was seconded from Cumann na mBan to take charge of the new organisation, with the rank of commandant' and oversaw expansion into Cobh and Douglas. According to her sister Peg, close to 200 girls joined the Clann na Gael Girl Scouts in Cork. Members learned military drill and first aid, elected their own officers, fundraised through collections and céilís, and helped the women of Cumann na mBan.[47]

Witness statements record a split in Cork's nationalist youth groups around late 1918/early 1919 due to the advent of rival organisations. The formation in Cork of the Citizen Army Boy Scouts and the Citizen Army Girl Guides apparently caused a split in the Fianna and Clann na Gael. The Citizen Army Girl Guides were led by the Misses Wallace of St Augustine Street. The Citizen Army Boy Scouts attracted about forty members, but apparently petered out by about 1920. All of these groups had a similar policy but sported slightly different uniforms. For instance, James A. Busby recalled that the Fianna wore a saffron scarf while the Citizen Army Scouts wore a blue scarf. The Cork Fianna maintained their numbers during this period through active recruitment of new members.[48]

PUBLIC DEFIANCE

In Hugo McNeill's view, the Fianna's involvement in 'minor incidents of defiance' played a 'useful' part 'in reviving national morale' after the 1916 Rising. In April 1917, the Fianna began to defy the British government's orders against marching and drilling when they openly paraded in uniform through the streets of Dublin, some members carrying hurleys. These parades led to clashes with the police, the most notable incident taking place in July 1917 when the entire Dublin Brigade marched in uniform through south Dublin city and county. 'Efforts were made by the DMP to stop the parade and break it up at Terenure and Rathmines Police Stations, but the police cordons were broken through at both points and the march continued in good order to the GPO [General Post Office] where the parade dismissed', reported McNeill. 'The Volunteers seemed quite willing – and rightly so – to sit back and note how this open defiance on the part of the younger organisation progressed.'[49] The Fianna's youth enabled them to challenge government authority more openly than their adult counterparts at this relatively early stage after the rebellion. The Fianna's acts of defiance would grow bolder over time. For instance, in November 1917 a Fianna special squad participated in an arms raid on a pawn shop, an activity that would become more common in 1920 once the War of Independence was well underway.[50]

The Fianna were among the republican organisations that increased their membership numbers and activities in response to the conscription crisis of the spring of 1918, though these new members did not necessarily remain once the threat diminished.[51] The crisis arose because the British government needed to find a way to boost numbers in its armed forces after the German army launched its final unsuccessful effort to win the war in Europe in March 1918. Contrary to the counsel of his Irish advisers, British Prime Minister Lloyd George started to consider extending conscription to Ireland. Although the Military Service Act of April 1918 was popular elsewhere in the United Kingdom, in Ireland it met with vehement opposition from every shade of political opinion except unionism.[52] According to George Hurley, the threat of conscription increased Fianna membership in Cork to about 200 boys in 1918.[53] J. E. Nolan recalled that the British government's unpopular efforts to apply conscription to Ireland helped to boost numbers in his local Fianna company, which met in an old warehouse on James's Street in Dublin and offered classes in musketry, the Irish language, signalling and first aid.[54]

The Dublin Brigade even formed an active service unit to oppose conscription.[55] 'This unit comprised picked members of the brigade, whose duty it was to cooperate with the Irish Volunteers in the event of conscription being enforced in Ireland', reported Joseph Reynolds. 'The boys were attached to the Volunteer Battalions under the control of a Fianna officer.' They were to be responsible for 'signalling and the use of small arms'.[56] Ultimately, Irish opposition to conscription proved so strong that the legislation was unenforceable. For the remainder of the Great War, the Fianna continued their military training programme and assisted in the ongoing advanced nationalist campaign against Irish recruitment into the British army.

THE 1918 GENERAL ELECTION

The end of the Great War in November 1918 was immediately followed by a general election in the soon-to-be disunited kingdom of Great Britain and Ireland. Although the *Fianna Handbook* had directed *sluaighte* not to get involved in party politics, Fianna members distributed election literature, posted bills ('sometimes at night during curfew') and undertook house-to-house collections for funds to support the Sinn Féin Party during the 1918 general election campaign.[57] Erroneously associated with the Easter Rising in the public mind, the Sinn Féin Party had slowly overtaken the champions of home rule, the Irish Parliamentary Party, as the most popular political party in Ireland between 1916 and 1918. During the 1918 election campaign, Sinn Féin candidates pledged to abstain from taking seats in the British parliament and instead to establish their own Irish legislative assembly in Dublin, which they duly did.

Fianna co-founder Countess Markievicz was among the seventy-three Sinn Féin candidates elected in December 1918, making her the first woman to win a seat in the British House of Commons, which she, of course, abstained from taking. Still imprisoned in Holloway jail in London, she was unable to attend the first meeting of Dáil Éireann, the new Irish legislative assembly, on 21 January 1919.[58] By coincidence, the opening shots of the Irish War of Independence (or Anglo-Irish War), a guerrilla war between the IRA and British government forces, rang out on the same day. The Irish parliament initially consisted of a unicameral assembly and a ministry (or cabinet) headed by a president. Markievicz became Minister for Labour. Despite being proscribed by the British government in September 1919, the Dáil continued to function throughout the guerrilla war.[59]

The foundation of Dáil Éireann created job opportunities for Dublin Fianna officers, such as Sean Harling and Sean Saunders, who were recruited to serve as couriers for the various Dáil departments. 'The Dáil Courier Service was recruited almost entirely from the Fianna Circle of the IRB', reported Saunders.[60] These young men had earned their positions of trust and responsibility through their membership in the IRB and their training in the Fianna, both of which demonstrated their commitment to the republican cause.

The start of the War of Independence necessitated some minor structural changes in the Fianna around the country. By 1919 there were Fianna *sluaighte* in 'every important sized town and village', recorded Hugo McNeill.[61] A report on the tenth annual Fianna *ard-fheis*, which was held in Dublin on 28 September 1919 with representatives of 100 *sluaighte* in attendance, indicates that the Headquarters' Staff had already been expanded to include directors of equipment and recruiting. The *ard-fheis* decided to add a director of education (Liam Langley) to the staff to promote knowledge of Irish language and history among members as well as to develop a code of 'moral ethics' to be observed by every member of the Fianna in hopes that the youth organisation 'would help to raise the moral standard of life' in Ireland.[62] The concern of this nationalist youth organisation for Irish morality is in keeping with Tom Garvin's assertion that 'like other European radicalisms, the Irish movement displayed a blend of romantic idealism, an exaggerated moralism and, commonly, a cult of youth'.[63]

After the 1919 *ard-fheis*, the director of organisation and training issued a series of circulars relating to schemes of military organisation and training for 1919–20. Troops around the country were ordered to reorganise themselves into companies, battalions and brigades with the requisite officers. Where a *sluagh* was not large enough to form a company, which consisted of seventy-eight members and a captain, the *sluagh* commander would have the same duties and responsibilities as a captain, though he could not hold this rank. A battalion was to consist of four to eight companies while a brigade was to cover 'the entire City and County strength with a Brigade Commandant'.[64] Frank MacMahon in Cork and Joe McKelvey in Belfast became the first brigade commandants outside of Dublin.[65]

Perhaps in response to comments at the 1919 *ard-fheis* that the training department had been inactive in 1918–19, the new director of training, Hugo McNeill, issued a circular outlining a new scheme of training for 1919–20. This was to include: lectures for officers beginning with talks on 'drill and discipline' and 'protection on the march'; officers' classes in larger centres such as Dublin, Cork, Belfast and Limerick; the circulation of training notes; examinations for commissioned officers; and the awarding of proficiency badges to officers, non-commissioned officers (NCOs) and boys reaching 'a certain standard' in skills such as signalling, first aid, scouting and musketry. McNeill hoped that 'with the earnest cooperation of every Fianna Officer in Ireland, the military efficiency of the Fianna will certainly reach a far higher standard than it has ever reached before'.[66]

In keeping with the changes ordered by Fianna Headquarters, the Belfast District Council decided in November 1919 to reconstitute itself as a Battalion Council, restructure the local *sluaighte* into two companies (A-B), which would have a right half for seniors and a left half for juniors, and begin collecting funds to buy arms. This may have been a response to an attempt by some older Fianna boys to form a Volunteer company, which the Belfast council had clamped down on two months earlier, considering it 'a breach of discipline' that would 'undermine its authority'. By July 1920, a growth in membership had necessitated a further restructuring with six companies divided between two battalions. This was scaled back in November 1920 to one battalion of five companies (A-E), two existing companies having been combined, with plans underway to form a new sixth company.[67]

Elsewhere in Ulster, Liam A. Brady, the leader of the Fianna company in Derry, undertook the organisation of the Fianna in County Donegal in the summer of 1920 at the request of Fianna Headquarters in Dublin. This led to the formation of branches in Letterkenny, Moville, Greencastle, Gweedore, Murlog and Raphoe. During the summers of 1920–21, the boys from these branches held camps at Fahan, County Donegal.[68]

The ongoing reorganisation of the Belfast Fianna and the earlier attempt by some boys to start a Volunteer company may be a reflection of tensions evident in Belfast in response to the increasing violence of the IRA's military campaign elsewhere in Ireland.[69] The summer of 1920 saw the outbreak of intense communal and sectarian violence in Belfast after loyalist workers expelled their Catholic co-workers from the Belfast shipyards and engineering works in July. They also expelled socialist Protestant workers, so-called 'rotten prods'. The expulsion was a reprisal for the IRA's assassination in Cork of Colonel Gerald Smyth, an Ulster-born police commissioner, and the subsequent refusal of southern Irish railway workers to transport his remains to his northern hometown. In August 1920, Dáil Éireann retaliated against the shipyard expulsions by introducing a boycott of Ulster businesses and banks in the vain hope that this action would not only demonstrate the north-east's economic dependence on the rest of Ireland but also lead to the reinstatement of Catholic workers.

Such tensions influenced activities undertaken by the Fianna in Ulster. In Derry, Fianna boys helped to print and distribute 'black lists' of businesses to be boycotted during the 'Belfast Boycott'.[70] In response to rioting in August 1920, the Belfast District Council decided that 'Fianna members in possession of arms [would] be posted where they [could] best defend Falls district from attack'.[71] Nineteen-year-old Fianna member John Murray died on 29 August 1920 after he was injured while engaged in defending the civilian population in the Ardoyne area of Belfast during an attack by government forces.[72]

The impact of the War of Independence on the Fianna was also evident in Cork, which was one of the most active theatres of the guerrilla war. In late 1920, an active service unit (ASU) of the Fianna was formed in Cork city. Under the leadership of Stephen Walsh, it 'consisted of 20 to 30 of the more senior boys', twelve of whom 'were armed with revolvers when occasion demanded'. Mainly drawn from the north side of the city, the unit assisted the 1st Battalion of the Cork IRA. A smaller ASU under Frank Nolan was established on the south side of the city to assist the 2nd Battalion of the IRA. As George Hurley noted, the main purpose of these units, which functioned on a part-time basis, 'was to have lads available for any sudden call from the IRA'. In addition, the Cork Fianna formed their own brigade staff in early 1921 with Frank McMahon as Officer Commanding (O/C), Jack Carey as Brigade Organiser and Vice O/C, Dan Scully as Adjutant, Michael O'Leary as Intelligence Officer and Edward Gamble as O/C City. The brigade consisted of two battalions, each containing several companies.[73]

There seems to be some debate about when the Fianna declaration was revised to reflect the political changes in Ireland brought about by the establishment of Dáil Éireann and the outbreak of the War of Independence in January 1919. Though Joseph Reynolds recalled that this occurred at the 1919 *ard-fheis*, contemporary sources suggest that a proposal made by the Belfast Battalion Council at the *ard-fheis* held on 1 August 1920 led to the declaration being changed to: 'I pledge my allegiance to Dáil Éireann, the Government of the Irish Republic, to do all in my power to force the withdrawal of the Army of Occupation, and to obey my superior officers.'[74] This replaced the previous declaration in which members promised 'to work for the Independence of Ireland, never to join England's armed forces, and to obey my superior officers'.[75] The revised wording of the declaration signalled the Fianna's support for the higher level of militancy now evident in the struggle for Irish independence.

The Belfast origin of the proposal made at the 1920 Fianna *ard-fheis* may have reflected anxieties about the impending partition of Ireland and the creation of Northern Ireland, which occurred in 1921 after the implementation of the Government of Ireland Act of 1920. Ironically, the six counties that comprised Northern Ireland were the only part of Ireland that accepted a home rule settlement, despite Ulster Unionist opposition to home rule having originated there. In the end, Ulster Unionists decided that the best way to secure their interests was to accept a devolved parliament for Northern Ireland within the United Kingdom. Anxieties regarding partition further heightened tensions in the north in the period 1920–22.

During the years of the War of Independence, the Fianna attracted its highest membership figures in Dublin, Limerick and counties Cork, Kerry, Tipperary and Clare.[76] For instance, the Fianna are reported to have attracted about 807 members in County Tipperary in the period 1917–23.[77] Numbers were also high in the cities of Belfast, Derry and Waterford and in counties Armagh and Wexford.[78] High membership figures in Munster counties probably correlate with the intensity of the War of Independence in that province, whereas the high numbers in parts of Ulster may reflect a desire to serve and protect the Catholic nationalist community there.

Conditions during the War of Independence impacted on the ability of the Fianna to function effectively as an organisation. Although 'a profit of £10.9.6 on the year's trading' of equipment was reported at the 1919 *ard-fheis*, it was noted that it had become difficult to secure necessary equipment at reasonable prices.[79] In March 1920, Eamon Martin admitted that the Fianna's work, certainly in Dublin, had been 'greatly hampered by lack of funds, arrests, etc. and we find it almost impossible to carry out all the work we have set out for ourselves'.[80] It was difficult to replace Headquarters' Staff who had been arrested because, as Adjutant Barney Mellows later admitted: 'We could not induce the elder boys to remain in the Fianna.'[81] Instead, they wished to transfer to the Volunteers. Even maintaining records could be a challenge. For instance, in November 1920 the Belfast District Council noted that the October reports from its affiliated companies 'had been taken by the British Crown Forces'.[82]

Communication between Fianna Headquarters and units around the country became increasingly difficult due to the conflict. In Waterford, Patrick Hearne could find 'no record of communications being received here from Fianna Headquarters' from the latter part of 1920 until the Truce in July 1921: 'We were seemingly on our own.' Furthermore, relations between the Fianna and the Irish Volunteers were also problematic in certain parts of the country, such as Waterford. 'We were rather anxious for a better understanding with the IRA here, but it did not seem to get very serious consideration in City circles', noted Hearne.[83]

Both the Fianna and their flamboyant frontwoman Countess Markievicz increasingly found themselves on the radar of the British authorities. In December 1920, Markievicz was court-martialled for 'conspiracy', informing her sister Eva that the conspiracy in question was the Fianna. She added, 'I can't see myself how any one with a sense of humour could seriously regard a child's organisation as a "conspiracy", but any stick does to beat the Irish rebel with!'[84]

Markievicz compared her court martial to a Gilbert and Sullivan comic opera:

> Isn't it Gilbertian to pretend that the Fianna is a conspiracy? It was started in 1909, and has always been open and never secret. I asked then could they point to one 'cowardly act' on the armed forces of the Crown by little boys. It was an awful performance: after being shut up alone for two months to be suddenly brought up before eight 'judges', plus prosecutors, be-wigged barristers, enemy witnesses, etc, and surrounded by bayonets![85]

The ostensible reason for Markievicz's incarceration in 1920–21 was just as disingenuous as her dismissal of the Fianna as 'a child's organisation' and its members as 'little boys', considering the involvement of its adolescent members in military operations against British government forces during the Easter Rising and the War of Independence. As discussed in chapter 8, involvement in military action could have fatal consequences, with at least twenty-eight serving members of the Fianna losing their lives between 1916 and 1923.

THE RELATIONSHIP BETWEEN THE FIANNA AND THE IRA

Over time, tensions between the IRA and the Fianna became apparent due to lack of communication about planned operations. For instance, in July 1920, a representative of the North Louth Battalion of the IRA expressed disquiet about the activities of a Fianna company in Dundalk, of which a dozen adolescent members were armed with revolvers. Complaining that 'several jobs [had] been carried out by them without information to, or sanction from any Volunteer Officer', he cited the example of a recent arms raid on a private house in the town, which had proved 'fruitless'. 'As a result of the raid one little girl has since been suffering from shock and unable to sleep – at least so her father a S.[inn] Feiner states', he added.[86] His letter provides the sense that the local IRA not only wanted clarification of the relationship between the two forces but also for the Fianna unit in Dundalk to be brought under the IRA's control. Interestingly, the agenda for the next Fianna *ard-fheis*, which was held on 1 August 1920, indicates that the Dundalk *sluagh* gave notice of the following motion: 'that the Fianna be united with the Irish Volunteers'.[87]

Recognition of the potentially dangerous consequences of overlapping arms raids by the Fianna and the IRA, which had occurred in the autumn of 1920, finally led to negotiations between Dáil Éireann's Ministry of Defence and Fianna Headquarters. As a result, a formal link between the Fianna and the IRA was forged in early 1921 to facilitate cooperation.[88] Eamon Martin viewed this arrangement as 'merely a formal recognition of a condition which had, for all essential purposes, existed since the foundation of the Volunteers'.[89] Under the agreement, the Fianna was 'recognised as one of the units at the disposal of the Republican Government' and responsible for assisting the Irish Volunteers 'in every manner possible' under their own officers. Though the Fianna would act in cooperation with the Irish Volunteers, it would 'remain in most respects a separate organisation'.[90] The Fianna leadership ceded a degree of control in hopes of receiving more assistance from the IRA in building up the youth movement and securing better communications channels between Fianna Headquarters in Dublin and companies around the country.

As a result of the agreement between the Fianna and the IRA, a composite council was created that consisted of three General Headquarters (GHQ) officers from each organisation. Barney Mellows, Garry Holohan and Liam Langley represented the Fianna while the Volunteer officers were Diarmuid O'Hegarty, Gearóid O'Sullivan and Eamon Price. A nominee of the Minister for Defence chaired meetings of the composite council.[91]

The agreement between the two organisations led to other developments as well. The Dáil's Department of Defence began to give the Fianna a monthly grant and paid a salary to Adjutant-General Barney Mellows 'who had given up his civilian employment'. In addition to the youth organisation's intelligence and communications duties, the Fianna started to be utilised as an official training corps for the Volunteers.[92] In particular, Fianna boys were to be trained in dispatch carrying, which included the correct delivery of verbal messages, as well as signalling in Morse code and reconnaissance. Furthermore, 'specially selected boys of good physique' would also be trained in such skills as bombing and rifle exercises where such opportunities existed.[93] The Fianna's Dublin Brigade was also reorganised to correspond to the structure of the IRA, expanding from two battalions to five.[94]

As a result of the scheme, the Fianna were required to assist 'the Army of Ireland in operations', with each Fianna unit working under their own officer who was responsible to the Irish Volunteer officer in charge of operations. Fianna battalion areas were to correspond to those of the Irish Volunteers. Each Fianna Battalion would have a Battalion Commandant who was responsible for giving instructions to the various companies and for carrying out certain operations authorised by the relevant Irish Volunteer Battalion or Brigade Commandant. Thus, the Fianna Battalion Commandant would serve as the Liaison Officer between the two organisations. In areas where the Fianna had not reached battalion strength, the senior Fianna officer in the area would serve as the liaison. To prevent overlapping and extra work, the Fianna were not permitted to 'carry out operations without having previously obtained (through the Fianna Battalion Commandant) sanction from Irish Volunteer Battalion Commandant'. In keeping with previous practice, Fianna members would transfer to the Volunteers once they had reached the age of eighteen, unless their services were essential for the successful management of their company.[95] These arrangements remained in place until the truce on 11 July 1921.[96]

Even after the agreement between the two organisations, relations between the Fianna and the IRA remained better in Dublin, Cork and Belfast, in particular, than elsewhere in Ireland.[97] For instance, minutes of brigade council meetings attended by Belfast Fianna officers in the latter half of 1921 suggest increased cooperation with the IRA. In August 1921 at the behest of the local IRA, Fianna members attended the funeral of a Volunteer and participated in IRA manoeuvres. At a meeting held on 9 October 1921, it was recorded that the Divisional Commandant of the IRA had complained about the conduct of certain Fianna members 'in Craobh Ruadh [Red Branch] the previous Sunday night'. In their defence, it was pointed out that the master of ceremonies and others in attendance at the event had provoked the disturbance which had involved Volunteers and civilians as well as Fianna members.[98] In his witness statement, John McCoy, a northern IRA leader, mentioned using Fianna members as scouts and their involvement in arms raids.[99]

Elsewhere in Ireland, however, relations between the Fianna and the IRA could be strained, a situation that had the potential to hamper the transfer of Fianna members to the Volunteers. 'We have found that in most cases the IV [Irish Volunteers] have not made the slightest attempt to avail themselves of the advantages of boys over men, and that the general opinion is that the Fianna are only youngsters and should be treated like children', reported Barney Mellows. Though there were many cases where the IRA were genuinely unable to assist in the formation of Fianna troops, in others the Volunteers apparently feared that the Fianna would draw them into premature military action.[100] Patrick Hearne reported that in Waterford, Fianna members were entrusted with dispatch carrying and regularly transferred to the IRA, but 'beyond this we did not seem to be making great progress towards coordination'. Frustrated at being left out of IRA operations, Fianna members in Waterford appear to have exacerbated the problem by undertaking their own operations, such as arms raids.[101]

In the wake of the national agreement between the two organisations, a new report form was developed to facilitate keeping track of how many Fianna members transferred to the IRA. The form was so new in August 1921 that the only figure available was 150 transfers covering Dublin, Belfast and Dundalk. Barney Mellows recommended that all Fianna members who transferred to the IRA should 'be placed in the same company or squad … as boys and men fight better when they know their partners'.[102]

THE TRUCE PERIOD

The Truce beginning on 11 July 1921 suspended open hostilities between the IRA and British government forces and paved the way for the negotiation of the Anglo-Irish Treaty. Figures contained in the Military Service Pensions Collection (MSPC) indicate that the Fianna had at least 4,437 members on the date of the Truce. An additional 1,322 members were recorded for unspecified dates between 1917 and 1923.[103] Prior to the Truce, Barney Mellows was aware of sixty-three Fianna units around the country; after the cessation of hostilities he received reports of forty more, some of which were newly created. During the Truce, the Fianna undertook a concerted recruiting campaign with some success, though Mellows was unsure how much support was being received from the IRA around the country.[104] In County Waterford, for example, there were Fianna companies in Waterford city, Tramore, Ferrybank and Portlaw at the time of the truce, with a further four companies being formed at Mount Sion, Dunkett-Sallypark, Ballyduff and Passage in the period after the Truce.[105]

Files in the MSPC suggest that Fianna membership figures grew in some places and dipped in others between the Truce on 11 July 1921 and the outbreak of the Irish Civil War on 28 June 1922. Numbers increased in Dublin city and county, Limerick city and counties Armagh, Kerry and Waterford,[106] while they decreased in the Mid Clare 1st Battalion and counties Mayo, Sligo and Wexford.[107] County Louth was mixed with numbers going up in Dundalk and down in Drogheda.[108] Membership in Cork city and county remained steady at 895 boys.[109] The collection does not contain comparative figures for all counties where the Fianna existed, so it is not possible to gain a complete picture of trends around the country.[110]

During the period of the Truce, the Fianna continued to expand in east Ulster where civil unrest and sectarian violence remained problematic. By August 1921 there were again two battalions in Belfast, which increased to three by December of that year. Organisational work in counties Down and Antrim was underway in October 1921. By December there were twelve Fianna units outside of Belfast. They were located in Ballycastle, Loughguile, Glenravel, Randalstown and Moneynick in County Antrim, in Armagh and Lurgan in County Armagh, and in Newry, Downpatrick, Castlewellan, Kilcoo and Crossgar in County Down.[111]

The Fianna were not the only republican organisation which increased its numbers once hostilities ceased. In County Clare, the

Irish Volunteers, Cumann na mBan and the Fianna all expanded during this period.¹¹² Numbers in the Fianna, however, would dip again in the Mid Clare Brigade's 1st Battalion, which included companies in Clooney, Ennis and Doora, by the time the Civil War was underway in mid-1922.¹¹³

A report from August 1921 records the existence of 132 Fianna units in Ireland, including those affiliated with the Dublin Brigade and Cork and Belfast battalions. Outside of these three cities, the number of units was 103. The report lists units in twenty-four counties across the four provinces. There were no units listed in counties Laois and Longford at the time. Fianna headquarters had received no information either way on six other counties. The official membership figure at that time stood at 2,738 males, but as Barney Mellows noted, this figure did not 'represent the number of boys who are working with the Irish Volunteers as there are many districts' which had not communicated with headquarters, 'in which the Fianna exists in a more or less disorganised state'.¹¹⁴ The Dublin Brigade alone consisted of 785 members, representing nearly 29% of the Fianna's reported total membership at the time.¹¹⁵

Even once the Truce was underway, the poor system of communications made it difficult to ascertain true numbers or exercise a degree of control over Fianna units around the country. Fianna Headquarters tried to use covering addresses as much as possible, but there were parts of the country for which the leadership did not have such addresses. Monthly reports from units around Ireland were meant to come through IRA lines, but often the Volunteers refused 'to accept them for transmission to Dublin'.¹¹⁶

During the Truce, the Fianna intensified their training programme in anticipation of a resumption of hostilities with British government forces. For instance, the Dublin Brigade held training camps at Finglas, Dollymount, Portmanock and Loughlinstown at which instruction in the use of arms 'formed the bulk of the training'.¹¹⁷ The Fianna also held a national training camp on 10–17 September 1921 at Loughlinstown, County Dublin, which was attended by about 150 Fianna officers and NCOs. To help make it possible for all officers to attend, Fianna Headquarters covered the cost of railway fares so that attendees only had to pay a nominal sum of fifteen shillings for provisions.¹¹⁸ A second national camp had been planned for 18–24 September, but was deemed unnecessary.¹¹⁹ While these training activities were going on, a treaty between Great Britain and the twenty-six southern Irish counties was being negotiated by political leaders in London.

THE IMPACT OF THE ANGLO-IRISH TREATY AND THE IRISH CIVIL WAR

The Irish War of Independence concluded with the signing of the Anglo-Irish Treaty on 6 December 1921. The terms of this agreement between the British and southern Irish governments proved highly contentious, particularly because the dominion status granted to the new Irish Free State meant that it would remain subordinate to the British crown – at least for the time being. The Sinn Féin Party and the IRA split between those who felt that the treaty was the best settlement that could be achieved at that time and those who rejected it because it fell short of the aim to achieve an independent republic. Although a small majority in Dáil Éireann (sixty-four to fifty-seven) voted in favour of ratifying the treaty on 7 January 1922, the treaty split set the scene for the outbreak of the Irish Civil War in June of that year. The Civil War was fought between the pro-Treaty National Army and other security forces of the Irish provisional (later Free State) government and the anti-Treaty IRA.

Dáil Éireann's acceptance of the Anglo-Irish Treaty on 7 January 1922 had disruptive repercussions for the Fianna as well as for the Sinn Féin Party and the IRA. On 10 January 1922, Barney Mellows informed Fianna officers that 'the present political situation [could not] be allowed to interfere with Fianna work', asserting that 'political discussions of any nature [were] strictly prohibited in Drill Halls, or at any Fianna meetings'. Plans were underway 'to hold an Ard-Fheis as soon as possible to decide the future of the organisation'. Until the meeting of the *ard-fheis*, all ranks of the Fianna were exhorted to 'STOP THE TALK AND GET ON WITH THE WORK'.[120]

The *ard-fheis* was initially planned to take place in Dublin on 12 March 1922 in order to discuss suggested changes to the Fianna constitution and other issues. It was proposed that the *ard-fheis* would express the anti-Treaty resolution of the Chief Scout Countess Markievicz

> that we Fianna Éireann, the organised youth of Ireland, re-affirm our allegiance to the Irish Republic and offer the strength of our bodies, the powers of our minds, and the truth that lies in the soul of each one of us to our Country in her distress. We here and now place on record our appreciation of those members of An Dáil who opposed the Subversion of the Republic, and we are prepared to stand on their side in the gap of danger.[121]

In the end, the date of the *ard-fheis* was postponed ostensibly due to concerns that the cost of railway fares would prevent many companies from sending delegates to Dublin to voice their views at such a critical time. Instead, a Munster Convention was to be held in Cork city on 17 March 1922. Delegates from this convention would then represent the Munster perspective at the *ard-fheis*, which would be held at a later date.[122]

On 16 April 1922, shortly after the occupation of the Four Courts in Dublin by the anti-Treaty IRA, Barney Mellows finally presided over the long awaited *ard-fheis*. A report on the event indicated that 187 delegates representing Fianna units in twenty-five counties were in attendance.[123] At this *ard-fheis*, most delegates 'declared their allegiance to the republic in unqualified terms'.[124] 'Practically the entire Dublin Brigade staff, officers commanding the Dublin battalions, and the vast majority of the rank and file of the Dublin Brigade Fianna opposed the Treaty', asserted Sean Saunders.[125] In contrast, most of the officers in the Belfast Brigade supported the Treaty.[126] Unlike the IRA, however, there was no split in the Fianna because members who were pro-Treaty quietly left the youth organisation, many to join the National Army. 'No attempt was made to maintain a pro-Treaty organisation', reported Hugo McNeill, who joined the National Army in February 1922 and went on to a distinguished career in the Irish Defence Forces. 'The [Fianna] organisation as such took the anti-Treaty side.'[127]

In June 1922, the month in which the Civil War broke out, Fianna membership was reported as 26,000.[128] This appears to be an inflated figure given that files contained in the MSPC indicate that there were at least 4,374 members of the Fianna on 1 July 1922.[129] The Fianna may have succeeded in maintaining their unity as an organisation, but membership figures were soon decimated as companies around the country collapsed, including four in south County Dublin.[130] For instance, in January 1922 membership in the Dublin Brigade was reported as 2,525, but by 1 July 1922 numbers were down to 788.[131] The members who abandoned the youth group may have done so because they were uncertain of whether to support the pro- or anti-Treaty sides or disheartened by the turn of political events.

By the end of 1922, what remained of the Fianna organisation had been further devastated by the Civil War. Most of the Headquarters' Staff had been arrested by the end of September: Garry Holohan, Eamon Martin, Liam Langley and Joe Reynolds were arrested between July and September 1922, followed by Barney Mellows in December of that year. The loss of the organisation's centre contributed to the collapse of its periphery units.[132] Furthermore, the circumstances of the Civil War made it almost impossible to recruit new members, parade, train or disseminate propaganda.[133] Even before the outbreak of the armed conflict in June 1922, the Quartermaster-General had admitted that 'the Fianna were practically without funds'. Plans for fundraising outlined at the 1922 *ard-fheis* were disrupted by hostilities between pro- and anti-Treaty forces.[134]

After the IRA's ceasefire on 30 April 1923 and the triumph of the pro-Treaty side in the Civil War, Markievicz undertook the task of reorganising the Fianna with the help of George Plunkett, who succeeded her as Chief Scout after her death in 1927.[135] George Plunkett was a brother of Joseph Mary Plunkett, who was executed for his leading role in the Easter Rising. George had fought in the GPO alongside Joseph and another brother, Jack, in 1916.[136] Markievicz and Plunkett virtually had to rebuild the youth group from scratch, shifting the Fianna's focus from military action back to the recruitment, training and education of a new generation of republicans.[137]

Plans for such a shift in focus were already evident prior to the outbreak of the Civil War. The 1922 *ard-fheis* amended the Fianna constitution, stating that the object of the organisation was 'to organise the Boys of Ireland and train them, mentally and physically, that their services may be utilised in the interests of the Republic, and to maintain the unity of Ireland'. To achieve this object, the boys would be taught scouting and military exercises, Irish history and the Irish language. Membership was open to all boys between the ages of twelve and eighteen who endorsed the Fianna constitution and made the declaration of the Fianna.[138] A new intermittent edition of the *Fianna* paper, this time billed as 'the official organ of Fianna Éireann', called on the organisation to 'devote more of our time to the training of the mind and the body' through such activities as qualifying to wear the Fáinne as a sign of skill in the Irish language or organising 'inter-company athletic competitions' and Gaelic games. The reappearance of the paper in June 1922 was billed as being part of a revival in the educational side of the Fianna's programming.[139] The outbreak in hostilities later that month ensured that the organisation's plans to focus more on educational than military activities had to be put on hold for another year.

After the Civil War, supporters of the republican movement maintained varying degrees of hostility towards the Irish Free State and Northern Ireland. The June 1926 issue of *Fianna* highlighted the perceived continuing need for the republican youth group alleging that there were 50,000 Freemasons and 36,000 Boy Scouts in Ireland, who represented 'the Vanguard of British imperialism in this country'.[140] Though such membership figures, especially in relation to the Baden-Powell Scouts, were based more on inflated perception than reality, the apparent need remained the same.[141] Irish Catholics, who formed the majority of the Fianna's membership, had long seen Freemasonry as an alleged 'part of an international anti-Catholic plot'.[142] As the Fianna had been founded as an Irish nationalist alternative to the Boy Scouts, they also found it frustrating that Baden-Powell's British import still outnumbered them after independence.

The subsequent history of the Fianna has tended to reflect the fortunes of (and splits within) the republican movement in Ireland.[143] For instance, the Fianna aligned themselves with the Provisional IRA during the Troubles, the period of political violence in Northern Ireland that lasted from 1969 until the Good Friday Agreement of 1998.[144] In more recent years, the organisation has promoted itself as an 'independent republican youth movement'.[145]

NOTES

1. Patrick Hearne, witness statement, 18 Aug. 1958 (MA BMH, WS 1,742).
2. Garry Holohan, witness statement, 17 Jan. 1950 (MA, BMH, WS 336).
3. Hugo McNeill, witness statement, 20 Mar. 1956 (MA, BMH, WS 1,377).
4. *Ibid*. The Dublin *sluaighte* and their leaders were: No. 1 – Camden St. – P. Cassidy; No. 2 – Dolphins Barn – Seamus Pounch; No. 3 – Inchicore – Robert Holland; No. 4 – Blackhall St. – Liam Staines; No. 5 – Merchants Quay – Theo Fitzgerald; No. 6 – North Frederick St. – P. Brown; No. 7 – Ranelagh / Rathmines – Hugo McNeill; and No. 8 – Fairview / Dollymount – M. Henderson.
5. Joseph Reynolds, witness statement, 31 Jan. 1949 (MA, BMH, WS 191).
6. The following witness statements outline the situation in Kerry: Michael O'Leary, witness statement, 17 May 1955 (MA, BMH, WS 1,167); Thomas Pelican, witness statement, 7 Mar. 1955 (MA, BMH, WS 1,109); Thomas O'Connor, witness statement, 15 June 1955 (MA, BMH, WS 1,189).
7. Patrick Hearne, witness statement, 18 Aug. 1958 (MA, BMH, WS 1,742).
8. Edward Fullerton, witness statement, 16 Sept. 1953 (MA, BMH, WS 890).
9. Liam A. Brady, witness statement, 1 May 1952 (MA, BMH, WS 676).
10. Margaret Ward, 'Fianna Éireann' in Brian Lalor (ed.), *The Encyclopedia of Ireland* (Dublin: Gill and Macmillan, 2003), p. 386.
11. Constance Markievicz to Eva Gore-Booth, 16 May 1916, quoted in Constance Georgina Gore-Booth de Markievicz, *Prison Letters of Countess Markievicz* (New York: Kraus Reprint, 1970), p. 139.

12 Markievicz to Gore-Booth, 9 June 1917, 21 Sept. 1917, in Markievicz, *Prison Letters*, pp. 152, 174–5.
13 An unflattering description of Hobson is included in *The Police Gazette or Hue-and-Cry*, 7 Nov. 1916, p. 3.
14 Claire Hobson, witness statement, n.d. (MA, BMH, WS 685); Mary Hobson, 'Bulmer family chronicle from before 1050 to 1936' (NLI, MS 5220); parish marriage register, Rathfarnham (NLI, microfilm no. P 8972).
15 C. C. Trench, diary entry, 21 May 1916, in Hilary Pyle (ed.), *Cesca's Diary* (Dublin: Woodfield Press, 2005), p. 228.
16 Maxwell to Asquith, 3 Aug. 1916, quoted in Michael Laffan, *The Resurrection of Ireland: The Sinn Féin Party, 1916–1923* (Cambridge: Cambridge University Press, 1999), p. 46.
17 See Marnie Hay, 'Kidnapped: Bulmer Hobson, the IRB and the 1916 Easter Rising', *Canadian Journal of Irish Studies*, 35:1 (2009), pp. 53–60; Marnie Hay, 'The mysterious "disappearance" of Bulmer Hobson', *Studies: An Irish Quarterly Review*, 98:390 (2009), pp. 185–95.
18 Marnie Hay, 'A "republic of learning": Bulmer Hobson, nationalism and the printed word' in Marnie Hay and Daire Keogh (eds), *Rebellion and Revolution in Dublin: Voices from a Suburb, Rathfarnham, 1913–23* (Dublin: South Dublin Libraries, 2016), pp. 185–7.
19 Sean McLoughlin, witness statement, 26 Aug. 1949 (MA, BMH, WS 290). For more on McLoughlin, see Charlie McGuire, 'Sean McLoughlin: The boy commandant of 1916', *History Ireland*, 14:2 (Mar.–Apr. 2006), pp. 26–30; Charlie McGuire, *Sean McLoughlin: Ireland's Forgotten Revolutionary* (London: Merlin Press, 2011).
20 Cathleen McCarthy (née Ryan), witness statement, 31 Mar. 1954 (MA, BMH, WS 937).
21 Brendan Lynch to Marnie Hay, 9 Aug. 2010 (email in possession of the author). Ó Riain was Lynch's great uncle. See also Cathleen McCarthy (née Ryan), witness statement, 31 Mar. 1954 (MA, BMH, WS 937); Sean McLoughlin, witness statement, 26 Aug. 1949 (MA, BMH, WS 290).
22 Joseph Reynolds, witness statement, 31 Jan. 1949 (MA, BMH, WS 191).
23 Hugo McNeill, witness statement, 20 Mar. 1956 (MA, BMH, WS 1,377). The Dublin Battalion staff consisted of the following: Commandant – Barney Mellows; Vice-Commandant – Robert Holland; Adjutant – P. Cassidy; and Quartermaster – Seamus Pounch. The commandants of the other two battalions were Joe McKelvey in Belfast and Frank MacMahon in Cork. Niall MacNeill mentions the revival of the Rathfarnham company in his BMH witness statement dated 6 Jan. 1948 (MA, BMH, WS 69).
24 Joseph Reynolds, witness statement, 31 Jan. 1949 (MA, BMH, WS 191). During the period 1917–21, the Headquarters' Staff included:

Righ-Fheinnidhe – Eamon de Valera (1917–18), Constance de Markievicz (1918–21); Chief of Staff – Eamon Martin (1917–20), Frank MacMahon (1920–21, Cork); Adjutant General – Barney Mellows (1917–21); Quartermaster General – Garry Holohan (1917–21); Director of Organisation and Training – Eamon Martin (1917–20), Hugo McNeill (1920–21); and Director of Education – Liam Langley (c. 1918–21) (Hugo McNeill, witness statement, 20 Mar. 1956 (MA, BMH, WS 1,377)).

25 Joseph Reynolds, witness statement, 31 Jan. 1949 (MA, BMH, WS 191).
26 Pádraig Mac Fhloinn, 'The history and tradition of Fianna Éireann' in *Fianna Éireann Handbook* (Dublin: Fianna Éireann, 1988), p. 14; County Inspectors' Confidential Reports, June 1917 (TNA, CO 904/103). The reports for the month state that Fianna *sluaighte* existed in the following counties: Cork West Riding, Down, Galway West Riding, Mayo, Laois, Waterford and Wexford. There were five troops in County Down and three in County Wexford, while only one *sluagh* existed in each of the other areas listed.
27 County Inspectors' Confidential Reports, Nov. 1917 (TNA, CO 904/104).
28 Hugo McNeill, witness statement, 20 Mar. 1956 (MA, BMH, WS 1,377).
29 Joseph Reynolds, witness statement, 31 Jan. 1949 (MA, BMH, WS 191). The staff of the 1st Battalion (South Dublin) included: Commandant – Barney Mellows; Adjutant – Hugo McNeill; and Quartermaster – Derry McNeill. The staff of the 2nd Battalion (North Dublin) consisted of: Commandant – Theo Fitzgerald; Adjutant – Roddy Connolly (son of James Connolly); and Quartermaster – P. Byrne.
30 George Hurley, witness statement, 7 June 1957 (MA, BMH, WS 1,630).
31 Charles Meaney, witness statement, 11 June 1957 (MA, BMH, WS 1,631).
32 *Ibid.*
33 George Hurley, witness statement, 7 June 1957 (MA, BMH, WS 1,630).
34 Michael O'Leary, witness statement, 17 May 1955 (MA, BMH, WS 1,167); Thomas Pelican, witness statement, 7 Mar. 1955 (MA, BMH, WS 1,109); Thomas O'Connor, witness statement, 15 June 1955 (MA, BMH, WS 1,189).
35 Patrick Hearne, witness statement, 18 Aug. 1958 (MA, BMH, WS 1,742).
36 Liam A. Brady, witness statement, 1 May 1952 (MA, BMH, WS 676).
37 Inspector General's and County Inspectors' Monthly Confidential Reports, Jan.–Nov. 1917 (TNA, CO 904/102–4).
38 Inspector General's and County Inspectors' Monthly Confidential Reports, Mar. 1918 (TNA, CO 904/105).
39 Belfast District Council Minute Book, 1918–22 (MA, BMH, Lieutenant-Colonel J. M. MacCarthy Collection, CD 29/4/1). Attendance figures as of Feb. 1919 were as follows: Sluagh Cúchullain, Roll = 72, Average = 50;

Sluagh Ua Conghaile, Roll = 80, Average = 40; Sluagh Colbaird, Roll = 60, Average = 30.

40 Rosamond Jacob, diary entry, 6 July 1916 (NLI, Rosamond Jacob Papers, MS 32,582 (30)). I would like to thank Dr Clara Cullen for bringing the references from Jacob's diary to my attention.

41 Rosamond Jacob, diary entry, 10 Oct. 1916 (NLI, Jacob Papers, MS 32,582 (30)).

42 Leeann Lane, *Rosamond Jacob: Third Person Singular* (Dublin: UCD Press, 2010), p. 123.

43 John Kenny, witness statement, 6 Nov. 1957 (MA, BMH, WS 1,693).

44 Patrick Hearne, witness statement, 18 Aug. 1958 (MA, BMH, WS 1,742).

45 Moses Roche, witness statement, 17 Mar. 1955 (MA, BMH, WS 1,129).

46 Patrick Hearne, witness statement, 18 Aug. 1958 (MA, BMH, WS 1,742).

47 Statement by May Chadwick (née Kelly), 22 Feb. 1937 (MA, MSPC, MSP34REF20098); Anne O'Callaghan (née Duggan), pension file (MA, MSPC, MSP34REF8617); Peg Duggan, witness statement, 14 Feb. 1957 (MA, BMH, WS 1,576).

48 James A. Busby, witness statement, 6 June 1957 (MA, BMH, WS 1,628); Peg Duggan, witness statement, 14 Feb. 1957 (MA, BMH, WS 1,576). The 1911 census return for 3 St Augustine Street, Cork, lists three Wallace sisters: Julia, a twenty-one-year-old shopkeeper, Hannah, a twenty-nine-year-old shop assistant, and Norah, a fifteen-year-old scholar; available at www.census.nationalarchives.ie/reels/nai001876203/ (accessed 3 July 2018).

49 Narrative by Gen. McNeill included in a MS memo prepared by Colonel J. J. O'Connell (MA, Collins Collection, A/0780, Item 5).

50 Aodh MacNeill, 'Summary of operations, Dublin Brigade, Fianna Éireann, 1916–1921' in 'Addendum to Fianna Éireann, History and Development, 1909–1921' (MA, Collins Collection, A/0041/3). This document is also available in NLI, J. J. O'Connell Papers, MS 22,113.

51 In his witness statement Patrick Hearne seems to imply that the Fianna were one of the national organisations in the city that saw their membership increase as a result of the conscription crisis in early 1918, but once the threat diminished so did the numbers (MA, BMH, WS 1,742).

52 Marie Coleman, *The Irish Revolution, 1916–1923* (London: Routledge, 2014), pp. 37–9.

53 George Hurley, witness statement, 7 June 1957 (MA, BMH, WS 1,630).

54 J. E. Nolan, 'History of Anglo-Irish Conflict: 1913–1921. Personal Reminiscences of Captain J. E. Nolan' (MA, Collins Collection, A/0800/2).

55 Aodh MacNeill, 'Summary of operations, Dublin Brigade, Fianna Éireann, 1916–1921' in 'Addendum to Fianna Éireann, History and Development, 1909–1921' (MA, Collins Collection, A/0041/3).

56 Joseph Reynolds, witness statement, 31 Jan. 1949 (MA, BMH, WS 191).
57 Pádraic Ó Riain (ed.), *Fianna Handbook* (Dublin: Central Council of Fianna Éireann, 1914), p. 23; Charles Meaney, witness statement, 11 June 1957 (MA, BMH, WS 1,631); James A Busby, witness statement, 6 June 1957 (MA, BMH, WS 1,628).
58 Lindie Naughton, *Markievicz: A Most Outrageous Rebel* (Newbridge, Co., Kildare: Merrion Press, 2016), pp. 215–17. Markievicz won the St Patrick's Division with a total of 7,835 votes, ousting the Irish Parliamentary Party incumbent William Field who had held the seat for twenty-six years.
59 Deirdre McMahon, 'Dáil Éireann' in S. J. Connolly (ed.), *The Oxford Companion to Irish History* (Oxford: Oxford University Press, 1999), pp. 133–4.
60 Sean Saunders, witness statement, 4 June 1953 (MA, BMH, WS 854). Also see the following witness statements: Sean Saunders, 19 Mar. 1953 (MA, BMH, WS 817); Sean Harling, 30 Mar. 1954 (MA, BMH, WS 935).
61 Hugo McNeill, witness statement, 20 Mar. 1956 (MA, BMH, WS 1,377).
62 Fianna Éireann, Ard-Fheis Report 1919 (MA, BMH, Michael Kilmartin Collection, CD144/1/5).
63 Tom Garvin, 'Great hatred, little room: Social background and political sentiment among revolutionary activists in Ireland, 1890–1922' in D. George Boyce (ed.), *The Revolution in Ireland, 1879–1923* (Basingstoke: Macmillan Education, 1988), p. 98.
64 'Organisation Circular No.1, Fianna Éireann – Headquarters Staff, Scheme of Military Organisation, 1919–1920' (MA, BMH, Kilmartin Collection, CD 144/1/6); 'Organisation Circular No.2, Fianna Éireann – Headquarters Staff, Duties of Company Officers and NCOs' (MA, BMH, Kilmartin Collection, CD 144/1/7).
65 George Hurley, witness statement, 7 June 1957 (MA, BMH, WS 1,630); Hugo McNeill, witness statement, 20 Mar. 1956 (MA, BMH, WS 1,377).
66 'Supplementary Training Circular No. 1, Fianna Éireann – Headquarters Staff, Scheme of Training for 1919–20' (MA, BMH, Kilmartin Collection, CD 144/1/9).
67 Belfast District Council Minute Book, 1918–22 (MA, BMH, MacCarthy Collection, CD 29/4/1).
68 Liam A. Brady, witness statement, 1 May 1952 (MA, BMH, WS 676).
69 Belfast District Council Minute Book, 1918–22 (MA, BMH, MacCarthy Collection, CD 29/4/1).
70 Liam A. Brady, witness statement, 1 May 1952 (MA, BMH, WS 676).
71 Belfast District Council Minute Book, 1918–22 (MA, BMH, MacCarthy Collection, CD 29/4/1).
72 John Murray, pension file (MA, MSPC, 2RBSD107).

73 George Hurley, witness statement, 7 June 1957 (MA, BMH, WS 1,630). The staff of the Cork battalions and companies consisted of: 1st Battalion: O/C Dan Mulroy; A Coy O/C Stephen Walsh; B Coy O/C Denis Woods; C Coy O/C Con O'Leary; D Coy O/C Stephen Wall who was later replaced by Patrick Lynch; E Coy O/C Leo Cahill; G Coy O/C Daniel Gamble; and H Coy O/C Peter Young. (Hurley did not list the O/C of F Coy.) 2nd Battalion: O/C Edward Murray; Adjutant John Roynane; B Coy O/C Richard O'Leary; C Coy O/C William Quirke; D Coy O/C Sean Downey; E Coy O/C Frank Nolan; F Coy O/C Christopher Hurley; G Coy O/C Richard Noonan; H Coy O/C Charles Meaney. (The O/C of A Coy is not listed.)
74 Joseph Reynolds, witness statement, 31 Jan. 1949 (MA, BMH, WS 191); entry for 7 July 1920, Belfast District Council Minute Book, 1918–22 (MA, BMH, MacCarthy Collection, CD 29/4/1); 'Fianna Éireann Ardfheis. Sunday. August 1st, 1920. Agenda.' (MA, BMH, Kilmartin Collection, CD 144/1/15). For an undated copy of the revised constitution, see MA, BMH, Kilmartin Collection, CD 144/1/3.
75 Constitution of the Fianna (MA, BMH, Kilmartin Collection, CD 144/1/1).
76 Membership figures are included in the Fianna Éireann Series (MA, MSPC). See Dublin and General Headquarters (FE/1), Limerick City Mid Limerick Brigade (FE/17), Cork No. 1 Brigade (FE/5), Cork No. 4 Brigade (FE/6), Kerry No. 1 Brigade (FE/10), Tralee Battalion Kerry No. 1 Brigade (FE/11), Listowel Battalion Kerry No. 1 Brigade (FE/12), 4th (Castlegregory) Battalion Kerry No. 1 Brigade (FE/13), 5th (Annascaul) Battalion Kerry No. 1 Brigade (FE/14), Tipperary No. 3 Brigade (South Tipperary) (FE/16), Rathkeale Company 4th Battalion West Limerick Brigade (FE/18), 1st Battalion Mid Clare Brigade (FE/19), 4th Battalion Mid Clare Brigade (FE/20), Kilkee Company 5th Battalion West Clare Brigade (FE/38).
77 See Tipperary No. 3 Brigade (South Tipperary) (MA, MSPC, FE/16).
78 See MA, MSPC: 1st Battalion – Belfast Brigade (FE/34), Derry City (FE/36), Waterford Brigade (FE/9), 3rd (Armagh) Brigade (FE/24), Wexford Brigade (FE/30).
79 Fianna Éireann, Ard-Fheis Report 1919 (MA, BMH, Kilmartin Collection, CD144/1/5). This report only lists job titles not names.
80 Eamon Martin to Michael Kilmartin, 10 Mar. 1920 (MA, BMH, Kilmartin Collection, CD 144/1/12).
81 Fianna Éireann report, Aug. 1921 (UCDA, Richard Mulcahy Papers, P7/A/23/133).
82 Belfast District Council Minute Book, 1918–22 (MA, BMH, MacCarthy Collection, CD 29/4/1).

83 Patrick Hearne, witness statement, 18 Aug. 1958 (MA, BMH, WS 1,742).
84 Markievicz to Gore-Booth, 8 Dec. 1920, 20 Dec. 1920, quoted in Markievicz, *Prison Letters*, pp. 258, 261.
85 Markievicz to Gore-Booth, 24 Dec. 1920, quoted in Markievicz, *Prison Letters*, pp. 263–4.
86 Fragment of letter from North Louth Battalion IRA to Adjutant General, 3 July 1920 (MA, Collins Collection, A/0472/27).
87 'Fianna Éireann Ardfheis. Sunday. August 1st, 1920. Agenda.' (MA, BMH, Kilmartin Collection, CD 144/1/15).
88 Fianna GHQ Dublin to Fianna officers, Feb. 1921 (MA, BMH, Kilmartin Collection, CD 144/1/20); Joseph Reynolds, witness statement, 31 Jan. 1949 (MA, BMH, WS 191).
89 Eamon Martin, witness statement, 1 Oct. 1951 (MA, BMH, WS 591).
90 Fianna GHQ Dublin to Fianna officers, Feb. 1921 (MA, BMH, Kilmartin Collection, CD 144/1/20).
91 Joseph Reynolds, witness statement, 31 Jan. 1949 (MA, BMH, WS 191); Garry Holohan, witness statement, 17 Jan. 1950 (MA, BMH, WS 336).
92 Joseph Reynolds, witness statement, 31 Jan. 1949 (MA, BMH, WS 191).
93 Fianna GHQ Dublin to Fianna officers, Feb. 1921 (MA, BMH, Kilmartin Collection, CD 144/1/20).
94 Joseph Reynolds, witness statement, 31 Jan. 1949 (MA, BMH, WS 191). The new battalions and commandants were the following: 1st (North West Dublin) – A. Colley; 2nd (North East Dublin) – Sean Harling; 3rd (South East Dublin) – P. Byrne; 4th (South West Dublin) – Willie Rowe; and 6th (South County Dublin) – Nicholas Kelly. The numerical names and areas covered by the battalions were designed to correspond with their Volunteer equivalents. The 5th Battalion of the Dublin Brigade of the IRA was an Engineer Battalion. As the Fianna did not have an Engineer Battalion, it did not use the 5th as the name of a battalion.
95 Fianna GHQ Dublin to Fianna officers, Feb. 1921 (MA, BMH, Kilmartin Collection, CD 144/1/20).
96 At the time of the Truce the Fianna's Headquarters' Staff consisted of the following: Chief of the Fianna – Constance de Markievicz; Chief of Staff – Garry Holohan; Adjutant-General – Barney Mellows; Assistant Adjutant-General – Joseph Reynolds; Quartermaster-General – Garry Holohan; Assistant Quartermaster-General – Alf White; and Director of Organisation – Eamon Martin (Joseph Reynolds, witness statement, 31 Jan. 1949 (MA, BMH, WS 191)).
97 Fianna Éireann report, Aug. 1921 (UCDA, Mulcahy Papers, P7/A/23/126).
98 Belfast District Council Minute Book, 1918–22 (MA, BMH, MacCarthy Collection, CD 29/4/1).

99 John McCoy, witness statement, 16 Mar. 1951 (MA, BMH, WS 492).
100 Fianna Éireann report, Aug. 1921 (UCDA, Mulcahy Papers, P7/A/23/132–4).
101 Patrick Hearne, witness statement, 18 Aug. 1958 (MA, BMH, WS 1,742).
102 Fianna Éireann report, Aug. 1921 (UCDA, Mulcahy Papers, P7/A/23/134).
103 See Appendix IV for a list of Fianna units and their strengths *c*. 1921–22.
104 Fianna Éireann report, Aug. 1921 (UCDA, Mulcahy Papers, P7/A/23/132–4).
105 Waterford Brigade (MA, MSPC, FE/9).
106 Membership in the Dublin Brigade increased from 755 to 788 boys (MA, MSPC, FE/1). In Limerick city, numbers rose from 719 to 764 (MA, MSPC, FE/17). The battalions in Armagh and Lurgan increased from 282 to 311 (MA, MSPC, FE/24). Numbers rose from 460 to 669 in Co. Kerry (MA, MSPC, FE/10). In Waterford membership increased from 112 to 320 (MA, MSPC, FE/9).
107 Membership in the Clare 1st Battalion went from 206 boys to 150 (MA, MSPC, FE/19). In Ballinrobe, County Mayo, numbers decreased from 65 to 52 (MA, MSPC, FE/21). In County Sligo members dipped from 49 to 37 (MA, MSPC, FE/22). In County Wexford numbers dropped from 192 to 123 (MA, MSPC, FE/30).
108 In Dundalk membership rose from 136 to 216 (MA, MSPC, FE/23/1) while in Drogheda it decreased from 20 to 7 (MA, MSPC, FE/29).
109 Cork No. 1 Brigade (MA, MSPC, FE/5).
110 See Appendix IV.
111 Belfast District Council Minute Book, 1918–22 (MA, BMH, MacCarthy Collection, CD 29/4/1).
112 David Fitzpatrick, *Politics and Irish Life, 1913–1921* (Cork: Cork University Press, 1998), pp. 184–5.
113 See 1st Battalion Mid Clare Brigade (MA, MSPC, FE/19).
114 Fianna Éireann report, Aug. 1921 (UCDA, Mulcahy Papers, P7/A/23/132).
115 Fianna Éireann report, Aug. 1921 (UCDA, Mulcahy Papers, P7/A/23/129–31). In Munster, Fianna units existed in counties Clare, Cork, Kerry, Limerick, Tipperary and Waterford. In Ulster, units were in Antrim, Armagh, Donegal, Monaghan, Tyrone and possibly Down; Fianna Headquarters had no information about whether or not units existed in Cavan, Derry and Fermanagh. In Connacht, units were in Leitrim, Mayo and Roscommon, with no information on Galway and Sligo, though there was a Fianna organiser in the latter county at the time. In Leinster, Fianna units existed in Carlow, Dublin, Kildare, Louth, Meath, Offaly, Westmeath, Wexford and Wicklow, but there was no information regarding Kilkenny.
116 Fianna Éireann report, Aug. 1921 (UCDA, Mulcahy Papers, P7/A/23/132–4).
117 Sean Saunders, witness statement, 4 June 1953 (MA, BMH, WS 854).

118 Report of Fianna Éireann Training Camp held at Loughlinstown, 10–17 Sept. 1921 (MA, Collins Collection, A/0631, Group IX, Fianna Éireann, Item 1); Fianna Éireann. Training Camps for Officers: September 11–17 [&18 to 24] (MA, BMH, Kilmartin Collection, CD 144/1/22). Campers were to bring an extra shirt and pair of socks and boots, overcoat, toothbrush, comb, brush, soap, towel, one blanket, shaving utensils ('if needed'), field service pocket book, pencil, magnetic compass, writing materials, notebook, knife, fork, spoon, plate and mug. Leggings, breeches and a light weight waterproof ground sheet were also recommended, but not essential. Garry Holohan was the officer in charge of the training camp (MA, BMH, WS 336).
119 Adjutant General to O/C Ennistymon, 12 Sept. 1921 (MA, BMH, Kilmartin Collection, CD 144/1/23).
120 Adjutant General to all Fianna officers, 10 Jan. 1922 (MA, BMH, Kilmartin Collection, CD 144/1/24).
121 Fianna Éireann. 11th Annual Ard Fheis, 12 Mar. 1922. Amendment to Constitution (MA, BMH, Kilmartin Collection, CD 144/1/26).
122 Special Order from Barney Mellows, Adjutant General, to all O/Cs in Munster, 28 Feb. 1922 (MA, BMH, Kilmartin Collection, CD 144/1/27).
123 'Report of the Fianna convention', *Fianna*, June 1922, p. 5.
124 Mac Fhloinn, 'The history and tradition of Fianna Éireann', p. 17.
125 Sean Saunders, witness statement, 4 June 1953 (MA, BMH, WS 854).
126 John R. Watts, 'Na Fianna Éireann: A case study of a political youth organisation' (PhD thesis, University of Glasgow, 1981), p. 183.
127 Hugo McNeill, witness statement, 20 Mar. 1956 (MA, BMH, WS 1,377). For details of McNeill's career in the Irish Defence Forces, see Patrick Long, 'McNeill, Hugh Hyacinth ("Hugo")' in *DIB*.
128 'Report of the Fianna convention', *Fianna*, June 1922, p. 5.
129 See Appendix IV. This is a minimum figure because some of the reports for Fianna units do not refer to this specific date and there are some counties for which there is no record of Fianna membership.
130 Watts, 'Na Fianna Éireann', pp. 183, 188.
131 *Ibid.*, p. 185; Dublin and General Headquarters file (MA, MSPC, FE/1).
132 Watts, 'Na Fianna Éireann', pp. 194–6, 206.
133 *Ibid.*, p. 198.
134 'Report of the Fianna convention', *Fianna*, June 1922, p. 5.
135 J. Anthony Gaughan, *Scouting in Ireland* (Dublin: Kingdom Books, 2006), p. 58.
136 See Lawrence William White, 'Plunkett, George Oliver Michael' in *DIB*.
137 Watts, 'Na Fianna Éireann', pp. 199–200.

138 *Fianna Handbook* (2nd edn, Dublin: Central Council of Na Fianna Éireann, 1924), p. 143.
139 'Editorial', *Fianna*, June 1922, p. 3.
140 'Editorial', *Fianna*, June 1926, p. 1.
141 I would like to thank Dr Margaret Scanlon for pointing out the inflation of the figures for Baden-Powell Boy Scout membership.
142 Ben Novick, *Conceiving Revolution: Irish Nationalist Propaganda During the First World War* (Dublin: Four Courts Press, 2001), p. 157.
143 For an overview of the Fianna's history from the Civil War to the 1998 Good Friday Agreement, see Gaughan, *Scouting in Ireland*, pp. 55–74.
144 *Ibid.*, p. 68.
145 Fianna poster viewed on Dame Street, Dublin, 15 Mar. 2011 (photo in possession of Marnie Hay).

5   Who joined the Fianna?¹

> Many joined and fell away, but those who remained formed a close comradeship and became the nucleus of the Irish Army and were destined to see a free Ireland, the hope and aspiration of centuries.²

James Nolan (or Séumas Ó Nualláin, as he was also known) was a twelve-year-old student at Mount Sion Christian Brothers' School in Waterford city when he joined the Fianna in the latter half of 1912. His parents were in business, but after his mother died, he moved in with his uncle Willie Walsh who was a referee of Gaelic games and an IRB centre. James himself joined a Gaelic League class when he was about ten, displayed a talent for step-dancing, and won a prize for a history essay that he submitted to a competition in the republican newspaper *Irish Freedom*. Within his Fianna *sluagh*, he rose to the position of adjutant. He joined the IRB in early 1916 and then two years later transferred from the Fianna to the Irish Volunteers where he served as his company's intelligence officer.³

Meanwhile in Cork, P. J. Murphy also joined the Fianna in 1912. He too was initiated into Irish nationalism at an early age through his education at the Christian Brothers' Schools at Blarney Street and North Monastery and through his relationship with his uncles Harry and Eamonn Lorton. Harry was an IRB member who introduced his nephew to the Fianna, while Eamonn was active in the GAA, the Gaelic League, Sinn Féin and the trade union movement. Murphy left school in the summer of 1916 and became an engineering apprentice at the Haulbowline Naval Dockyard, but later lost his job as a result of his nationalist activism, for which he was imprisoned. In 1918 he transferred from the Fianna to C Company of the 1st Cork Battalion, Cork No. 1 Brigade of the IRA where he served in the engineering section. In later life, he achieved the rank of commandant in the Irish Defence Forces.⁴

Nolan and Murphy were typical of the boys who joined Na Fianna Éireann during the years of the Irish Revolution, as indicated by the preceding précis of their personal backgrounds and nationalist involvement. The initial decision to join the Fianna was often a result of previous exposure to advanced nationalism or republicanism through family connections and a Christian Brothers' education. The majority of Fianna members were Catholic and male. They often participated in cultural nationalist activities, such as those promoted by the Gaelic League. Their involvement in the Fianna frequently led to membership of the IRB and later the Irish Volunteers/IRA or the Irish Citizen Army. A small minority of Fianna members were female, some of whom later joined Cumann na mBan. For some members, the military training, leadership skills and social and political network developed through their membership in the Fianna proved useful in their future careers.

MEMBERSHIP PROFILE BASED ON THREE SAMPLES

This chapter will examine the membership of the Fianna between 1909 and 1923 in order to provide a general profile of who joined the Fianna during the revolutionary era. The research for this chapter is based on three samples of former Fianna members gleaned from Bureau of Military History (BMH) witness statements, entries from the *Dictionary of Irish Biography* (*DIB*) and applications from the Military Service Pensions Collection (MSPC). These three samples combined contain a total of 271 different individuals. Nineteen of these former members are included in more than one sample.[5] There are issues with each of these samples, which will be discussed in turn.

The first sample is from the BMH. The Irish government established the BMH in 1947 in order 'to assemble and co-ordinate material to form the basis for the compilation of the history of the movement for Independence from the formation of the Irish Volunteers on 25 November 1913 to the [signing of the Truce] 11 July 1921'.[6] The July 1921 'cut-off point [was] introduced primarily to appease Fine Gael/pro-Treaty hostility towards the Fianna Fáil initiated project, but the Bureau did not enforce the rule', explains Eve Morrison, an expert on the BMH collection. Thus, it also includes some limited material related to the Civil War.[7] Between 1947 and 1957 the Bureau collected 1,773 witness statements as well as contemporary documents, photographs, voice recordings and press cuttings.[8] Although copies of some witness statements were available among personal papers donated to various archives, the BMH collection was not opened to researchers until 2003 and since then has revolutionised the study of the Irish Revolution.

At least ninety-five former members or leaders of the Fianna provided witness statements to the BMH. These individuals were identified as former Fianna members or leaders on the basis of their listing as such in the BMH's online database, their reference to Fianna involvement in their witness statement, or my recognition of their membership from other primary sources. It is possible that there are other former Fianna members in this collection but they were not identified as such in their statements.[9]

This first sample comes from ninety-five BMH witness statements from former members or leaders of the Fianna. These statements discuss in varying degrees of detail the individual's involvement in the youth group, with some providing information about family background, education and employment. Not all former members mentioned their Fianna membership, however. In their joint statement, Theobald (Theo) Wolfe Tone Fitzgerald and Robert Henry (Harry) Walpole, for example, discussed the hoisting of a flag on the General Post Office (GPO) during the Easter Rising rather than their involvement in the Fianna.[10]

The second sample is from the *DIB*. It was published in nine volumes in 2009 by Cambridge University Press in collaboration with the Royal Irish Academy and is also available as an online searchable database.[11] It consists of forty-seven former Fianna members born between 1887 and 1912 whose achievements merited the inclusion of entries on them in the *DIB*.[12] Some of these individuals, such as Ina Connolly Heron and Brian MacNeill, do not have *DIB* entries of their own, but are included in a family member's entry.[13] As *DIB* entries were written by different authors who had access to differing amounts of source material, they do not always allow for a comprehensive comparison of the backgrounds of former Fianna members. Although some entries do not mention Fianna membership, I was able to confirm the individual's involvement through other sources.[14] This sample should not be seen as comprehensive because there may be other former Fianna members included in the *DIB* whose involvement with the youth group is not mentioned in their entry. Furthermore, new entries are being added to the online *DIB* database on an ongoing basis.[15]

The *DIB* sample includes Joseph and Seamus Robinson, who belonged to Hobson's original Fianna organisation founded in Belfast in 1902, on the basis that Joseph assumed a leadership role in the later incarnation of Na Fianna Éireann and both brothers were active during the struggle for independence. Michael Kevin O'Doherty did not join the Fianna until about 1929, but he is included because his birth year (1912) and family background fit the profile of so many Fianna members during the revolutionary period. He was the son of Seamus and Kitty O'Doherty who were both active in the Gaelic League and the struggle for independence.[16]

The third sample comes from the MSPC. Irish Military Archives began the phased online release of the MSPC in 2016.[17] This collection of pension applications and supporting documents initially arose as a result of the 1923 Army Pensions Act which was designed 'to recognise and compensate wounded members, and the surviving dependents of deceased members, of various groups that had participated in the events of 1916 to 1923 and were deemed and proven to have had "active service" during this time'.[18] The Cumann na nGaedheal government then took the unusual measure of introducing the 1924 Military Service Pensions Act to compensate other veterans of the Irish Revolution and the subsequent Civil War. As Marie Coleman has noted,

> The revolutionary generation consisted largely of young men in their late teens and early twenties who in other circumstances would have been starting careers, settling down in their personal lives, or pursuing studies towards a profession, all of which was interrupted by their involvement in revolutionary activity.

The new military service pensions were ostensibly to compensate these young men for their loss of earning potential so early in their careers. Coleman persuasively argues, however, that these military service pensions were actually a way of placating disgruntled members of the National Army who were being demobilised after the Civil War.[19]

Only male former Fianna members who had later served in the National Army, and thus had fought on the pro-Treaty side in the Civil War, were eligible for pensions under the 1924 legislation. In 1934 under the Fianna Fáil government, the legislation was amended and extended in order to include members of Cumann na mBan as well as individuals who had only served prior to the 1921 Truce or had supported the anti-Treaty side during the Civil War.[20] This gesture of reconciliation made pensions available to a wider group of former Fianna members.

This third sample consists of 155 male Fianna members whose files in the MSPC indicate that they or their family sought compensation from the Irish state for their service in the military conflicts of the Irish

Revolution.²¹ This sample by its very nature is skewed towards those Fianna members who were male and deemed themselves militarily active. The list was generated through an online search of the Military Service Pensions and Awards files using the term 'Fianna Éireann', but this search did not capture all of the Fianna members in the collection because some former members claimed on the basis of their involvement in other organisations, such as the Irish Volunteers/IRA or Cumann na mBan. For instance, Niall MacNeill, a son of Eoin MacNeill, did not appear on the list because he claimed for his service with the IRA and the National Army, rather than the Fianna.²² Furthermore, this search did not generate the names of the Connolly sisters, who had claimed for their service with Cumann na mBan and thus instead appeared on a search of that organisation's members. Ina mentioned in her pension application that she joined the Fianna in 1911, but Nora's application made no reference to her membership in the youth group.²³

The 'Fianna Éireann' search undertaken on 11 July 2018 actually generated 157 names, but the two additional individuals were not former members of the Fianna, so they were not included in the sample. In their pension applications, Ellen Sarah Bushell and Dorothy Hannafin indicated that they had played a support role for Fianna leaders or units but had not been members themselves. Thomas O'Donoghue recalled the attendance of 'Nellie Bushell of the Abbey [Theatre]' (presumably Ellen) at an early organisational meeting of the Fianna. Bushell made kilts for Fianna members and served as a courier for Con Colbert during the Easter Rising. Hannafin, whose brothers belonged to the Fianna, recorded that she was attached to the Fianna unit in Tralee, County Kerry, and engaged in such activities as distributing election and IRA propaganda, dispatch carrying and intelligence work. Bushell's application under the 1949 Military Pensions Act was successful whereas Hannafin's application under the more restrictive 1934 act was unsuccessful because the legislation was deemed not to apply in her case.²⁴

These three samples will be used to build up a general profile of Fianna membership during the revolutionary era. The chapter will explain how members were recruited and discuss who actually joined, highlighting factors such as family background, social class, religion, age and gender. It will highlight the use of the Fianna as a vehicle to recruit young men into the IRB. It will also consider what proportion of Fianna members transferred to the Irish Volunteers/IRA, the ICA, Cumann na mBan or the National Army when they reached adulthood, whether or not former members supported the pro- or anti-Treaty side during the Irish Civil War, and what careers former members pursued after the Irish Revolution.

RECRUITMENT INTO NA FIANNA ÉIREANN

Boys were encouraged to join the Fianna by nationalist schoolmasters, family members, friends and notices in nationalist newspapers. Eamon Martin attended the first public meeting of the Fianna at the urging of his former schoolmaster William O'Neill of St Andrew's National School on what is now Pearse Street in Dublin.[25] Markievicz had contacted O'Neill about her plans to start a nationalist youth group, asking him to recommend suitable boys, which he duly did.[26] After Liam Mellows joined the Fianna in 1911, he also brought his brothers Barney and Fred into the organisation. Garry Holohan was recruited into the Fianna by his friend Joe Connolly who belonged to the first 'Irish-Ireland family' that Holohan had ever met.[27] Irish-Irelanders like the Connollys advocated an Irish cultural nationalism grounded on Catholic and Gaelic values. Seamus Mac Caisin (also known as James Cashen) attended the inaugural meeting of the Fianna after he spotted an announcement about the event in the Gaelic League newspaper *An Claidheamh Soluis*.[28] Other potential recruits may have been intrigued by the flag-wielding Fianna boy who stood outside the organisation's

Figure 5 Na Fianna Éireann at their annual *ard-fheis* at the Mansion House in Dublin *c.* 1913.

main hall at 34 Lower Camden Street in Dublin, ready to answer queries about the organisation and to direct boys inside.[29]

Who exactly were the Fianna seeking to recruit through these various methods? The youth group initially purported to be a national organisation open to all Irish boys between the ages of eight and eighteen, no matter 'what class, creed, or party that they or their fathers belong[ed] to'.[30] There was a difference, however, between who was welcome to join the Fianna and who actually joined the organisation in the period 1909–23. Issues of political and religious affiliation, class, age and gender had varying degrees of impact on the Fianna's membership over time.

FAMILY, EDUCATION, ASSOCIATIONS AND EMPLOYMENT

As Tom Garvin has highlighted, a notable trait within European politics in the period 1890–1922 'was the rise of political movements of an often visionary and romantic character, commonly dominated by relatively well-educated young people from the middle reaches of society'. He describes how the Irish case fits into this pattern:

> The Irish nationalist revolution was dominated by young men from the new Catholic middle class, and many of the most energetic and articulate of them came from the lower fringes of the middle class and from the skilled working class. By the standards of the period they were very well educated.[31]

This description is applicable to Na Fianna Éireann, whose members tended to come from Catholic families of these classes and had received a formal education up to the age of at least fourteen.[32]

Most members of the Fianna were the product of skilled working-class or lower middle-class families. The *DIB* sample indicates that Fianna members were the offspring of labourers, carpenters, tailors, clerks, bookkeepers, merchants and farmers. The fathers of members included labour leader and 1916 insurrectionist James Connolly, journalist W. P. Ryan, university professor Eoin MacNeill and Harold's Cross builder George Walsh, who, like MacNeill, was a member of the Provisional Committee of the Irish Volunteers.[33]

Atypically, the fathers of Alfie White and Patrick O'Daly were members of the Dublin Metropolitan Police, one an inspector and the other a constable.[34] Another unusual case was the Mellows brothers whose father and paternal grandfather were soldiers in the British army. Despite being educated at military schools, Liam Mellows 'disappointed his father's wish that he join the [British] army' and instead became a clerk.[35] Any military impulses fostered by his upbringing were directed towards Irish paramilitary organisations. The Mellows brothers were not the only ones with a family connection to the British army: Liam Langley was the son of a retired army sergeant.[36]

Although some Fianna members, like Liam Mellows, may have rebelled against their father's expectations, most generally conformed to their family's nationalist outlook. Thus, members of the Fianna tended to be products of families with nationalist sentiments of various degrees. Of the forty-seven former Fianna members born between 1887 and 1912 whose achievements merited their inclusion in the *DIB*, thirteen definitely came from families that included Fenians or republicans while four had fathers who supported home rule. Joseph and Seamus Robinson fell into both categories in that their parents were home rulers, but their grandfathers had been exiled Fenians.[37]

There was a clear link between Fianna membership and republicanism. Thomas O'Donoghue observed that in Dublin 'many of the boys in the Fianna were sons of members of the IRB'.[38] Áine Ceannt, wife of 1916 insurrectionist Eamonn, recalled that 'only the most extreme families had enrolled their sons in the Fianna'.[39] Michael F. Ryan concurred. The self-confessed product of 'a rebel household' and grandson of a RIC member, Ryan described the Fianna in Waterford as 'a little advanced in outlook for the Nationalists of that day'. By 'Nationalists', he probably meant home rulers during the period *c.* 1912–18.[40] Occasionally, boys joined the Fianna despite parental opposition. For instance, Austin Hogan's father, a RIC pensioner, disapproved of republicanism.[41]

The Fianna may have attracted members from a wider nationalist spectrum after the establishment of the Irish Volunteers in November 1913 because many sons of Volunteers joined.[42] The Irish Volunteers included home rulers as well as republicans and Sinn Féiners prior to the split in the organisation in September 1914 between those who supported or opposed Irish Parliamentary Party leader John Redmond's call for Volunteers to fight in the First World War. For example, the sons and nephews of two founders of the Irish Volunteers, Eoin MacNeill and The O'Rahilly, became members of the Fianna. Niall and Brian MacNeill and their cousin Hugo McNeill (also known as Aodh MacNeill) founded the Ranelagh company of the Fianna around 1915, having previously formed 'a sort of private Boy Scout organisation of [their] own, called Na Ceithearnai Coille' (The Outlaws).[43] Mac and Aodogán

O'Rahilly and their cousin Emmet Humphreys were photographed in their Fianna uniforms around the same year.[44]

Some members had belonged to other uniformed youth groups prior to joining the Fianna, but switched organisations because they found the Fianna's Irish nationalist orientation more attractive. For instance, in Glasgow Seamus Reader had been a member of the Baden-Powell Boy Scouts, but joined the Fianna in 1911 after his brother told him the Irish youth group was better.[45] Another example is Liam O'Callaghan who originally joined the Boy Scouts in Cork, but switched to the Fianna and then later transferred to the Irish Volunteers.[46] In Ballybunion, County Kerry, troops of the Baden-Powell Boy Scouts and the Fianna competed for members when both rival organisations were established around the same time in 1913.[47]

Sometimes a shift in youth group membership signalled a deepening of nationalist sentiment. Michael F. Ryan, for example, had been a member of the Hibernian Boys' Brigade in Waterford before he joined the Fianna. In Ryan's admittedly hazy memory, the Hibernian Boys' Brigade did not last very long and was later replaced by the Fianna. Due to 'social snobbery' and the more advanced nationalism of the Fianna, few if any Hibernian boys other than himself made the transition between the two youth groups.[48]

Occasionally, Fianna members left to join other youth organisations, such as the Irish National Guards, 'an off-shoot of Fianna Éireann'.[49] Patrick Hearne saw them as 'similar to Fianna but of senior or more advanced status'.[50] Thomas O'Donoghue, Sean Kennedy, Seamus Bevan and Moses Roche were among the Fianna members who moved to the Irish National Guards in 1912.[51] James Connolly's son Roddy was an unusual case in that he joined the Fianna as well as the ICA Boy Scouts, reflecting his father's leading role in the latter organisation.[52]

Unlike other youth groups of the period, such as the various boys' brigades, religion played no official part in the Fianna, probably because its Protestant founders recognised how politically divisive religion was in Ireland and furthermore did not want Catholic parents to fear proselytism. As nationalism tended to be associated with Catholicism, the majority of Fianna members came from Catholic families, but nationalists of other religions also joined the organisation. The *DIB* sample includes Archie Heron, who was Presbyterian, George Gilmore and George and James Plant, whose specific Protestant denominations are not specified, and Robert Briscoe, who was Jewish.[53] The Protestant Plant brothers from Fethard, County Tipperary, were an unusual case because they were drawn to the Fianna and IRA after they had been beaten by members of the RIC while being questioned about two local republicans.[54] The religion of the others in the *DIB* sample is either stated or implied as being Catholic.

A family commitment to advanced nationalism or republicanism was often reinforced by the schools and clubs that Fianna boys attended. Twenty-two members of the *DIB* group attended Christian Brothers' schools, while four others went to St Enda's School set up by Patrick Pearse.[55] These schools were notable for their emphasis on providing an overtly Irish education for students, particularly through the teaching of history, geography and the Irish language.[56] Two other members of the *DIB* sample, Sean MacBride and Aodogán O'Rahilly, attended Mount St Benedict in Gorey, County Wexford, a Benedictine school whose headmaster and student body became increasingly republican in ethos from about 1917.[57] Many Fianna members, such as Eamon Martin and Patrick Ward, were also involved with cultural nationalist organisations such as the Gaelic League and hurling clubs.[58]

Some members of the Fianna had already left school and were serving apprenticeships or otherwise earning a living. This is not surprising given that in 1911 almost nineteen percent of the total workforce in the United Kingdom consisted of those aged between ten and twenty.[59] Over the course of his Fianna membership Patsy O'Connor made the transition from a twelve-year-old schoolboy to an eighteen-year-old electrician.[60] Seamus Kavanagh, who was in his early teens, had just left school and started working as an 'apprentice cash-boy' in a drapery shop on Camden Street when Markievicz encouraged him to join the Fianna. Thomas Pelican was a sixteen-year-old apprentice tailor when he joined the youth group in Listowel, County Kerry, in 1917.[61] The Connolly sisters worked at a wareroom as sewing machine operators while they were members of the Belfast Fianna.[62]

Fianna officers were generally in employment, especially as some remained in the youth group into their twenties. Examples include carpenter Patrick O'Daly, bookkeeper Liam Langley, and Con Colbert and Sean Heuston, who worked as clerks at Kennedy's Bakery and the Great Southern and Western Railway Company, respectively. In 1911, O'Daly, Langley and Colbert were twenty-three years of age while Heuston was twenty. [63]

Sometimes work commitments resulted in a member having to resign from the Fianna. James Rowan, who belonged to the Fianna *sluagh* in Ringsend in Dublin in 1913–14, left the youth group after he took up employment as a telegraph messenger in the postal service because his evening shifts conflicted with Fianna meetings. Working at the GPO when the 1916 Easter Rising broke out and residing on Bath Avenue, near Beggar's Bush Barracks, fifteen-year-old Rowan was a witness to the insurrection rather than a participant. This was in contrast to his former Fianna O/C Jackie O'Shea, who served in the Boland's Mill garrison. Rowan saw O'Shea being taken prisoner at the end of the rebellion.[64]

Some employers objected to their young employees' membership in the Fianna while others were supportive. In Dundalk, County Louth, Patrick McHugh's manager forced him to choose between his job as a monitor in a national school and Fianna membership; he chose the latter and instead became an apprentice fitter in the Great Northern Railway.[65] Liam Langley referred to a case in Tuam, County Galway, where a Fianna uniform was 'burnt to ashes by the employer of the Fianna boy concerned'.[66] In contrast, William Lynskey, who had worked as a clerk in the office of *The Cross*, a magazine published by the Passionist Fathers, found that the editor Fr Columban Tyne's awareness of his Fianna membership led to 'long conversations about the events of the time'.[67] The political sympathies of an employer probably governed their tolerance of Fianna membership.

AGE

The age range of Fianna members did not remain static throughout the period of 1909–23, nor was it as precise as the organisation's rules stipulated. The Fianna were initially aimed at boys aged between eight and eighteen. Apparently the parents of the younger boys were willing to allow their children to enrol because they found the presence of a woman in the leadership reassuring.[68] The formation of the breakaway National Guards in 1912, which stemmed from differences of opinion about Fianna policy, may have also reflected a desire on the part of older adolescents to distance themselves from the younger boys. By June 1922, only boys aged between twelve and eighteen were eligible for membership in the Fianna.[69] The restriction of membership to male adolescents in the later years of the Irish Revolution probably reflected the expectation after the experience of the 1916 Rising that Fianna members could or would become combatants.

Furthermore, some of the officers remained in the organisation into their twenties, even though the official age limit for Fianna membership was eighteen. For instance, the Fianna members who attacked the Magazine Fort in Dublin's Phoenix Park at the beginning of the Easter Rising were in their late teens and early twenties.[70] There was also some overlap between older members of the Fianna and the Volunteers. An example is Patrick O'Daly, who was already a member of the Volunteers when he moved to Tuam, County Galway, in his mid-twenties. There he found that the local Fianna *sluagh* was more actively engaged in military training than the Volunteers, so he joined the youth group and remained a member when he returned to Dublin.[71]

GENDER

Although the Fianna were officially for boys, some girls did get involved in the organisation in certain parts of the country for limited periods of time during the revolutionary era. Prior to 1916, there was a girls' *sluagh* in Belfast, in which James Connolly's daughters Nora and Ina played leading roles. The question of whether to admit girls to the organisation nationally was a source of controversy because many boys felt that there should be a separate organisation for girls. As noted in chapter 3, a 1912 *ard-fheis* decision to establish girls' troops was quickly reversed after the *ard-choisde* held a plebiscite in which the majority of *sluaighte* voted in favour of changing the constitution back to its original boys-only status.[72] Girls remained involved even if they had no official representation at the national level, though they did attend the annual *ard-fheis*.

Throughout Ireland girls showed interest in joining the Fianna. Molly Reynolds, for example, grew up in a home where 'there was always a good Irish atmosphere'. She became envious of her three brothers' involvement in the Dublin Fianna after she watched them practising their skills in first aid and fencing at home. One of these brothers, Percy, was a future chairman of Coras Iompair Éireann (CIÉ), the Irish state-owned transport company established in 1944. The 1901 Irish Census lists her father, John Richard Reynolds, as an accountant's clerk from County Tipperary who reported knowledge of both the English and Irish languages. He and his wife Mary only had three of their five children at home on census night: Augustus Percival (aged five), Mary Catherine (aged four) and Annie Georgeina (aged two). Over a decade later, Mr Reynolds, a bookkeeper, shared an office on D'Olier Street with Fianna co-founder Bulmer Hobson in 1913–14 and became auditor of the Irish Volunteers. Molly approached Hobson about forming 'a girls section in the Fianna'. He said the Fianna would help her if she started one herself, but she felt unequal to the task. Aged about seventeen, she joined Cumann na mBan, the women's auxiliary of the Irish Volunteers, when it was formed in 1914.[73]

Even after the 1916 rebellion, some girls still chose to join the Fianna, but their presence remained controversial. As discussed in chapter 4, between late 1916 and early 1918 girls under the age of eighteen belonged to the Fianna in Waterford city where Cumann na mBan and the Fianna shared premises.[74] In early 1918, however, Fianna Headquarters in Dublin informed the Waterford girls that they should join the Clann na Gael Girl Scouts instead.[75]

It was not until 1930 that Cumann na mBan established an alternative republican scouting organisation for girls. Cumann na gCailíní, or the Irish National Girl Scouts, sought to instil a republican ethos in girls between the ages of eight and sixteen, with the long-term goal of attracting new recruits to the ranks of the adult organisation.[76] The Fianna were still referring to Cumann na gCailíní as their female counterpart in 1964.[77]

It would be many years before girls could join the Fianna on an equal footing with the boys. The Fianna finally began to accept girls as members in 1968–69 in the context of the outbreak of the Troubles in Northern Ireland. An initiative was undertaken without the permission of the Fianna leadership to establish a girls' troop in Dundalk in 1968. Although there had been some discussion of admitting girls prior to this, the formation of the Dundalk branch was a *fait accompli*, in much the same way the foundation of the Belfast girls' *sluagh* had been in 1911. Girls became official members of the Fianna from 1969.[78] A statement from the leadership of the republican movement published in the 1988 *Fianna Éireann Handbook* hailed the opening of the organisation to young women and girls as one of the most welcome and progressive moves within the Fianna, remarking that 'there could not be a more appropriate memorial to your founder, Constance Markievicz'.[79]

RECRUITMENT INTO THE IRB

Although the Fianna ostensibly welcomed Irish boys from all political persuasions, Bulmer Hobson clearly intended the organisation to foster future republicans. It was his 'personal aim to recruit suitable members of the new Fianna into the IRB' from the youth group's inception in 1909.[80] He even started a special Fianna circle of the IRB in 1912 after his election as the Dublin centre of that secret society. Con Colbert and Pádraic Ó Riain, who were already members of the IRB, became the centre and secretary, respectively, of this new circle, which was known as the John Mitchel Literary and Debating Society. According to

Ó Riain's sister Cathleen, the 'society' met regularly at her family's home at 48 Clonliffe Road in Drumcondra. Other members included Eamon Martin, Paddy Ward, Michael Lonergan, Liam and Barney Mellows, Garry and Paddy Holohan, Archie Heron, Sean Heuston, Desmond Ryan, Frank Burke and Eamonn Bulfin, the latter three students at Pearse's St Enda's School.[81]

The link between the Fianna and the IRB was probably strongest in Dublin, but Fianna members elsewhere also joined the brotherhood. For instance, thirteen out of twenty-three former Fianna members in the BMH sample who said they joined the IRB were from Dublin; the others lived in Belfast, Limerick, Tuam, Westport, Waterford and Glasgow.[82] IRB member Joseph Melinn, who formed a Fianna *sluagh* in Tralee in 1912, may have done so as part of his wider endeavours to expand the brotherhood in County Kerry.[83]

Some Fianna members chose not to join the IRB or displayed an antipathy towards the secret society. 'I was asked by Eamon Martin, Con Colbert and Martin Murphy on different occasions to join, but declined to do so on conscientious grounds', reported Seamus Pounch.[84] In Dundalk, Patrick McHugh's determination not to have anything to do with the IRB was influenced by his father's tales of the Land League and his uncle's membership in Clan na Gael in America: 'Truly, secret societies only breed traitors and informers.'[85] In his witness statement, Thomas O'Donoghue expressed a negative attitude towards the brotherhood, claiming that due to 'IRB influence' parents took their sons out of the Fianna *sluagh* led by him and that he left the Volunteer company based at Larkfield because it was 'dominated by the IRB'.[86]

The IRB also appear to have had a hand in the Irish National Guards. O'Donoghue recorded that the IRB supported the formation of the National Guards and that many members of this Fianna off-shoot belonged to the brotherhood. 'I was not a member of the IRB, though I knew all about it', he asserted.[87]

TRANSFER TO ADULT PARAMILITARY ORGANISATIONS

By the latter part of 1913, the Fianna had become a fertile training and recruiting ground for future members of adult paramilitary organisations, a situation that continued throughout the years of the Irish Revolution. Once the Irish Volunteers were established in November 1913, Fianna members who had reached the age of eighteen and for whom there was no officer position available, such as Patrick Ward, were asked to transfer to the adult paramilitary organisation.[88] In

Belfast, Fianna girls could transfer to the branch of Cumann na mBan established in the northern city in 1914.[89]

Alternatively, Fianna members loyal to the labour movement gravitated to the ICA, which had been formed earlier in November 1913 to protect striking workers during the Dublin Lockout of that year. Andy Dunne, Thomas O'Donoghue and Joe Connolly are examples of Fianna members who joined the ICA and later served with Markievicz as part of the St Stephen's Green garrison during the Easter Rising.[90] Another former Fianna member, Frederick Ryan, was also serving with the ICA when he was killed in action on 27 April 1916 during the rebellion.[91]

Fianna members often maintained an association with the youth group even after they joined the Irish Volunteers. John A. Caffrey, James Carrigan and Sean McLoughlin, who had been Fianna members in Dublin, indicated in their witness statements that they did not sever their link with the Fianna after they transferred to the Volunteers. When Liam McCabe joined his local Volunteer company *c.* 1917, he remained captain of the Fianna *sluagh* in Ballybunion, County Kerry.[92] Such individuals provided an important, even if informal, connection between the youth and adult organisations.

It was not until early 1921 that the Fianna and the Irish Volunteers/IRA finally forged a formal link to facilitate better cooperation. Recognition of the potentially dangerous consequences of overlapping arms raids by the two organisations in the autumn of 1920 had led to negotiations between Dáil Éireann's Ministry of Defence and Fianna Headquarters. These negotiations resulted in the formal link and an agreement of how the two organisations would work together, an arrangement that remained in place during the rest of the War of Independence until the Truce on 11 July 1921.[93] In keeping with previous practice, interested Fianna members continued to transfer to the Volunteers once they had reached the age of eighteen, unless their services were essential for the successful management of their company.[94] In the wake of the agreement between the two organisations, a new report form was developed to facilitate keeping track of how many Fianna members transferred to the IRA. The form was so new in August 1921 that the only figure available was 150 transfers covering Dublin, Belfast and Dundalk.[95]

BMH witness statements suggest that the general trend was indeed for Fianna members to transfer to the Volunteers/IRA, the ICA or Cumann na mBan when they reached the appropriate age. For instance, two former Fianna members from County Cork, Kevin Murphy of Cobh and John C. Murphy of Mallow, both refer to Fianna members transferring to the Volunteers in their witness statements.[96] Of the BMH sample of former Fianna members, sixty-eight joined the Irish Volunteers or IRA, with Thomas O'Donoghue joining both the Irish Volunteers and the ICA.[97] Among the forty-seven ex-Fianna members in the *DIB* sample, thirty-seven are listed in their entries as joining the Irish Volunteers or the IRA, while the two Connolly sisters joined Cumann na mBan.[98]

Other nationalist youth groups also followed this trend. Members of the Clann na Gael Girl Scouts, such as May Kelly, May Murray, Nellie Lambert and Margaret Fagan, later joined Cumann na mBan.[99] Similarly, members of the Irish National Guards joined either the Irish Volunteers or the ICA.[100]

Sometimes there was a break between an individual's membership in the Fianna and later involvement in the Volunteers. For instance, James Fulham began attending Fianna meetings in the Camden Street hall in Dublin *c*. late 1912/early 1913 where he received training in signalling and Morse code. Too young to appreciate this form of training, he left the Fianna, but later joined the Irish Volunteers in 1917 and served with the 4th Battalion of the Dublin Brigade until 1921. He eventually became a commandant in the Irish Defence Forces.[101]

Not every Fianna member who wanted to transfer to the Volunteers was permitted to do so. An example is Patrick Hearne who rose to become commandant in the Waterford City Battalion of the Fianna. He applied three times for transfer to the IRA in the period 1917–21, but was refused even though he was between the ages of nineteen and twenty-three during those years.[102] It would appear that his work with the Fianna was deemed more valuable than any contribution he might make to the IRA.

Further evidence for the common transfer of members from the Fianna to adult paramilitary organisations is provided by the military service pension sample, which is made up of 155 males. It indicates that ninety-six former Fianna members also joined the Irish Volunteers/ IRA, comprising 61.9% of the sample.[103] Out of these ninety-six men, twenty-eight also went on to join the National Army to fight on the pro-Treaty side during the Irish Civil War. Most of those who are not listed as joining the Volunteers/IRA received a pension solely on the basis of their Fianna involvement.[104] Others joined only the Fianna and the National Army.[105] Overall, 71.6% of this sample (111 males) graduated from the Fianna to adult organisations including the Irish Volunteers/ IRA, ICA, National Army and the police force, An Garda Síochána. This high percentage is not surprising given that the sample is derived from military service pension applications.

ATTITUDE TOWARDS THE ANGLO-IRISH TREATY

The 1921 Anglo-Irish Treaty established an Irish Free State with dominion status within the British Commonwealth rather than a completely independent republic. This distinction contributed to a slide into Civil War between former nationalist comrades, including those of the Fianna. Given that Na Fianna Éireann as an organisation took the anti-Treaty side in the Civil War, it is not surprising that 53.5% of the military service pension sample (eighty-three males) supported the anti-Treaty side during the conflict. Some serving and former members of the Fianna, however, instead chose to fight on the pro-Treaty side. Thus, 25.2% of the pension sample (thirty-nine males) joined the National Army and/or An Garda Síochána in support of the pro-Treaty side during the Civil War. Two individuals appear to have had mixed feelings about the situation. William Roe initially joined the National Army, but then switched to the anti-Treaty IRA. Stephen Donnelly joined the National Army in April 1922 and served during the Civil War, but there were allegations that he secretly aided the anti-Treaty side during this time. Both men later joined An Garda Síochána.[106] The remaining 21.3% (thirty-three males) either died before the Civil War or did not claim for Civil War service.[107]

Within the *DIB* sample, of the thirty-seven ex-Fianna members who joined the Volunteers/IRA or Cumann na mBan, twenty-nine are identified as anti-Treaty and six as pro-Treaty. The pro-Treaty individuals in this sample either went on to notable careers in the Irish Defence Forces or were active in the Labour Party. Those who were anti-Treaty covered a wider spectrum of political party affiliations and future careers, though this group also included labour activists and members of the Irish Defence Forces.[108]

FUTURE CAREERS

In its early years, Na Fianna Éireann fostered a revolutionary vanguard of youth, some of whom were able to capitalise in their future careers on the connections made through their involvement in the struggle for independence. For instance, Eamon Martin was one of several Irish revolutionaries employed by former government minister Joseph McGrath at the Hospitals Trust Limited, which operated the Irish Hospitals Sweepstake to raise money to fund public hospitals in Ireland. Martin became controller of sales.[109]

Many former Fianna members who joined during the years of the Irish Revolution went on to notable careers after independence. Of the *DIB* sample, thirteen became deputies in Dáil Éireann, two for Sinn Féin, six for Fianna Fáil, three for the Labour Party and one for Clann na Poblachta.[110] Sean MacBride of Clann na Poblachta and Fianna Fáilers Thomas Derrig and John Ormonde even held cabinet portfolios.[111] Four of the group became senators.[112] Seven were active in local government as councillors with two, Robert Briscoe and John McCann, both serving as Lord Mayor of Dublin.[113] Eleven were left-wing political activists either in the trade union movement or espousing socialism or communism, including – not surprisingly – Roddy Connolly and his sister Nora.[114] Others continued their activism in the republican movement in the years after the Civil War. For instance, George Plant remained a member of the IRA and was executed by the state in 1942 for the murder of a fellow IRA associate.[115] Given the ideology propagated by the Fianna, it is not surprising that the politically active former Fianna members in the *DIB* sample overwhelmingly supported parties that were republican or left wing in nature.

Other former Fianna members pursued notable careers beyond politics. Four joined the National Army or the Irish Defence Forces. For instance, Michael Brennan served as Army Chief of Staff between 1931 and 1940 and Hugo McNeill retired as a major general.[116] Five ex-Fianna members in the sample became journalists, another five became businessmen, and two others were teachers before they entered politics.[117] Some supported Irish culture and sport through their endeavours. Dan Dowd and Martin Walton promoted Irish traditional music, not only as musicians but also as an uilleann pipe-maker (Dowd) and the owner of several music businesses (Walton).[118] John Joe 'Purty' Landers and John Joe Sheehy distinguished themselves as Gaelic footballers.[119] One former member, Maurice MacGonigal, went on to become a celebrated artist and is buried in Roundstone, Connemara, next to Hobson, who was responsible for encouraging him to join the youth group.[120]

The type of training and experience gained through involvement in the Fianna may have contributed to the decision of some former members to work in the Irish security forces in the years after the Civil War. Twelve individuals in the pension sample remained in the Irish Defence Forces after 1924 or later rejoined it, six of these during the Emergency, as the period of the Second World War was known in Éire.[121] Five other individuals in the pension sample served in An Garda Síochána.[122]

Of course, not everyone who joined the Fianna and participated in the events of the Irish Revolution found this experience beneficial for their future careers and by extension their financial stability. Military pensions granted on the basis of disability or service provided helpful financial assistance for some. Pension applications demonstrate how important this potential income could be at a time before there was a proper social welfare safety net in Ireland. For example, in a letter dated 3 December 1925, a secretary in the Department of Defence asked the Army Finance Officer to hasten the application of Walter Leo Holland for a service pension because his family had been experiencing financial difficulties over the past two years and was facing eviction. One of four Holland brothers from Inchicore who were active in the struggle for independence, Walter had served with the Fianna, the Irish Volunteers and the National Army and was granted a pension of £70 per year.[123] Even notable figures could find themselves fallen on hard times. Diarmaid Ferriter and Marie Coleman have both highlighted the case of Nora Connolly O'Brien. 'After her husband, who worked as an agent for a British firm, lost his job through the adverse effects of the Economic War with Britain and the Second World War on British trade in Ireland', the O'Briens were in dire financial straits.[124] In July 1941 Nora wrote:

> I am at my wits end. We are absolutely on the rocks. This week will see the end of us unless I have something definite to count upon. Seamus [her husband] has had no luck in finding any kind of job. I was hoping that the pension business could be hurried up and what I could get might tide us over this bad spell.[125]

For those former Fianna members who qualified, military pensions not only recognised service during the struggle for independence but also helped to ease the financial pressure that some faced later in life.

NOTES

1 This chapter builds upon and revises material contained in two previously published articles: Marnie Hay, 'Moulding the future: Na Fianna Éireann and its members, 1909–1923', *Studies*, 100:44 (2011), pp. 441–54; Marnie Hay, 'An Irish nationalist adolescence: Na Fianna Éireann, 1909–1923' in Catherine Cox and Susannah Riordan (eds), *Adolescence in Modern Irish History* (Basingstoke: Palgrave Macmillan, 2015),

pp. 103–28. The present chapter discusses a larger sample of former Fianna members who merited entries in the *DIB* for two reasons; not only have more relevant entries been added since I published those articles, but I have become aware of more former members whose involvement in the Fianna is not mentioned in their entries.

2 Seamus Pounch, witness statement, 15 June 1949 (MA, BMH, WS 267).
3 James Nolan, witness statement, 10 Mar. 1956 (MA, BMH, WS 1,369).
4 P. J. Murphy, witness statement, 14 Apr. 1953 (MA, BMH, WS 869).
5 The following former members are included in more than one sample group: Dick Balfe, Michael Brennan, Ina Connolly Heron, Nora Connolly O'Brien, Roddy Connolly, Stephen Donnelly, Theo Fitzgerald, Archie Heron, Garry Holohan, Paddy Holohan, Sean McLoughlin, Hugo McNeill, Eamon Martin, Patrick O'Daly, Seamus Reader, Joseph Reynolds, Seamus Robinson, P. J. Stephenson and Harry Walpole.
6 Quoted in Jennifer Doyle et al., *An Introduction to the Bureau of Military History* (Dublin: Military Archives, 2002), p. 1.
7 Eve Morrison, 'The Fr Louis O'Kane interviews in context' in Dónal McAnallen (ed.), *Reflections on the Revolution in Ulster* (Armagh: Cardinal Tomás Ó Fiaich Library and Archive, 2016), p. 34.
8 Doyle et al., *An Introduction to the Bureau of Military History*, p. 1.
9 See list in Appendix II. BMH witness statements are available online at www.militaryarchives.ie/collections/online-collections/bureau-of-military-history-1913-1921.
10 Joint witness statement by Theobald Wolfe Tone Fitzgerald and Robert Henry Walpole, 10–11 Apr. 1949 (MA, BMH, WS 218).
11 James McGuire and James Quinn (eds), *Dictionary of Irish Biography* (Cambridge: Cambridge University Press, 2009); see also http://dib.cambridge.org.
12 The *DIB* sample was generated by a database search at http://dib.cambridge.org on 7–8 Feb. 2011 and 31 May 2017. See Appendix I for a list of individuals included in this sample.
13 Ina Connolly Heron is mentioned in the *DIB* entries for her sister Nora Connolly O'Brien and husband Archie Heron while Brian MacNeill is noted in the entry for his father Eoin MacNeill. Garry Holohan, James Plant and John Walsh are further examples of former Fianna members included in their brothers' entries. In Walsh's case, he was mentioned in an entry for his younger brother, Waterford newspaper editor Joseph James Walsh (1905–92).
14 For instance, Roddy Connolly's *DIB* entry does not mention his Fianna membership, but other sources confirm it. See Charlie McGuire, *Roddy Connolly and the Struggle for Socialism in Ireland* (Cork: Cork University Press, 2008), pp. 10–11, 14, 19.

15 For example, entries on Eamon Martin, Sean McLoughlin, Joseph Robinson and Patrick Joseph Stephenson were added to the *DIB*'s online database after I completed my research for Hay, 'An Irish nationalist adolescence: Na Fianna Éireann, 1909–1923'.
16 Terry Clavin, 'O'Doherty, (Michael) Kevin' in *DIB*. See also Michael Kevin O'Doherty, *My Parents and Other Rebels* (Dublin: Errigal Press, 1999).
17 The MSPC is available online at www.militaryarchives.ie/collections/online-collections/military-service-pensions-collection-1916-1923.
18 Diarmaid Ferriter, '"Always in danger of finding myself with nothing at all": The military service pensions and the battle for material survival, 1925–55' in Diarmaid Ferriter and Susannah Riordan (eds), *Years of Turbulence: The Irish Revolution and Its Aftermath* (Dublin: UCD Press, 2015), p. 194.
19 Marie Coleman, 'Military service pensions for veterans of the Irish Revolution, 1916–1923', *War in History*, 20:2 (2013), pp. 205–6. In this article Coleman provides a detailed explanation of how the pension scheme operated.
20 Coleman, 'Military service pensions for veterans of the Irish Revolution', pp. 215–16; Ferriter, 'The military service pensions and the battle for material survival', p. 195. For a detailed discussion of the gender dimension of the pension scheme, see Marie Coleman, 'Compensating Irish female revolutionaries, 1916–1923', *Women's History Review*, 26:6 (2017), pp. 915–34.
21 This sample was generated online at www.militaryarchives.ie/collections/online-collections/military-service-pensions-collection-1916-1923 on 11 July 2018. See Appendix III for a list of pension applicants included in this sample.
22 For details of Niall MacNeill's successful application, see his pension file (MA, MSPC, 24SP10285). Other random examples of former Fianna members who were not captured by this search are Thomas Crimmins (MA, MSPC, MSP34REF16809) and Frederick Maurice Shelley (MA, MSPC, 24SP13284).
23 For details of their successful pension applications under the 1934 Military Service Pension Act, see Nora Connolly-O'Brien, pension file (MA, MSPC, MSP34REF59637) and Ina Connolly-Heron, pension file (MA, MSPC, MSP34REF21565). As James Connolly's daughters, they also received dependant's allowances under the 1923 Army Pensions Acts.
24 Ellen Sarah Bushell, pension file (MA, MSPC, MSP34REF22326); Dorothy Hannafin, pension file (MA, MSPC, MSP34REF16986); Thomas O'Donoghue, witness statement, n.d. (MA, BMH, WS 1,666); Seamus Kavanagh, witness statement, 9 Sept. 1957 (MA, BMH, WS 1,670).

25 Eamon Martin, witness statement, 1 Oct. 1951 (MA, BMH, WS 591).
26 Anne Marreco, *The Rebel Countess* (London: Weidenfeld and Nicolson, 1967), p. 114; Sean McGarry, witness statement, 13 Apr. 1950 (MA, BMH, WS 368).
27 Garry Holohan, witness statement, 7 Dec. 1949 (MA, BMH, WS 328).
28 Seamus Mac Caisin, witness statement, 8 June 1947 (MA, BMH, WS 8).
29 Seamus Pounch, witness statement, 15 June 1949 (MA, BMH, WS 267).
30 Pádraic Ó Riain (ed.), *Fianna Handbook* (Dublin: Central Council of Na Fianna Éireann, 1914), p. 23.
31 Tom Garvin, 'Great hatred, little room: Social background and political sentiment among revolutionary activists in Ireland, 1890–1922' in D. George Boyce (ed.), *The Revolution in Ireland, 1879–1923* (Basingstoke: Macmillan Education, 1988), pp. 91–2.
32 Unsurprisingly, the Fianna's profile was similar to that of the IRA. See Peter Hart, 'The social structure of the Irish Republican Army, 1916–1923', *Historical Journal*, 42:1 (Mar. 1999), pp. 207–31.
33 Eamon Martin, witness statement, 1 Oct. 1951 (MA, BMH, WS 591).
34 Robert Holland, *A Short History of Fianna Éireann*, 14 Aug. 1949, p. 10 (NLI, MS 35,455/3/12A); Lawrence William White, 'O'Daly (Daly), Patrick' in *DIB*.
35 Marie Coleman and William Murphy, 'Mellows, William Joseph ('Liam')' in *DIB*.
36 According to his family's 1901 census return, William 'Liam' Langley, who was born in Sydney, Australia, was the son of Michael Langley, an 'army sergeant pensioner', and his wife Margaret, an upholsteress; available at www.census.nationalarchives.ie/pages/1901/Galway/Tuam_Town_in_31_files/Church_View/1401559/ (accessed 9 July 2018).
37 Michael Brennan, Con Colbert, the three Connolly siblings, Joe Groome, Sean MacBride, Sean McLoughlin, Peter O'Connor, Michael Kevin O'Doherty, the Robinson brothers and Martin Walton are listed as coming from families with Fenian/republican sympathies. The fathers of Robert Briscoe, the Robinson brothers and John Walsh were supporters of home rule. The political persuasion of the subject's family is not always included in *DIB* entries. See Eamon Murphy, 'Robinson, Joseph' in *DIB*.
38 Thomas O'Donoghue, witness statement, n.d. (MA, BMH, WS 1,666).
39 Áine Ceannt, witness statement, 27 May 1949 (MA, BMH, WS 264).
40 Michael F. Ryan, witness statement, 9 Dec. 1957 (MA, BMH, WS 1,709).
41 See Lawrence William White, 'Briscoe, Robert Emmet', Diarmaid Ferriter, 'Heron, Archibald ('Archie')' and Lawrence William White, 'Plant, George' in *DIB*.
42 Holland, *A Short History*, p. 19 (NLI, MS 35,455/3/12A).

43 Niall MacNeill, witness statement, 6 Jan. 1948 (MA, BMH, WS 69).
44 A photograph of the three young boys in uniform is included in Aodogán O'Rahilly, *Winding the Clock: O'Rahilly and the 1916 Rising* (Dublin: Lilliput Press, 1991), p. 110.
45 Seamus Reader, witness statement, 28 Dec. 1951 (MA, BMH, WS 627).
46 Liam O'Callaghan, witness statement, 4 Oct. 1947 (MA, BMH, WS 47).
47 William (Liam) McCabe, witness statement (MA, BMH, WS 1,212).
48 Michael F. Ryan, witness statement, 9 Dec. 1957 (MA, BMH, WS 1,709).
49 John Kenny, witness statement, 6 Nov. 1957 (MA, BMH, WS 1,693).
50 Patrick Hearne, witness statement, 18 Aug. 1958 (MA, BMH, WS 1,742).
51 Thomas O'Donoghue, witness statement, n.d. (MA, BMH, WS 1,666); Sean Kennedy, 1 May 1953 (MA, BMH, WS 842); Seamus Bevan, witness statement, 7 Jan. 1955 (MA, BMH, WS 1,058); Moses Roche, 17 Mar. 1955 (MA, BMH, WS 1,129).
52 McGuire, *Roddy Connolly*, p. 11.
53 See Diarmaid Ferriter, 'Gilmore, George Frederick', 'Heron, Archibald ('Archie')' and White, 'Briscoe, Robert Emmet', 'Plant, George' in *DIB*.
54 White, 'Plant, George' in *DIB*; Joost Augusteijn, 'Accounting for the emergence of violent activism among Irish revolutionaries, 1916–21', *Irish Historical Studies*, 35:139 (May 2007), p. 330.
55 The following former Fianna members attended Christian Brothers' schools: Sean Brady, Con Colbert, Roddy Connolly, Thomas Derrig, Joe Groome, Stephen Hayes, Sean Heuston, Austin Hogan, John Joe 'Purty' Landers, John McCann, Maurice MacGonigal, Sean McLoughlin, Eamon Martin, Tommy O'Brien, Peter O'Connor, John Ormonde, Percy Reynolds, Joseph and Seamus Robinson, Desmond Ryan, John Joe Sheehy and P. J. Stephenson. The ex-St Enda's pupils were Hugo McNeill, Thomas Mullins, Michael Kevin O'Doherty and Desmond Ryan.
56 For a discussion of the education provided by these schools, see Barry M. Coldrey, *Faith and Fatherland: The Christian Brothers and the Development of Irish Nationalism, 1838–1921* (Dublin: Gill and Macmillan, 1988); Elaine Sisson, *Pearse's Patriots: St Enda's and the Cult of Boyhood* (Cork: Cork University Press, 2004); Brendan Walsh, *The Pedagogy of Protest: The Educational Thought and Work of Patrick H. Pearse* (Bern: Peter Lang, 2007).
57 Caoimhe Nic Dháibheid, 'Schooling the national orphans: The education of the children of the Easter Rising leaders', *Journal of the History of Childhood and Youth*, 9:2 (2016), pp. 269–70.
58 Eamon Martin, witness statement, 1 Oct. 1951 (MA, BMH, WS 591).
59 John Springhall, *Coming of Age: Adolescence in Britain, 1860–1960* (Dublin: Gill and Macmillan, 1986), p. 65.

60 Willie Nelson [Pádraic Ó Riain], 'Fianna Éireann', *IV*, 26 June 1915, p. 8; Interment record for Patrick O'Connor, died 15 June 1915, Glasnevin Cemetery, available at www.glasnevintrust.ie/genealogy/ (accessed 22 Mar. 1914).
61 Seamus Kavanagh, witness statement, 9 Sept. 1957 (MA, BMH, WS 1,670); Thomas Pelican, witness statement, 7 Mar. 1955 (MA, BMH, WS 1,109).
62 Ina Connolly Heron, witness statement, 25 Jan. 1954 (MA, BMH, WS 919). Ina's first job in Belfast was at a laundry.
63 Robert Holland, witness statement, 18 July 1949 (MA, BMH, WS 280); Patrick O'Daly, witness statement, 6 Apr. 1949 (MA, BMH, WS 220); David Murphy, 'Heuston, Sean (John J.)' in *DIB*; 1911 census return for William Thomas Langley, Tuam, Co. Galway, available at www.census.nationalarchives.ie/pages/1911/Galway/Tuam_Urban__part_of_/Tierboy_Road/548537/ (accessed 9 July 2018).
64 James Rowan, witness statement, 25 June 1953 (MA, BMH, WS 871).
65 Patrick McHugh, witness statement, 15 May 1952 (MA, BMH, WS 677).
66 Liam Langley, witness statement, 19 Mar. 1953 (MA, BMH, WS 816).
67 William Lynskey, witness statement, 12 Nov. 1951 (MA, BMH, WS 1,749).
68 Helena Molony, witness statement, 19 May 1950 (MA, BMH, WS 391).
69 'HQ Notes and Orders', *Fianna*, June 1922, p. 2.
70 Patrick O'Daly, witness statement, 6 Apr. 1949 (MA, BMH, WS 220).
71 *Ibid*.
72 For more detail on the gender controversy, see Marnie Hay, 'The foundation and development of Na Fianna Éireann, 1909–16', *Irish Historical Studies*, 36:141 (May 2008), pp. 60–1.
73 Molly Reynolds, witness statement, 3 Feb. 1949 (MA, BMH, WS 195); 1901 census return for the Reynolds family, 13 York Street, Dublin, available at www.census.nationalarchives.ie/pages/1901/Dublin/Mansion_House/York_Street/1343997/ (accessed 9 July 2018); Shaun Boylan, 'Reynolds, Augustus Percival Harald ("Percy")' in *DIB*.
74 Rosamond Jacob, diary entries, 6 July 1916, 10 Oct. 1916 (NLI, Rosamond Jacob Papers, MS 32,582 (30)).
75 Leeann Lane, *Rosamond Jacob: Third Person Singular* (Dublin: UCD Press, 2010), p. 123.
76 Ann Matthews, *Dissidents: Irish Republican Women, 1923–1941* (Cork: Mercier Press, 2012), p. 202.
77 *The Young Guard of Erin: The Fianna Handbook* (Dublin: Na Fianna Éireann, 1964), p. 145.
78 John R. Watts, 'Na Fianna Éireann: a case study of a political youth organisation' (PhD thesis, University of Glasgow, 1981), pp. 295–6.
79 *Fianna Éireann Handbook* (Dublin: Fianna Éireann, 1988), pp. 1–2.

80 Bulmer Hobson, witness statement, 15 Oct. 1947 (MA, BMH, WS 31).
81 *Ibid.*; Bulmer Hobson, 'The IRB and the Fianna' in F. X. Martin (ed.), *The Irish Volunteers, 1913–1915: Recollections and Documents* (Dublin: James Duffy, 1963), p. 21; Eamon Martin, witness statement, 1 Oct. 1951 (MA, BMH, WS 591); Cathleen McCarthy (née Ryan), witness statement, 31 Mar. 1954 (MA, BMH, WS 937).
82 Dublin members included Richard (Dick) Balfe, John A. Caffrey, Sean Harling, Robert Holland, Garry Holohan, Sean McLoughlin, Eamon Martin, Patrick O'Daly, Dónal O'Hannigan, Pádraic Ó Riain, Joseph Reynolds, Sean Saunders and Patrick Ward. Archie Heron and David McGuinness were members in Belfast while Michael Brennan, James Nolan and Thomas Kettrick were members in Limerick, Waterford and Westport, respectively. In Tuam, there were Patrick Dunleavy, Thomas Nohilly and Sean O'Neill. Seamus Reader and Seamus Robinson joined the IRB in Glasgow.
83 Joseph Melinn, witness statement, 21 Dec. 1948 (MA, BMH, WS 168).
84 Seamus Pounch, witness statement, 15 June 1949 (MA, BMH, WS 267).
85 Patrick McHugh, witness statement, 15 May 1952 (MA, BMH, WS 677).
86 Thomas O'Donoghue, witness statement, n.d. (MA, BMH, WS 1,666).
87 *Ibid.*
88 Eamon Martin, witness statement, 1 Oct. 1951 (MA, BMH, WS 591); Patrick Ward, witness statement, 30 Mar. 1955 (MA, BMH, WS 1,140).
89 Nora Connolly O'Brien, witness statement, 21 July 1949 (MA, BMH, WS 286).
90 Seamus Kavanagh, witness statement, 9 Sept. 1957 (MA, BMH, WS 1,670); Thomas O'Donoghue, witness statement, n.d. (MA, BMH, WS 1,666).
91 'Fianna Roll of Honour' in Holland, *A Short History*, p. 25 (NLI, MS 35,455/3/12A). For a list of ICA members in 1916, see Ann Matthews, *The Irish Citizen Army* (Cork: Mercier Press, 2014), pp. 188–211.
92 John Anthony Caffrey, witness statement, 14 Sept. 1951 (MA, BMH, WS 569); James Carrigan, witness statement, 26 Nov. 1951 (MA, BMH, WS 613); Sean McLoughlin, witness statement, 26 Aug. 1949 (MA, BMH, WS 290); William (Liam) McCabe, witness statement, 25 July 1953 (MA, BMH, WS 1,212).
93 Fianna GHQ Dublin to Fianna officers, Feb. 1921 (MA, BMH, Michael Kilmartin Collection, CD 144/1/20); Joseph Reynolds, witness statement, 31 Jan. 1949 (MA, BMH, WS 191).
94 Fianna GHQ Dublin to Fianna officers, Feb. 1921 (MA, BMH, Kilmartin Collection, CD 144/1/20).
95 Fianna Éireann report, Aug. 1921 (UCDA, Richard Mulcahy Papers, P7/A/23/134).

96 For instance, Kevin Murphy and John C. Murphy both refer to Fianna members transferring to the Volunteers in their witness statements. See Kevin Murphy, witness statement, 7 June 1957 (MA, BMH, WS 1,629); John C. Murphy, witness statement, 28 July 1955 (MA, BMH, WS 1,217).

97 The Fianna members from the BMH sample who indicated that they had joined the Irish Volunteers/IRA, or for whom I was able to confirm membership from the MSPC, were: Richard (Dick) Balfe, Michael Brennan, Patrick Burke, James A. Busby, Joseph Byrne, John A. Caffrey, James Carrigan, William Christian, Dominic Doherty, John Donnelly, Stephen Donnelly, Patrick Dunleavy, Patrick Egan, Theo Fitzgerald, James Fulham, Edward Fullerton, Sean Healy, Archie Heron, Robert Holland, Garry Holohan, Edward Horgan, Sean Kennedy, Thomas Kettrick, Michael Lonergan, William (Liam) McCabe, William J. McCarthy, Roger McCorley, David McGuinness, Patrick McHugh, Sean McLoughlin, Hugo McNeill, Niall MacNeill, Tomás Malone, William Mullins, John. C. Murphy, Kevin Murphy, P. J. Murphy, Joseph Murray, Thomas Nohilly, James Nolan, Denis O'Brien, William (Liam) O'Brien, Liam O'Callaghan, Patrick O'Connell, Patrick O'Daly, Felix O'Doherty, Thomas O'Donoghue, Charles J. O'Grady, Dónal O'Hannigan, Michael O'Leary, Peadar O'Mara, Sean O'Neill (Dublin), Sean O'Neill (Tuam), Pádraic Ó Riain, John O'Riordan, James Ormond, Joseph O'Shea, Dermot O'Sullivan, Thomas Pelican, Sean Prendergast, Seamus Reader, Amos Reidy, James M. Roche, Moses Roche, Michael J. Ryan, Robert Henry (Harry) Walpole, Patrick Ward and Patrick Whelan.

98 The *DIB* lists the following former Fianna members as having joined either the Irish Volunteers or the IRA: Sean Brady, Michael Brennan, Robert Briscoe, Con Colbert, Roddy Connolly, Thomas Derrig, George Gilmore, Joe Groome, Stephen Hayes, Archie Heron, Sean Heuston, the Holohan brothers, John Joe 'Purty' Landers, Sean MacBride, Maurice MacGonigal, Joseph McKelvey, Sean McLoughlin, Brian MacNeill, Hugo McNeill, Eamon Martin, Liam Mellows, Thomas Mullins, Tommy O'Brien, Peter O'Connor, Patrick O'Daly, Aodogán O'Rahilly, Cathal O'Shannon, the Plant brothers, Joseph and Seamus Robinson, Desmond Ryan, Eugene Sheehan, John Joe Sheehy, P. J. Stephenson and Martin Walton.

99 Mary (May) Chadwick (née Kelly), pension file (MA, MSPC, MSP34REF20098); May Murray, pension file (MA, MSPC, 49SP7805); Ellen (Nellie) Stynes (née Lambert), pension file (MA, MSPC, MSP34REF56696); Margaret Mary MacSherry (née Fagan), pension file (MA, MSPC, MSP34REF54707).

100 John Kenny, pension file (MA, MSPC, 24SP2573); John Kenny, witness statement, 6 Nov. 1957 (MA, BMH, WS 1,693); Frank Robbins, witness statement, 10 Sept. 1951 (MA, BMH, WS 585).

101 James Fulham, witness statement, 3 Jan. 1952 (MA, BMH, WS 630).
102 Patrick Hearne, witness statement, 18 Aug. 1958 (MA, BMH, WS 1,742).
103 The figure of ninety-six includes the ninety-three former Fianna members in the sample who definitely joined the Volunteers/IRA, as well as two who claimed they joined the IRA (James Delea and Ralph J. Lynch) and one other individual (Leo Rea) who may have joined the IRA.
104 The forty-four pension applicants (or subjects of applications by family members) whose military service was listed as solely with the Fianna were: William Barrett, Frank Burke Jr, John Burke, Patrick William Cashman, Philip Cleary, Sean Cole, Martin Considine, John Desmond, Michael Doyle, Albert Dyas, Michael Edgeworth, Daniel D. Foley, Stephen Gethings, Patrick Hanley, Patrick. J. Hanlon, Patrick J. Hannafin, John Healy, Arthur Hughes, Joseph Hurson, Denis Kavanagh, James Keating, Gerald Landers, John Lawlor, Thomas Lowe, Micheál S. MacEochaidh, Christopher McEvoy, Eamon Martin, James Mooney, Thomas Moriarty, Michael Moynihan, Francis Murphy, John Murray, Michael O'Brien, Henry O'Connor, Daniel O'Driscoll, John O'Leary, Joseph W. Reed, Joseph F. Reynolds, Percy Reynolds, Michael J. Ryle, Michael Sheahan, Thomas Slattery, William Toal and Patrick Tubridy.
105 The fifteen pension applicants (or subjects of applications by family members) whose military service was listed as being with the Fianna and the National Army were: Francis Leo Byrne, John Devoy, Richard J. Doherty, John Dooley, Michael Finnegan, James Fleming, Patrick Flynn, Patrick Hanly, Christopher Martin, John Martin, Michael Mulkerrins, Joseph O'Riordan, Thomas Sheehan, Anthony Swan and Patrick Young.
106 See William Charles Roe, pension file (MA, MSPC, MSP34REF21737); Stephen Donnelly, pension file (MA, MSPC, 1924A22).
107 The following individuals in the pension sample made no claim for Civil War service: Richard Balfe, John Caffrey, Patrick William Cashman, Albert Dyas, Christopher Feekery, Stephen Gethings, Denis Kavanagh, Micheál Mac Eochaidh, Christopher McGrane, Percy Reynolds and P. J. Stephenson. The following individuals, whose families made applications for dependants' allowances, died before the Civil War: Joseph Burns, Thomas Doyle, John (Sean) Healy, Patrick Hanley, Patrick J. Hannafin, Joseph A. Hurson, Gerald A. Keogh, John Lawlor, Christopher McEvoy, Peter Meade, Thomas Moriarty, Francis Murphy, John Murray, Michael O'Brien, Daniel O'Driscoll, John O'Leary, Leo Rea, Joseph Reed, Thomas Slattery, William F. Staines and William Toal. It was unclear whether John O'Leary was still active with the Fianna at the time of his death from phthisis and heart failure on 8 Sept. 1922, so I was unable to determine whether he was pro- or anti-Treaty (see MA, MSPC, 1D372).

108 The anti-Treatyites were: Sean Brady, Robert Briscoe, Roddy Connolly, Thomas Derrig, Dan Dowd, George Gilmore, Joe Groome, Stephen Hayes, the Holohan brothers, John Joe Landers, Sean MacBride, Brian MacNeill, Joseph McKelvey, Sean McLoughlin, Eamon Martin, Liam Mellows, Thomas Mullins, Nora Connolly O'Brien, Peter O'Connor, Aodogán O'Rahilly, John Ormonde, the Plant brothers, the Robinson brothers, Eugene Sheehan, John Joe Sheehy and Martin Walton. The pro-Treatyites were: Michael Brennan, Archie Heron, Hugo McNeill, Patrick O'Daly, Cathal O'Shannon and Desmond Ryan.

109 Marie Coleman, *The Irish Sweep: A History of the Irish Hospitals Sweepstake, 1930–87* (Dublin: UCD Press, 2009), p. 31.

110 The following former Fianna members became deputies of Dáil Éireann: Sean Brady (Fianna Fáil), Robert Briscoe (Fianna Fáil), Roddy Connolly (Labour), Thomas Derrig (Fianna Fáil), Archie Heron (Labour), Sean MacBride (Clann na Poblachta), John McCann (Fianna Fáil), Liam Mellows (Sinn Féin), Thomas Mullins (Fianna Fáil), John Ormonde (Fianna Fáil), Cathal O'Shannon (Labour) and Seamus Robinson (Sinn Féin).

111 MacBride, the leader of the Clann na Poblachta Party, served as Minister for External Affairs in the first Irish 'inter-party' government. Derrig served in three ministries, Education, Lands, and Posts and Telegraphs, while Ormonde also held the latter portfolio. See Ronan Keane, 'MacBride Sean', Pauric J. Dempsey, 'Derrig, Thomas (Ó Deirig, Tomás)' and Anne Dolan, 'Ormonde, John Michael' in *DIB*.

112 The senators were Thomas Mullins (Fianna Fáil), Nora Connolly O'Brien (Independent), John Ormonde (Fianna Fáil) and Seamus Robinson (Fianna Fáil).

113 The councillors were Sean Brady, Michael Brennan, Robert Briscoe, John McCann, Thomas Mullins, John Ormonde and John Joe Sheedy.

114 The following are listed as labour or trade union activists, socialists or communists (however briefly): Roddy Connolly, George Gilmore, Archie Heron, Austin Hogan, Paddy Holohan, Sean McLoughlin, Nora Connolly O'Brien, Peter O'Connor, Cathal O'Shannon, Desmond Ryan and P. J. Stephenson.

115 Examples include George Gilmore, Stephen Hayes, John Joe 'Purty' Landers, Sean MacBride, Peter O'Connor and the Plant brothers. See White, 'Plant, George' in *DIB*.

116 The following individuals served in the National Army or the Irish Defence Forces: Michael Brennan, Paddy Holohan, Hugo McNeill and Patrick O'Daly. See James Quinn, 'Brennan, Michael' and Patrick Long, 'McNeill, Hugh Hyacinth ('Hugo')' in *DIB*.

117 The journalists were Basil Clancy, John McCann, Tommy O'Brien, Cathal O'Shannon and Desmond Ryan. The businessmen were Sean Brady, Robert Briscoe, Joe Groome, Percy Reynolds and Martin Walton, while Thomas Derrig and John Ormonde were teachers before entering politics.
118 Paul Rouse, 'Dowd (O'Dowd), Dan' and Lawrence William White, 'Walton, Martin' in *DIB*.
119 Sean Kearns, 'Landers, John Joe ('Purty')' and Marie Coleman, 'Sheehy, John Joe' in *DIB*.
120 Carmel Doyle and Lawrence William White, 'MacGonigal, Maurice Joseph' in *DIB*; email from Ciarán MacGonigal to Ivar McGrath, 17 Nov. 2009 (email in possession of Marnie Hay).
121 Denis Begley, Sylvester J. Doyle and Henry V. Staines remained in the Irish Defence Forces until the late 1920s; Staines returned briefly in 1939, but was later court-martialled. Joseph Cullen stayed on until 1945 while Hugo McNeill and Anthony Swan did not retire until the 1950s. The following six rejoined the defence forces during the Emergency: Denis Begley, Sylvester J. Doyle, Patrick J. Dunne, Patrick Holohan, Patrick O'Daly and Robert Henry Walpole.
122 The following five joined the police force either during the Civil War or later: Stephen Donnelly, Edward J. Murray, William C. Roe, James Staines and Patrick J. Young.
123 See Walter Leo Holland, pension file (MA, MSPC, 24SP10402).
124 Coleman, 'Compensating Irish female revolutionaries', p. 928.
125 Nora Connolly O'Brien to 'Seamus', 9 July 1941, quoted in Ferriter, 'The military service pensions and the battle for survival', p. 199; Coleman, 'Compensating Irish female revolutionaries', p. 928.

6 The Fianna experience

> The annual Ard Fheis or Convention was a big event in our lives. Then we would meet boys from various parts of Ireland and have our big 'pow wow' in the Mansion House, Dawson St. Each sluagh sent its delegate or delegates, and on each occasion our photograph was taken by the reputable Keogh's of Dorset St. In the night time a céilidhe or reception would be held.[1]

Sean Prendergast's description of the Fianna's *ard-fheis* in Dublin evokes the sense of occasion surrounding the youth group's annual national convention, providing a taste of only one of the many activities that formed the Fianna experience in the period 1909–23. Fianna members were involved in a seeming whirlwind of instruction in military drill and scouting skills, classes in Irish language and history, Sunday route marches, summer camping trips and evening concerts and céilís. Participation in these activities gave members the chance to make friends and join various nationalist networks. Members who progressed to the officer level gained hands-on experience in governance and administration. Some Fianna members assisted their adult counterparts in the nationalist movement by serving as stewards and guards of honour at various events, participating in protests or disseminating print propaganda. As the Irish Revolution progressed, some members also engaged in activities with potentially serious consequences, such as smuggling weapons, carrying dispatches while under gunfire or conducting arms raids.

This chapter will provide an overview of the Fianna's activities in the period 1909–23 in order to gain an insight into the value and appeal of the Irish youth group and to provide a comparison to other European youth organisations of the period. It will discuss Fianna activities that fit into the following four categories: military training and scouting; Irish history and culture; social contacts and nationalist networking;

and adolescent mayhem. Two other specific areas of Fianna activity merit chapters of their own: the involvement of the Fianna in the production and dissemination of print propaganda will be discussed in chapter 7, while the Fianna's military contribution to the 1914 Howth gunrunning, the 1916 Easter Rising, the Irish War of Independence (1919–21) and the Irish Civil War (1922–23) will be covered in chapter 8.

PHASES OF FIANNA ACTIVITIES

The activities of the Fianna can be slotted into three main time frames, corresponding to phases within the Irish Revolution. The first phase covers the period from the youth group's inception in 1909 up to the 1916 Easter Rising. During this period the organisation developed from a nationalist scouting organisation with a cultural dimension to an outright military training body for nationalist youth. In the second phase between 1916 and 1918, the Fianna continued their military training and scouting programme and lent their support to the various propagandist activities of their adult counterparts in the advanced nationalist movement. During the third phase, covering the years of the War of Independence and the Civil War, the Fianna carried on in this vein, with some older members also providing support services to the IRA and engaging in some military action of their own.

The Cork Fianna provide a useful snapshot of continuity and change within the youth group's activities during the three phases of the Irish Revolution. Formed by members of the O'Growney branch of the Gaelic League in 1910, the Cork Fianna initially offered classes in Irish language and history as well as training in military drill, first aid and scouting skills such as map reading, knot tying, Morse code, semaphore, tent-pitching and tracking. In addition, route marches were held most Sundays (except in winter) and camping trips usually took place at Easter, Whitsuntide and during the summer.[2] Over time, the language and history classes appear to have been abandoned and replaced by rifle and revolver practice as the *sluagh* and its members began to acquire firearms in 1915. Up to that point, the Cork Fianna had been 'purely a Scout movement', but after that date 'it became more of a military body and training ground for the Irish Volunteers', recalled former members.[3]

After the 1916 Easter Rising, the growing number of Cork *sluaighte* focused on drilling, route marching and instruction in signalling, first aid and the use of revolvers and rifles. At the same time, the Cork Fianna continued to assist their adult counterparts in the nationalist movement with such activities as pasting up (and tearing down) posters, disseminating print propaganda, fundraising and participating in anti-military recruitment protests just as they had done prior to the rebellion.[4] During the War of Independence, some Fianna boys not only volunteered as scouts and dispatch carriers for the IRA but also raided private homes for arms, destroyed the stores of British government forces and attacked individuals whom they deemed 'enemy personnel'.[5] The changes in the activities in which Cork Fianna members engaged illustrate the youth group's shift over time from a scouting organisation imbued with cultural and political nationalism to a military training and support body.

Elsewhere in the country, a similar shift in the Fianna's activities and their character also took place in response to the changing phases of the Irish Revolution. Certain activities, however, remained continuous throughout the three phases. These include the Fianna's provision of training in military drill, signalling and first aid, participation in route marches and involvement in several types of propagandist work. The various activities offered by the Fianna will be discussed in turn, keeping in mind differing contexts of time and place. Dublin is a prime example of this. Given that it was the centre of the Fianna movement, not only were a wider range of activities on offer, but changes in the organisation were initiated there first.

MILITARY TRAINING AND SCOUTING

Many of the activities undertaken by the Fianna, particularly those associated with military training and scouting skills, overlapped with those offered by other European youth groups of the period. For example, in Germany 'high esteem for the military' inspired 'tens of thousands of male youths [to join] recreational associations that taught shooting and organized war games' during the years leading up to and during the First World War.[6] In Britain and Ireland, the various boys' brigades also provided training in military drill and discipline, but with a view to fostering the religious and moral development of their members.[7] The Boys' Brigade had always used 'dummy rifles for drill', but this was later joined by marksmanship and rifle shooting practice in anticipation of the outbreak in 1914 of the First World War.[8] Baden-Powell's Boy Scouts usually did not engage in military drill, except when influenced by the conditions of the Great War, but they did learn the kind of scouting skills that formed part of a soldier's training. In fact, the interest shown by boys in his army training manual, *Aids to*

Scouting, was one of the factors that inspired Baden-Powell to establish the youth group.[9]

Many of these scouting skills also applied to camping, an activity whose links to both military life and outdoor adventure appealed to members of scouting associations and boys' brigades. In Germany and in the German-speaking areas of Austria-Hungary, the Wandervögel (Wandering Birds) were also avid young campers, but for this network of middle-class hiking clubs their interest in camping was not associated with militarism. As Andrew Donson explains, 'they imagined themselves escaping the sordid urban world of their elders by exploring the countryside – that is, their Heimat (local geography)'.[10] The Wandervögel thus 'placed themselves in symbolic opposition to the militarism of the German upper classes'.[11]

While the Wandervögel eschewed the military ethos of many contemporary youth groups, they did share the Fianna's commitment to celebrating indigenous national culture during their open-air activities. For instance, the Wandervögel championed German folklore and 'sang traditional folk songs to the accompaniment of lutes' around the campfire.[12] Both youth organisations also wore clothing that reflected their national cultures. While some Fianna members sported a kilt as part of their uniform, the Wandervögel chose to wear 'the folkloric German dress of decorated shirtfronts, flamboyant hats, and leather shorts or flowery skirts'.[13]

For its part, from the outset the Fianna offered members a mixture of military training, including marksmanship, as well as the outdoor adventure side of scouting and camping. As the founders of the Fianna envisaged the youth group as the nucleus of a future Irish army, the first activity to be provided twice a week at the Fianna's Camden Street hall was training in military drill, which was designed to instil order and discipline in the boys.[14] Con Colbert was the troop's first instructor in elementary drill formations. 'He was no great expert at this time', reported Eamon Martin. 'By intense swotting, however, he improved as the weeks went on, and, consequently, so did the Sluagh.' The troop later secured the voluntary services as drill instructor of an ex-member of the British army named Sean Kavanagh. Like Colbert, Michael Lonergan also showed officer potential from the beginning and he too became 'a natural instructor'. Early Fianna officers were mainly self-taught, having assiduously studied British army manuals. Pádraic Ó Riain, who later compiled the first *Fianna Handbook*, issued stencilled sheets from British army manuals to the company and section leaders of every *sluagh* and encouraged them to recruit ex-soldiers as drill instructors.[15] According to Eamon Martin, 'in a comparatively short time we had left the "form fours" stage behind us, and had advanced to section and company formations, to signalling and all the rest of a fairly comprehensive course'.[16] To progress within the Fianna, members had to demonstrate knowledge of squad, company and ambulance drill as well as an understanding of commands given in the Irish language.[17]

With training in military drill underway, plans were soon in place to provide instruction in scouting skills and organise route marches and camping trips. In February 1910, *Bean na hÉireann* reported that the boys were already 'making rapid progress' in aspects of scouting such as map drawing.[18] The 1914 *Fianna Handbook* outlines the scouting skills that Fianna members were expected to master. To earn the colour-coded shoulder cords that indicated an individual's class (first, second or third) within the organisation, members needed to demonstrate their knowledge of first aid, signalling (semaphore and Morse code), knot tying, tracking, field sketching and local topography and general geography of Ireland. They were also expected to know how to read and make a scout's map, pitch a tent, light a wood camp fire and cook on it, read a compass and find north using only the sun and the stars, make a camp latrine, and swim and save someone who was drowning.[19] Members of other scouting organisations would have learned such skills too.

Fianna members received tuition in these scouting skills at weekly meetings and from 1914 onwards they could also refer to the *Fianna Handbook* and articles in the *Irish Volunteer* for instruction. For instance, Pádraic Ó Riain contributed a series of articles to the paper on the duties of military scouts, training in observation, map reading and field sketching between December 1915 and March 1916. The paper had previously run articles on tracking, dispatch carrying and map making.[20]

First aid appears to have been the only area of expertise for which the Fianna issued a specific badge. In Cork, boys who qualified in first aid were entitled to wear a red cross on their sleeve and carry a first aid kit in a pouch on their belt.[21] The Fianna recruited local doctors to provide first aid instruction, though as members became more adept they might be called upon to share their knowledge with their peers.[22] Nora Connolly is a prime example. 'I taught the Fianna and the Volunteers first-aid', she recalled. 'There was a young doctor … he took me and gave me the lesson; next day, I gave it to the Cumann na mBan, next day to the Fianna, and next day to the Volunteers.'[23]

Instruction in signalling, both in semaphore and Morse code, was provided at Fianna meetings as well as in the organisation's publications. Such training did not appeal to everyone, however, as attested by James Fulham who only attended Fianna meetings in Dublin for a brief period beginning around late 1912/early 1913. By his own admission, he did not appreciate the value of instruction in signalling until he later joined the IRA and served during the War of Independence, ultimately becoming a commandant in the Irish Defence Forces.[24]

Instruction in the use of firearms was the most controversial aspect of the Fianna's training programme. In Dublin, Markievicz provided instruction in marksmanship from an early stage. For training purposes, a Lee Enfield rifle was used outdoors and an air rifle indoors.[25] The quality of such training is open to question. According to Sean Kennedy, he was placed on guard duty at a weekend Fianna camp at Belcamp Park when he was about fourteen years of age and given a .22 rifle which he did not know how to handle.[26] Elsewhere in Ireland instruction in the use of firearms seems to have started at a later date, as for example, in 1915 in Cork.

Not all nationalists, let alone Fianna members, were comfortable with this aspect of the Fianna's training programme. Fianna member Thomas O'Donoghue, a future Catholic priest, 'objected to boys being trained to use arms' and left the Fianna *c.* 1912 to help form a

Figure 6 Fianna Éireann scouts carrying out signalling training with flags.

breakaway group called the Irish National Guards because he wanted 'youths, not boys, trained in the use of arms', though he did not define at what age boys became youths.[27] O'Donoghue was not alone in his view. Writer and nationalist activist Rosamond Jacob did not 'think boys under 16 ought to be let use arms at all; it can't but be bad for them'.[28] Like Hobson, Jacob's parents came from a Quaker background. She recognised the potential value of the Fianna, but she had concerns about the nature of Markievicz's leadership and its impact on members: 'Madame is a bloodthirsty woman … and the boys seem the same in theory. Now if some humane person had charge of the Fianna what a lot of good might be done.'[29] Jacob later became honorary president of a troop of Fianna girls in Waterford.[30]

Fianna boys also practised rifle drill, bayonet fighting and fencing with single sticks.[31] These and other skills acquired through involvement in the youth group were demonstrated by members at outdoor public events such as *aeraíochtaí* (open-air entertainments) and drill competitions. When Dublin Fianna members Seamus Kavanagh and Percy Reynolds presented an exhibition of fencing with single sticks in Castlebar, County Mayo, more than their skill ended up on display. The exhibition took place on a platform about five feet above the ground, with both boys wearing kilts. During this fencing match Kavanagh became convinced that Reynolds was trying to keep him at the edge of the platform in order to push him off, not realising that Reynolds was actually trying to stay away from the edge because he was not wearing any 'shorts' under his kilt. Kavanagh decided to manoeuvre Reynolds to the edge instead. Reynolds tried to avoid a lunge that Kavanagh made at him but forgot that he was so close to the edge of the platform and fell back on the ground. Realising the embarrassing situation Reynolds was in, Fianna officer Pádraic Ó Riain brought the exhibition to an immediate end.[32]

Fianna members had opportunities to practice their scouting skills while on route marches, camping trips and other visits to the local countryside. For instance, from the spring of 1910 Dublin members honed their skills and built up their physical fitness during regular Sunday route marches into the Dublin Mountains and north County Dublin, an activity that according to Liam Mellows particularly appealed to 'city boys'.[33] Similarly, in early 1914 Belfast members planned to go to Black Mountain, which was close to their headquarters, to practise scout-work.[34] Cork members recalled that tests in these skills were held at regular intervals and that 'the Scoutmaster was very strict in maintaining a high standard in them'.[35]

The Dublin route marches, often ten to fifteen miles in length, were full-day outings that began early in the morning and ended late at night. 'We never used trams or other modes of travelling on our way out, and only on rare occasions on the return journey', recalled Sean Prendergast. 'Distance seldom upset us as we boasted the fact that we were young and active. Besides we were always sure of a halt on the way for refreshments and a rest of sorts.' As they marched, Fianna members sang 'songs of an Irish and national character', often 'to the accompaniment of mouth organ, bagpipe or the modest tin whistle'. Like many Irish nationalist organisations of the time, the Fianna sought to combat Irish assimilation into British culture. Thus, music hall songs or those deemed to be English were 'taboo'.[36] Among the Fianna's favourite marching songs were the future Irish national anthem, 'The soldier's song', as well as 'Step together' and 'The green flag'. Popular Irish-Ireland poet Brian O'Higgins even composed a marching song for the Fianna, which was published in *Irish Freedom*.[37]

Once the Fianna reached their destination, members lit fires, brewed tea and ate an open-air meal. Then they spent the next few hours engaged in scouting exercises or climbing mountains. The sights and sounds of the return journey inspired Prendergast to wax lyrical in his memoir: 'It was ... romance to the soul marching down the mountainside in the dusk of a fine summer evening, our steady tramp, tramp, tramp breaking the peace and quietude of the countryside.' Below them, he and the other boys could see their 'own beloved Dublin' basking in the 'crimson glow of the setting sun'.[38]

From the Fianna's inception, camping was one of the organisation's regular summer activities. In 1909, early members of the Dublin Fianna spent six days 'camping on the slopes of Three Rock Mountain', with Hobson and some other Fianna members joining the campers on the Sunday to play 'scouting' games. During 'the damp evenings' the campers sang Irish songs and talked of Irish heroes to pass the time.[39] While Markievicz and Molony were in possession of Belcamp Park, it was a regular camping destination for Fianna members. For instance, the grounds of the house served as the venue for camping and sports on the August bank holiday in 1910.[40] After Markievicz and Molony vacated Belcamp Park, Malahide or Baldoyle became Dublin's north-side camping destinations. The Fianna also camped in the Dublin Mountains south of the city at Balally and Ticknock (where Markievicz had a cottage), Glendue, Kilmashogue and the Hell-Fire Club. Once Pearse moved his school St Enda's to the site of the Hermitage in Rathfarnham that too became a popular spot for camping trips and route marches.[41]

As the Fianna's annual *ard-fheis* often coincided with their July holidays, Belfast delegates sometimes extended their stay in the Dublin area to include a camping vacation with the countess.[42]

Fianna troops elsewhere in Ireland also had their favourite camping spots. For instance, the Cork Fianna often camped at Blarney, Ballincollig, Healy's Bridge, Knocknahorgan or Clash.[43] Joseph O'Shea's recollection of a camp at Healy's Bridge in 1914 provides an insight into the Fianna's relations with the local communities in which they camped and the occasional benefits of mistaken identity:

> The lady who owned the land came and invited us up to the house. Sean Healy, Liam Óg and I went up. She was very kind to us and gave us eggs and milk free, but as Union Jacks and pictures of the Royal family were prominent in the house I think she must have been under the impression that we belonged to the Baden Powell Scouts.[44]

This friendly landowner recognised that camping was an activity embraced by many uniformed youth groups of the period, though she could not tell the difference between the various organisations. These weekend outings with their combination of camaraderie, vigorous physical activity, fresh air and scenic views provided city youths with a welcome break from their usual urban environment and the daily routine of school or work – hence their appeal to the members of scouting organisations, boys' brigades and the German Wandervögel.

The growing number of Fianna troops in Dublin soon made it possible to organise inter-*sluagh* scouting games, such as the one held in Scholarstown on 6 November 1910. On this occasion, the games were conducted as follows:

> An Chead Sluagh and Sluagh Wolfe Tone will jointly defend the citadel which comprises about 400 square yards of Mr Jolley's land in Scholarstown. The attackers, composed of sluaighte on the north side of the Liffey, shall endeavour to enter the citadel without being captured. When a member of the attacking force enters the precincts of the defender's territory he is free from any molestation from the defenders and cannot be captured. It will be defenders' business to intercept and capture the attackers before reaching the citadel. Marks shall be awarded by the umpires for good scouting work, the capturing of scouts and for those who succeed in entering the citadel uncaptured. The attackers shall be known by the

red bands on their arms and the defenders shall wear the white bands.⁴⁵

Such war games enabled members to put their new skills to the test in a simulated setting in preparation for the real thing, adding an exciting element of competition to proceedings.

Over time, there were an increasing number of opportunities for Fianna members to practice their new skills in real-life situations. For instance, members, most notably Patsy O'Connor, utilised their first aid skills during the 1913 Dublin Lockout. O'Connor had been administering first aid to an injured worker during a protest when he himself was batoned by the police and sustained a head injury after which he was subject to headaches. A Fianna commentator reported that O'Connor's premature death in June 1915 was an indirect result of this injury.⁴⁶ Liam Mellows recorded the following account of O'Connor's injury and subsequent death:

> During the great Dublin strike in 1913, Patsy received a severe blow on the head from a police baton while trying to administer first aid to an old man who had been badly hurt during one of the baton charges. After superficial treatment at a hospital Patsy thought he was all right as the wound healed up rapidly. But two years later he arrived home one evening complaining of a pain in his head and after drinking a cup of tea suddenly collapsed and died almost immediately. A clot of blood had congealed on the brain and two years after the blow had burst.⁴⁷

However, the record of O'Connor's interment in Glasnevin Cemetery indicates the alleged cause of the eighteen-year-old's death was pneumonia.⁴⁸ Whatever the cause of O'Connor's death, his name is the first on a 1981 Fianna Roll of Honour, which lists the names of members 'who gave their lives for Ireland's freedom'.⁴⁹ A commemorative headstone was finally erected on his grave in 2015.⁵⁰

In another incident of skills being put to real use, on Sunday, 27 July 1913, four Fianna members intervened in a drowning incident while on a camping trip on Three Rock Mountain. Peter Doyle, a young man from the local area, got out of his depth while bathing in the Barnacullia quarry pool, which was as deep as twenty feet in places. Seeing that he was in difficulty, Doyle's younger brother and his companions ran to the neighbouring houses looking for help, but none of the occupants could swim. Hearing of the accident, the Fianna

Figure 7 Fianna Éireann scouts engaged in field medical training.

campers rushed to the scene and immediately began diving to try to find Doyle. After two hours with no success they were exhausted. They then built a raft and took turns searching for the body by which time the police had arrived. A Fianna commentator claimed that the police, instead of aiding in the actual search, produced notebooks in order to 'investigate'. Thomas Crimmins finally found the body and brought it to the surface. It was apparently at this stage that the police sought to intervene, but the boys insisted on carrying Doyle's 'body home across the mountains in their own stretcher and to his grief-stricken parents'. 'At the inquest the jury highly commended the action of the Fianna and paid a compliment to the efficiency of the boys', reported Liam Mellows in the *Gaelic American*. The local community held a meeting at Ballaly, Sandyford, County Dublin, on 10 August 1913 at which Fianna members Harry Walpole, Thomas Crimmins, Edward (sometimes known as Eamon) Murray and Thomas McCabe were presented with gold medals and certificates to recognise their bravery in assisting during the drowning incident. The meeting also led to the formation of a Fianna troop in Sandyford.[51]

On another occasion in Limerick, it was a Fianna member who lost his life in a rescue attempt. 'A number of small boys were fishing in a pond near the railway when one of them named Killeen fell into deep water', explained Liam Mellows. 'A Fianna boy named Willie Davern, aged thirteen, jumped in to rescue him and succeeded in getting his comrade to safety, but fell back exhausted himself and was drowned.'[52] The preceding incidents illustrate how the Fianna fostered the practical skills and service mentality that enabled members to lend a hand in emergencies. The willingness to volunteer assistance to people in need was not unique to the Fianna, however, with 'lend a hand' being the motto of the Brownies, a branch of guiding that was formed in 1914 to cater for girls aged between eight and eleven years.[53]

This willingness to help out was also evident in less critical situations. The Fianna's training in military drill and discipline and their uniformed appearance proved useful to adult nationalists on many public occasions. Just as today, military forces and uniformed youth groups were often called on to participate in parades and other events that required an air of order and pageantry. For example, when a public meeting was held on 25 November 1913 at the Rotunda in Dublin to form the Irish Volunteers, Fianna boys were 'equipped with pads of enrolment forms' and served as stewards.[54] Irish nationalists recognised the value of children and youth, particularly those in uniform, as potent symbols of the future nation state and often used them in different types of public displays. Up to 1916, the Cork *sluagh* served as the guard of honour for the Blessed Sacrament at the annual procession at Wilton Church, a more overtly religious use of the nationalist youth group than was usually the case.[55] Fianna members also participated in the annual Manchester Martyrs events held in different parts of the country to mark the hanging of three Fenians in Manchester in 1867.[56] For example, as part of these commemoration proceedings Fianna boys in Cork used to lay wreaths on Fenian graves while in 1911 the Belfast girls' troop presented an exhibition of drill.[57]

The public presentation of the Fianna, particularly male members, was echoed in other contexts both in Ireland and abroad. Elaine Sisson has noted that St Enda's School 'secured national identity to the body of the male youth and paraded youthful male bodies as a visual metaphor for the nation state'. She adds that this exercise 'was reflected in European-wide practices of annexing the "physical culture" of masculinity to moral strength'.[58] St Enda's and Na Fianna Éireann both displayed young male bodies as 'a visual metaphor for the nation state', demonstrating an uncomfortable link with an aspect of fascism. For instance, at the St Enda's fête held at Jones's Road in June 1913 to raise money for the school's building fund, St Enda's students performed in the pageant 'The Fianna of Fionn', while Fianna boys participated in a different type of performance – a display of tent-pitching, camp work, skirmishing and drill.[59] Rather than feeling like poster boys for Irish nationalism, Fianna members probably took pride in being chosen to participate in such public displays.

The increasing militarisation of the Fianna happened most rapidly in Dublin, possibly spurred on by the formation of the Irish Volunteers and the involvement of certain senior Fianna members in the adult paramilitary organisation. By March 1914 Cadet Corps classes, which were designed for 'officers and supernumeraries', were being held on Wednesdays at 8 pm at 6 Harcourt Street in Dublin.[60] In October 1914, plans were announced to start a Fianna Officer Training Corps, an initiative that had been recommended in Pádraic Ó Riain's Honorary Secretary's Report at the *ard-fheis* earlier that year.[61] In November 1914, fifty cadets enrolled in the new corps which held lectures twice weekly at 41 Kildare Street under the leadership of Ó Riain.[62] Also known as the Fianna Cadet Corps, this group was designed for boys between ages fifteen and eighteen.[63]

J. J. 'Ginger' O'Connell, one of the few leaders of the Irish Volunteers with previous military experience, recalled delivering 'a series of tactical lectures' to the Fianna cadets. 'These were boys well on in their teens and most intelligent as, indeed, one might expect considering that they were picked from a large number', he reported. 'It could not be the lot of any instructor to have better material than these boys, all of whom in drill and training, and many of whom in action, definitely proved of what soldierly stuff they were made.'[64] O'Connell clearly recognised the value of the youth organisation in preparing future members and leaders of the Irish Volunteers/IRA.

The creation of the Cadet Corps also reflected Ó Riain's concern that individual Fianna troops were trying to cater to an age range of boys that was too wide, given that a *sluagh* might include boys between the ages of eight and eighteen. 'The governing and training of boys from eight to twelve years of age ought to be very different from that of boys between the ages of thirteen and sixteen years', he asserted in the *Irish Volunteer* newspaper. He recommended that the Fianna be divided into three groups with the Scout period covering ages eight to twelve years, the Fianna or Soldier period for twelve to sixteen years, and the Cadet or Officer period for ages sixteen to eighteen.[65] As a Fianna leader, Ó Riain had observed how stages of child development impacted on members' attitudes towards authority and responsibility: 'Boys generally up to twelve or thirteen accept the authority of their officer without question and leave it to him to settle all the disputes and difficulties that arise in connection with the sluagh.' Older boys, in contrast, were more 'self-assertive and eager for the responsibilities of office'. They became more interested 'in the working of the sluagh' and thus required a different course of training from 'the kids'.[66] Extant sources do not indicate whether Ó Riain's recommendations were fully implemented.

The Fianna shifted into its second phase of activity in 1916 within the wider context of the First World War of 1914–18. This war impacted on the membership and activities of youth organisations in European countries. Many older male members of youth groups enlisted in their states' armed forces. In Britain and Ireland, older members of the boys' brigades and the Boy Scouts enlisted in the British armed forces. Even a few Fianna members joined the British forces, despite their pledge not to do so.[67] Girl Guides supported the war effort by joining Voluntary Aid Detachments (VADs). Although the British War Office had started the VAD scheme in August 1909 in order to 'supplement the medical organization of the Territorial Force', VADs became better known 'for their role in providing auxiliary military nursing staff during World War I'.[68] From its inception, the VAD scheme, which was open to males and females, had recruited local youth groups including Boy Scouts and Girl Guides to help with its work.[69] In Germany, the war years saw an increase in female membership of the Wandervögel as well as more young women taking up leadership positions within the organisation at the local and regional levels while male members were away serving in the armed forces.[70]

Other members of youth groups engaged in new areas of instruction and different types of voluntary work in order to support the war effort. In Belfast, for instance, some of the Baden-Powell Boy Scouts participated in 'rifle drill and firing practice as part of their training in a "Scouts' Defence Corps for Home Services"'.[71] Irish Boy Scouts contributed to the British war effort in other ways as well. They undertook a variety of voluntary duties, such as delivering telegrams, letters and orders for the military authorities, coast-watching, serving as hospital orderlies and raising funds 'to provide a rest centre for soldiers near the front in France'.[72] Girl Guides also supported the war effort through voluntary work. In Britain, they knitted socks for soldiers, collected sphagnum moss for wound dressings, volunteered in hospitals and on farms, distributed military recruitment leaflets, raised funds to provide the troops in France with a motorised ambulance and 'a recreation hut', and formed uniformed guards of honour at 'the dedication of war shrines or monuments to the dead'.[73] In Germany, the type of activities undertaken by the Wandervögel also changed, with members 'helping with the harvest, collecting scrap metals, and at-home paramilitary activities'.[74]

Like the Boy Scouts and the Girl Guides, the Fianna promoted a service ethos during the Great War era, though the 'war effort' they served differed. Scouts and Guides in Britain and Ireland supported the British war effort while the Fianna prioritised the struggle for Irish independence. Thus, while the Fianna undertook voluntary work during the Irish Revolution that was similar to that performed by the Boy Scouts and Girl Guides during the First World War, its purpose differed fundamentally. For instance, Fianna members took food and clothing to republican prisoners in Cork Gaol in 1917 and collected money for prisoner aid funds.[75] During the War of Independence, Fianna boys served as letter carriers for 'a secret post office service' that was established in Dublin to enable people to boycott the British postal service and avoid the interception of republicans' letters by the British authorities. 'Several shops in the Dublin area were designated as posting centres where letters could be left', explained Sean Prendergast. 'A team of "postmen" which consisted of selected men of the IRA and boys of the Fianna looked after the delivery service.'[76]

After 1916, during the second and third phases of the Irish Revolution, the Fianna continued to provide military training and instruction in scouting skills at weekly meetings and on route marches and camping trips, as outlined previously. Some members also distributed Sinn Féin propaganda, provided support services to the Irish Volunteers/IRA by acting as dispatch carriers and scouts, and undertook military operations of their own such as arms raids.[77] By the time of the truce in July 1921, Fianna camps could be a far cry from the outdoor adventure weekends led by Markievicz in the youth group's early days.

Some became full-fledged military training camps as described in a detailed report on a camp held in Loughlinstown, County Dublin, on 10–17 September 1921. About 150 Fianna officers and NCOs arrived at the training camp at 11:10 pm on Saturday, 10 September 1921. After a meal of tea, bread and butter, they bedded down in six bell tents and one marquee, with about twenty-two young men per tent, and spent a 'very restless night owing to overcrowding'. The first full day of the camp on Sunday, 11 September stretched from 6 am to 11 pm and the main activity was drill. Faced with yet another meal of tea, bread and butter on Monday morning, the section leaders of each tent complained about the unsatisfactory 'food conditions' to the O/C Frank MacMahon and another senior officer Garry Holohan. As a result, the young men were allowed two hours to leave the camp in search of a better breakfast. Holohan's defence for the poor provisions was the inability 'to get proper supplies for camp owing to short notice'. Aside from the impromptu breakfast break, Monday's activities included physical exercises, more drill, and a lecture on protection of a unit at rest.[78]

Over the course of the week, senior Fianna officers MacMahon, Holohan, Jack Carey and Liam Langley presented lectures on different methods of taking cover, signalling with Morse code, and the use of prismatic and magnetic compasses and of explosives. Trained 'gunners' came to give a lecture on the Thompson machine gun that covered 'dissecting and building [stripping and assembling], also how to use gun to best effect, and cover most suitable for its use'. Attendees were also instructed to go into districts where the Fianna did not have a presence and to start new companies. On Friday, officers from IRA Headquarters inspected the camp and interviewed a Fianna representative from each area of the country. After the camp finished at lunchtime on Saturday, the attendees took the train back to Dublin. On arrival at 46 Parnell Square at 1:30 pm, however, the young men were ordered back to camp for another week's training, though anyone who could supply a valid reason for returning home was allowed to do so. In the end, thirty-two officers and NCOs returned to Loughlinstown at 8 pm to restart the fires and pitch two tents.[79]

In the Fianna's early years, the youth group struck a balance between military training and Irish educational and cultural activities, but the increasingly violent nature of the struggle for independence and subsequent Civil War disturbed this equilibrium. An editorial in the June 1922 edition of the *Fianna* paper highlights how the impact of the War of Independence had narrowed the range of activities originally offered by the youth group:

> Conditions in recent years rendered it necessary that the Fianna should act more like a military organisation than they would be expected to do in normal times. The educational side of our programming has been completely neglected. For instance, how many of our officers or boys have qualified to wear the Fáinne? ... While still keeping in view military training we must devote more of our time to the training of the mind and body. Physical training has had to be cut out; Gaelic games have been neglected, both necessary if we are to raise up strong and virile Irishmen fit to take a soldier's part in the national struggle of tomorrow.[80]

The implication that few members had qualified for the Fáinne, a pin symbolising proficiency in Irish, indicated that the Fianna's Irish language classes had been abandoned. Furthermore, the organisation's provision of activities to promote physical fitness and sport had waned over time. During the third phase of the Irish Revolution in particular, the Fianna's main focus was on the military side of its remit with far less emphasis on the Irish cultural activities that had also played an important part in the youth group's appeal at an earlier stage of its development.

IRISH HISTORY AND CULTURE

From the Fianna's inception in 1909, teaching members about Irish history from an overtly Irish nationalist perspective was an important part of the youth group's education programme, though as already demonstrated this seems to have diminished after 1916. Troops organised weekly history classes as well as special lectures on people who Irish republicans viewed as historical role models, such as the 'boy heroes' of the 1798 rebellion, Robert Emmet and the Manchester Martyrs.[81]

The Society of United Irishmen, whose revolutionary activities culminated in risings in various parts of Ireland in 1798, were the source of many role models for Irish republicans. Robert Emmet (1778–1803) was one of the new leaders of the United Irishmen to emerge after the 1798 rebellion and was executed for spearheading the July 1803 insurrection in Dublin. The Fenians of the latter half of the nineteenth century also provided republicans with heroic inspiration. The Manchester Martyrs were William O'Meara Allen, Michael Larkin and William O'Brien who were hanged for their involvement in an attack on a police van that was transporting two Fenian prisoners from the Manchester courthouse to the county jail in 1867.

Markievicz often delivered lectures on such topics, linking historical events to contemporary issues. A prime example is her lecture on the women of the 1798 rebellion, which *Bean na hÉireann* summarised:

> After speaking of the brave women who took an active part in the national struggle she told of many who suffered from the brutality of the conquering army, and wound up by telling how the Irish of that day lost all sense of honour and chivalry by serving under the English flag, and urged the need of a much stronger anti-enlisting movement in Ireland at this moment.[82]

Markievicz herself mobilised members of the Fianna to disseminate print propaganda urging Irishmen not to enlist in the British forces.[83]

Similarly, in her lecture on the Manchester Martyrs, Markievicz provided an 'account of the Fenian movement and previous revolutionary movements', before informing her young Belfast audience that 'many men who died for Ireland were little more than boys themselves' and that 'she wanted the Fianna to work for Ireland and to build up a great army for Ireland'.[84] Thus, Irish history was presented as a form of nationalist propaganda with particular emphasis on the history of battles and insurrections. As Eamon Martin explained, 'in this way the boys were being given a reason for their own military training'.[85]

The Fianna's history classes were designed to help members prepare for the series of tests that would enable them to progress upwards to the level of a First-Class *Fiannaidhe*, entitling them to wear a green, white and orange cord on the right shoulder of their uniform.[86] However, *Irish Freedom* reported that 'much difficulty has been experienced in conducting history classes on account of the lack of suitable textbooks covering the periods required for the test'.[87] To help overcome this difficulty – at least in the short term – P. S. O'Hegarty, a nationalist associate of Hobson's, contributed a series of articles on Irish history from 1782 to 1803 to the paper in 1914 in order to help Fianna members prepare for their Third-Class Fianna test.[88] The second-class test expanded the range of general historical knowledge required from 1782 to 1870 while the first-class test covered the period from the arrival of St Patrick in Ireland to 1782.[89]

Fianna members were also encouraged to participate in the Irish cultural revival in the areas of language, sport, theatre and music either through activities organised by Na Fianna Éireann or by joining the various branches of the Gaelic League or local hurling clubs around the country. Participation in such cultural activities helped members to nurture a sense of a separate Irish national identity. From an early date, for example, many Dublin Fianna *sluaighte* offered weekly Irish language classes to their members.[90] In 1911, however, the Dublin District Council decided to form a Fianna branch of the Gaelic League in order to centralise the teaching of Irish, seeing this as being 'more effective than teaching it' in each individual troop.[91] Fianna members had to pass Irish language tests based on the levels set down in Fr Eugene O'Growney's textbooks in order to progress upwards in the organisation and earn their colour-coded shoulder cords.[92] O'Growney was the author of the standard Irish language textbooks used in the early twentieth century.

In the late nineteenth and early twentieth centuries, youth groups emulated public schools in adopting 'the ideology of athleticism', which viewed sport as 'a highly effective means of instilling social and educational values such as physical and moral courage, loyalty, teamwork, fairness and the capacity to accept defeat while teaching boys how both to obey and to command'.[93] For instance, the Boys' Brigade promoted association football among its Irish members, with teams attached to its companies in Belfast and Dublin. 'In providing football, the leaders were attracted by the values attributed to playing the game, but they were also motivated to acquire a supervisory role over the leisure time of their members', notes Brendan Power.[94] The Fianna's leaders also wished to instil these values, but also wanted to ensure the availability of leisure activities with an Irish nationalist flavour. Thus, the Fianna promoted physical culture through games nights and sports days. Some *sluaighte*, such as one in Wexford town, even had their own hurling teams.[95] A hurling league for Fianna members in Dublin was formed in early 1914.[96]

The prominent role of theatre in the Irish literary revival as well as the importance of music in traditional Irish culture ensured that Fianna members with the requisite talent and inclination had many opportunities to display their dramatic and musical abilities. A Dublin-based drama group called the Fianna Players, which at least one member deemed 'successful', performed a number of Irish plays including Padraic Colum's *The Saxon Shilling*.[97] Colum's play had been rejected by the Irish National Theatre Society, a forerunner of the Abbey Theatre, on the grounds that it was merely anti-military recruitment propaganda, but this theme suited the Fianna Players because it chimed with the promise made by Fianna members not to join Britain's armed forces.[98] Elsewhere, Sluagh John McHale in Tuam, County Galway, held a dramatic class and Belfast Fianna members performed in two plays at their annual concert in 1914.[99]

The Fianna also lent their talents to fundraising events, such as the Lang Benefit Concert held in Dublin in early 1915 at which members were among the performers of mainly Irish songs, dances, recitations and sketches. Some of the songs performed at this concert referenced Germany at a time when it was at war with Britain. For instance, the concert programme featured the German patriotic song, 'Die Wacht am Rein' ('The Watch/Guard on the Rhine'), as well as two new songs, 'Brit-Huns' and 'Ireland to Germany', written by Countess Markievicz and poet Maeve Cavanagh, respectively.[100] Showing sympathy for Germany was a way of protesting against Ireland's political union with Britain.

The Fianna hall on Camden Street and the meeting rooms of other *sluaighte* served as the venues for céilís and other social occasions 'at which nothing but Irish songs and dances were permitted'. According to Sean Prendergast, hosting such events helped the Fianna to gain 'friends among even those older than ourselves, and among the cailíní [girls]'.[101] Céilís provided the perfect opportunity to promote Irish culture while fostering sociability. These events also raised much needed funds for the youth group.

In the aftermath of Easter Week 1916, Cork Fianna members Seamus Courtney and Sean Healy decided to organise a concert 'to revive the spirit of the people and to change their apathetic attitude'. Among the songs performed was 'The wearing of the green'. As Bridie Conway sang the line 'High above their shining weapons hung their own beloved green', she turned to the wings from where Fianna member 'Liam Óg O'Callaghan marched on to the stage carrying a green flag with harp' escorted by a two-man Fianna guard of honour 'with rifles and bayonets at the slope, and in full uniform'. This apparently sent the audience 'absolutely mad with enthusiasm'. As there were police detectives present, the organisers convinced girls to smuggle the rifles in and out of the hall, presumably under their skirts. Healy and O'Callaghan continued to take pride in the success of this spirit-raising event years later.[102]

Like their adult counterparts in the nationalist movement, the Fianna formed marching bands, which not only provided members with a sociable recreational activity but also added to the pageantry and popular appeal of nationalist events such as public processions. 'Irish marching bands emerged amid an international "brass band movement" during the middle and late nineteenth century', explains John Borgonovo. 'From the late eighteenth century, amateur, non-élite musical groups had become increasingly common in Britain and Ireland, and were associated with a steady growth of military, church and village bands.'[103] In Ireland, such bands were often harnessed to political causes as exemplified by bands associated with the Fianna and with companies of the Irish Volunteers. For instance, Sluagh Emmet on Dublin's north-side had its own bugle band.[104]

Brian Callender is credited with establishing the Fianna Pipers, a Dublin-based war pipe band, which was in existence by early 1911, though the band's first incarnation appears to have petered out.[105] In 1914, twelve Fianna members 'were sent to a Mr McKenzie in Bolton Street to learn the war pipes', but after about six months of lessons this number dwindled to three: William Christian, Tommy Crimmins and

Eddie Murray. With the leadership of Thomas O'Donoghue and the addition of three drummers and several more pipers, the band staged a revival in 1915 and went on to compete in that year's Oireachtas, an annual Gaelic cultural festival.[106]

The Fianna Pipers so impressed members of the Thomas Francis Meagher Sluagh on a visit to Dublin in 1915 that the boys decided to form their own band when they returned home to Waterford. With the help of the Irish National Foresters' Pipers' Band and the driving force of Thomas Walsh, the Waterford Fianna had developed 'a well-trained pipers' band of twelve before Easter 1916'.[107] James Nolan recalled that 'a Fianna pipers' band was started' in Waterford in 1917, but this may have been a revival of the band after the disarray caused by the Easter Rising.[108] Dr Vincent White, a Sinn Féin candidate in the Waterford by-election and general election of 1918, praised the Waterford Fianna band for its 'valiant work for us at every public function held under Sinn Féin auspices for years'.[109]

Fianna involvement in bands was evident elsewhere in Ireland. Joseph O'Shea reported that Tomás Mac Curtain tried to form a Fianna band in Cork, 'but it fell through'.[110] Members of the Fianna in that city later joined the Brian Boru Pipers Band, which was associated with the Irish Volunteers and whose members claimed to be 'the first kilted band in the country'.[111]

Links between pipe bands and nationalist militias were also apparent in Dublin where members of the Fianna Pipers saw themselves as soldiers as well as musicians. William Christian recalled:

> We were a special section of the Fianna and we were not satisfied being just members of the band, so we made a rule that all members of the band over 18 years of age should join a company [of the Irish Volunteers] and we scattered ourselves among the different battalions not intentionally, it just worked out that way.[112]

O'Donoghue later became a founding member of the Fintan Lalor Pipers, which were associated with the Irish Citizen Army.[113]

The Fianna were not the only youth group of the period that sought to build up its members physically through athletics and sport, and form bands as part of the range of activities on offer, but what each organisation sought to achieve through such activities could differ. Elsewhere, the London Regiment of the Jewish Lads' Brigade held athletic contests in which boys competed in running and field events, included gymnastics in its public displays, and formed a brass band, a drum and fife band and a bugle band.[114] While the Fianna used the Irish language, hurling and pipe bands to assert their Irish national identity in the face of British cultural assimilation, the Jewish Lads' Brigade focused on sportsmanship because it 'was seen as playing a key role in creating a more anglicized Jew'.[115] The Fianna and the Jewish Lads' Brigade thus had very different attitudes towards the issue of assimilation. The Fianna wanted to assert the separateness of Irish culture as part of the nationalist campaign for independence from Britain whereas the Jewish Lads' Brigade wanted its members, who were 'Russian and Polish immigrant Jewish boys', to assimilate into British culture while retaining their religious heritage.[116]

SOCIAL CONTACTS AND NATIONALIST NETWORKING

An important part of membership in any youth group is the opportunity it provides for social contact. 'Whatever our shortcomings in worldly wealth or influence [these] were amply counter-balanced by the quality and value of friendships made and reciprocated', noted Sean Prendergast in reference to Fianna membership.[117] He appears to be referring to friendships between individual Fianna members as well as to those between Fianna members and adults in the advanced nationalist movement.

Informal social contacts could be as important as the Fianna's formal education and training initiatives and print propaganda in influencing the minds of the organisation's young members. For instance, Garry Holohan often spent weekends at Bulmer Hobson's cottage at Balroddery near Tallaght, County Dublin, with Hobson and fellow Fianna members Pádraic Ó Riain and Frank Reynolds. It was during these weekends away that Holohan first read Ethna Carbery's poetry, later reporting that:

> I can assure you they [Carbery's poems] did much to fan the fires of patriotism to white heat. From now on my outlook on life was completely changed. The Fianna was no longer a mere pastime or social function. It became a sacred duty, and I started to bend my every effort towards the freeing of Ireland. No task was too great or time too long.[118]

Carbery herself had influenced Hobson in his youth, helping to lay the foundations for his future career as a nationalist.[119]

Thus, joining the Fianna enabled members to become part of a nationalist social network of like-minded individuals. Older members were often recruited into another nationalist network: the Irish Republican Brotherhood (IRB), a secret society committed to the establishment of an Irish republic through the use of physical force if necessary. The IRB served a social as well as a political function for members. The Fianna's increasingly militant stance coincided with recruitment of selected senior members into the IRB when they had reached the age of seventeen. Pádraic Ó Riain and Con Colbert joined at an early stage. Eamon Martin and Patrick Ward became members in 1911, while Liam Mellows, Michael Lonergan and Garry Holohan were sworn in the following year.[120] In 1912, Hobson formed a special Fianna circle of the IRB, following his election as the Dublin centre of the secret society. This new circle was known as the John Mitchel Literary and Debating Society, with Colbert as its head. The membership included Ó Riain, Martin, Lonergan, Holohan, Sean Heuston, Desmond Ryan and the Mellows brothers, Liam and Barney.[121] Martin claimed that by 1913 practically every senior Fianna officer throughout the country had become a member of the IRB. The annual Fianna *ard-fheis* often served to endorse decisions already made at meetings of the Fianna circle of the IRB held the night before.[122]

An alternative social network revolved around Markievicz who disapproved of secret societies like the IRB.[123] A small group of Fianna members regularly gathered at her home on Leinster Road in Rathmines in Dublin and became known as 'Madam's Boy's' or 'the Surrey House clique'. According to Seamus Pounch, the group consisted of himself, Patsy O'Connor, Harry Walpole, Jack Shallow, Eddie Murray and Andy Dunne.[124] Some of these boys – Walpole, Shallow, O'Connor and Pounch himself – featured in a short story by Percy Reynolds about a group of Fianna members who went Christmas carolling in Rathmines in 1914 only to be arrested as alleged German spies.[125] Although Pounch chose not to join the IRB on conscientious grounds, he was no less militaristic than his Fianna colleagues who belonged to the secret society. He served at Jacob's Biscuit Factory during the Easter Rising, later recalling that after the surrender 'I dumped my gun with the rest and it was the saddest parting I can remember'.[126]

Brimming with books and works of art, Surrey House was a busy meeting place for Markievicz's various associates, which included suffragettes, Sinn Féiners, labour activists and many young members of *An Chéad Sluagh*. 'Seldom a night passed without its quota of Fianna boys showing up for a sing-song or other form of revelry', recalled Sean

Prendergast, who once stayed at the house while convalescing from an illness. Apparently, the neighbours were not amused by such comings and goings: 'It was said that the house, and those who frequented it, were looked upon with deep disgust and condemnation by the inhabitants of that most law-abiding and respectable locality … of Rawthmines.'[127] 'Rawthmines' was Prendergast's way of denoting the posh accent associated with the wealthier inhabitants of Rathmines at the time.

ADOLESCENT MAYHEM

As many members of the Fianna were adolescents, it is unsurprising that they engaged in certain kinds of behaviour associated with that period of life. Historians have debated how far back an awareness of adolescence can be traced, with some citing 'a number of institutions, nearly all of them male, that fulfilled in the [more distant] past at least some of the functions – mainly violence and mayhem – that we now attribute to adolescence'.[128] Such institutions served to channel such violence and mayhem, helping not only to reinforce order but also to propose alternatives to the existing order.[129] The Fianna promoted order through its provision of training, education and discipline for nationalist youth, but in advocating a new political order in Ireland many members, particularly adolescents, experienced both violence and mayhem during the years of the Irish Revolution.

Mayhem ranged from the boys playing 'rude tricks' on Markievicz's beloved dog Poppit or the Holohan brothers, Paddy and Garry, beating each other up on the floor of their *sluagh*'s meeting rooms to aggressive behaviour towards the Royal Irish Constabulary and attacks on Baden-Powell Boy Scouts or members of the Boys' Brigade who carried Union Jacks.[130] For instance, during a raid on a boy scout camp in Crumlin, the Fianna captured flags and military equipment and ordered English scouts back home to Liverpool.[131] Even Fianna girls joined in the mayhem. In the summer of 1913, some British soldiers were marching back to Dublin after manoeuvres in counties Carlow and Wicklow when they approached Markievicz's cottage in the Dublin Mountains and asked the Belfast Fianna girls staying there to fill their canteens with water. Instead, the girls stuffed the canteens with anti-enlistment leaflets and gave them back to the thirsty soldiers. 'The soldiers must have been greatly astonished when they opened the lids to take a drink and found something not to their taste at all', quipped Liam Mellows in his account of the incident.[132] But these were just mere youthful hijinks in comparison to what was to come. Between 1916 and 1923, in particular, many Fianna members experienced violence first-hand either as witnesses, victims or perpetrators.[133]

NOTES

1 Sean Prendergast, witness statement, 3 Nov. 1952 (MA, BMH, WS 755).
2 Sean Healy and Liam Ó Callaghan, joint witness statement, 4 Oct. 1947 (MA, BMH, WS 47). Whitsuntide refers to the period around Whit Sunday, the seventh Sunday after Easter.
3 *Ibid.*
4 George Hurley, witness statement, 15 July 1957 (MA, BMH, WS 1,630).
5 Charles Meaney, witness statement, 11 June 1957 (MA, BMH, WS 1,631).
6 Andrew Donson, *Youth in the Fatherless Land* (Cambridge, MA: Harvard University Press, 2010), p. 4.
7 Richard A. Smith, 'Boys' Brigade' in John Cannon (ed.), *The Oxford Companion to British History* (Oxford: Oxford University Press, 1997), p. 119.
8 Paul Wilkinson, 'English youth movements, 1908–30', *Journal of Contemporary History*, 4:2 (Apr. 1969), p. 5; Richard A. Voeltz, '"…A good Jew and a good Englishman": The Jewish Lads' Brigade, 1894–1922', *Journal of Contemporary History*, 23:1 (Jan. 1988), p. 122.
9 Richard A. Smith, 'Boy Scouts' in Cannon (ed.), *Oxford Companion*, p. 119.
10 Donson, *Youth in the Fatherless Land*, p. 35.
11 John R. Gillis, 'Conformity and rebellion: Contrasting styles of English and German youth, 1900–33', *History of Education Quarterly*, 13:3 (1973), p. 250.
12 Donson, *Youth in the Fatherless Land*, p. 35.
13 *Ibid.*
14 One of the Fianna, 'Na Fianna Éireann (National Boys' Brigade)', *B na hÉ*, Sept. 1909, pp. 8–9.
15 Eamon Martin, witness statement, 1 Oct. 1951 (MA, BMH, WS 591); Pádraic Ó Riain (ed.), *Fianna Handbook* (Dublin: Central Council of Na Fianna Éireann, 1914), p. 18.
16 Eamon Martin, witness statement, 1 Oct. 1951 (MA, BMH, WS 591).
17 Ó Riain, *Fianna Handbook*, pp. 13–20.
18 'Fianna na h-Éireann', *B na hÉ*, Feb. 1910, p. 7.
19 Ó Riain, *Fianna Handbook*, pp. 13–21.
20 For tracking, see 'Boy Scouts', *IV*, 10 Oct. 1914, p. 16. *Irish Volunteer* also published articles on dispatch carrying (31 Oct. 1914, p. 16), map making (21 Nov. 1914, pp. 15–16) and field sketching (28 Nov. 1914, p. 15).

21 Healy and O'Callaghan, witness statement, 4 Oct. 1947 (MA, BMH, WS 47).
22 The 1914 *Fianna Handbook* advised *sluaighte* to find a local doctor to provide first aid instruction (p. 18). For instance, in Cork Dr D. J. O'Sullivan taught first aid to the Fianna (Healy and O'Callaghan, witness statement, 4 Oct. 1947 (MA, BMH, WS 47)).
23 Nora Connolly O'Brien, witness statement, 21 July 1949 (MA, BMH, WS 286).
24 James Fulham, witness statement, 3 Jan. 1952 (MA, BMH, WS 630).
25 Seamus Mac Caisin, witness statement, 8 June 1947 (MA, BMH, WS 8).
26 Sean Kennedy, witness statement, 1 May 1953 (MA, BMH, WS 842).
27 Thomas O'Donoghue, witness statement, n.d. (MA, BMH, WS 1,666).
28 Rosamond Jacob, diary entry, 1 Nov. 1917, quoted in Leeann Lane, *Rosamond Jacob: Third Person Singular* (Dublin: UCD Press, 2010), p. 122.
29 Rosamond Jacob, diary entry, 30 July 1911, quoted in Lane, *Rosamond Jacob*, p. 64.
30 Lane, *Rosamond Jacob*, p. 122.
31 Seamus Mac Caisin, witness statement, 8 June 1947 (MA, BMH, WS 8); Seamus Pounch, witness statement, 15 June 1949 (MA, BMH, WS 267).
32 Seamus Kavanagh, witness statement, 9 Sept. 1957 (MA, BMH, WS 1,670).
33 'Fianna na h-Éireann', *B na hÉ*, Mar. 1910, p. 8; Liam Mellows, 'The Irish Boy Scouts by an Irish Volunteer officer – Chapter I' (MA, Colonel Dan Bryan Collection, CD 129/1).
34 'Boy Scouts organising notes', *IV*, 7 Mar. 1914, p. 16.
35 Healy and O'Callaghan, witness statement, 4 Oct. 1947 (MA, BMH, WS 47).
36 Sean Prendergast, witness statement, 3 Nov. 1952 (MA, BMH, WS 755).
37 Liam Mellows, 'The Irish Boy Scouts by an Irish Volunteer officer – Chapter V' (MA, BMH, Colonel Dan Bryan Collection, CD129/1).
38 Sean Prendergast, witness statement, 3 Nov. 1952 (MA, BMH, WS 755).
39 One of the Fianna, 'Na Fianna Éireann (National Boys' Brigade)', *B na hÉ*, Sept. 1909, p. 9.
40 'Na Fianna Éireann', *B na hÉ*, [July or Aug.?] 1910, p. 10.
41 Sean Prendergast, witness statement, 3 Nov. 1952 (MA, BMH, WS 755).
42 Nora Connolly O'Brien, witness statement, 21 July 1949 (MA, BMH, WS 286).
43 Healy and O'Callaghan, witness statement, 4 Oct. 1947 (MA, BMH, WS 47).
44 Joseph O'Shea, witness statement, n.d. (MA, BMH, WS 21).
45 'Na Fianna Éireann', *B na hÉ*, Nov. 1910, p. 11.

46 Willie Nelson, 'Na Fianna Éireann', *IV*, 26 June 1915, p. 8.
47 Liam Mellows, 'The Irish Boy Scouts by an Irish Volunteer officer – Chapter VII' (MA, BMH, Colonel Dan Bryan Collection, CD129/1).
48 Interment record for Patrick O'Connor, died 15 June 1915, Glasnevin Cemetery, available from www.glasnevintrust.ie/geneaology/ (accessed 22 Mar. 2014).
49 'Fianna roll of honour' in Robert Holland, *A Short History of Fianna Éireann*, [c. 1981], pp. 25–6 (NLI, MS 35,455/3/12A). Na Fianna Éireann produced this photocopied booklet, which features Holland's memoir written in 1949.
50 Jason Walsh-McLean, 'A headstone for Patsy O'Connor: Fianna scout and forgotten Lockout martyr', *Saothar* 41 (2016), pp. 294–7.
51 'Sad drowning accident at the Three Rock Mountain', *FJ*, 29 July 1913; Liam Mellows, 'The Irish Boy Scouts by an Irish Volunteer officer – Chapter IV' (MA, BMH, Colonel Dan Bryan Collection, CD129/1); 'Sandyford drowning tragedy; National Boy Scouts honoured', *FJ*, 12 Aug. 1913. Also see Eamon Murphy, 'Fianna Éireann and Three Rock Mountain', 14 Jan. 2014, available at https://fiannaeireannhistory.wordpress.com/2014/01/14/wm_2235-jpg/ (accessed 15 Feb. 2017).
52 Liam Mellows, 'The Irish Boy Scouts by an Irish Volunteer officer – Chapter IV' (MA, BMH, Colonel Dan Bryan Collection, CD129/1).
53 Richard A. Smith, 'Girl Guides' in Cannon (ed.), *Oxford Companion*, p. 417.
54 Bulmer Hobson, *Ireland Yesterday and Tomorrow* (Tralee: Anvil Books, 1968), p. 45. IRB men also served as stewards at this meeting.
55 Joseph O'Shea, witness statement, n.d. (MA, BMH, WS 21); Healy and O'Callaghan, joint witness statement, 4 Oct. 1947 (MA, BMH, WS 47); James A. Busby, witness statement, 6 June 1957 (MA, BMH, WS 1,628).
56 See Neal Garnham, 'Manchester martyrs' in S. J. Connolly (ed.), *The Oxford Companion to Irish History* (Oxford: Oxford University Press, 1999), p. 343.
57 Healy and O'Callaghan, witness statement, 4 Oct. 1947 (MA, BMH, WS 47); Pádraic Ó Riain, 'Na Fianna Éireann', *IF*, Dec. 1911, p. 6.
58 Elaine Sisson, *Pearse's Patriots* (Cork: Cork University Press, 2005), p. 113.
59 Róisín Ní Ghairbhí and Eugene McNulty (eds), *Patrick Pearse: Collected Plays* (Dublin: Irish Academic Press, 2013), p. 18; 'Touching the St Enda's Fete', *An Macaomh*, May 1913, p. 46.
60 'Boy Scouts organising notes', *IV*, 7 Mar. 1914, pp. 8, 16.
61 'Boy Scouts', *IV*, 24 Oct. 1914, p. 16.

62 'National boy scouts', *IV*, 21 Nov. 1914, p. 15.
63 Willie Nelson, 'Na Fianna Éireann', *IV*, 19 Dec. 1914, p. 8.
64 J. J. O'Connell, 'Memoir of the Irish Volunteers, 1914–16, 1917', ed. Daithí Ó Corráin in *Analecta Hibernica*, 47 (2016), p. 21. During a brief spell living in the United States, O'Connell had 'served in the 69th (New York Irish) Regiment from 1912 to 1914' (Ó Corráin, 'Introduction' to O'Connell, 'Memoir of the Irish Volunteers, 1914–16, 1917', p. 4).
65 Willie Nelson, 'Na Fianna Éireann', *IV*, 30 Jan. 1915, p. 8.
66 Willie Nelson, 'Na Fianna Éireann', *IV*, 6 Feb. 1915, p. 8.
67 Examples of Fianna members who joined the British forces during the First World War are discussed in chapter 3.
68 Anne Summers, 'Scouts, guides and VADs: A note in reply to Allen Warren', *English Historical Review*, 102:405 (Oct. 1987), p. 944.
69 *Ibid.*, pp. 944–6.
70 Elizabeth Heineman, 'Gender identity in the Wandervogel movement', *German Studies Review*, 12:2 (May 1989), p. 260.
71 J. Anthony Gaughan, *Scouting in Ireland* (Dublin: Kingdom Books, 2006), p. 11.
72 *Ibid.*, pp. 10–11.
73 Richard A. Voeltz, 'The antidote to "Khaki Fever"? The expansion of the British Girl Guides during the First World War', *Journal of Contemporary History*, 27:4 (Oct. 1992), pp. 629–30.
74 Heineman, 'Gender identity in the Wandervogel movement', p. 260.
75 James A. Busby, witness statement, 6 June 1957 (MA, BMH, WS 1,628); George Hurley, witness statement, 15 July 1957 (MA, BMH, WS 1,630).
76 Sean Prendergast, witness statement, 3 Nov. 1952 (MA, BMH, WS 755).
77 The Fianna's increasing involvement in propagandist and military activities during phases two and three will be discussed in more detail in Chapters 7 and 8.
78 Report of Fianna Éireann Training Camp held at Loughlinstown, 10–17 Sept. 1921 (MA, Collins Collection, A/0631, Group IX, Fianna Éireann, Item 1).
79 *Ibid.*
80 'Editorial', *Fianna*, June 1922, p. 3. The Fáinne is a pin symbolising proficiency in the Irish language.
81 One of the Fianna, 'Na Fianna Éireann (National Boys' Brigade)', *B na hÉ*, Oct. 1909, p. 8.
82 One of the Fianna, 'Fianna na h-Éireann', *B na hÉ*, Dec. 1909, p. 9.
83 This will be discussed in the next chapter.
84 Ruaidhri, 'Na Fianna Éireann', *B na hÉ*, Jan. 1911, p. 13.
85 Eamon Martin, witness statement, 1 Oct. 1951 (MA, BMH, WS 591).

86 Ó Riain, *Fianna Handbook*, p. 21.
87 'Na Fianna Éireann', *IF*, June 1914, p. 2.
88 Pádraic Ó Riain, 'Na Fianna Éireann', *IF*, May 1914, p. 6. The first instalment of the series appeared the following month: Lucan, 'An outline of Irish history from the Volunteers to Emmet', *IF*, June 1914, p. 2.
89 Ó Riain, *Fianna Handbook*, pp. 19, 21.
90 One of the Fianna, 'Na Fianna Éireann (National Boys' Brigade)', *B na hÉ*, Oct. 1909, pp. 8–9.
91 Oscar, 'Na Fianna Éireann', *IF*, Sept. 1911, p. 7.
92 Ó Riain, *Fianna Handbook*, pp. 18–21.
93 Brendan Power, 'The functions of association football in the Boys' Brigade in Ireland, 1888–1914' in Leeann Lane and William Murphy (eds), *Leisure and the Irish in the Nineteenth Century* (Liverpool: Liverpool University Press, 2016), p. 43.
94 Power, 'The functions of association football in the Boys' Brigade in Ireland, 1888–1914', p. 51.
95 Liam Ó Maoil Íosa [Liam Mellows], 'Boy Scouts organising notes', *IV*, 7 Feb. 1914, p. 14.
96 'Boy Scouts organising notes', *IV*, 14 Feb. 1914, p. 16. The teams in the league were: Éire Óg Pipers, Sluaighte Willie Nelson and William Orr, Clann na bhFiann, Clann Ruadhraigh and Wolfe Tone ('Boy Scouts organising notes', *IV*, 7 Mar. 1914, p. 16). For a wider discussion of Irish youth and sport in the early twentieth century, see Richard McElligott, '"A youth tainted with the deadly poison of Anglicism"? Sport and childhood in the Irish independence period' in Ciara Boylan and Ciara Gallagher (eds), *Constructions of the Irish Child in the Independence Period* (Basingstoke: Palgrave Macmillan, 2018), pp. 279–305.
97 Seamus Mac Caisin, witness statement, 8 June 1947 (MA, BMH, WS 8). Mac Caisin lists the members of the group as: himself, Percy Reynolds, Con Colbert, Theo Fitzgerald, Sean (Jack?) Shallow, [?] MacGowan, Andy Dunne, Harry Walpole and Brian Callendar as well as Countess Markievicz and Helena Molony.
98 Robert Welch (ed.), *The Concise Oxford Companion to Irish Literature* (Oxford: Oxford University Press, 2000), pp. 64–5.
99 Liam Ó Maoil Íosa [Liam Mellows], 'Boy Scouts organising notes', *IV*, 7 Feb. 1914, p. 14; 'Boy Scouts organising notes', *IV*, 28 Mar. 1914, p. 9.
100 Photocopy of Lang Benefit Concert Programme (MA, BMH, James FitzGerald Collection, CD 91/5).
101 Sean Prendergast, witness statement, 3 Nov. 1952 (MA, BMH, WS 755).
102 Healy and O'Callaghan, witness statement, 4 Oct. 1947 (MA, BMH, WS 47).

103 John Borgonovo, 'Politics as leisure: Brass bands in Cork, 1845–1918' in Lane and Murphy (eds), *Leisure and the Irish in the Nineteenth Century*, p. 24.
104 Sean Prendergast, witness statement, 3 Nov. 1952 (MA, BMH, WS 755).
105 'Piobairi na bhFiann (Fianna War Pipe Band)', *B na hÉ*, Feb. 1911, p. 5; Seamus Mac Caisin, witness statement, 8 June 1947 (MA, BMH, WS 8); Sean Prendergast, witness statement, 3 Nov. 1952 (MA, BMH, WS 755); Thomas O'Donoghue, witness statement, n.d. (MA, BMH, WS 1,666). See also William Christian, witness statement, 5 Feb. 1952 (MA, BMH, WS 646); Seamus Kavanagh, witness statement, 9 Sept. 1957 (MA, BMH, WS 1,670). Over the years, members of this band included Brian Callender, Percy Reynolds, Jack Reynolds, Barney Murphy, Peadar Kearney, Thomas O'Donoghue, Tommy Crimmins, Tony O'Carroll, William (Billy) Christian, Eddie Murray, Jack Murphy, Joe Coffey, Jack and Paddy Norris, Andy Dunne and Billy 'Bully' Roberts.
106 William Christian, witness statement, 5 Feb. 1952 (MA, BMH, WS 646).
107 Patrick Hearne, witness statement, 18 Aug. 1958 (MA, BMH, WS 1,742).
108 James Nolan, witness statement, 10 March 1956 (MA, BMH, WS 1,369).
109 Dr Vincent White, witness statement, Dec. 1958 (MA, BMH, WS 1,764).
110 Joseph O'Shea, witness statement, n.d. (MA, BMH, WS 21).
111 James A. Busby, witness statement, 6 June 1957 (MA, BMH, WS 1,628); Borgonovo, 'Politics as Leisure: Brass bands in Cork', p. 38.
112 William Christian, witness statement, 5 Feb. 1952 (MA, BMH, WS 646).
113 Thomas O'Donoghue, witness statement, n.d. (MA, BMH, WS 1,666).
114 Voeltz, '"…A good Jew and a good Englishman": The Jewish Lads' Brigade, 1894–1922', pp. 122–3.
115 *Ibid.*, p. 123.
116 *Ibid.*, p. 125.
117 Sean Prendergast, witness statement, 3 Nov. 1952 (MA, BMH, WS 755).
118 Garry Holohan, witness statement, 7 Dec. 1949 (MA, BMH, WS 328).
119 Hobson, *Ireland*, pp. 2–3.
120 Eamon Martin, witness statement, 1 Oct. 1951 (MA, BMH, WS 591); Patrick Ward, witness statement, 30 Mar. 1955 (MA, BMH, WS 1,140); Garry Holohan, witness statement, 7 Dec. 1949 (MA, BMH, WS 328).
121 Bulmer Hobson, 'The IRB and the Fianna' in F. X. Martin (ed.), *The Irish Volunteers, 1913–1915: Recollections and Documents* (Dublin: James Duffy, 1963), p. 21.
122 Eamon Martin, witness statement, 1 Oct. 1951 (MA, BMH, WS 591).
123 Jacqueline Van Voris, *Constance de Markievicz in the Cause of Ireland* (Amherst, MA: University of Massachusetts Press, 1967), pp. 89–90.
124 Seamus Pounch, witness statement, 15 June 1949 (MA, BMH, WS 267).

125 A. P. H. R. [Percy Reynolds], 'The Christmas Carol Singers', *Nodlaig na bhFiann*, Dec. 1914, pp. 6–8.
126 Seamus Pounch, witness statement, 15 June 1949 (MA, BMH, WS 267).
127 Sean Prendergast, witness statement, 3 Nov. 1952 (MA, BMH, WS 755).
128 Colin Heywood, *A History of Childhood* (Cambridge: Polity Press, 2005), p. 28.
129 Natalie Zemon Davis, 'The reasons of misrule: Youth groups and charivaris in sixteenth-century France', *Past and Present*, 50 (1971), p. 74.
130 Sean Prendergast, witness statement, 3 Nov. 1952 (MA, BMH, WS 755); Elizabeth Colbert, witness statement, 8 June 1953 (MA, BMH, WS 856); Garry Holohan, witness statement, 7 Dec. 1949 (MA, BMH, WS 328).
131 Seamus Pounch, witness statement, 15 June 1949 (MA, BMH, WS 267).
132 Liam Mellows, 'The Irish Boy Scouts by an Irish Volunteer officer – Chapter IV' (MA, BMH, Colonel Dan Bryan Collection, CD129/1).
133 The involvement of the Fianna in military action during this period will be discussed in chapter 8.

7 Moulding minds and marketing martyrdom

> The inheritance of chivalry is with us still – a motherland to serve, a fair country to be freed. For this we shall need all the chivalry of the Irish heart, all the training and manhood of the Irish body, all the service, devotion, and self-sacrifice of our boys and young men. The true knight is he who keeps the boy's heart in the trained body of the man.[1]

Apprentice compositor Liam O'Brien joined the Emmet branch of the Fianna in 1910. While he was attending a weekend camp at Belcamp Park, Countess Markievicz informed him that she possessed a small letterpress printing machine with some type which could be used to produce 'propagandist literature for the Fianna' and recruited him for the job.[2] The Fianna's propagandist literature would disseminate messages like the one contained in the previous quotation from Roger Casement. By September 1911, O'Brien had come to the attention of the Dublin Metropolitan Police who noted that he took 'a great interest in the promotion of the Sinn Féin propaganda' and 'although very young is reputed to hold extreme political views'.[3] As a result of his propagandist work for Markievicz, O'Brien was introduced to James Connolly in 1915 and began working for him, helping to produce and print the *Worker's Republic* newspaper. A year later, O'Brien, by then a member of the Irish Volunteers, set the type and printed the 1916 Proclamation.[4] O'Brien's example demonstrates how adults recruited and utilised youth within the advanced Irish nationalist movement. Members of the Fianna like O'Brien not only helped to create and distribute nationalist print propaganda such as posters, leaflets and newspapers but were also the target of propagandist messages designed to influence their personal and political philosophies and by extension their actions.

For the purposes of this chapter, the term 'propaganda' refers to written material intended to influence the attitude and opinion of readers.[5]

As members of the Fianna tended to come from families with advanced nationalist and/or republican views, Fianna propaganda was more likely to reinforce or intensify an existing nationalist sentiment rather than convert readers to nationalism. In addition, much of the youth-oriented material under consideration was designed to provide an Irish nationalist alternative to popular British publications, such as Robert Baden-Powell's *Scouting for Boys* (1908) and periodicals like the *Boy's Own Paper*, by subverting the conventions of such literature.[6]

A VOLUNTEER DISTRIBUTION FORCE

From an early stage, the Fianna played a prominent role in campaigning against Irish recruitment into the British army. The Boer War (1899–1902) had heightened the issue of military recruitment as a source of nationalist anxiety. Advanced Irish nationalists supported the Boers in this colonial war and took particular pride in the Irish brigade, which had been raised in the Transvaal in September 1899 to fight alongside them. By the early twentieth century, 'the anti-recruitment campaign … had a permanent place on the nationalist agenda', with advanced nationalist organisations such as Inghinidhe na hÉireann (Daughters of Erin) and the three groups that amalgamated as Sinn Féin (Cumann na nGaedheal, the National Council and Bulmer Hobson's Dungannon Clubs) actively crusading against Irish enlistment in the British army.[7] Markievicz and Hobson were closely connected to these organisations, which supported Arthur Griffith's Sinn Féin policy of Irish self-reliance. Thus, it is not surprising that in October 1909, shortly after the Fianna's inception, the police reported that the pair hoped their new youth group would 'advance the campaign against enlistment in the army'.[8]

Markievicz and her friend Helena Molony recognised from an early stage that boys like Liam O'Brien were an invaluable volunteer force for spreading advanced nationalist propaganda, especially anti-recruitment literature. At the pair's request, Fianna boys camping at Belcamp Park placarded the surrounding area with leaflets urging Irishmen not to join the police or the British armed forces. Fianna member Dónal O'Hannigan, whose older brother Donnchadh managed the short-lived market gardening enterprise at the house, recalled:

> On many occasions all the members of the RIC of Santry and Raheny Stations spent several hours nightly trying to catch us in the act of posting up the leaflets, leaving only the Orderly in the

Barracks. They would return to find the windows and doors of the barracks plastered with our literature.⁹

A local police sergeant stopped Markievicz and Molony on the road one day to discuss the problem. According to their friend Sydney Czira, 'Helena, pretending to sympathise with his difficulties, clapped him on the back as she was leaving him, at the same time sticking on a notice which appealed to young Irishmen not to join the British Armed Forces or Police'.¹⁰ It would seem that the pair never missed an opportunity to spread their message – or have a laugh.

Fianna members also participated in similar propagandist activities elsewhere in the country. In Cork, Fianna boys not only pasted up anti-recruiting posters and 'distributed handbills advising men not to join the British army' but also created disturbances at British army recruitment meetings.¹¹ For instance, at the instigation of three Gaelic Leaguers, a group of Fianna boys threw eggs at the screen of the Palace Theatre during the showing of a British military recruitment film around 1912–13; the boys were disappointed that they were unable to find any rotten eggs to use.¹² In addition to protesting against military recruitment, Cork Fianna members regularly 'pasted up posters concerning meetings, concerts and public parades' and tore down 'enemy' posters and proclamations, presumably material emanating from the British government and its supporters in Ireland.¹³

The Fianna were involved in the distribution of a variety of nationalist print propaganda. In 1910–14, Dublin members folded and stamped copies of the separatist, republican paper *Irish Freedom* and then took them to the post office so the paper could be dispatched around the country.¹⁴ They also circulated Roger Casement's 1913 pamphlet *Ireland, Germany and the next war*, which discussed the approaching First World War and its implications for Ireland.¹⁵ Fianna members also distributed Sinn Féin literature and posters during the 1918 general election campaign.¹⁶ Such activities continued during the War of Independence. For instance, Thomas O'Connor, who belonged to the Fianna in Tralee, recalled that 'one of my last actions before the Truce was to paste up around the town printed posters setting out the names of RIC men and Black and Tans who had been sentenced to be shot by the IRA for their activities against the IRA and people generally'.¹⁷ Thus, the Fianna proved instrumental in helping their adult colleagues to disseminate print propaganda during the years of the Irish Revolution, while at the same time gaining practical hands-on experience that enabled them to produce and circulate their own publications.

FIANNA PRINT PROPAGANDA

From its inception in 1909 up until the 1916 Easter Rising, the official Fianna organisation, as well as individual members, published propaganda aimed mainly at boys in their pre-teen and teen years in advanced nationalist newspapers, such as *Bean na hÉireann* (1908–11), *Irish Freedom* (1910–14), the *Irish Volunteer* (1914–16) and *Fianna* (1915–16), as well as in the first *Fianna Handbook* (1914) and the 1914 Christmas publication *Nodlaig na bhFiann*. There appears to have been a lull in Fianna publications during the period between the Rising and the establishment of the Irish Free State because the youth organisation was preoccupied with re-grouping in the wake of the 1916 rebellion and then making an active contribution to the War of Independence. In addition, many of the adult publications that had published Fianna material prior to 1916 were associated with Hobson, who found himself banished to the side lines of the nationalist movement as a result of his opposition to the insurrection. After the Rising, he worked initially in book publishing before becoming a civil servant in the new Irish Free State. Without the Hobson connection, the Fianna may have found it difficult to secure a regular outlet in adult advanced nationalist newspapers, which faced the challenge of censorship by the British government during the years of the Great War and subsequent Irish War of Independence.[18] From about 1922 onwards, propagandist publications, such as a revived version of the *Fianna* paper, souvenir programmes from commemorative events and a new edition of the *Fianna Handbook* (1924), began to appear again.

Although the newspapers *Bean na hÉireann*, *Irish Freedom* and the *Irish Volunteer* were primarily aimed at an adult audience, they provided a forum for Na Fianna Éireann to report its news and views.[19] Hobson was associated with all of these papers as a writer, editor or manager. He and Markievicz were contributors to *Bean na hÉireann* (Woman of Ireland), a monthly paper that was published by the nationalist women's organisation Inghinidhe na hÉireann and edited by Fianna supporter Helena Molony. Hobson was one of the editors of *Irish Freedom*, the monthly mouthpiece of the IRB, to which various Fianna members and supporters contributed articles. From December 1914 onwards, he served as business manager and unofficial editor of the *Irish Volunteer*, the weekly official organ of the Irish Volunteers, for which Fianna officers Liam Mellows and Pádraic Ó Riain wrote regular columns.

From the Fianna's inception, *Bean na hÉireann* published monthly coverage of the youth group's views, activities and growth, making the paper an important primary source for the organisation's early history. Most of the Fianna articles were written pseudonymously. In September 1909, a Fianna member reported that '[s]ome Nationalists think that the boys don't count in the nation, but the founders of Na Fianna Éireann rightly consider them of supreme importance. They are the recruits of the future armies of Ireland, and on them the future of Ireland must depend.'[20] Pleas for nationalists to support the work of the new youth group appeared in both Fianna articles and Molony's editorials.[21] Belfast readers were even encouraged to send their younger brothers down to the local Fianna hall to join the organisation.[22]

Bean na hÉireann's Fianna articles provided readers of all ages with information about how to join local *sluaighte* as they spread around the country. They also kept readers abreast of events such as classes in military drill, route marches, camping trips, history lectures and concerts. For instance, an early report from September 1909 described a recent camping trip, recording that the 'Red Branch' section

> spent a most enjoyable six days' camping on the slope of Three Rock Mountain. On Sunday they were joined by the President [Hobson] and some other members, and 'scouting' games were played. The damp evenings were passed quickly with the singing of Irish songs and talks of Irish heroes.[23]

Markievicz had set up the Red Branch section prior to the official launch of the Fianna in August 1909.

In some cases, reports of these events may have been enticing enough to attract new members to the youth group. A report from November 1910 offered a taste of the excitement in store at the Dublin Fianna's forthcoming inter-*sluagh* scouting games at which *An Chéad Sluagh* and Sluagh Wolfe Tone would defend a 'citadel' in Scholarstown against attackers from the city's north-side *sluaighte*. The defenders had 'to intercept and capture the attackers before [they reached] the citadel'. 'Umpires' would award marks 'for good scouting work, the capturing of scouts and for those who succeed in entering the citadel uncaptured'. The article went on to boast of the 'steady progress' that the Fianna were making throughout Ireland, claiming that 'Irishmen who are alive to the needs of their country are slowly realising the necessity of training the coming generation to be a well-disciplined, strong people, imbued with intense national pride in their country's past, and with the proper sentiments as to their rights of independence'.[24]

Similar coverage in *Irish Freedom* and the *Irish Volunteer* kept current and potential Fianna members up to date on the activities of troops around the country and changes to official policy, with the latter paper also publishing instruction on topics such as field sketching and map reading. According to Sean Prendergast, Fianna members came to look upon *Irish Freedom* 'as a kind of official organ' that 'put us on a new plane': 'It revolutionised our movement which advanced with the spread of this paper throughout the country – new branches were springing up in various parts of Ireland'.[25] The *Irish Volunteer* later served a similar purpose for the Fianna.

Irish Freedom also ran a monthly column for youth under twenty, entitled 'Grianán na nÓg' ('the Sunroom of Youth'). Its author was identified only as 'Neasa'. The column featured monthly writing competitions on Irish topics, some of which attracted entries by Fianna members, such as Barney Mellows and Sean Prendergast from Dublin and James Nolan from Waterford. Prendergast and Nolan were so pleased with the paper's public commendation of their entries that they mentioned their competition successes in their Bureau of Military History witness statements.[26] Neasa also suggested practical ways in which young people could further the struggle for Irish independence, such as was proposed on one occasion, by joining the Fianna or setting up a similar organisation for girls.[27]

It is impossible to say for certain how many members of the Fianna read these papers, which were probably purchased by older family members. Hobson's estimate that there were over 1,500 members of the IRB in 1912 suggests that *Irish Freedom* had a potential adult audience of at least that number.[28] Contemporary police reports surmised that the *Irish Volunteer* had at the very least a total circulation of 3,937 in November 1915 and 4,615 in February 1916.[29]

In 1914, the Fianna started to produce its own publications to disseminate propaganda aimed at youth, particularly boys. Its first venture was the launch of the *Fianna Handbook*, which was issued by the Fianna's Central Council and compiled by Honorary General Secretary Pádraic Ó Riain.[30] Hobson helped Ó Riain to negotiate with the government publication agent, who had attempted to break a verbal contract with the Fianna after he realised it was not affiliated with the Baden-Powell movement.[31]

The *Fianna Handbook* was billed as 'the first, the largest and the only illustrated military publication issued for the use of Irish nationalists', implying that its content would be of use to adults (such as the Irish Volunteers) as well as youth.[32] It was designed to replace Baden-Powell's 1908 book *Scouting for Boys* and British War Office manuals, which were the few written sources for instruction previously available to the Fianna. Priced at one shilling, the handbook provided detailed information about the Fianna organisation, such as its aims, structure, rules and tests of skill, and practical instruction in military drill, rifle exercises, camping, knot-tying, signalling, first aid and swimming.[33] While Markievicz's introduction was directed towards 'young people' in general, the remainder of the text referred to boys only, highlighting the controversy over female membership in the organisation.[34] Prominent nationalists such as Patrick Pearse, Douglas Hyde and Roger Casement also contributed chapters. The handbook's editor proudly reported that Catherine M. Mahon, the former president of the Irish National School Teachers' Organisation Society, had not only written a favourable review of the book but urged 'all national school teachers to read [it] and to set about starting branches of the Fianna in connection with local Volunteer corps'.[35]

In addition to the appearance of the first handbook, the year 1914 witnessed the publication of a Fianna Christmas publication entitled *Nodlaig na bhFiann* (The Fianna Christmas). Edited by Fianna members Percy Reynolds and Patsy O'Connor, it resembled a Christmas annual in genre. Although it was not issued by Fianna Headquarters, *Nodlaig na bhFiann* did have official sanction.[36] The Christmas publication may have been the first business venture of Reynolds who was then aged nineteen. Following his imprisonment in the wake of the 1916 Rising, Reynolds went on to a successful career first as an accountant and then as an executive in the transportation industry, most notably as the first chairman of CIÉ in the latter half of the 1940s. He later owned Abbeville, a mansion set in 120 acres, racehorses, including a 1941 Irish Derby winner, and an art collection featuring the work of Nathaniel Hone and Jack B. Yeats.[37] His co-editor O'Connor is notable for quite a different reason. O'Connor's is one of the first names on the Fianna Roll of Honour, which lists the names of members 'who gave their lives for Ireland's freedom'.[38] His premature death in 1915 was believed to have resulted from a head injury that he sustained when he was batoned by the police while administering first aid to a worker during the 1913 Dublin Lockout.[39]

Nodlaig na bhFiann featured a mix of articles, short stories, poetry, cartoons and plenty of advertising designed to appeal to Christmas shoppers. The Fianna's two founders wrote articles for the publication with Markievicz sharing her memories of how the Fianna was first established and Hobson reflecting on the organisation's first five years. 'Corporal Willie Nelson' (probably Pádraic Ó Riain) provided a firsthand account of the Fianna's role in the Howth gunrunning in July 1914. Labour leader James Connolly, the father of three Belfast Fianna members, contributed an opinion piece on the tensions between boys and their parents. He encouraged boys not to be content to conform to the 'beaten paths travelled intellectually, nationally or socially' by their parents, who in turn were urged to allow their children to develop in new directions.[40] *Nodlaig na bhFiann*'s short fiction included a mystery set in the ranch country of the American wild west and a ghost story surrounding the body of an 'Esquimaux' woman being transported on a ship returning from an arctic expedition.[41] A. E. (George Russell), Maeve Cavanagh and others contributed poems while Grace Gifford, the future bride of 1916 insurrectionist Joseph Mary Plunkett, provided some of the cartoons and other illustrations.

The Christmas publication proved a financial success, but it drew criticism from Ó Riain who deemed it 'the most unboyish boys' paper I have ever seen'. He criticised 'two rather heavy articles' by Connolly and Hobson ('The chief merit of both is that they are brief') and complained that the publication's title was the only line of Irish that appeared in it. On a more positive note, Ó Riain praised Markievicz's article on the formation of the Fianna and enjoyed reading 'an amusing escapade of four members of the Dublin Fianna' who decided to annoy 'the aristocracy of Rathmines and neighbourhood' through their carol singing.[42]

Although Ó Riain liked this story by Percy Reynolds, readers outside of Dublin may not have appreciated its in-jokes and personal details about Walpole, Kavanagh, 'Mac' and John Shallow.[43] For instance, Harry Walpole 'did not want any of his lady friends to see him carol singing in Rathmines' while John Shallow lit his 'Golden Spangled'.[44] (Ironically, the future Fianna Code of Honour would urge members to cut out 'the poisonous "nicotine"'.[45]) Set against the backdrop of the Great War, the Fianna quartet apparently went carolling in disguise only to be arrested as German spies for singing a song in English called 'The Good Comrade' which unbeknownst to them was originally German. Despite the Fianna's official policy of welcoming members of all creeds, Kavanagh's costume is derided for making him look 'like a little Jew'.[46]

The Christmas publication having been deemed a success, Reynolds and O'Connor continued to take heed of Hobson's recommendation that 'every boy in the Fianna should be a propagandist for the Irish nation'.[47] The pair went on to launch *Fianna*, a monthly paper for boys, in February 1915, 'without any Capital'.[48] Hobson probably served as advisor to these young entrepreneurs and may have helped to edit the paper, possibly after O'Connor abandoned the project to concentrate on his local *sluagh*.[49] The paper initially circulated in Dublin, but by April Reynolds was tapping into a network of nationalist contacts to find stockists to circulate the fledgling paper nationally. For instance, he asked John Southwell, a member of the IRB and the Irish Volunteers,

> Would you mind stocking it, displaying a poster and pushing it for me in Newry, I am prepared if you think it wise, to send you some back numbers which you can give away free as specimen copies, and this should insure you of a good sale of future copies.[50]

Even as an adolescent, Reynolds was already a businessman in the making.

The paper published fiction, poetry and jokes, articles on Irish history and folklore and Fianna news and views. Although it was not an official organ of Na Fianna Éireann, it helped to keep members around the country in touch with the centre of the movement.[51] Ó Riain's criticism regarding the absence of Irish in the Christmas publication was addressed by including a monthly column on folklore written in Irish. Among the serials that the paper ran was *The Wandering Hawk*, a school story by Patrick Pearse about a popular teacher in a Catholic boys' boarding school who was a Fenian on the run, and 'The Boys of Wexford', a series of tales about 'a brave band of boys' who fought during the 1798 Rebellion.[52] These stories were designed to provide an Irish nationalist alternative to the content of popular British boys' periodicals, such as the *Boys' Friend*.

Fianna's editors found it difficult to compete against the seductive allure of British youth publications. Despite attempts to boost circulation by offering incentives such as free copies of the *Fianna Handbook* to readers who attracted four new subscribers, they were forced to widen their target audience to include adult men as well as boys from July 1915 onwards.[53] Another youth paper, *Young Ireland/Éire Óg*, which first appeared in April 1917, also had to broaden its target audience to include adults within a year of its inception. *Fianna*'s content now included articles on weightier topics such as Irish industry. Neasa, having been forced out of Grianán na nÓg after the demise of *Irish Freedom*, re-emerged in 'Neasa's nook' with a column and monthly competition for readers between the ages of six and seventeen.[54] By November 1915, the British authorities estimated that the paper had a circulation of at least 859, which grew to 1,094 by February 1916.[55]

The *Fianna* paper went into abeyance after the 1916 Rising, Reynolds having been imprisoned as a result of his participation in the rebellion. Upon his release he focused on building a career as an accountant.[56] In 1922, Fianna Headquarters revived the paper in a new format.

In general, the Fianna appear to have produced less of their own print propaganda between 1916 and 1922. The loss of Hobson as a conduit between the youth group and adult advanced nationalist newspapers may have been a factor. More significantly, after the Rising the Fianna were preoccupied with rebuilding their network of branches around the country and then participating in the War of Independence. This left little time for the production of print propaganda. The Fianna organisation may not have been circulating much of its own print propaganda during these years, but (as noted previously) its members continued to distribute posters, pamphlets and handbills generated by their adult counterparts in the nationalist movement, such as 1918 general election campaign literature.

During these years, the need for some sort of promotional vehicle was certainly felt by some Fianna members. Prior to the 1919 *ardfheis*, the Waterford *sluagh* suggested that the Fianna should try to procure an 'official space' for reports in either *Nationality* or *Young Ireland*.[57] If such an attempt was made, it was unsuccessful, as neither paper included an official Fianna column, though *Young Ireland* occasionally published content that would resonate with Fianna members. For instance, it published abridged versions of articles by Pearse and Casement, which originally appeared in the 1914 *Fianna Handbook*, as well as a translation of Fionn MacCumhaill's words to MacLugach outlining the duties of a true member of the Fianna and an extract from a letter found on the body of a German soldier. The letter, which had been quoted by Baden-Powell during a recent public address, praised the courage of a French boy scout about to be executed.[58]

The need for Fianna publications continued to be discussed, but little was done to address this concern. The Belfast Fianna briefly considered starting their own paper. On 20 April 1920, the Belfast District Council of the Fianna appointed an editorial staff for a paper whose content would be generated by the boys themselves, but within less than a month it abandoned the project 'owing to the amount of work to be done and the trouble and expense in running a journal'.[59] Although the need for a revised and reprinted *Fianna Handbook* to serve as a training manual was highlighted at the annual *ard-fheis* in August 1920, a new edition did not appear until 1924.⁶⁰

Some members of the Fianna appear to have believed that the youth group had a role to play in influencing Irish morality during the War of Independence. At the instigation of the Belfast contingent, delegates to the 1919 Fianna *ard-fheis* decided that the organisation should develop a code of 'moral ethics' to be observed by every member of the Fianna in hopes that the youth group 'would help to raise the moral standard of life' in Ireland. Delegates to the *ard-fheis* were to send their suggestions for the code to the Adjutant Barney Mellows.⁶¹ The resulting Fianna Code of Honour was inspired by what its (unnamed) author believed to be the moral code that was 'generally observed in Ireland in the days of Cuchulain and the Red Branch Knights and the Fianna of Finn'. As part of their daily lives, members of the modern-day Fianna were urged to live up to the new code's twelve points by being patriotic, reliable, diligent, kind, obedient, cheerful, thrifty, brave, clean, humble, temperate and punctual.⁶² By promoting such qualities, the Fianna sought to uphold its members' morals or ethics as well as their military efficiency.

The *Fianna* paper pioneered by Reynolds and O'Connor was later revived as an official organ of the youth group in June 1922. Its editor outlined some of the challenges facing the organisation not only in the previous years but also in light of the changed circumstances in a (partially) independent Ireland:

> The educational side of our programming has been completely neglected. ... To develop on educational lines a paper is more needed than ever. While still keeping in view military training we must devote more of our time to the training of the mind and body ... if we are to raise up strong and virile Irishmen fit to take a soldier's part in the national struggle of tomorrow.⁶³

This paper, which appeared on an occasional basis, included the usual Fianna news and views, as well as poetry, competitions and articles about republican heroes, old and new, such as the father of Irish republicanism Theobald Wolfe Tone (1763–98) and former Fianna officer Liam Mellows (1892–1922).⁶⁴

A competition in the June 1922 edition betrayed the organisation's continuing sexist attitude towards the role of females in the nationalist movement, despite Markievicz's position as Chief of the Fianna and the notable contributions made by women to the Irish Revolution in the preceding years.⁶⁵ The premise of the competition was that Kathleen, 'a good Irish cailín', needed help in choosing a husband on the basis of the answers provided by her suitors Kevin, Lorcan and Brendan to the question 'Why did you become a soldier of the IRA?' Entrants were to write an essay arguing which soldier gave the best answer to the question and by extension which man Kathleen should marry.⁶⁶ The competition depicted young women as potential marriage partners with republican loyalties rather than activists in their own right, echoing the organisation's unwillingness to include girls among its ranks.

In keeping with the Fianna's renewed commitment to education and training, which it was not in a position to address until after the Civil War, the organisation issued a second edition of the *Fianna Handbook* in 1924, with the content remaining largely the same as the earlier version. A key difference, however, was the declaration made by new Fianna members, which reflected the changed political circumstances in Ireland and post-Treaty divisions within Irish nationalism. In 1914, Fianna members promised 'to work for the independence of Ireland, never to join England's armed forces, and to obey [their] superior officers'.⁶⁷ Ten years later members of what was now an anti-Treaty youth organisation pledged their 'allegiance to the Irish Republic and promise[d] to do all in [their] power to protect her from all enemies, whether foreign or domestic, and not to relax [their] efforts until the Irish Republic is universally recognised'. The promise to obey their superior officers remained the same.⁶⁸ New editions of the handbook appeared in 1964 and 1988, both with complete revisions of their content.⁶⁹

PURPOSE OF FIANNA PRINT PROPAGANDA

At a basic level, Fianna publications provided current and potential members with information about the organisation's policies and activities, serving as a forum for communication. At a deeper level, these publications assisted the organisation in its aim to educate and influence young people along nationalist lines in order to prepare them for their role in the struggle for Irish independence. Like other examples of Irish nationalist children's culture, Fianna print propaganda sought to educate members about Irish history and folklore in order to teach them about their own unique heritage, to familiarise them with the nationalist vision of Ireland's long struggle against British rule, and to introduce them to Irish heroes and heroines worthy of imitation. Education was also provided through practical instruction in areas such as scouting skills and military training. Such propaganda promoted specific role models as well as an idealised image of Irish nationalist youth that members were encouraged to emulate. It also offered an Irish nationalist alternative to popular British youth publications.

Irish history, folklore and language were among the topics that featured in Fianna publications. *Fianna* included a monthly calendar of significant dates in Irish history and ran articles on aspects of Irish history and folklore. Pearse contributed a chapter to the *Fianna Handbook* in which he traced the three traditions of the Fianna in Ireland – Fionn Mac Cumhaill's Fianna, the Fenians of the nineteenth century and the Fianna boy scout organisation – before focusing on the tradition surrounding Fionn's Fianna. Although these publications did not provide any Irish language instruction, they did urge Fianna members to learn Irish, using Fr O'Growney's textbooks. The *Fianna Handbook* included a chapter in Irish by Douglas Hyde, a founder of the Gaelic League, while *Fianna* ran a monthly column on Irish folklore written in Irish.

In 1910 a Fianna member, writing in *Irish Freedom*, predicted that the final settlement of the 'Irish question' would fall to 'those of us who are growing up boys and girls'.[70] In order to prepare boys for their future role in the settlement of the Irish question, the *Fianna Handbook* asserted that 'their first work must be to train themselves to be fit citizens of a free nation'. To render service to Ireland, they needed to be trained in mind and body. The study of Irish language and history helped to train the mind while military training and physical fitness drilled the body. The book provided instruction on topics ranging from military drill to swimming. Such practical instruction on topics such as map reading was also the subject of Fianna articles included in the *Irish Volunteer*.[71] In taking the initiative to produce *Nodlaig na bhFiann* and *Fianna*, Reynolds and O'Connor demonstrated that Fianna membership could help youths to develop the ability and self-confidence to communicate the message of Irish nationalism and separatism to their own age cohort.

As the boys themselves were responsible for the running of the organisation, the *Fianna Handbook* also outlined the policy, organisational structure and constitution of the Fianna.[72] This taught members how to govern themselves, preparing them for citizenship, perhaps even leadership, in an independent Ireland of the future.

Advanced nationalist propaganda promoted an idealised image of Irish nationalist youth. Patriotism and morality were among the most important traits embodied in the ideal young nationalist. For instance, he or she was loyal to God and Ireland, not to the newly crowned

King George V or the British Empire. As the children's columnist Neasa pointed out, 'the allegiance of the boys and girls of Ireland is due to God and their Motherland alone'.[73] Such loyalty had wider benefits because, according to Neasa, 'the boy or girl who is true to the Motherland will be true to home and friends, true to everything noble and holy and good'.[74] In keeping with the organisation's secular nature, propaganda generated by the Fianna usually avoided any religious connotation and referred only to Ireland. The implication that there was a moral dichotomy between Britain and Ireland is typical of nationalist propaganda from the period.[75] Ben Novick has suggested that such propaganda 'sought to both create an idealised (and fictive) revolutionary and highlight as a sharp contrast the degenerate and debased nature of British and pro-British people'.[76]

Advanced nationalist publications aimed at youth, such as those produced by the Fianna, communicated the messages of the Sinn Féin and Irish-Ireland schools of thought by showing how the patriotism of the ideal young nationalist could be expressed through knowledge of certain subjects and choice of pastimes and consumer goods. He or she knew their Irish history (from a nationalist viewpoint, of course), tried to master the Irish language, read Irish publications, bought products made in Ireland and resisted the 'Anglicising force' of foreign dances, songs and games, instead choosing to dance traditional Irish dances, sing Irish songs and play Irish games like hurling.[77]

The ideal nationalist boy joined Na Fianna Éireann in order to prepare himself mentally and physically to play an active role in the fight for Irish independence. Ironically, in light of the so-called moral dichotomy between Britain and Ireland, the Baden-Powell Boy Scouts and the Fianna shared core values such as discipline, trust, obedience, loyalty, manliness, service and self-sacrifice.[78] The editors of *Fianna*, however, freely admitted that 'you can learn something from the enemy'.[79] Among the benefits of such core values were their usefulness in moulding future soldiers.

Fianna propaganda promoted the importance of not only patriotism and morality but also self-sacrifice. A Fianna member was to learn 'all about his country, its history and language, its resources and industries, and his one aim in life [was] to serve it to the best of his ability'. He should also keep his body and mind 'clean and pure'.[80] Such propaganda urged members never to 'do anything that would bring discredit upon Ireland or upon the Fianna'.[81] They also had to be prepared to make the ultimate sacrifice to attain Irish independence. In her introduction to the 1914 *Fianna Handbook*, Markievicz predicted that members of the Fianna would not 'flinch' if the 'path to freedom' led to their death, as it had for Wolfe Tone and Robert Emmet.[82]

Those serving or former members of the organisation who died as a result of their involvement in the Irish Revolution were not only praised in post-1916 Fianna propaganda but promoted as worthy role models for future generations.[83] For instance, a 1922 Easter Week commemoration souvenir programme declared that Fianna officers Sean Heuston and Con Colbert, who were executed for their roles in the 1916 Rising, 'met their deaths, happy that it was for Ireland, sure of the heaven that awaited them. In boyish simplicity and purity, and with manly courage, they faced the firing squad.'[84] Markievicz's foreword to the second edition of the *Fianna Handbook* encouraged members to follow 'the example and teachings of our heroic dead'. She reported that Liam Mellows 'always urged on the Fianna the importance of educating and training their minds, in the principles and ideals that governed Gaelic Ireland'.[85] Mellows was executed in 1922 during the Civil War by the Irish Free State as a reprisal for the murder of a Dáil Éireann deputy. Future Fianna propaganda continued to glorify martyrs to the cause, with a Fianna Roll of Honour issued in 1981 listing the names of fifty-four members 'who gave their lives for Ireland's freedom' between 1915 and 1981.[86]

The *Fianna Handbook*, the Christmas publication *Nodlaig na bhFiann* and the boys' paper *Fianna* were designed to provide Irish nationalist alternatives to British popular literature for boys, which was also imbued with militarism, patriotism and heroism in this period.[87] The Irish versions remained true to the genres of their British counterparts, but adapted their content to suit an Irish nationalist audience. For instance, *Fianna* published an example of the classic school story genre in a serial entitled *The Wandering Hawk* by Patrick Pearse, which remained unfinished when the paper ceased publication in early 1916. Set in St Fintan's, a fictitious Catholic boys' boarding school, it tells the tale of a group of boys whose inspirational new schoolmaster turns out to be a Fenian on the run from the authorities.[88] '*The Wandering Hawk* promotes the very qualities – bravery, loyalty, athleticism – fostered in public schools, promulgated through popular adventure stories, and associated with the *esprit de corps* and aggressive model of masculinity that underpinned British imperialism', asserts Anne Markey. She further notes that this serial is a revision and expansion of Pearse's play *Owen*, which was first staged in Irish in the winter of 1913 and published as an English translation in *Fianna* in December 1915. Like Na Fianna Éireann itself, the play and the serial make a clear link between education and 'the promotion of violent republicanism and … preparation for military action'.[89]

As noted earlier, the *Fianna Handbook* replaced Baden-Powell's 1908 book *Scouting for Boys* as a source of instruction. Both books covered such topics as camping, first aid, chivalry and patriotism. However, the interpretation of the latter two topics differed.

Originating in the Middle Ages, chivalry was a gentlemanly code of behaviour 'demanding personal honour, generosity, loyalty and courage'.[90] It was often associated with Arthurian romances, which had seen a resurgence in popularity in the nineteenth century as a result of romanticism and medievalism. These cultural trends reflected a nostalgic longing for a simpler, pastoral past in a world that was becoming more rational, industrialised and urban. Given that both youth groups were concerned with influencing – possibly even controlling – their members' behaviour, it is not surprising that both books covered the topic of chivalry. Baden-Powell discussed it in the context of medieval knights. In contrast, Casement hearkened back to the chivalry of Fionn MacCumhaill's Fianna:

> The inheritance of chivalry is with us still – a motherland to serve, a fair country to be freed. For this we shall need all the chivalry of the Irish heart, all the training and manhood of the Irish body, all the service, devotion, and self-sacrifice of our boys and young men. The true knight is he who keeps the boy's heart in the trained body of the man.[91]

He depicted Ireland as a damsel in distress (a recurring metaphor in Irish literature) and made a clear connection between Ireland's legendary past and the present youth group.

Patriotism was also a concern for both organisations. Baden-Powell's emphasis on patriotism reflected the anxieties generated by the approaching European war while the Fianna were openly preparing for a future Irish war of independence. In *Scouting for Boys* Baden-Powell promoted patriotism in the context of the British Empire. He exhorted boys not to 'be disgraced like the young Romans, who lost the Empire of their forefathers by being wishy-washy slackers without any go or patriotism in them'.[92] The Fianna rejected such imperialistic patriotism, instead encouraging Irish boys to direct their patriotic impulses towards the foundation of an independent Irish state.

In further contrast to *Scouting for Boys*, the *Fianna Handbook* included a section on rifle exercises, revealing the militant nature of the Irish organisation.⁹³ Illustrations in the two books emphasise this difference between the groups. While Baden-Powell's scouts were portrayed holding walking sticks, the Fianna were shown handling rifles.

Although Fianna members were encouraged to express their nationalism by buying and reading only Irish publications, the lure of popular British literature was hard to counteract. In February 1915 Pádraic Ó Riain, writing in the *Irish Volunteer*, estimated that 'nearly every boy from twelve to sixteen years of age' read at least one boys' story-paper per week. Despite the launch of two Irish monthly papers for boys, the Christian Brothers' *Our Boys* in 1914 and *Fianna* in 1915, Irish boys were still subscribing to weekly magazines imported from Britain.⁹⁴ When the editors of *Fianna* declared that 'English boys' periodicals' were 'killing Irish Nationalism', there is a sense that what they really meant was that British boys' magazines were killing their paper.⁹⁵

The stereotypical image of the Irish and the imperialist message in these British publications incensed advanced nationalists. A particularly striking example can be found in 'The legions of the Kaiser', a timely war serial that appeared in the *Boys' Friend* between June and September 1914. It tells the story of Roy Kildare, the young squire of an estate on the border of County Donegal, who 'was generally either laughing or fighting'. Although he was 'an Ulsterman and a Protestant', Roy supported home rule and 'came of the old native Irish race'. Politics, however, 'bored him stiff, though he liked elections, for there were always some merry ructions'.⁹⁶ Roy's dichotomous identity as a home ruler from Ulster and a Protestant of native Irish stock broke down some Irish stereotypes, yet he was still portrayed as a stereotypical Irishman – jocular and pugnacious. His boredom with politics may have been British wishful thinking at a time when the Ulster question dominated the Westminster parliament.

In the serial, German soldiers invade Ireland hoping to team up with Irish nationalists in order to use the island as a base to attack Great Britain.⁹⁷ Roy responds to this threat by helping to bring home rulers and Ulster Volunteers together to oust their common foe.⁹⁸ By the time this has been achieved, Roy is happy to be called a 'Britisher' and exclaims 'God save the King!'⁹⁹ Despite its positive depiction of Irish nationalists and unionists working together, the story's pro-British, anti-German message would have been unacceptable to advanced nationalists. By July 1915, even the Christian Brothers' magazine *Our Boys* came under fire in the pages of *Fianna* for including 'such war articles' and being no better than a British story-paper.¹⁰⁰

In addition to objecting to the imperialist message of British youth papers, Irish nationalists also accused them of being immoral. *Neasa* published 'The poisoned bowl', a poem by a young correspondent, which encouraged the rejection of 'degrading and denationalising publications sent over from England to corrupt the minds and morals of Ireland's youth'.[101] Advanced nationalists were particularly scathing in their condemnation of the (ironically) Irish press baron Alfred Harmsworth (Lord Northcliffe), who published the *Boys' Friend*.[102]

The Fianna were seen by themselves and others as having a part to play in combating the alleged immorality of British imports. For instance, Fianna members were portrayed as Irish moral crusaders in a serial entitled 'The Fianna, or Irish Boy Scouts', which ran in the Christian Brothers' magazine *Our Boys* between October 1919 and March 1920.[103] The Fianna heroes lead a protest against the local cinema's showing of 'objectionable pictures', including one featuring a scantily clad 'ballet girl' performing 'antics … [that] were not only indecent but shocking'.[104] The boycott escalates into a courtroom battle that the Fianna boys win, striking a blow for 'Catholic moral rectitude'.[105] That the Fianna featured in an *Our Boys*' serial not only shows the impact that the War of Independence was having on the magazine's editorial policy by late 1919/early 1920 but also suggests that the advanced nationalist youth group had entered the Irish mainstream (at least for a little while). The overt Catholicism of the fictional members' moral crusade, however, was not in keeping with the Fianna's official policy.

EFFECTIVENESS OF FIANNA PRINT PROPAGANDA

The nature of propaganda is such that it is difficult to provide an empirical assessment of its effectiveness. There are, however, indications that advanced nationalist propaganda aimed at youth was effective to some degree. That the editors of *Bean na hÉireann*, *Irish Freedom*, the *Irish Volunteer* and *Fianna* chose to publish, and continued to publish, propaganda aimed at youth, and members of the Fianna in particular, suggests that they believed there was a potentially receptive audience for their message. Participation in *Neasa*'s competitions shows that entrants had absorbed and could reiterate in their own words her advanced nationalist message. Although *Fianna* clearly failed in its attempt to provide a successful Irish nationalist alternative to popular British boys' papers, it made gains in circulation after it widened its focus to become a paper geared towards boys and men. After the outbreak of the First World War, the authorities at Dublin Castle were so concerned about the effect of such 'seditious' newspapers that they suppressed *Irish Freedom*, issued a warning to the printer of the *Irish Volunteer* – though the youth columns in these papers were probably the least of their worries – and began tracking the rising circulation of *Fianna*.[106]

That some serving and former members of the Fianna participated in various military capacities in the Easter Rising, the War of Independence and the Civil War also attests to the effectiveness of Fianna propaganda. For instance, nine serving and former Fianna members died as a result of the Rising with many more losing their lives during the struggle for independence in the period 1919–23.[107] In many ways, Sean Heuston exemplified the success of Fianna propaganda with the following words: 'Whatever I have done as a soldier of Ireland is what I believe to be my country's best interest. I have, thank God, no vain regrets.'[108] Such propaganda probably contributed to the role of youth and the predominance of young men within the IRA, which has been noted in recent studies of the Irish Revolution.[109]

Clearly, however, Fianna propaganda was not always successful. Boys continued to consume aspects of British popular culture, such as story-papers. More significantly, not all members of the Fianna heeded the organisation's call for young Irish men not join the British armed forces. Instead, some Fianna members, such as Christy Moynihan and Thomas Barr, chose to serve in the British army during the First World War.[110]

NOTES

1. Roger Casement, 'Chivalry' in Pádraic Ó Riain (ed.), *Fianna Handbook* (Dublin: Central Council of Na Fianna Éireann, 1914), p. 86.
2. Liam O'Brien, witness statement, 19 Nov. 1949 (MA, BMH, WS 323).
3. Précis of reports relative to secret societies, etc in the DMP district, Sept. 1911 (TNA, CO 904/119).
4. Liam O'Brien, witness statement, 19 Nov. 1949 (MA, BMH, WS 323).
5. An earlier draft of material covered in this chapter was published as Marnie Hay, 'The propaganda of Na Fianna Éireann, 1909–26' in Mary Shine Thompson (ed.), *Young Irelands: Studies in Children's Literature* (Dublin: Four Courts Press, 2011), pp. 47–56.
6. See Lieut.-General R.S.S. Baden-Powell, *Scouting for Boys: A Handbook for Instruction in Good Citizenship*, fifth impression (London: C. Arthur Pearson, 1908). For more on Irish nationalist children's culture, see Ríona

Nic Congáil, 'Young Ireland and *The Nation*: Nationalist children's culture in the late nineteenth century', *Éire-Ireland*, 46:3 & 4 (2011), pp. 37–62; Marnie Hay, 'What did advanced nationalists tell Irish children in the early twentieth century?' in Ciara Ní Bhroin and Patricia Kennon (eds), *What Do We Tell the Children? Critical Essays on Children's Literature* (Cambridge: Cambridge Scholars Publishing, 2012), pp. 148–62; Marnie Hay, 'This treasured island: Irish nationalist propaganda aimed at children and youth, 1910–16'; Michael Flanagan, '"There is an Isle in the western ocean": The Christian Brothers, *Our Boys* and Catholic/nationalist ideology' in Mary Shine Thompson and Celia Keenan (eds), *Treasure Islands: Studies in Children's Literature* (Dublin: Four Courts Press, 2006), pp. 33–52; Marnie Hay, 'Children and the Irish cultural revival', podcast and script for UCD Scholarcast Series 12, Modalities of Revival, 24 Feb. 2015, available at: www.ucd.ie/scholarcast/scholarcast46.html.
7 Terence Denman, '"The red livery of shame": The campaign against army recruitment in Ireland, 1899–1914', *Irish Historical Studies*, 29:114 (Nov. 1994), p. 219.
8 Police intelligence reports, Oct. 1909 (TNA, CO 904/119), quoted in Denman, '"The red livery of shame"', p. 228.
9 Dónal O'Hannigan, witness statement, 2 Dec. 1948 (MA, BMH, WS 161).
10 Sydney Czira, witness statement, 29 Dec. 1953 (MA, BMH, WS 909).
11 Sean Healy and Liam O'Callaghan, joint witness statement, 4 Oct. 1947 (MA, BMH, WS 47); George Hurley, witness statement, 7 June 1957 (MA, BMH, WS 1,630). An adult nationalist activist, Sean O'Hegarty, gave them the posters and paste.
12 Joseph O'Shea, witness statement, n.d. (MA, BMH, WS 21).
13 George Hurley, witness statement, 7 June 1957 (MA, BMH, WS 1,630).
14 Garry Holohan, witness statement, 7 Dec. 1949 (MA, BMH, WS 328); Sean Prendergast, witness statement, 3 Nov. 1952 (MA, BMH, WS 755).
15 Alfred White, witness statement, 12 July 1955 (MA, BMH, WS 1,207).
16 Patrick Hearne, witness statement, 18 Aug. 1958 (MA, BMH, WS 1,742); Charles Meaney, witness statement, 11 June 1957 (MA, BMH, WS 1,631).
17 Thomas O'Connor, witness statement, 15 June 1955 (MA, BMH, WS 1,189).
18 For a brief discussion of censorship during this period, see Peter Martin, *Censorship in the Two Irelands, 1922–1939* (Dublin: Irish Academic Press, 2006), pp. 7–12.
19 For an example of these Fianna news reports, see Ruaidhri, 'Na Fianna Éireann', *B na hÉ*, Jan. 1911, pp. 12–13, which discusses the drawing of the Goose Club prizes at the Fianna Hall on Camden Street in Dublin and the recent growth and activities of three Belfast troops.

20 One of the Fianna, 'Na Fianna Éireann (National Boys' Brigade)', *B na hÉ*, Sept. 1909, p. 8.
21 One of the Fianna, 'Na Fianna Éireann (National Boys' Brigade)', *B na hÉ*, Nov. 1909, p. 8; 'Editorial notes', *B na hÉ*, Jan. 1910, p. 8.
22 C. Ua S. (probably Cathal O'Shannon), 'Volunteers' Branch', *B na hÉ*, Mar. 1910, p. 8.
23 *B na hÉ*, Sept. 1909, p. 9.
24 'Na Fianna Éireann', *B na hÉ*, Nov. 1910, p. 11.
25 Sean Prendergast, witness statement, 3 Nov. 1952 (MA, BMH, WS 755).
26 Hay, 'This treasured island', p. 35; Sean Prendergast, witness statement, 3 Nov. 1952 (MA, BMH, WS 755); James Nolan, witness statement, 10 Mar. 1956 (MA, BMH, WS 1,369). Prendergast wrote an address to the King of England while Nolan submitted a history essay.
27 Neasa, 'Grianán na nÓg', *IF*, June and July 1912, p. 3.
28 Bulmer Hobson, *Ireland Yesterday and Tomorrow* (Tralee: Anvil Books, 1968), p. 36.
29 Breandán Mac Giolla Choille (ed.), *Intelligence Notes 1913–16* (Dublin: Republic of Ireland State Papers Office, 1966), p. 163.
30 Bulmer Hobson, witness statement, 15 Oct. 1947 (MA, BMH, WS 31).
31 *Ibid.*
32 'Boy Scouts', *IV*, 12 Sept. 1914, p. 3.
33 See Ó Riain (ed.), *Fianna Handbook*.
34 Countess Markievicz, 'Introduction' in Ó Riain (ed.), *Fianna Handbook*, pp. 6–8. For a discussion of this controversy, see Marnie Hay, 'The foundation and development of Na Fianna Éireann, 1909–16', *Irish Historical Studies*, 36:141 (May 2008), pp. 60–2; Margaret Ward, *Unmanageable Revolutionaries* (London: Pluto Press, 1995), pp. 104–6.
35 'Boy Scouts', *IV*, 24 Oct. 1914, p. 16.
36 Liam Mellows, 'Boy Scouts organising notes', *IV*, 21 Nov. 1914, p. 15.
37 See Shaun Boylan, 'Reynolds, Augustus Percival Harald ("Percy")' in *DIB*, available from http://dib.cambridge.org.
38 'Fianna roll of honour' in Robert Holland, *A Short History of Fianna Éireann* [c. 1981], pp. 25–6 (NLI, MS 35,455/3/12A). Na Fianna Éireann produced this photocopied booklet, which features a memoir written in 1949. O'Connor's name comes first on the list in this booklet, but his is second on a more recent list available at https://nafiannaeireann.files.wordpress.com/2014/09/nfe_rollofhonor.pdf (accessed 18 July 2018).
39 Willie Nelson [Pádraic Ó Riain], 'Na Fianna Éireann', IV, 26 June 1915, p. 8.
40 James Connolly, 'Boys and parents', *Nodlaig na bhFiann*, Christmas 1914, p. 13.

41 See Lisheen Gifford, 'Frank Desmond, Deputy Sheriff', pp. 4–5 and S. M., 'The doctor's secret', pp. 9–10, both in *Nodlaig na bhFiann*.
42 Willie Nelson (Pádraic Ó Riain), 'Na Fianna Éireann', *IV*, 19 Dec. 1914, p. 8.
43 A. P. H. R. [Percy Reynolds], 'The Christmas Carol Singers' in *Nodlaig na bhFiann*, pp. 6–8. These Fianna members were Robert Henry (Harry) Walpole, (probably) Seamus Kavanagh and John (or Jack) Shallow, but I was unable to identify 'Mac'. Walpole and Kavanagh gave statements to the BMH. Fianna lieutenants Patsy O'Connor (Reynolds' co-editor) and J. J. Puinse (Seamus Pounch) are also mentioned in the story.
44 A. P. H. R., 'The Christmas Carol Singers', p. 6.
45 Fianna Code of Honour (NLI, MS 10,910).
46 A. P. H. R., 'The Christmas Carol Singers', p. 6.
47 Fergus Mac Leda (Bulmer Hobson), 'Letters to members of Na Fianna Éireann', *IF*, Mar. 1913, p. 6.
48 A. P. Reynolds to John Southwell, 14 Apr. 1915 (MA, BMH, John Southwell Collection, CD 212).
49 Contemporary newspaper articles identified Reynolds and O'Connor as the initial editors of the paper. O'Connor resigned from the editorship sometime prior to his death in June 1915 (Willie Nelson, 'Na Fianna Éireann', *IV*, 9 Jan. 1915, 26 June 1915, p. 8; 'In memoriam', *Fianna*, July 1915, p. 3). Reynolds may have secured another editorial partner after O'Connor's departure. Although Virginia E. Glandon and Ben Novick have cited Hobson as editor of *Fianna*, Hobson does not verify this in his memoirs. See Virginia E. Glandon, *Arthur Griffith and the Advanced Nationalist Press: Ireland, 1900–1922* (New York: Lang, 1985), p. 269; Ben Novick, *Conceiving Revolution: Irish Nationalist Propaganda During the First World War* (Dublin: Four Courts Press, 2001), p. 30; Bulmer Hobson, witness statement, 15 Oct. 1947 (MA, BMH, WS 31).
50 A. P. Reynolds to John Southwell, 14 Apr. 1915 (MA, BMH, Southwell Collection, CD 212).
51 Patrick Hearne in Waterford and William McCabe in Ballybunion remembered receiving the paper regularly. See Hearne, witness statement, 18 Aug. 1958 (MA, BMH, WS 1,742); McCabe, witness statement, 25 July 1955 (MA, BMH, WS 1,212).
52 Pearse's serial started in the Feb. 1915 issue of *Fianna* while 'The Boys of Wexford' by Croghan Kinsella began in April of that year.
53 'Killing Irish Nationalism', *Fianna*, Mar. 1915, p. 4; 'From the editors', *Fianna*, June 1915, p. 3.
54 See A. P. Reynolds, 'Our industries', *Fianna*, July 1915, pp. 4–6; Neasa, 'Neasa's nook', *Fianna*, July 1915, p. 12.
55 Mac Giolla Choille (ed.), *Intelligence Notes*, p. 163.

56 Boylan, 'Reynolds, Augustus Percival Harald ("Percy")'. According to his biographical entry, Reynolds served at the Royal College of Surgeons during the Rising and was imprisoned first at Wormwood Scrubs and then at Frongoch camp in Wales.
57 Ard Fheis 1919 Agenda (MA, BMH, Michael Kilmartin Collection, CD 144/1/4).
58 See P. H. Pearse, 'The Fianna of Fionn', *YI*, 10 Nov. 1917, p. 3; Roger Casement, 'Chivalry', *YI*, 8 Dec. 1917, p. 2; 'A ballad history of Ireland. Songs of the Fianna', *YI*, 29 Sept. 1917, p. 5; 'Fianna Éireann!', *YI*, 18 May 1918, p. 7.
59 Belfast District Council minute book, entries for 20 Apr. 1920 and 4 May 1920 (MA, BMH, Lieutenant-Colonel J. M. MacCarthy Collection, CD 29/4/1).
60 Fianna Éireann Ardfheis. Sunday, 1 August 1920. Agenda (MA, BMH, Michael Kilmartin Collection, CD 144/1/15).
61 Fianna Éireann, Ard-Fheis Report 1919 (MA, BMH, Kilmartin Collection, CD144/1/5).
62 Fianna Code of Honour (NLI, MS 10,910). The name and address of Liam Langley, who became the Fianna's new Director of Education at the 1919 *ard-fheis*, are listed on this copy of the Fianna Code of Honour, which was donated to the NLI by historian Alice Stopford-Green.
63 'Editorial', *Fianna*, June 1922, p. 3.
64 'Tone: Episodes in his life', 'The objects of Tone', *Fianna*, June 1922, pp. 8–9; 'Liam Ó Maoil Íosa', *Fianna*, June 1926, p. 1.
65 For instance, see Ward, *Unmanageable Revolutionaries*, chapters 3–5; Ann Matthews, *Renegades: Irish Republican Women, 1900–1922* (Cork: Mercier Press, 2010), chapters 4–12; Ruth Taillon, *When History was Made: The Women of 1916* (Belfast: Beyond the Pale Publications, 1996); Cal McCarthy, *Cumann na mBan and the Irish Revolution* (Cork: The Collins Press, 2007).
66 'Fianna-tion', *Fianna*, June 1922, p. 10.
67 Ó Riain, *Fianna Handbook*, p. 13.
68 *Fianna Handbook* (2nd edn, Dublin: Central Council of Fianna Éireann, 1924), p. 7.
69 See *The Young Guard of Erin: The Fianna Handbook* (Dublin: Na Fianna Éireann, 1964) and *Fianna Éireann Handbook* (Dublin: Fianna Éireann, 1988).
70 Art, 'The Fianna', *IF*, Nov. 1910, p. 7
71 For instance, Pádraic Ó Riain contributed a series of articles on map reading. See Ó Riain, 'Na Fianna Éireann', *IV*, 22 Jan. 1916, 29 Jan. 1916, 5 Feb. 1916, 12 Feb. 1916, p. 8.

72 Ó Riain, *Fianna Handbook*, p. 14.
73 Neasa, 'Grianán', *IF*, July 1911, p. 3.
74 Neasa, 'Grianán', *IF*, Nov. 1910, p. 3.
75 Novick, *Conceiving Revolution*, p. 132.
76 *Ibid.*, p. 169.
77 Na Fianna Éireann, *The Constitution of Na Fianna Éireann as Amended by the Ard-Fheis, 1912* (Dublin: Na Fianna Éireann, 1912), p. 6; Rap., 'Practical patriotism', *Fianna*, Jan. 1916, p. 3. A young reader named Máire Ní Cheallaigh wrote to Neasa about the necessity of rejecting foreign dances because they were 'an Anglicising force' (quoted in Neasa, 'Grianán', *IF*, Sept. 1911, p. 3). Séumas Ó Connghalaigh urged his fellow readers to 'dance no English dances; play no English games; and sing no West British ditties' (quoted in Neasa, 'Grianán', *IF*, June 1912, p. 3).
78 Baden-Powell, *Scouting for Boys*, p. 266. These values are also promoted in the *Fianna Handbook* and the Fianna Code of Honour.
79 'From the editors', *Fianna*, Mar. 1915, p. 3.
80 Fianna Code of Honour (NLI, MS 10,910).
81 Ó Riain, *Fianna Handbook*, p. 14.
82 Markievicz, 'Introduction' in Ó Riain (ed.), *Fianna Handbook*, p. 8.
83 See *Easter Week 1916–1922 Commemoration Aeridheacht Souvenir Programme, 23 April 1922* (Dublin: Fianna Éireann Dublin Brigade, 1922); Cathal O'Shannon (ed.), *Souvenir of the Golden Jubilee of Fianna Éireann, Aug. 16, 1909–Aug. 16, 1959* (Dublin: Na Fianna Éireann, 1959).
84 *Easter Week 1916–1922 Commemoration Aeridheacht Souvenir Programme*, 23 April 1922, p. 7.
85 Countess Markievicz, 'Foreword', in Ó Riain (ed.), *Fianna Handbook*, 2nd edn, pp. 4–5.
86 'Fianna roll of honour' in Holland, *A Short History*, pp. 25–6 (NLI, MS 35,455/3/12A).
87 John M. MacKenzie, *Propaganda and Empire: The Manipulation of British Public Opinion, 1880–1960* (Manchester: Manchester University Press, 1984), pp. 199, 213.
88 For the first instalment of this serial, see *Fianna*, Feb. 1915, pp. 4–7.
89 Anne Markey, 'Patrick Pearse: Literary pioneer and propagandist' in Eugene McNulty and Róisín Ní Ghairbhí (eds), *Patrick Pearse and the Theatre* (Dublin: Four Courts Press, 2017), pp. 44–8.
90 Anne Curry, 'Chivalry' in John Cannon (ed.), *The Oxford Companion to British History* (Oxford: Oxford University Press, 1997), pp. 202–3.
91 Casement, 'Chivalry', p. 86.
92 Baden-Powell, *Scouting for Boys*, p. 240.
93 See Ó Riain, *Fianna Handbook*, pp. 53–74.

94 Willie Nelson, 'Na Fianna Éireann', *IV*, 13 Feb. 1915, p. 8.
95 'Killing Irish Nationalism', *Fianna*, Mar. 1915, p. 4.
96 John Tregellis, 'The legions of the Kaiser', *Boys' Friend*, 13 June 1914, p. 34.
97 Tregellis, 'The legions of the Kaiser', *Boys' Friend*, 20 June 1914, p. 50.
98 Tregellis, 'The legions of the Kaiser', *Boys' Friend*, 27 June 1914, p. 66.
99 Tregellis, 'The legions of the Kaiser', *Boys' Friend*, 19 Sept. 1914, p. 266.
100 Dalcassian, 'From a long way to Bodenstown', *Fianna*, July 1915, p. 2.
101 Neasa, 'Grianán', *IF*, Mar. 1911, p. 3.
102 Novick, *Conceiving Revolution*, p. 167.
103 For a discussion of this serial, see Flanagan, 'There is an Isle in the western ocean', pp. 49–51.
104 'The Fianna, or Irish Boy Scouts', *Our Boys*, Oct. 1919, p. 35, quoted in Flanagan, 'There is an Isle in the western ocean', p. 50.
105 Flanagan, 'There is an Isle in the western ocean', p. 50.
106 Mac Giolla Choille (ed.), *Intelligence Notes*, pp. 116, 163.
107 Chapter 8 includes a discussion of Fianna deaths in the period 1916–23.
108 *Easter Week Commemoration Programme*, 1932, p. 12 (MA, BMH, Kathleen Clarke Collection, CD 163/4).
109 For instance, see Peter Hart, *The IRA and Its Enemies* (Oxford: Clarendon Press, 1998); Joost Augusteijn, *From Public Defiance to Guerrilla Warfare* (Dublin: Irish Academic Press, 1996); Marie Coleman, *County Longford and the Irish Revolution* (Dublin: Irish Academic Press, 2003); David Fitzpatrick, *Politics and Irish Life, 1913–1921* (Cork: Cork University Press, 1998).
110 Joseph O'Shea, witness statement, n.d. (MA, BMH, WS 21); Patrick Hearne, witness statement, 18 Aug. 1958 (MA, BMH, WS 1,742). O'Shea noted that a few of the older Cork Fianna members served in the First World War.

8 Youth in arms

> The dream of Freedom rose in beauty out of the thoughts and hopes of our young people, and many a lad trained and disciplined in the Fianna took up his gun for Ireland. Two of our noblest and best loved, Con Colbert and Sean Heuston, faced the firing squad in 1916, and won a martyr's crown. Many more noble lads of the rank and file suffered and died that Ireland might be free. We know how the goal was nearly won, when treachery and ignorance again played their part, and riveted the chains around the neck of Caitlin ni Houlihan yet once more at the bidding of England.[1]

This was the romanticised view of the Fianna's military contribution to the struggle for Irish independence promoted by Countess Markievicz in the 1924 edition of the *Fianna Handbook*. Her words, written in the immediate aftermath of the Irish Civil War, reflected her view, and that of the republican youth group, that the Irish Revolution was unfinished, having been betrayed by those Irish people who supported the Anglo-Irish Treaty. Some of those people were former members of the Fianna. Young men and boys who had fought together during the Easter Rising and the War of Independence later found themselves fighting on opposite sides during the Civil War.

Despite Markievicz's lofty words, one former Fianna officer asserted over thirty years later that the youth organisation had not received enough credit for its military contribution to the Irish Revolution. 'In the stories and histories of the period 1913 to 1921 which have been published to date [1955], scant mention has been made of the part played by the boys of Fianna Éireann, and my interest in making this [witness] statement is solely to show how that organisation, in at least one small country district, could and did assist the Irish Volunteers and the Irish Republican Army', claimed William O'Flynn, who had been captain of the Fianna *sluagh* in Fethard, County Tipperary.[2]

The purpose of this chapter is to fill the gap in the historiography highlighted by O'Flynn's BMH witness statement. The chapter examines and assesses the military contribution of the Fianna to the Irish Revolution during the years between the foundation of the Irish Volunteers in November 1913 and the end of the Civil War in 1923. During these years, many (but not all) members of the Fianna undertook a variety of military roles, experiencing violence first-hand either as witnesses, victims or perpetrators. Such military activism could result in job losses, imprisonment, poor health, wounding or even death.

Members of the Fianna served during the main military events of the Irish Revolution: the Howth and Kilcoole gunrunning episodes on 26 July and 1 August 1914; the Easter Rising of 24–9 April 1916; the Irish War of Independence (or Anglo-Irish War), which lasted from 21 January 1919 until the Truce on 11 July 1921; and the Irish Civil War, which broke out on 28 June 1922 and came to a ceasefire on 30 April 1923.

The purpose of running German guns and ammunition into Howth, County Dublin, and Kilcoole, County Wicklow in the summer of 1914 was to arm the Irish Volunteers. These arms and ammunition were later used during the Easter Rising. The Military Council of the IRB was responsible for organising this rebellion, utilising the Irish Volunteers, the Irish Citizen Army, the Hibernian Rifles, Na Fianna Éireann and Cumann na mBan in its effort to strike a blow against British rule in Ireland while Britain was preoccupied fighting the Great War in continental Europe. Although the Rising itself was a failure, the British government's repressive measures in its wake, such as the execution of sixteen leading rebels, including Con Colbert and Sean Heuston of the Fianna, helped to gain mass support for a more advanced form of nationalism than home rule.

It was only by coincidence that the first shots of the Irish War of Independence were fired on the day that Dáil Éireann met for the first time. This guerrilla campaign, which was fought between British government forces and the Irish Volunteers, who became known as the Irish Republican Army, can be divided into three main phases. The first phase in 1919 mainly involved the sporadic seizure of arms and attacks on individual policemen by republican forces. The campaign shifted into higher gear in 1920 with IRA attacks on police barracks, raids and ambushes. The British government responded to this challenge by deploying military troops and creating two new forces, the Black and Tans and the Auxiliaries, to bolster the Royal Irish Constabulary (RIC). The Black and Tans were ex-British soldiers and sailors who got their nickname from the mixed uniform of 'khaki military trousers and dark green police tunics' with which they were initially issued due to a shortage of RIC uniforms. Demobilised British army officers were recruited for the Auxiliary Division (or Auxiliaries) of the RIC. Late 1920 saw a steep escalation of violence and the emergence of 'flying columns', which were armed groups of IRA men on full-time active service. Throughout the conflict, the British government's increasingly harsh security policy only served to disaffect the civilian population without curbing the IRA's activities.[3]

The 1921 Anglo-Irish Treaty, which was negotiated during the Truce that began in July of that year, established an Irish Free State with dominion status within the British Commonwealth, rather than a completely independent republic. This distinction contributed to a slide into civil war between former republican comrades. Both Sinn Féin and the IRA split over the issue of the treaty. The Irish Civil War was fought between the pro-Treaty forces of the Provisional Government, most notably the National Army, and the anti-Treaty IRA, who were referred to as the Irregulars. Unlike the IRA, disagreement over the acceptance of the Treaty did not lead to a split within the Fianna. As an organisation, the Fianna opposed the Treaty and supported the anti-Treaty IRA during the Civil War. Fianna members who were pro-Treaty quietly left the youth group, some choosing to join the National Army.

The active involvement of children and youth in military conflict was nothing new in the early twentieth century and has only grown in global prominence since then. Alcinda Honwana's work on child soldiers in Mozambique and Angola highlights comparisons and contrasts that help to put the Fianna's military contribution to the Irish Revolution in perspective. She notes:

> Recent civil wars tend to obliterate distinctions between civilians and belligerents in ways hardly witnessed before. In these kinds of civil wars the separation between the 'battlefield' and the 'home front' becomes blurred. ... Children, sometimes referred to as 'easy prey,' are particularly vulnerable to military recruitment in these conflicts.[4]

The 'irregular' nature of the Irish War of Independence and the subsequent Civil War meant that it was difficult for government forces to distinguish between civilians and belligerents. The young age of Fianna members ensured that they were less likely to be suspected of subversive activity, which heightened their value in providing military support to the Irish Volunteers/IRA through their service as scouts, dispatch carriers and couriers. This value was probably lessened during the Civil War because Irish government forces were more likely to recognise Fianna members even out of uniform.

The difference between young Fianna activists in the early twentieth century and the child soldiers of recent years is that Fianna members chose to be militarily active, tended to be adolescents, and were not likely to perform combat roles until they were in their later teens or early twenties. 'The majority of children who participated in the wars in Mozambique and Angola were forcibly recruited, many at a very tender age', reports Honwana. 'Children were abducted from their homes and schools to fight.'[5] As discussed in Chapter Five, the ideological environment of the homes and schools from which Fianna members emerged was likely to foster their active involvement in the independence movement.

Once recruited, children and youth in both cases were moulded through training and propaganda in preparation for the roles they would assume within these military conflicts. As Honwana points out, one reason for 'the systematic preference for children as soldiers is based on the assumption that children make good soldiers because they are especially susceptible to ideological conditioning; they are easier to manipulate and control'.[6] In establishing Na Fianna Éireann, Markievicz and Hobson demonstrated their recognition of the importance of indoctrinating future Irish nationalists from a young age. Some IRA members, however, would have questioned how easy it was to control Fianna boys during the War of Independence.

In what follows, this chapter will identify and discuss the Fianna's performance of different military functions or tasks in turn, illustrating each with examples from different events of the Irish Revolution. The personal price paid by Fianna members for their activism will also be examined. The chapter will also assess the value of the Fianna's military contribution to the Irish Revolution and consider how this contribution was recognised by the Irish state and others in subsequent years.

PROVISION OF TRAINED MILITARY PERSONNEL

The most important military contribution that the Fianna made to the Irish Revolution was the youth group's role as a recruiting and training ground for future members of adult paramilitary and auxiliary organisations and later the National Army. This role was arguably at its most significant in the period 1909–16 when the Fianna's founders Hobson and Markievicz were at their most influential and the youth group's membership was at its most concentrated in terms of numbers and dedication to the advanced nationalist cause.

Militarily Na Fianna Éireann were in the vanguard within the Irish nationalist movement in the early twentieth century. As Patrick Pearse asserted in February 1914 in the pages of the republican newspaper *Irish Freedom*:

> We believe that Na Fianna Éireann have kept the military spirit alive in Ireland during the past four years, and that if the Fianna had not been founded in 1909, the Volunteers of 1913 would never have arisen. In a sense, then, the Fianna have been the pioneers of the Volunteers; and it is from the ranks of the Fianna that the Volunteers must be recruited.[7]

From its inception in 1909, the Fianna provided its members with instruction in military drill, signalling, first aid and marksmanship.[8] Involvement in the Fianna also enabled the group's older members to develop leadership skills because they, not its adult founders, assumed responsibility for the administration of the organisation. The youth group also promoted a militant mindset that glorified fighting and dying for Ireland. Sean Heuston, who was executed for his role in the Easter Rising, exemplified the success of Fianna propaganda with the following words: 'Whatever I have done as a soldier of Ireland is what I believe to be my country's best interest. I have, thank God, no vain regrets.'[9]

The military training and leadership skills of senior Fianna members enabled them to assume the role of instructors when adult paramilitary and auxiliary organisations, such as the Irish Volunteers, Irish Citizen Army and Cumann na mBan, were formed in 1913–14. For instance, Michael Lonergan, Pádraic Ó Riain, Con Colbert and Eamon Martin were members of the Fianna circle of the IRB and served as drill instructors when members of the IRB in Dublin began training in military drill in the summer of 1913. Hobson had instigated such training in preparation for the establishment of a nationalist military body to counter the Ulster Volunteer Force, which had been formed in January of that year in opposition to the impending implementation of home rule in Ireland. Drilling took place at 41 Parnell Square in Dublin, the base of the Irish National Foresters, where Ó Riain's father worked as caretaker.[10] Lonergan later boasted that he 'was the first man in Ireland who taught Patrick Pearse to "form fours".[11] Pádraic Ó Riain, Con Colbert and Seamus Pounch were also called into service to train members of Cumann na mBan after it was formed as a women's counterpart to the Volunteers in April 1914.[12] In contrast, Cumann na mBan member Margaret Skinnider, one of the few women to undertake a combat role during the Easter Rising, trained and drilled the Fianna in Glasgow.[13]

Fianna officers also assumed leadership roles within the Irish Volunteers and Cumann na mBan. When Hobson helped to form the Irish Volunteers in November 1913, he recruited five senior members of the Fianna to the Provisional Committee of the new body: Ó Riain, Colbert, Martin, Lonergan and Liam Mellows. These young men visited various halls in the evenings, instructing the Volunteer officers and directing the course of training. These Fianna officers had previously trained some of the Volunteer officers, the ones who were also members of the IRB.[14] As in the case of the IRB, there was an unofficial link between the Fianna and the Irish Volunteers from the inception of the latter organisation. However, although cooperation between the two organisations was naturally close, there was no formal affiliation between the two until the latter part of the War of Independence.[15]

In Belfast, Nora Connolly was among the organisers of a branch of Cumann na mBan, using what was then the only Fianna troop for girls, the Betsy Gray *sluagh*, as a recruiting ground for the new women's organisation.[16] Connolly's influence and Fianna training helped to ensure that the Belfast members were reputed to be the best shots in Cumann na mBan.[17]

J. J. 'Ginger' O'Connell, one of the few Volunteer officers with professional military experience, was impressed by the high calibre of the Fianna officers who later became officers in the Volunteers. He first met many of these young men when he delivered lectures on military tactics to the Fianna Cadet Corps formed in November 1914.[18] He recalled:

> In general, it was my experience everywhere that those boys who had been officers in the Fianna were subsequently among the very best officers of the Volunteers. This, I do not attribute altogether to the training they received, though that went for much. But even more the boys selected boys with the touch of iron essential for leadership, whereas the men commonly selected someone because he was popular or distinguished in some sphere or other. The Fianna, in short, were primarily soldiers; the raw Volunteers were primarily friends and neighbours.[19]

Thus, the value of the military training and militant mindset propagated by the Fianna was evident from the outset of the Irish Revolution.

The Fianna not only provided adult paramilitary organisations with trained instructors and officers but also with rank and file members. The general trend was for Fianna members to transfer to adult paramilitary and auxiliary organisations when they reached an appropriate age.[20] Around late 1913/early 1914, the Fianna introduced a new rule by which members who had reached the age of eighteen but had not achieved the rank of lieutenant were automatically transferred to the Volunteers. Eamon Martin deemed the arrangement a success: 'It gave to the Volunteers [recruits] who were already fully trained and for the Fianna it solved the problem of the young men of eighteen years and over, for whom there were not sufficient officer positions.'[21]

Involvement in the Fianna brought members into close contact with the Irish Volunteers in Dublin, especially the ones in their local units, and as the boys grew up they transferred into these Volunteer units. Some assumed positions of leadership. As a result, serving and former Fianna members were well represented at the various garrisons around Dublin city centre during the Easter Rising. Others were assigned roles outside of Dublin, such as Liam Mellows who took command in County Galway and Pádraic Ó Riain who was sent to County Tyrone with Commandant Eimar O'Duffy to direct operations there.[22]

A similar though numerically smaller link was forged between the Fianna and the ICA. Fianna members whose dominant loyalty lay with the labour movement chose to join the ICA rather than the Volunteers. Examples include Andy Dunne, Thomas O'Donoghue, Joe Connolly and Fred Ryan, all of whom served with Markievicz as part of the St Stephen's Green garrison during the Easter Rising.[23]

In the years after the Rising, Na Fianna Éireann continued in its role of providing military training to boys, many of whom later transferred to the Irish Volunteers/IRA. Drilling, parading and instruction in the use of firearms were the most common activities in which Fianna members participated in the post-1916 period. As the guerrilla war between the IRA and British government forces intensified over the course of the period 1919–21, the Fianna increasingly had to hold its training classes in what they hoped were secret locations. In 1921, the Fianna in Limerick 'ran regular arms instruction classes for the members', which were usually held somewhere a short distance from the city, such as 'a small wood in Rosbrien'. It was there, however, in May 1921 that twelve members of the class were captured by the RIC. Thomas Dargan reported that the captives were marched to William Street RIC

Barracks where they were locked in a single cell, roughed up during an interrogation parade held by the Black and Tans, and finally sentenced to three years penal servitude.[24] This episode demonstrates the serious challenges faced by the Fianna as the Irish Revolution developed into its later phases.

THE MILITARY ACTIVITIES OF THE FIANNA

While all members of the Fianna received some form of military training, not all were militarily active during the Irish Revolution. This is not surprising given the age cohort of the youth group. The age range of Fianna members was neither static throughout the period of 1909–23, nor as precise as the organisation's rules stipulated. The youth group was initially aimed at boys aged between eight and eighteen, though some of the officers remained involved into their twenties and some girls joined in Belfast and Waterford for short periods of time.[25] By June 1922, only boys aged between twelve and eighteen were eligible for membership in the Fianna.[26]

The restriction of membership to male adolescents in the later years of the Irish Revolution probably reflected the expectation after the experience of the 1916 Rising that Fianna members were likely to be drawn into military action. Even before the Rising, the Fianna leadership appears to have recognised that it would be inappropriate for younger boys to participate in military action. To that end, a Fianna camp was arranged for the Easter weekend in 1916 in order to keep the younger members of the youth group out of danger during the planned rebellion.[27]

There continued to be a link between age and involvement in active service during the War of Independence. In the city of Cork, for example, only a limited number of Fianna members could be deemed militarily active during this guerrilla war. 'Quite a number of the boys, because of their youth, would not be called on for any hazardous tasks', explained Charles Meaney.[28] And yet the relatively young age of Fianna members was what could make their services valuable to the IRA. 'Being a youth of 15 years I did not come under suspicion and was able to move around more freely than an adult', noted P. J. Murphy. He recalled carrying out such tasks as serving as a contact in the purchase of rifles and revolvers from soldiers or, prior to a raid, gaining entrance to premises, such as the Grammar School, where the presence of an adolescent would not be considered suspicious.[29] Only a small number of Fianna members would have provided such services, however. 'As the struggle developed in the years 1920–21, the really active members of the Fianna in Cork [city] could be said to number not more than 30', reported Meaney. Of these, only a fraction was armed with no more than 'a dozen revolvers' among them.[30]

The arming of Fianna boys was controversial because of the potential consequences. 'The use of arms by the Fianna in Cork was frowned on by the IRA leaders in the city; possibly it was thought that we were too young and irresponsible and that independent action by us might in some way cut across IRA plans', noted Meaney, adding that the IRA in Cork issued an order in 1920 that forbade the Fianna from using arms unless they had 'prior permission from the local Volunteer leaders'. 'It is not to be understood from this that we were "pulling against" the IRA', he insisted, 'on the contrary, we acted in close cooperation with the city units, but the question of carrying and using arms against the enemy was regarded as one for decision by the IRA'. Despite this, some Fianna members continued to carry a gun even without permission.[31]

The IRA's willingness to engage the support services of Fianna members was connected to their trust in the individual in question. William O'Flynn noticed that of the fifteen or so boys in the Fethard *sluagh*, only about five were given duties by the local IRA in 1920–21: 'This was not due to any lack of enthusiasm on the part of the other boys for the work, but simply to the fact that they were not asked to do it by the officers of the Volunteer Company.' O'Flynn, who was aged fourteen or fifteen, may have inspired a degree of trust because his father was a Sinn Féin politician and his brother an officer in the Tipperary No. 3 Brigade of the IRA. 'At that time the enemy forces did not pay much attention to boys of my age so I was often entrusted with the care or conveyance of small arms', he reported.[32]

In some places, such as Dublin, Cork and Waterford, the Fianna established active service units.[33] Two such units were formed in Cork city in late 1920 in order 'to have lads available' on a part-time basis 'for any sudden call from the IRA' for assistance.[34] In contrast, the Fianna formed an ASU in Waterford in 1921 as a response to members' frustration that the IRA in that city was not making full use of their services.[35]

The potential for Fianna members to be militarily active during the Irish Revolution also depended on where they were located.[36] It is not surprising that Fianna members in Dublin were the most likely to participate in the Easter Rising as the majority of action during the rebellion took place in that city. As the War of Independence was at its most intense in the province of Munster, Fianna members in counties like Cork and Kerry, for instance, had greater opportunities to play an active part in that conflict.

In light of all of these considerations, the ultimate value of the military duties undertaken by the Fianna during the events of the Irish Revolution is open to different interpretations. To what extent adult activists valued the contributions of their young comrades, often depended on whether Fianna members were operating independently or under IRA orders. The following section highlights some of the military duties performed by the youth group and some of the consequences for individual members.

THE MAIN MILITARY DUTIES UNDERTAKEN BY FIANNA MEMBERS, 1914–21

One of the challenges in assessing the Fianna's military contribution to the Irish Revolution is how to define 'active service' in the military sense. This was an issue faced by the assessors of applicants for military service pensions. As Marie Coleman has highlighted, the 1924 legislation on military service pensions did not provide a clear definition of what constituted 'active service'. It was not until 1955 that the Department of Defence generated a definition, but it was not applicable to Na Fianna Éireann and Cumann na mBan. An applicant who had served with the IRA, for instance, had to have 'participated in an engagement against enemy forces, such participation being in the immediate area of operations and as an integral part of the operating force'.[37] Duties that constituted 'active service' included: 'attacking the enemy, obstructing communications, acquiring and transporting arms and ammunition, guarding prisoners, attending training camps and battalion or brigade meetings, carrying despatches, providing first aid, and assisting volunteers on the run'.[38] Even though the 1955 definition did not apply to Na Fianna Éireann, members of the youth group actually performed many of these duties.

The following sub-sections assess the Fianna's involvement in performing relevant duties from this list, as well as other related tasks, between 1914 and 1921. Primary sources covering these years are richer in detail than those describing the Fianna's military service during the Civil War of 1922–23. Hence, the Fianna's military duties during the Civil War will be discussed in a separate section.

Acquiring and transporting arms and ammunition

Throughout the Irish Revolution, the Fianna played a role in acquiring and transporting arms and ammunition that was sometimes controversial even among their colleagues in the independence movement. The value placed on this role was dependent on coordination with their counterparts in the Irish Volunteers/IRA.

From an early stage, Fianna members were involved in gunrunning as well as the smuggling of weapons and ammunition, most famously as part of the Howth and Kilcoole gunrunning episodes in the summer of 1914, but also on other less spectacular occasions. Adolescent male Fianna members had the opportunity to put their skills and training to work in a real-life military manoeuvre when they helped the Irish Volunteers in the landing of a consignment of 1,500 rifles and 45,000 rounds of ammunition at Howth, County Dublin, on 26 July 1914. About 200 male members of the Fianna over the age of twelve participated in the event.[39] Hobson, who organised the landing, instructed them to bring their trek-cart loaded with wooden batons to Howth and to distribute these batons to the Volunteers for protection in case of police interference. Six Fianna members were responsible for signalling, both in Morse code and semaphore, to the Asgard from the Hill of Howth.[40] When the yacht, the Asgard, docked at the pier, the Fianna were ordered to fill their trek-cart with 2,000 rounds of ammunition and bring it back to Dublin. For Hobson, the Fianna 'were the only body with sufficient discipline to be entrusted with ammunition' at that time.[41] When a second shipment of arms arrived in Kilcoole on the night of 1 August 1914, Garry Holohan and Patrick Ward were among the Fianna members who helped to land the cargo and transport it to Dublin.[42]

Hobson excluded Markievicz and the female members of the Fianna from the Howth gunrunning, provoking their anger and disappointment. During the weekend in which the gunrunning took place, Markievicz was supervising a Fianna camp in the Dublin Mountains attended by the Connolly sisters as well as boys under twelve. Ina Connolly was angry and disappointed that the girls had been excluded, recalling that 'it really looked as if we were not trusted ... Had I been a boy I would not have been overlooked'.[43] Ina and her sister Nora, however, were later asked to smuggle guns up to Belfast, a risky task that they completed successfully.[44] Transportation of arms was a task often entrusted to women. It was among the duties carried out by members of Cumann na mBan during the War of Independence.[45]

Figure 8 Members of the Fianna and the Irish Volunteers at the Howth gunrunning on 26 July 1914.

Fianna members were sometimes given the task of smuggling weapons and ammunition because their youth made them less likely than adults to be suspected of such activities. On occasion, however, the police received information that led to the arrest of these young couriers. For instance, on 25 November 1917 two Fianna boys, Michael O'Carroll and John Nelson, were arrested in Belfast when they alighted from the Glasgow boat carrying about fifty pounds of explosives. Joseph Robinson, a prominent member of the Irish Volunteers in Glasgow and a former Fianna member himself, had given the boys the explosives and some letters to convey to an unnamed man at Amiens Street Station (now Connolly Station) in Dublin. Robinson and the two boys were prosecuted in Glasgow. According to the Inspector-General's monthly report, the police had been aware for some time that 'Countess Markievicz and the Irish Citizen Army [were] endeavouring to procure explosives in Glasgow', but it now appeared 'from information supplied by an agent of the [RIC] in Glasgow that the IRB [were] engaged in procuring explosives through the Scottish circles of the Brotherhood'.[46] The arrest of the trio was a result of such police intelligence.

Fianna members later proved useful to the IRA in serving as couriers to transport arms and ammunition. For example, Thomas O'Connor 'took part in collecting and delivering rifles, revolvers and ammunition' between the various battalions and the ASU in the Kerry No. 1 Brigade in 1920–21.[47]

The Fianna found different ways to acquire their own weapons and ammunition. For instance in Tralee, the father of Fianna member Billy Myles worked as a general carpenter in the military barracks at Ballymullen and occasionally managed to obtain 'revolvers, ammunition and bombs' from soldiers stationed at the barracks. These were used by the boys for practice in the use of revolvers and Mills bombs.[48]

Fianna members were also involved in raids to acquire arms, either in conjunction with the Volunteers or operating independently. For instance, in November 1917 a Fianna special squad participated in an arms raid on a pawn shop in Dublin, an activity that would become more common in 1919–20 once the War of Independence was underway.[49] In late 1919, senior members of the Fianna in Limerick 'decided it was time some effort was made to collect guns', though 'this did not meet with the wholehearted approval' of their officers. Despite this, the senior members began to plan and execute arms raids. Thomas Dargan reported:

> Most of the raids were carried out by two groups and our success at the beginning was anything but good, due principally to lack of good information. It must be remembered that at the time the average age of the Fianna raiding parties was about 15 years and they were starting out without any experience. Nevertheless, a certain amount of success came our way and as time went on we were gaining valuable experience which proved very useful in 1920 and 1921, when activities on the war front were every day gaining momentum.[50]

Fianna members elsewhere in Ireland were also keen to gain experience acquiring their own arms.

Charles Meaney recorded that during the War of Independence small groups of Cork Fianna members armed with a revolver carried out night-time raids on the homes of 'pro-British people who were suspected of having guns'.[51] Meaney's description of his first such raid reveals a combination of bumbling inexperience and sheer good luck. In March 1920, he was making his daily delivery of bread to the home of 'a retired British army colonel' in the Douglas area of Cork when he 'noticed a few shotguns inside'. That night, he returned to the house with four other Fianna boys all wearing 'cloth masks'. They knocked at the door and the housekeeper let them in, but they were unable to find the shotguns. While their search for arms was underway, Meaney's mask fell from his face and the housekeeper recognised him. The young raiders left the house immediately.

Early the next morning, the RIC raided Meaney's home and he was taken to the Bridewell where he found two of his Fianna comrades in custody. He recalled:

> Head Constable Browne of the RIC, who was in charge of the Bridewell, knew me well and told me he would 'look after me'. He asked me if I had anything incriminating in my possession and I told him I had a toy revolver in my pocket. He took the revolver from me. When we were paraded next day for identification, to our great surprise, nobody from the colonel's house came to identify us. We were released the following day.

Meaney later discovered that Browne had 'tipped off' some IRA men who visited the retired colonel and informed him that 'he would be shot if he, or his housekeeper, came along to identify [the Fianna boys] as the raiders'.[52] Meaney and his Fianna comrades went on to participate in more successful arms raids.

Patrick Hearne's BMH witness statement indicates that relations between the Fianna and the IRA were problematic in Waterford, with the acquisition of arms and ammunition a particular source of tension. Frustrated that they had been left out of arms raids during 1920, the Fianna there decided to undertake their own armament, which then consisted of a single .45 revolver in Hearne's possession. Having struggled to raise the £7 necessary to buy 'two new long .45 Webley revolvers', they began raiding 'Loyalist houses', railway linesmen's huts and quarry storehouses for arms. 'We arranged our own dump at the County Kilkenny side of the [river] Suir and by the end of a month or two we had several revolvers, shotguns, one Lee Enfield rifle, [and] one .22 rifle', recalled Hearne. Unfortunately, however, they often found that the IRA had preceded them in raids or vice versa.[53]

The morning after successful raids on two businesses, Hearne was summoned to Brigade Headquarters of the IRA where he was questioned about the raids. 'I was then handed a list of the goods seized and found it did not correspond with mine insofar as their list contained much more than I had had listed by our Quartermaster, Joe Tobin, as being taken in the raid', reported Hearne. 'After some days we had found that four of those who had been on the raids, had set aside some of the fuse, detonators, one revolver and some trenching tools.' These items were recovered and the four Fianna members were severely reprimanded and from then on were kept under close watch by their officers to ensure they were excluded from future operations.[54]

Such an incident, despite the steps taken to neutralise the culprits, was unlikely to boost the IRA's confidence in the Waterford Fianna. Thus it is not surprising that in December 1920 the Fianna were instructed to hand over their arms, ammunition and 'any other war material' to the 4th Battalion IRA. After a heated debate that nearly led to the disintegration of the Fianna battalion, the instruction was carried out, though officers who possessed their own arms were allowed to keep them. Thus, the Waterford Fianna began 1921 with only 'four revolvers and very little ammunition'. Relations between the Fianna and the IRA in Waterford remained somewhat strained, with Fianna officers being excluded from an ambush at Picardstown, Tramore, in January 1921, much to their chagrin. To counter dissatisfaction in their ranks, the Fianna organised their own ASU independent of the IRA in Waterford city and began a special training course for 'twenty of the oldest members and officers'.[55]

The situation in Waterford illustrates why the IRA was at times reluctant to make full use of the Fianna as a human resource and sought to bring the youth group to heel. It was recognition of the potentially dangerous consequences of overlapping arms raids by the Fianna and the IRA that finally led to negotiations between Dáil Éireann's Ministry of Defence and Fianna Headquarters. As a result, a formal link between the Fianna and the IRA was forged in early 1921 to facilitate cooperation – and control.[56] Under the agreement, the Fianna was 'recognised as one of the units at the disposal of the Republican Government' and responsible for assisting the Irish Volunteers 'in every manner possible' under their own officers. Though the Fianna would act in cooperation with the Irish Volunteers, it would 'remain in most respects a separate organisation'.[57]

Participating in engagements against enemy forces

Some older members of the Fianna, usually those in their later teens and in their twenties, took part in combat during the events of the Irish Revolution. Often these individuals held overlapping memberships in the Fianna and the Irish Volunteers/IRA. This was particularly the case for Fianna officers who might also be members of adult paramilitary organisations.

One of the most famous examples of the Fianna in combat occurred during the 1916 Easter Rising. A combination of Irish Volunteers and Fianna officers, who were in their late teens and early twenties, were responsible for attacking the Magazine Fort in the Phoenix Park at the beginning of the Rising. With an assumed air of innocence, the young men kicked a football around in front of the fort before they rushed the sentry at the entrance. They proceeded to disarm the guards in the guardroom and seize their rifles and bayonets. Garry Holohan and Barney Mellows had orders 'to take the sentry on the parapet'. Holohan recalled:

> I rushed straight through the fort, which is rather a large place, and I had some difficulty in locating him. I eventually saw him looking at me over a roof. I rushed towards him, calling on him to surrender. He came towards me with his bayonet pointed towards me. I fired a shot and he fell, and at that moment Barney came along the parapet. The poor sentry was crying, 'Oh, sir, sir, don't shoot me. I'm an Irishman and the father of seven children'.[58] Barney tried to stand him up but his leg must have been broken. We told him not to be afraid as we would do him no harm and we would send his companions to attend him.[59]

As this incident highlights, many of the members of the British government forces whom the rebels fought were actually their fellow Irishmen. As for the Magazine Fort, Paddy O'Daly (also known as Daly) had orders to blow it up. Unable to find the key to the high-explosives store, he set the charges in the small-arms ammunition store instead. Thus, what was meant to be a massive explosion to mark the start of the Rising ended up being a much smaller blast.[60]

The attacking party released their prisoners, who included the fort commander's wife Mrs Playfair and her two sons, and everyone managed to clear out of the fort before the detonation. The prisoners had been warned that anyone who headed towards any of the several nearby barracks to report the incident would be shot. However, the fort commander's eldest son, George Playfair, ignored the warning and was shot and fatally wounded by the Fianna Quartermaster Garry Holohan as he ran to alert a policeman to the attack.[61] Both Holohan and Playfair were both twenty-three years of age at the time.[62]

In contrast, Seamus Pounch, who was about twenty-two years of age, saw less action at the garrison located at Jacob's Biscuit Factory, though on one occasion he 'was dispatched to the biscuit loft to direct fire' at British troops who were advancing from the park beside St Patrick's Cathedral. According to Pounch, the British troops fled in disorder when he and his comrades opened fire. He also recalled that 'during a lull in the fighting in Jacob's we held a miniature ceilidh – Volunteers and Fianna, Cumann na mBan, Clan na Gael Girl Scouts … a real welcome break in the serious business we had in hand'.[63] As these examples show, the roles played by Fianna members during the Easter Rising could depend both on the intensity of military action experienced by their garrison as well as their age profile.

Serving as dispatch carriers, couriers and orderlies

Among the most common military duties assigned to members of the Fianna was serving as dispatch carriers, couriers and orderlies. Members of Cumann na mBan and the Clann na Gael Girl Scouts also undertook such duties. The age and/or gender of members of these organisations made them less likely to be suspected by government authorities of subversive activities. For instance, the youth and gender of fifteen-year-old Clann na Gael Girl Scout, Mary McLoughlin, facilitated her contribution as a courier during the Easter Rising in Dublin. She was responsible for delivering messages and ammunition.[64]

Members of the Fianna also served as dispatch carriers and couriers during the Easter Rising. Charles MacMahon later claimed that he was only eleven years of age when he delivered food and dispatches during the Easter Rising.[65] Among the various duties that Seamus Pounch carried out during the rebellion was delivering supplies to the garrison at the Royal College of Surgeons.[66] One of the youngest Fianna boys to serve as a dispatch carrier during the Rising was Tommy Keenan, who was about twelve years of age. According to Pounch, Keenan 'came to Jacob's with dispatches and by his youth and innocent appearance he had no trouble in getting around'.[67] Keenan himself recorded that the British troops allowed him to traverse the city without question because 'I said I was going to relations'.[68] Another Fianna member was not so lucky. Sean Healy had just turned fifteen when he was shot by British troops close to his Phibsborough home in north Dublin. Garrison commander Thomas MacDonagh had sent the boy home from Jacob's 'because he was too young to fight'. It has been suggested that he may have asked Healy to deliver a message warning of 'an ambush at the bridge in Phibsborough'.[69]

During the Rising, Fianna members also served as orderlies, a role that involved carrying orders or running errands for a senior officer.

The experience of one such orderly highlights how the youthfulness of the Fianna could have its humorous side even in a combat situation. According to Thomas Meldon, who served at Jacob's Biscuit Factory during the Easter Rising, 'A Fianna boy, who was attached to HQ as orderly, discovered in a display case an extra-rich cake which he disposed of with remarkable speed and with dire results, but although very ill, he refused to go home'.[70]

Fianna members outside of Dublin also carried out similar duties during the rebellion. Michael Mulkerrins, who served in the Athenry area of County Galway, was responsible for dispatch carrying, scout duty and driving a horse and cart loaded with rations during the Rising. His 1916 service resulted in the loss of his job as a pantry boy at Rockfield House as well as his arrest, though he was released within a day because of his youth.[71]

Fianna members also undertook similar tasks for the IRA during the War of Independence. 'The carrying of IRA dispatches was part of the routine work of the Fianna, but nonetheless important', reported Charles Meaney in reference to Cork city. 'Boys were available at all times to carry out this work in cooperation with Cumann na mBan, and, so far as I am aware, the job was done efficiently and quickly, without interference by the enemy.'[72] Volunteer officer Jeremiah Whelan had already recruited several local boys to carry dispatches for the IRA company in Fethard, County Tipperary, before a Fianna *sluagh* was formed there in 1920.[73] After the Kerry No. 1 Brigade of the IRA formed an ASU in late 1920, Thomas O'Connor found himself increasingly involved in dispatch carrying. 'From then to the Truce, with other members of the Fianna, I was constantly on the road carrying dispatches to and from the different battalion officers in the area, Brigade Active Service Unit and Brigade staff', he noted.[74]

The Fianna Battalion Council in Limerick controlled a dispatch service that 'was going full swing in 1920'. The 'operational centre' for this service was located at the Irish Transport and General Workers' Union Hall on O'Connell Street, which was also the IRA Brigade HQ. The Fianna collected 'all dispatches from [IRA] GHQ which arrived in Limerick at the railway station'. 'The messages, which usually were carried by the train staff, were handed over to a contact in the Railway office and then collected by our members and brought to IRA Brigade HQ', explained Thomas Dargan. 'Messages for HQ were delivered at the station and then forwarded to Dublin by the same procedure.' The Fianna in the city of Limerick were responsible for delivering 'GHQ dispatches for mid-Limerick, East Limerick, West Limerick and

Clare'. Fianna messengers had to cycle many miles to places such as Annacrotty, Castleconnell, Caherconlish and Patrickswell, all in County Limerick, and Cratloe, County Clare, to get the dispatches on their way. 'In the end of 1920 and in 1921 these roads became very dangerous for cyclists as British military, Black and Tans and Auxiliaries were practically continuously on them, but during the whole period only one dispatch was captured', noted Dargan.[75]

In Waterford, the Fianna also played an important role in the collection and delivery of dispatches. A Fianna member, who worked as a junior clerical officer at the Great Southern Railway, North Station, collected dispatches 'enclosed in envelopes addressed to O/C, Waterford', which had been sent by rail 'with the Stationmaster's official correspondence'. He then arranged for them to be sent to Fianna leader Tom McDonald's hairdressing salon on The Mall from where a team of Fianna cyclists would set off to deliver dispatches.[76]

Scouting and intelligence gathering

The Fianna played an important role in scouting and intelligence gathering during the Easter Rising and War of Independence. Members of Cumann na mBan also engaged in intelligence gathering for the IRA particularly during the latter conflict.[77] Fianna scouts were valuable for reconnaissance because their youth made them less likely than adults to be suspected of subversive activity when they were sent out to obtain information, for example, about a specific building, a geographic area or the movements of police or military personnel. Fianna members carried out scouting and other intelligence gathering at the request of their own officers or of the Irish Volunteers/IRA. Sometimes Fianna scouts were attached to IRA ASUs.

Joseph Reynolds reported that he served as a scout, gathering information about military barracks in Dublin prior to and during the Easter Rising. In late 1915, Fianna officer Barney Mellows approached Reynolds about carrying out this task because Reynolds regularly visited the Marlboro (now McKee) and Royal (now Collins) Barracks to deliver 'feeding for the officers' dogs' from the abattoir where his father worked. While there, Reynolds 'had practically the run of the Barracks'. He recalled:

> Barney asked me would I concentrate on the Marlboro Barracks and get as much information as possible regards the entrances, exits, and all the military stores appertaining to the Barracks. From

time to time I supplied Barney with various details regarding the Barracks. I continued doing this up to the Rising.⁷⁸

On the mornings of Easter Sunday and Monday 1916, Reynolds was asked to 'watch the movements of the British troops in and around the [Marlboro] Barracks … I went to the railway bridge at Blackhorse Lane from where I could observe all movements in the Barracks'. He saw 'nothing unusual' from this vantage point on either day. Later on Monday, he was on his way to Church Street when he spotted 'British troops marching down Aughrim Street towards the Quays'. His report of this sighting apparently resulted in an order to strengthen a barricade in the area.⁷⁹

Fianna members played an important role during the War of Independence by serving as scouts for the IRA and engaging in other intelligence gathering. William O'Flynn, for example, made use of two school friends, the sons of sergeants in the RIC and the military barracks in Fethard, County Tipperary, to help him gather information for the IRA. 'By chumming with these two boys I was able to gain easy access into both the RIC and military barracks, and whenever I was in either barracks I always kept my ears and eyes open', he recalled. 'I took particular notice of any unusual police or military activity, memorised the registration numbers of motor cars or lorries which I saw in the barracks, got the names of prisoners or hostages brought in in lorries, and made a mental note of the times at which patrols or parties of police or military left or entered the barracks.' He passed this information on to two Volunteer officers of his acquaintance.⁸⁰

According to George Hurley and Charles Meaney, the Fianna in Cork city frequently undertook scouting duty for the IRA. They watched military and police barracks in order to observe the movements of troops, Black and Tans and police, tracked the movements of 'suspected spies' and reported any relevant information obtained to the IRA.⁸¹ For example, Fianna boys often acted as scouts for IRA units that were waiting in preparation for an ambush or any other attack. 'Our job was to give warning of the approach of enemy forces', noted Meaney.⁸²

The Fianna also undertook these duties in County Kerry. Thomas O'Connor recalled that when the IRA attacked Camp RIC Barracks in February 1920, they mobilised the Tralee Battalion of the Fianna who were placed at strategic points between Ballymullen Military Barracks and Blennerville Bridge. 'Our duty was to warn the IRA taking part in the attack of the approach of enemy reinforcements', he explained. O'Connor and other members of the Fianna in Tralee also shadowed individuals, such as ex-British soldiers, who were suspected of 'giving information to the enemy'. In 1921, intelligence provided by O'Connor and his colleagues resulted in the IRA's decision to shoot dead a Major J. A. MacKinnon while 'he was playing a round of golf'.[83]

Elsewhere in Kerry, Thomas Pelican, the O/C of the Listowel Battalion of the Fianna, ordered two Fianna company captains, Patrick Flaherty of Listowel and James Sullivan of Ballylongford, to keep a Mrs Wallace of Ballylongford under observation and report her movements to him. Pelican had heard that Mrs Wallace, the wife of an imprisoned IRA man, 'was friendly with the enemy garrison in Ballylongford Barracks'. Information provided by the two Fianna captains resulted in Pelican and two IRA men holding up Mrs Wallace and obtaining two letters signed by the Head Constable of Listowel. The letters contained information that the RIC were planning to arrest and shoot an IRA officer and that a Miss O'Carroll, whom the IRA thought was friendly towards their cause, was also helping the police. In response to this intelligence, the IRA warned their comrade to go on the run and placed the woman under arrest.[84]

Fianna members often gathered valuable information for the IRA as a result of their civilian employment. 'Several of our members had obtained employment in the local post office, where, on numerous occasions, they got possession of telegrams in code passing from Dublin Castle and vice versa to the various military and police barracks in the area', recorded Thomas O'Connor of Tralee. The Fianna members passed these messages to IRA officers who had a key for decoding them before the telegrams 'were delivered to the enemy'. O'Connor assisted in decoding these messages.[85]

On another occasion in Listowel, a Fianna member who was employed as a telegraph messenger in the local post office provided information to Thomas Pelican, who was attached to both the IRA and the Fianna. John Kiely had seen Maurice Enright-Egan pass two letters to a Black and Tan sergeant. Enright-Egan 'worked as a carrier delivering goods daily between Ballylongford and Listowel'. Pelican had already warned him about the potential consequences of 'helping the enemy'. Acting on Kiely's information, Pelican held up Enright-Egan twice in two days:

> As the monthly reports of the enemy in outlying districts usually came into Listowel on the last or first day of each month I waited outside Ballylongford on the last day of the month and again held up Enright-Egan as he was leaving the village. This time he had no

enemy communications on him, so I let him go about his business. On the following day, however, I held him up again and took from him the official monthly report from Ballylongford RIC Barracks together with a letter from a Sergeant Gilhooley addressed to Head Constable Smyth in Listowel. I again warned him, saying that he would be shot if he continued working for the enemy.

Pelican gave the report and the letter to the O/C of his local IRA column. He did not record whether Enright-Egan heeded his warnings.[86]

Acquiring provisions and other items

Fianna members were responsible for commandeering items or carrying out raids in order to acquire provisions and other goods for redistribution or destruction. For instance, during the Easter Rising in Dublin Seamus Pounch's duties included commandeering lard, potatoes and several trays of bread from shops located close to the garrison at Jacob's Biscuit Factory.[87] Thomas O'Reilly, who served on the north side of the city, reported that he 'took stuff out of the houses' in order to build barricades, which he then defended.[88]

During the War of Independence, the Fianna engaged in similar activities. In April 1920, the Fianna in Waterford took part in a successful raid on the income tax office on Parnell Street, which was close to the Manor Street RIC Barracks. The 'books and documents' seized in the raid 'were burned in the Gaelic Field immediately afterwards', recalled Patrick Hearne.[89]

The Fianna also 'carried out daylight raids on shops and vans containing provisions and various other goods being dispatched to military barracks in Cork'.[90] For instance, Charles Meaney recalled 'a daylight hold-up of a lorry' which had just been loaded up with provisions outside of Dobbyn's shop on Alford Street. The Fianna boys commandeered the lorry and drove it to Hardwick Street where they 'emptied the contents (jam and other provisions) into a store' and later distributed these to the relatives of IRA men in prison.[91]

In Cork city, the Fianna not only 'held up and destroyed' 'military stores in transit' but also 'held up individual soldiers or Black and Tans and took their equipment'.[92] 'Three or four of us waylaid soldiers and Black and Tans who were sometimes in the company of girls, or, perhaps, leaving a public house in a drunken condition', recalled Meaney. 'Whenever the opportunity offered, we attacked them, took their equipment and, in quite a good few instances, got revolvers as well.'[93]

The IRA in Cork and Waterford instructed the Fianna to commandeer bicycles from civilians and the military for use by dispatch riders and IRA flying columns. Charles Meaney reported that he and his comrades managed to collect about forty bicycles from 'certain houses of loyalists' in Cork city during 'one day's raiding' and took them to a shed in Sawmill Street where a man repainted them to prevent identification.[94]

Bicycles were also a valuable commodity in Limerick where the Fianna found that dispatch carrying was getting to be such a big job that it required one. In 1920 the local Fianna started 'to capture bicycles' first from the British military, who soon got wise to their raids, and then from shops in O'Connell Street. Thomas Dargan estimated that they 'must have taken 50 or 60 bicycles'. 'Sometimes our members were armed, but in most cases we depended on speed of operation to get us through', he recorded, adding that two Fianna members were arrested and sentenced to two years in prison because of their bicycle stealing. 'The bicycles, on being captured, were brought to the Fianna Hall where they were immediately stripped of all military equipment and repainted.' On the night in 1920 when the Black and Tans burned the Fianna Hall, 'about 14 bicycles in the course of being changed-over were destroyed'.[95]

The Fianna used their experience in raiding to support the Belfast Boycott. In August 1920, the cabinet of Dáil Éireann had retaliated against the expulsion of Catholic workers from Belfast shipyards by introducing a boycott of Ulster businesses and banks in the vain hope that this action would not only demonstrate the northeast's economic dependence on the rest of Ireland but also lead to the reinstatement of Catholic workers. The boycott continued until the outbreak of the Civil War. 'The Fianna was particularly active in enforcing the boycott of Belfast goods being sold in shops', reported George Hurley. 'Daylight raids were of frequent occurrence; goods were removed from shops and the owners warned that the practice of selling such goods should stop.' He deemed the Fianna's actions as 'very effective in "tightening" the boycott campaign in Cork city'.[96]

Other duties as assigned

Fianna members were often called upon to undertake other duties as assigned. In addition to his duties as a dispatch carrier and courier during the Easter Rising, Patrick Daly also helped to erect barricades in the North King Street area of Dublin and 'regulate the crowd' seeking bread from Monks' Bakery.[97] In some places, Fianna members worked in cooperation with the IRA to obstruct communications. For instance, Thomas Sheehan, a Fianna member in Carlow, was involved in road blocking and wire-cutting during the War of Independence as well as the more usual Fianna tasks of scouting and dispatch carrying. He was arrested in March 1921 for blocking roads and sentenced to one year in Wandsworth Prison in London. After his release under the general amnesty in January 1922, he resumed his duties with the Fianna and then joined the National Army in April of that year.[98]

MILITARY DUTIES DURING THE IRISH CIVIL WAR, 1922–23

Na Fianna Éireann as an organisation supported the anti-Treaty side during the Civil War. Fianna members who were pro-Treaty left the youth group, some, like Thomas Sheehan in Carlow, choosing to join the National Army. Such a choice may have been motivated as much by the prospect of regular pay as by a commitment to the pro-Treaty side.[99] As discussed in chapter 4, Fianna membership dropped drastically after the outbreak of the Civil War and the youth organisation barely survived the conflict.

During the Civil War, some of the remaining members of the Fianna carried out military duties in support of the anti-Treaty IRA. These duties were much the same as those undertaken during the previous events of the Irish Revolution, such as scouting, serving as dispatch carriers and couriers, and sometimes participating in combat. The circumstances surrounding the deaths of Fianna members during the Civil War provide insight into the ages of militarily active members and the roles they assumed during this bitter conflict between former comrades.

Nineteen-year-old Patrick Tubridy, for example, was helping to garrison the O'Curry Street Barracks in Limerick on 12 May 1922 when he was accidentally shot by his comrade Thomas Dargan and died in hospital later that day. Michael J. Ryle was scouting for the anti-Treaty IRA when he was killed in an engagement with the National Army on 5 August 1922 in Ballycarthy, County Kerry. The eighteen-year-old had also served as a dispatch carrier prior to his death. William Barrett was returning to his home in Castlebar, County Mayo, after delivering a dispatch when he was knocked down by a truck driven by members of the National Army. He died in hospital on 24 March 1923.[100] Other Fianna members, such as eighteen-year-old James Mooney, served as couriers for the anti-Treaty IRA and took part in fighting against the National

Army. Nineteen-year-old Michael Moynihan, for instance, died of gunshot wounds that he received in action against the National Army at the Telephone Exchange Building in Limerick on 12 July 1922.[101] These examples suggest that Fianna members who were militarily active during the Civil War were usually in their late teens.

The Fianna's active service in support of the anti-Treaty side also led to the arrest and internment of members. In some cases, unhealthy conditions in prisons and involvement in hunger strikes contributed to poor health and ultimately death. Eighteen-year-old Martin Considine's death from acute pneumonic phthisis in December 1923 was attributed to his service with the Fianna and his subsequent imprisonment in Limerick Jail and Harepark Camp. In the same year, the deaths of Daniel D. Foley, aged seventeen, and Arthur Hughes, aged nineteen, from tuberculosis were also deemed attributable to their service and imprisonment. Gerald Landers, who had been attached to an ASU in Kerry before his arrest in September 1922, was recorded as having gone on hunger strike twice while imprisoned, but did not die of tuberculosis until 1927.[102]

FIANNA DEATHS, 1916–23

As noted in the preceding pages, many members of the Fianna lost jobs, were jailed or suffered wounds or ill health due to their activism. Still others paid the ultimate price and died either as a result of their active service or as collateral damage. The Military Service Pensions Collection (MSPC) contains records relating to at least sixty-nine serving or former Fianna members who died in the period 1916–23, most as a result of their military service. Of these sixty-nine individuals, twenty-eight were still members of the Fianna at the time of their death. Table 1, based on the MSPC sample discussed in chapter 5, shows how many serving or former Fianna members died in each relevant year between 1916 and 1923.[103] These numbers suggest that the majority of serving or former Fianna members who died during the Irish Revolution lost their lives in the context of the Civil War.

Table 1 Deaths of serving and former Fianna members in the MSPC sample, 1916–23.

Year	1916	1918	1919	1920	1921	1922	1923
Deaths	2	2	2	4	4	38	17

The twenty-eight youths in the MSPC sample who were members of the Fianna at the time of their death were killed in a variety of circumstances relating either to their military service or the conflicts of the time.[104] For example, several Fianna members were killed on active service during the War of Independence or died as a result of wounds sustained in incidents in early 1922. Thomas Moriarty was accidently shot and killed on 5 September 1920 at Faha, County Kerry, while he was scouting during a raid for an RIC man who had been ordered to leave the area.[105] Daniel O'Driscoll was shot and killed by British forces at Ardfert, County Kerry, on 9 April 1921 while he was engaged in scouting at Liscahane Bridge.[106] Elsewhere in Kerry, tensions between British government forces and republicans remained evident during the Truce period. Patrick (Percy) J. Hannafin was shot in the head by the Black and Tans during an encounter on Edward Street in Tralee on 20 January 1922 and died a week later. Fellow Fianna member Michael Mullaly was also wounded in the incident, but recovered.[107] Percy Hannafin's mother's application for a dependant's allowance or gratuity under the Army Pensions Act (APA) was initially rejected because 'the wounds which resulted in his death were not received while he was engaged in military service (despite acting on the instructions of his O.C., P. Hannafin was engaged in an unlawful act and was wounded during the period of suspension of hostilities)'.[108] In a further incident that occurred during the uneasy months leading up to the Civil War, Henry O'Connor was accidentally killed by an IRA comrade on 27 April 1922 while carrying out an arms raid in Ferns, County Wexford.[109]

Accidents while handling firearms also led to the deaths of some Fianna members. In Cork in November 1918, Joseph W. Reed was cleaning his revolver when it accidentally discharged and wounded him; he died a week later.[110] Earlier that year, another Fianna member with a similar name died from wounds received when the revolver he was cleaning accidentally discharged. James A. Busby recalled that the incident occurred when a Fianna boy named Joe Reid was cleaning his revolver in preparation for the firing party that would render military honours at the funeral of Fianna officer Seamus Courtney in July 1918.[111] Courtney's comrades attributed his death to 'imprisonment and poor health', as he had taken part in a hunger strike by political prisoners in Cork Gaol in 1917 while imprisoned there.[112] Another fatal accident occurred in April 1922. Thomas Slattery, a seventeen-year-old lieutenant with the Limerick City Battalion of the Fianna, was giving instruction in the use of a revolver when he accidentally shot himself and died the next day.[113]

As the guerrilla war between the IRA and British government forces descended into tit-for-tat violence, some Fianna members became the victims of reprisals. On 17 November 1920, two Fianna members suffered the results of 'a reprisal by government forces for the shooting of an RIC sergeant named O'Donoghue by the IRA earlier on the same night'. A man wearing a policeman's uniform broke into the Broad Street home of seventeen-year-old Fianna member Patrick Hanley just before midnight. Having heard a commotion, Hanley, clad 'in his night attire', opened his bedroom door only to be confronted by the uniformed gunman. Hanley apparently said 'Don't shoot; I am an orphan and my mother's only support', but the gunman fired anyway, the first bullet missing the youth but the second hitting him above the heart and killing him instantly.[114] On the same night that Hanley was killed, the RIC shot another Fianna member by the name of O'Brien during another reprisal raid, this one in the Grattan Street area of Cork city. O'Brien, however, recovered from his wound.[115]

Extremely high levels of violence in Belfast in the first half of 1922 provided the context for the deaths of at least three serving Fianna members. The Anglo-Irish Treaty was meant to normalise relations between north and south, but instead it heightened tensions. In the spring of 1922, the pro- and anti-Treaty forces of the IRA pursued an anti-partitionist strategy by planning a northern offensive that ultimately failed due to poor coordination. The Ulster Unionist government in Northern Ireland responded by bringing in the Special Powers Act to combat the IRA. Under this legislation, Na Fianna Éireann was one of the organisations 'deemed to be unlawful'.[116] Fianna member William Toal died in hospital on 26 May 1922, having been shot in the chest by British forces in the Ardoyne district while he was trying to deliver dispatches between IRA units during an attack by British and Northern Ireland government forces.[117] Continuing unrest led to the deaths of two members of 'A' Company of the Belfast Fianna. Leo Rea, a seventeen-year-old messenger from Leeson Street, was fatally wounded on the morning of 23 June 1922. The official report was that he was shot on his way to work, though there is some question about whether he might have been on duty for the IRA at the time. There was a lot of gunfire in Belfast that day because the previous day in London the IRA had assassinated Sir Henry Wilson, a military advisor to the northern administration and Unionist Member of Parliament (MP). Eleven days later, on 4 July 1922, Joseph Aloysius Hurson, a sixteen-year-old apprentice cabinet maker, was standing at the front door of his Unity Street home when he was shot in the head by a sniper.[118]

Thus, Fianna members were as likely as any other youths in Ireland to be innocent victims caught in the crossfire during times of conflict. James Kelly, aged fifteen, died of a fatal gunshot wound to the head sustained on 25 April 1916, the second day of the Easter Rising. Evidence uncovered by RTÉ broadcaster Joe Duffy suggests that James Kelly, unlike his brother Francis, was not involved in the Rising. According to his grand-nephew Paul Brady, James Kelly was killed at Blacquiere Bridge in Phibsborough, close to his workplace 'in the nearby Broadstone railway yard where he was serving an apprenticeship'.[119] In contrast, Kelly's mother Teresa stated in her claim for compensation after his death that her son 'was killed whilst playing outside Phibsborough Chapel in the field'. She burned his Fianna uniform and remained silent about his membership in the youth group in her compensation claim, knowing that it would be rejected if his membership were known.[120] A link to the Fianna would have fuelled suspicions of misconduct during the rebellion. Despite her efforts to burn the evidence, British soldiers apparently raided the family's home, 'leaving bullet marks that were visible in the cottage at 205 Phibsborough Road, opposite All Saints Church, until it was demolished in 1980'.[121]

Fianna deaths became more common as a result of the Civil War. Poor preparation for war on both sides may have contributed to the higher death count during this later conflict. The new National Army, for example, suffered from 'a lack of sound officers' and an excess of troops with 'no military knowledge and experience'.[122] Fifteen pension applications were made by family members whose sons' deaths between 1922 and 1928 were either claimed or deemed to have been attributable in some way to their Fianna service during the Civil War. Some of these Fianna members died in combat, others in prison and still others due to illness after their release from prison.[123]

One of the most notorious incidents in which members of the Fianna were killed during the Civil War was the murder of officers Sean Cole and Alf Colley on 26 August 1922 only days after Michael Collins, commander-in-chief of the National Army, was shot dead in the Béal na Bláth ambush in County Cork. Cole's MSPC file records that the pair were coming home 'from a meeting to set up a Fianna Éireann Dublin Brigade active service unit' when they 'were stopped, searched and taken away in a car from Newcomen Bridge by a number of armed men who [were] alleged to have been members of the National Forces wearing trench coats over National Army uniforms'. The bodies of Cole and Colley were 'later found with gunshot wounds' at Yellow Lane in Whitehall, Dublin. Although the 'inquest on 28 August 1922 returned a verdict of wilful murder against some person or persons unknown', a letter from the Department of Defence, which was dated 19 October 1922, stated that nineteen-year-old Cole was killed by anti-Treaty forces ('Irregulars') because he refused to obey orders.[124] At the inquest, Alderman Michael Staines testified that 'my brother [Vincent] said to me that young Cole had told him he was leaving the Irregulars'.[125] It appears that both sides tried to blame the other for the killing of the two Fianna officers. Cole's funeral was an emotional public affair featuring the pageantry of full Fianna military honours whereas Colley's family instead chose a private funeral. Both young men were buried in Glasnevin Cemetery, with Cole's cortège passing Collins' grave.[126]

Less than two months later three teenaged former Fianna members, then attached to the IRA, also died in murky circumstances. On the night of 6 October 1922, Edwin (Eamonn) Hughes, Joseph Rogers and Brendan Houlihan, all aged between sixteen and seventeen, were caught with republican posters in their possession when they were arrested on Clonliffe Road in Drumcondra and taken away for interrogation by three men wearing National Army uniforms. The next day the youths' bodies were found at Red Cow near Clondalkin, County Dublin. An inquest determined that they had died 'from gunshot wounds inflicted by some person or persons unknown', despite allegations that Commandant Charles Dalton of the National Army had been involved in the incident.[127] In the charged atmosphere of the Civil War, posting print propaganda in opposition to the pro-Treaty side could be as potentially hazardous as involvement in military confrontation.

STATE RECOGNITION OF THE FIANNA'S MILITARY SERVICE

In the years after the Irish Revolution, the Irish state recognised the military contribution of Na Fianna Éireann to the struggle for independence through the awarding of service pensions and medals to former members and providing financial compensation to dependants of members who had died as a result of their military service. Service pension recipients automatically received medals for their service. Medals were also awarded to individuals whose service was not of a pensionable standard.

Of the 155 former Fianna members in the MSPC sample, sixty-three received service pensions; the applications of ten others were unsuccessful.[128] In the Fianna sample, 85.7% of service pension recipients were from Dublin (or had served there) and 81% had participated in the Easter Rising, which highlights the importance of service during that rebellion for the receipt of pensions. The vast majority of Fianna members who served during the Rising did so in Dublin, but four pension recipients participated in action outside of the capital. Michael Mulkerrins served in Athenry, County Galway, while Mícheál S. Mac Eochaidh (Michael J. Kehoe), James O'Brien and Pádraic Toibin took part in the rebellion in Enniscorthy, County Wexford.[129] As Marie Coleman has noted, 'those who participated in the Rising in Dublin – both men and women – had a much easier time securing service pensions'. It was much harder for Cumann na mBan veterans to get credit for their activities during the War of Independence and Civil War, and the same appears to be true for the Fianna.[130]

The pension paid to recipients was based on a calculation of their length of pensionable service combined with their pension grade (A-E), which was determined by their military rank. Thus, individuals of higher rank and longer service received larger pensions. Under the 1924 Military Service Pensions Act (MSPA), the lowest pension grade was designated as A (for privates and NCOs) while the highest was E (for ranks higher than major general). These pension grades were reversed under the 1934 legislation, with E becoming the lowest grade.[131] Table 2 shows the categories of military ranks of the sixty-three successful applicants in the sample.

These categories of military ranks determined an individual's pension grade and related to service not just in the Fianna, but also in the ICA, the Irish Volunteers/IRA and the National Forces. Patrick O'Daly, for example, was awarded a high ranking D grade pension under the 1924 Act mainly on the basis of his service with the Volunteers and the National Army.[132]

The MSPC sample also includes seventy-nine applications made by family members of deceased Fianna members for dependants'

Table 2 Military ranks of service pension recipients in the MSPC sample of former Fianna members.

Ranks	Private/ NCO	Lieutenant/ Captain	Commandant/ Major	Colonel/ Major General	Higher than Major General
Number of recipients	31	23	6	1	2
Percentage of total recipients	49.2	36.5	9.5	1.6	3.2

allowances and gratuities or, in rare cases, widow's allowances under the APA. A total of fifty-eight of these applications (73.4%) were successful while twenty (25.3%) were not. The outcome of one application was unclear.[133] Claims were rejected if the Fianna member's death was not deemed attributable to their military service or the applicant, usually a parent or a sibling, was not found to have been financially dependent on the deceased. In the cases of a stepmother and a mother of an 'illegitimate' son, it was decided that the legislation did not apply.[134] In addition, three other former Fianna members in the sample made applications under the APA and were awarded disability pensions or a wound pension and allowance to compensate them for injuries they sustained while on active service.[135] One applicant was refused a wound pension or gratuity because the injury he sustained while serving with the National Army was due to his own negligence.[136] Some of the service pension recipients also received compensation for injuries.

In addition, the state recognised the military service of former Fianna members through the awarding of medals. A search of the MSPC Pensions and Awards database for the organisation 'Fianna Éireann' revealed that 1,702 medals were awarded to former Fianna members who were not pension recipients.[137] Five of these individuals were awarded 1916 Medals.[138] Twenty received the Service (1917–1921) Medal with Bar.[139] The remaining 1,677 received the Service (1917–1921) Medal without Bar, which was awarded to individuals who had played limited roles that were not of a pensionable standard.

The male gender of most Fianna members and their tendency to transfer to adult organisations, such as the ICA, Irish Volunteers/IRA and National Army, meant that they undertook a wider variety of military roles during the Irish Revolution and received compensation from the state for their service from an earlier date than members of Cumann na mBan. Some former Fianna members were eligible for service pensions under the 1924 legislation because they had also served with the National Army. In contrast, Cumann na mBan members had to wait until 1934 for recognition of their service in the form of pensions. Although both Cumann na mBan and Na Fianna Éireann were limited under the 1934 legislation 'to the two lowest possible ranks for pension purposes – D and E', the ability of Fianna members to later transfer to the ICA, the Irish Volunteers/IRA and the National Army meant that they had the opportunity to serve in ways that incurred greater risks, but also received greater recognition and financial compensation by the state.[140]

NOTES

1 Countess Markievicz, 'Foreword by chief of the Fianna' in *Fianna Handbook* (Dublin: Central Council of Fianna Éireann, 1924), p. 4.
2 William O'Flynn, witness statement, 29 Aug. 1955 (MA, BMH, WS 1,235).
3 'Anglo-Irish War', p. 15, 'Black and Tans', p. 47 and 'Auxiliaries', p. 32, in S. J. Connolly (ed.), *The Oxford Companion to Irish History* (Oxford: Oxford University Press, 1999).
4 Alcinda Honwana, 'Children's involvement in war: Historical and social contexts', *Journal of the History of Childhood and Youth*, 1:1 (2008), p. 141.
5 *Ibid.*, p. 145.
6 *Ibid.*, p. 146.
7 Patrick Pearse, 'To the boys of Ireland', *IF*, Feb. 1914, p. 6.
8 For more on the Fianna's military training programme, see chapter 6.
9 *Easter Week Commemoration Programme*, 1932, p. 12 (MA, BMH, Kathleen Clarke Collection, CD 163/4).
10 Bulmer Hobson, *Ireland Yesterday and Tomorrow* (Tralee: Anvil Books, 1968), p. 18; Bulmer Hobson, 'The IRB and the Fianna' in F. X. Martin (ed.), *The Irish Volunteers, 1913–1915: Recollections and Documents* (Dublin: James Duffy, 1963), pp. 21–2.
11 Michael Lonergan, witness statement, 1 Aug. 1948 (MA, BMH, WS 140).
12 Marnie Hay, 'The foundation and development of Na Fianna Éireann', *Irish Historical Studies*, 36:141 (May 2008), pp. 62–3.
13 Daniel Branniff, witness statement, 14 Oct. 1948 (MA, BMH, WS 222).
14 Eamon Martin, witness statement, 1 Oct. 1951 (MA, BMH, WS 591).
15 Hobson, *Ireland*, p. 18; Hobson, 'IRB and Fianna', p. 22.
16 Nora Connolly O'Brien, witness statement, 21 July 1949 (MA, BMH, WS 286).
17 Denis McCullough, witness statement, 11 Dec. 1953 (MA, BMH, WS 915); Margaret Ward, *Unmanageable Revolutionaries* (London: Pluto Press, 1995), p. 104.
18 For more on O'Connell and the Fianna Cadet Corps, see chapter 6.
19 J. J. O'Connell, 'Memoir of the Irish Volunteers, 1914–16, 1917', ed. Daithí Ó Corráin in *Analecta Hibernica*, 47 (2016), p. 21.
20 This trend is demonstrated in chapter 5 in its examination of sample cohorts of former Fianna members.
21 Eamon Martin, witness statement, 1 Oct. 1951 (MA, BMH, WS 591).
22 *Ibid.*
23 Seamus Kavanagh, witness statement, 9 Sept. 1957 (MA, BMH, WS 1,670); 'Irish Citizen Army Membership, 1916' in Ann Matthews, *The Irish Citizen Army* (Cork: Mercier Press, 2014), pp. 188–211.

24 Thomas Dargan, witness statement, 24 Apr. 1956 (MA, BMH, WS 1,404).
25 The controversies surrounding girls in the Fianna are discussed in chapters 3–5.
26 'HQ Notes and Orders', *Fianna*, June 1922, p. 2.
27 Joseph Reynolds, witness statement, 31 Jan. 1949 (MA, BMH, WS 191).
28 Charles Meaney, witness statement, 11 June 1957 (MA, BMH, WS 1,631).
29 P. J. Murphy, witness statement, 14 Apr. 1953 (MA, BMH, WS 869).
30 Charles Meaney, witness statement, 11 June 1957 (MA, BMH, WS 1,631).
31 *Ibid.*
32 William O'Flynn, witness statement, 29 Aug. 1955 (MA, BMH, WS 1,235).
33 'Addendum to Fianna Éireann – history and development, 1909–1921' (NLI, J. J. O'Connell Papers, MS 22,113).
34 George Hurley, witness statement, 7 June 1957 (MA, BMH, WS 1,630).
35 Patrick Hearne, witness statement, 18 Aug. 1958 (MA, BMH, WS 1,742).
36 For a map of the location of Fianna troops, *c.* 1909–22, see Marnie Hay, 'Na Fianna Éireann' in John Crowley *et al.* (eds), *Atlas of the Irish Revolution* (Cork: Cork University Press, 2017), p. 174.
37 Memorandum, 'Military service pensions and service (1917–1921) medals without bar', 13 Oct. 1955 (UCDA, Sean MacEoin Papers, P151/519), quoted in Marie Coleman, 'Military service pensions for veterans of the Irish revolution, 1916–1923', *War in History*, 20:2 (2013), p. 211.
38 Coleman, 'Military service pensions for veterans of the Irish revolution', p. 211.
39 Robert Holland, witness statement, 18 July 1949 (MA, BMH, WS 280).
40 *Ibid.*
41 Hobson, 'IRB and Fianna', p. 22.
42 Garry Holohan, witness statement, 7 Dec. 1949 (MA, BMH, WS 328).
43 Ina Connolly Heron, witness statement, 25 Jan. 1954 (MA, BMH, WS 919).
44 Ward, *Unmanageable Revolutionaries*, pp. 105–6.
45 Marie Coleman, 'Compensating Irish female revolutionaries, 1916–1923', *Women's History Review* 26:6 (2017), p. 916.
46 Inspector-General's Report, Nov. 1917 (TNA, CO 904/104).
47 Thomas O'Connor, witness statement, 15 June 1955 (MA, BMH, WS 1,189).
48 *Ibid.*
49 Aodh MacNeill, 'Summary of operations, Dublin Brigade, Fianna Éireann, 1916–1921' in 'Addendum to Fianna Éireann, history and development,1909–1921' (MA, Collins Collection, A/0041/3). This document is also available in NLI, J. J. O'Connell Papers, MS 22,113.
50 Thomas Dargan, witness statement, 24 Apr. 1956 (MA, BMH, WS 1,404).
51 Charles Meaney, witness statement, 11 June 1957 (MA, BMH, WS 1,631).

52 *Ibid.*
53 Patrick Hearne, witness statement, 18 Aug. 1958 (MA, BMH, WS 1,742).
54 *Ibid.*
55 *Ibid.*
56 Fianna GHQ Dublin to Fianna officers, Feb. 1921 (MA, BMH, Michael Kilmartin Collection, CD 144/1/20); Joseph Reynolds, witness statement, 31 Jan. 1949 (MA, BMH, WS 191).
57 Fianna GHQ Dublin to Fianna officers, Feb. 1921 (MA, BMH, Kilmartin Collection, CD 144/1/20).
58 Fearghal McGarry, *Rebels: Voices from the Easter Rising* (Dublin: Penguin Ireland, 2011), p. 162.
59 Joe Duffy, *Children of the Rising* (Dublin: Hachette Books Ireland, 2015), p. 20.
60 *Ibid.*, p. 20.
61 Garry Holohan, statement regarding Easter Week 1916 (MA, BMH, John F. Shouldice Collection, CD 20/8); Shane Hegarty and Fintan O'Toole, *The Irish Times Book of the 1916 Rising* (Dublin: Gill and Macmillan, 2006), p. 44.
62 Duffy, *Children of the Rising*, p. 20.
63 Seamus Pounch, witness statement, 15 June 1949 (MA, BMH, WS 267). According to the Pounch family's 1911 census return (misspelled Paunch), James (also known as Seamus) was then aged seventeen; available at www.census.nationalarchives.ie/pages/1911/Dublin/Fitzwilliam/Charlemont_Street/73316/ (accessed 17 July 2018).
64 Mary McLoughlin, witness statement, *c.* Feb. 1954 (MA, BMH, WS 934).
65 Charles Eugene MacMahon, pension file (MA, MSPC, 24SP6134).
66 Seamus Pounch, witness statement, 15 June 1949 (MA, BMH, WS 267).
67 *Ibid.*
68 Thomas Patrick Keenan, pension file (MA, MSPC, MSP34REF303).
69 Duffy, *Children of the Rising*, p. 226.
70 McGarry, *Rebels*, p. 190.
71 Michael Mulkerrins, pension file (MA, MSPC, 24SP906).
72 Charles Meaney, witness statement, 11 June 1957 (MA, BMH, WS 1,631). George Hurley also mentioned the Fianna's involvement in dispatch carrying (MA, BMH, WS 1,630).
73 William O'Flynn, witness statement, 29 Aug. 1955 (MA, BMH, WS 1,235).
74 Thomas O'Connor, witness statement, 15 June 1955 (MA, BMH, WS 1,189).
75 Thomas Dargan, witness statement, 24 Apr. 1956 (MA, BMH, WS 1,404).
76 Patrick Hearne, witness statement, 18 Aug. 1958 (MA, BMH, WS 1,742).
77 Coleman, 'Compensating Irish female revolutionaries', p. 916.

78 Joseph Reynolds, witness statement, 31 Jan. 1949 (MA, BMH WS 191).
79 *Ibid.*
80 William O'Flynn, witness statement, 29 Aug. 1955 (MA, BMH, WS 1,235).
81 George Hurley, witness statement, 7 June 1957 (MA, BMH, WS 1,630); Charles Meaney, witness statement, 11 June 1957 (MA, BMH, WS 1,631).
82 Charles Meaney, witness statement, 11 June 1957 (MA, BMH, WS 1,631).
83 Thomas O'Connor, witness statement, 15 June 1955 (MA, BMH, WS 1,189).
84 Thomas Pelican, witness statement, 7 Mar. 1955 (MA, BMH, WS 1,109).
85 Thomas O'Connor, witness statement, 15 June 1955 (MA, BMH, WS 1,189).
86 Thomas Pelican, witness statement, 7 Mar. 1955 (MA, BMH, WS 1,109).
87 Seamus Pounch, witness statement, 15 June 1949 (MA, BMH, WS 267).
88 Thomas O'Reilly, pension file (MA, MSPC, MSP34REF33197).
89 Patrick Hearne, witness statement, 18 Aug. 1958 (MA, BMH, WS 1,742).
90 George Hurley, witness statement, 7 June 1957 (MA, BMH, WS 1,630).
91 Charles Meaney, witness statement, 11 June 1957 (MA, BMH, WS 1,631).
92 George Hurley, witness statement, 7 June 1957 (MA, BMH, WS 1,630).
93 Charles Meaney, witness statement, 11 June 1957 (MA, BMH, WS 1,631).
94 Patrick Hearne, witness statement, 18 Aug. 1958 (MA, BMH, WS 1,742); Charles Meaney, witness statement, 11 June 1957 (MA, BMH, WS 1,631).
95 Thomas Dargan, witness statement, 24 Apr. 1956 (MA, BMH, WS 1,404).
96 George Hurley, witness statement, 7 June 1957 (MA, BMH, WS 1,630).
97 Patrick Daly, pension file (MA, MSPC, MSP34REF5541).
98 Thomas Sheehan, pension file (MA, MSPC, 24SP794). The duties undertaken by the Fianna in Carlow are also outlined in a letter from P. P. O'Farrell to the Office of Director of Artillery, Dept. of Defence, 18 July 1934 (MA, Collins Collection, A/0800/16).
99 Michael Hopkinson, *Green against Green: The Irish Civil War* (Dublin: Gill and Macmillan, 1988), p. 136.
100 Patrick Tubridy, pension file (MA, MSPC, DP6554); Michael J. Ryle, pension file (MA, MPSC, DP24836); William Barrett, pension file (MA, MSPC, DP668).
101 James Mooney, pension file (MA, MSPC, DP7488); Martin Considine, pension file (MA, MSPC, DP156); Michael Moynihan, pension file (MA, MSPC, DP8157).
102 Martin Considine, pension file (MA, MSPC, DP156); Daniel D. Foley, pension file (MA, MSPC, DP3596); Arthur Hughes, pension file (MA, MSPC, DP4576); Gerald Landers, pension file (MA, MSPC, 2RBSD506).
103 See Appendix III for a list of those included in this sample, which was generated on 11 July 2018. The Fianna Roll of Honour only lists the

names of thirty-seven Fianna members who died between 1916 and 1923. See https://nafiannaeireann.files.wordpress.com/2014/09/nfe_roll ofhonor.pdf (accessed 18 July 2018).
104 The twenty-eight Fianna members in this sample who died between 1916 and 1923 are: William Barrett (died 1923), Sean Cole (1922), Martin Considine (1923), Michael Doyle (1923), Daniel D. Foley (1923), Patrick Hanley (1920), Patrick J. Hanlon (1923), Patrick (Percy) J. Hannafin (1922), John (Sean) Healy (1916), Arthur Hughes (1923), Joseph Hurson (1922), John Lawlor (1921), Christopher McEvoy (1919), James Mooney (1923), Thomas Moriarty (1920), Michael Moynihan (1922), Francis Murphy (1919), John Murray (1920), Michael O'Brien (1921), Henry O'Connor (1922), Daniel O'Driscoll (1921), John O'Leary (1922), Leo Rea (1922), Joseph Walton Reed (1918), Michael J. Ryle (1922), Thomas Slattery (1922), William Toal (1922) and Patrick Tubridy (1922).
105 Thomas Moriarty, pension file (MA, MSPC, DP3424).
106 Daniel O'Driscoll, pension file (MA, MSPC, DP9697).
107 'British truce-breakers in Tralee by Volunteer' in J. J. Lee (ed.), *Kerry's Fighting Story, 1916–21: Told by the Men Who Made It* (Cork: Mercier Press, 2009), pp. 318–19.
108 Patrick J. Hannafin, pension file (MA, MSPC, DP4142).
109 Henry O'Connor, pension file (MA, MSPC, DP7242).
110 Joseph Walton Reed, pension file (MA, MSPC, 1D103).
111 James A. Busby, witness statement, 6 June 1957 (MA, BMH, WS 1628). The Fianna Roll of Honour lists Seamus Courtney and Joseph Reid as dying on 18 and 20 July 1918, respectively. See https://nafiannaeireann.files.wordpress.com/2014/09/nfe_rollofhonor.pdf (accessed 18 July 2018).
112 P. J. Murphy, witness statement, 14 Apr. 1953 (MA, BMH, WS 869); James A. Busby, witness statement, 6 June 1957 (MA, BMH, WS 1,628).
113 Thomas Slattery, pension file (MA, MSPC, DP5715).
114 George Hurley, witness statement, 7 June 1957 (MA, BMH, WS 1,630); Patrick Hanley, pension file (MA, MSPC, DP4150).
115 George Hurley, witness statement, 7 June 1957 (MA, BMH, WS 1,630).
116 Robert Lynch, *The Northern IRA and the Early Years of Partition, 1920–1922* (Dublin: Irish Academic Press, 2006), p. 226.
117 William Toal, pension file (MA, MSPC, DP6722).
118 Leo Rea, pension file (MA, MSPC, 2D504); Joseph Aloysius Hurson, pension file (MA, MSPC, 2D502); Alan F. Parkinson, *Belfast's Unholy War* (Dublin: Four Courts Press, 2004), pp. 258, 299.
119 Duffy, *Children of the Rising*, pp. 196–8, 244.
120 *Ibid.*, pp. 197, 213.
121 *Ibid.*, p. 197.

122 Hopkinson, *Green against Green*, pp. 128, 136.
123 The MSPC contains pension applications in relation to the following Fianna members who died between 1922 and 1928: William Barrett (DP668), Sean Cole (DP3749), Martin Considine (DP156), Michael Doyle (DP8502), Daniel D. Foley (DP3596), Patrick J. Hanlon (3D25), Arthur Hughes (DP4576), James Keating (DP9571), Gerald Landers (2RBSD506), James Mooney (DP7488), Michael Moynihan (DP8157), John O'Leary (1D372), Michael J. Ryle (DP24836), Michael Sheahan (DP24083) and Patrick Tubridy (DP6554).
124 Sean Cole, pension file (MA, MSPC, DP3749).
125 'Alderman's statement', *Nationalist and Leinster Times*, 2 Sept. 1922, p. 6.
126 'Comrades' last tribute', *FJ*, 31 Aug. 1922, p. 4.
127 'Hold-up at Clonliffe Road', *FJ*, 19 Oct. 1922, p. 5; 'Officer's narrative', *Irish Independent*, 19 Oct. 1922, p. 6; 'Open verdict at inquest', *Irish Independent*, 16 Nov. 1922, p. 7; *I gCuimhne* (Dublin: Irish Republican Soldiers Memorial Committee, 1926) (NLI, EPH, A371); Eamonn Patrick Hughes, pension file (MA, MSPC, DP4559); Brendan M. Holohan, pension file (MA, MSPC, DP4496).
128 See Appendix III. The list used for this sample was generated through an online search of MSPC files on 11 July 2018 at www.militaryarchives.ie/collections/online-collections/military-service-pensions-collection-1916 –1923.
129 Michael Mulkerrins, pension file (MA, MSPC, 24SP906); Micheál S. Mac Eochaidh (Michael J. Kehoe), pension file (MA, MSPC, MSP34REF23991); James O'Brien, pension file (MA, MSPC, MSP34REF4836); Pádraic Toibin, pension file (MA, MSPC, MSP34REF21379).
130 Coleman, 'Compensating Irish female revolutionaries', p. 926.
131 Catriona Crowe (ed.), *Guide to the Military Service (1916–1923) Pensions Collection* (Dublin: Óglaigh na hÉireann, 2012), p. 175.
132 See Patrick O'Daly, pension file (MA, MSPC, 24SP424).
133 The claim was made by the parents of Gerald Landers, a Fianna member who was imprisoned during the Civil War and died of pulmonary tuberculosis in 1927 (MA, MSPC, 2RBSD506).
134 The application by Richard Twohig's stepmother was rejected because she was not his birth mother (MA, MSPC, DP5824), while the application made by Thomas Greehy's mother was rejected because she had not been married to his father (MA, MSPC, DP1837).
135 Christopher Feekery, pension file (MA, MSPC, DP54521); Ralph J. Lynch (MA, MSPC, MSP34REF84); Joseph Marrinan, pension file (MA, MSPC, DP3018).
136 Patrick Flynn, pension file (MA, MSPC, 4P121).

137 This search was undertaken on 17 July 2018 at www.militaryarchives.ie/collections/online-collections/military-service-pensions-collection-1916–1923.
138 James Cleary, Ernest Nunan, Cormac McGinley, Sean McGuinness and James (also known as Seamus) Pounch were awarded 1916 Medals.
139 The following men were awarded the Service (1917–21) Medal with Bar: Robert Brendan Bonfield, James Cleary, Alfred Leo Colley, Sean Doyle, Leo Basil Craig, Patrick Cuddihy, William Devine, Leo Dooley, George Kearns, John Keogh, George McClean, Sean McDarby, Cormac McGinley, Robert Leahy, Francis O'Connor, Patrick O'Sullivan, James Pounch, John Anthony Stack, David Tormey and Thomas White.
140 Coleman, 'Compensating Irish female revolutionaries', p. 924.

Conclusion

Uniformed youth groups are a form of associational culture that arose in the late nineteenth and early twentieth centuries as a response to societal anxieties associated with the coming war in Europe. Na Fianna Éireann, or the Irish National Boy Scouts, were an Irish nationalist manifestation of this trend. Countess Constance Markievicz and Bulmer Hobson founded the Fianna in Dublin in 1909 as an Irish nationalist antidote to Robert Baden-Powell's Boy Scout movement formed in the previous year. The Fianna went on to play a notable role in the struggle for Irish independence in the years before and after the Easter Rising of 1916.

In the early twentieth century, youth groups in many European countries offered members various combinations of military training, instruction in scouting and other practical skills, hiking and camping trips, cultural activities with a national flavour, opportunities for volunteering and social companionship. The Fianna were no different. Involvement in Fianna activities could be a source of education, empowerment and excitement – it could even be fun. And from that point of view, the Fianna's appeal was similar to many other youth groups of the period. Where the Fianna experience could differ from that of many other youth organisations was the increased potential for members to kill or be killed.

The Fianna also played an important role in the production and distribution of advanced Irish nationalist print propaganda. In some cases, members served as a volunteer labour force for the distribution of propaganda generated by adult colleagues in the nationalist movement. In other cases, the Fianna were responsible for producing and disseminating their own publications. The propaganda produced by the Fianna in its early years served a similar purpose to advanced nationalist propaganda aimed at children and youth in general. It provided Fianna members with an Irish nationalist education and with military instruction. It promoted specific role models as well as an idealised image of Irish nationalist youth that members could emulate. Just like the Fianna organisation itself, it offered an Irish nationalist alternative to British popular youth culture. Participation in the production and distribution of print propaganda empowered Fianna members, helping them to gain hands-on experience and providing them with a public voice. Such propaganda, however, also sought to mould the minds and bodies of members into a tool to be used by adult nationalists in the struggle for independence and to portray martyrdom as an attractive destiny.

Markievicz and Hobson may have instigated the youth group, but most of the hard work of keeping the organisation going was done by the boys and young men themselves. Older members of the Fianna who took on leadership roles within the youth group gained practical experience in governance and administration. They learned how to run meetings, instruct members and manage all aspects of the organisation. They undertook such tasks as fundraising and organising events. Even for those members who did not assume positions of leadership, the chance to learn and practise new skills, to participate in events like camping trips or public parades, and to be entrusted with various tasks must have boosted self-esteem and self-confidence.

During the period 1909–23, members of Na Fianna Éireann were mainly male adolescents from Irish Catholic nationalist families who had been influenced not only by the Irish cultural revival of the late nineteenth and early twentieth centuries but also by the cult of discipline, training and manliness that grew out of the increasing anticipation of the First World War. Although some girls joined the Fianna in Belfast and Waterford during the revolutionary era, their presence was controversial. Undoubtedly, young people who already harboured advanced nationalist or republican views were attracted to the Fianna. But it would be surprising if involvement in the organisation did not reinforce or intensify these views.

Adult nationalists made use of the Fianna as a source of voluntary workers and symbols of the future nation state. The activities offered by the Fianna were clearly designed (in modern parlance) to groom members to play an active role in the struggle for Irish independence, though an active role did not necessarily mean a life-threatening role. The voluntary work undertaken by members could be more political than military in nature. It is evident, however, that Fianna members were not only utilised by adults in the Irish nationalist movement but also empowered by their involvement in that movement. In the longer term, some former Fianna members grew up to become political, military and business leaders as well as individuals who were in a position to shape public opinion through their employment in journalism and education. Others contributed to the cultural life of the new Irish state.

Over a decade after the foundation of the Fianna, Markievicz found herself imprisoned in 1920–21, ostensibly because her leading role in the youth group's establishment was viewed as a conspiracy against British authority in Ireland within the later context of the Irish War of Independence of 1919–21. The apparent reason for her arrest said as much about her high profile as a radical nationalist as it did about the transformation of the Irish nationalist youth group into a training ground and military support body for the Irish Volunteers/IRA.

In a letter to her sister Eva Gore-Booth, Markievicz contrasted her own treatment to that of Baden-Powell:

> It rather amused me to see that for starting the Boy Scouts in *England* Baden Powell was made a Baron. I have always heard that he did not really start them but that it was a woman. I suppose, though, that he more or less ran them and made them a success. I bet he did not work as hard as I did from 1909–1913.[1]

She highlighted the irony that a man who started a British uniformed youth group was knighted while a woman who started an Irish one was incarcerated. Her comments also assert her feminist viewpoint – and perhaps imply some resentment towards her male co-founder Hobson, who had used the Fianna as a recruiting ground for the IRB.

The years that Markievicz associated with her own hard work were also significant. Without her endeavours, the Fianna would never have been established in 1909. Though she remained the organisation's flamboyant frontwoman until her death in 1927, Markievicz was probably at her most influential in the period 1909–13. The year 1913 was a turning point in two ways. Firstly, at that year's *ard-fheis* Fianna officers who were also members of the IRB gained control of the youth group and remained at the helm until 1923, after which Markievicz regained control of the youth group. Secondly, 1913 was also the year that witnessed the formation of the adult paramilitary organisations, the Irish Volunteers and the Irish Citizen Army. From their inception in 1909, the Fianna had been in the military vanguard of the Irish nationalist movement through their provision of military training and promotion of a militant mindset. Thus, Fianna members were well prepared to assume an active role in these new adult militias when they were old enough. From 1913 onwards, the youth group's fortunes tended to be inextricably linked to trends in the adult republican movement.

The period 1909–16 witnessed the slow and often unsteady development of the Fianna. During those years, Markievicz and Hobson oversaw the emergence of a cadre of young revolutionaries. The Fianna in Dublin city and county were the trailblazers within this increasingly republican youth group. Organisational changes in the Dublin area set the trend for those that would occur elsewhere in the country. Ultimately, the Dublin Fianna would provide the youth organisation with its strongest republican core during the revolutionary era.

The Easter Rising of 1916 was another turning point for the Fianna. Serving and former members of the Fianna played a prominent part in the rebellion. Some lost their lives as a result, most famously Con Colbert and Sean Heuston, who were executed for their roles in the Rising. As the advanced nationalist movement gained in popularity in the post-1916 period, so did the Fianna. The youth group attracted an increasing number of members around Ireland particularly from 1917 onwards. Prior to the rebellion, the Fianna had balanced their focus on military training and scouting with Irish cultural activities. During the subsequent War of Independence, this balance would tip in favour of military training for all members and participation, for some, in military action, mainly in support roles.

During the period 1916–23, the Fianna went from being one of the first military organisations to begin regrouping after the Easter Rising to almost completely collapsing. The organisation's survival throughout this period was due to the efforts of its young officers, not its co-founders Markievicz and Hobson. Markievicz's freedom was frequently curtailed during this time and she could not resume anything other than a nominal leading role until the end of the Civil War in 1923, whereas Hobson, by force of circumstances, chose to retreat from the nationalist movement after the Rising.

Former Fianna member Charles Meaney summed up the youth group's military contribution to the War of Independence in Cork city in the following statement: 'The efforts of the Fianna were mainly concentrated on causing as much trouble to the enemy as was possible, having regard to our age, our numbers, the few weapons at our disposal and the reluctance of the IRA to let us use what weapons we had.'[2] His statement highlights many of the issues related to the Fianna's military contribution throughout the Irish Revolution.

Factors such as age, geographic location, willingness to engage in risky activities and the quality of relationships with adult paramilitary groups, most notably the Irish Volunteers/IRA, all impacted on the military roles undertaken by the Fianna and the value placed on these roles by their older comrades during the years of the Irish Revolution. Where there was trust, respect and coordination between the Fianna and adult paramilitary organisations, Fianna members often played an essential support role. When mutual trust and cooperation broke down, the Fianna could be viewed by their adult counterparts as immature and irresponsible interlopers. Ultimately, the most valuable and least ambiguous military contribution of the Fianna to the Irish Revolution was the youth group's role in providing trained personnel to adult paramilitary organisations. The Irish state's provision of medals, service pensions and financial compensation to those who were injured or to the dependants of those who died demonstrated its recognition of the contributions and sacrifices made by serving and former Fianna members during the struggle for Irish independence.

The unsettled conditions that prevailed during the War of Independence and the Irish Civil War increasingly impacted on the Fianna's ability to function effectively due to such factors as arrests, limited funds and poor communications. In contrast to Sinn Féin and the IRA, the 1921 Anglo-Irish Treaty did not lead to a split within the Fianna, which as an organisation took an anti-Treaty stance. Instead, pro-Treaty members quietly left the youth group.

The Civil War nearly destroyed Na Fianna Éireann. Former comrades fought against one another. Membership numbers collapsed, the leaders as well as many members were imprisoned, and there was a steep rise in Fianna deaths. In the aftermath of the Civil War, Markievicz practically had to rebuild the republican youth group from scratch. If revolutions are what happens to wheels, Na Fianna Éireann went full circle between 1909 and 1923.

NOTES

1. Constance Markievicz to Eva Gore-Booth, 1 Jan. 1921, quoted in Constance Georgina Gore-Booth de Markievicz, *Prison Letters of Countess Markievicz* (New York: Kraus Reprint, 1970), p. 266.
2. Charles Meaney, witness statement, 11 June 1957 (MA, BMH, WS 1,631).

Appendix I

Former Fianna members in the *DIB* who were born in the period c. 1888–1912

List No.	Name	Years of birth and death	Type of entry/notes
1	Sean Ernest Brady	1890–1969	Own entry
2	Michael Brennan	1896–1986	Own entry
3	Robert Emmet Briscoe	1894–1969	Own entry
4	Basil Clancy	1907–96	Own entry
5	Cornelius 'Con' Colbert	1888–1916	Own entry
6	Ina Connolly Heron	1896–1980	Mentioned in the entries for her sister Nora Connolly O'Brien and her husband Archie Heron, whom she married in 1919.
7	Nora Connolly O'Brien	1893–1981	Own entry
8	Roderic James 'Roddy' Connolly	1901–80	Own entry
9	Thomas Derrig (Tomás Ó Deirig)	1897–1956	Own entry
10	Dan Dowd (O'Dowd)	1903–89	Own entry
11	George Gilmore	1898–1985	Own entry
12	Joe Groome	c. 1908–77	Own entry
13	Stephen Hayes	1902–74	Own entry
14	Archibald 'Archie' Heron	1894–1971	Own entry; married Ina Connolly in 1919.
15	Sean (John J.) Heuston	1891–1916	Own entry
16	Austin Hogan (né Dilloughery)	1906–74	Own entry
17	Garry Holohan	1894–1967	Mentioned in his brother Paddy Holohan's entry.
18	Patrick 'Paddy' Holohan (Houlihan)	1897–1946	Own entry
19	John Joe 'Purty' Landers	1907–2001	Own entry

230 Appendix I

List No.	Name	Years of birth and death	Type of entry/notes
20	Sean MacBride	1904–88	Own entry
21	John McCann	1905–80	Own entry
22	Maurice Joseph MacGonigal	1900–79	Own entry
23	Joseph McKelvey	c. 1885 [1898]–1922	Own entry; may have been a member of the Fianna.
24	Sean McLoughlin	1895–1960	Own entry
25	Brian MacNeill	c. 1900–1922	Mentioned in his father Eoin MacNeill's entry.
26	Hugh Hyacinth 'Hugo' McNeill	1900–63	Own entry
27	Eamon Martin	1892–1971	Own entry
28	William Joseph 'Liam' Mellows	1892–1922	Own entry
29	Thomas Lincoln Joseph Mullins	1903–78	Own entry
30	Thomas 'Tommy' O'Brien	1905–88	Own entry
31	Peter O'Connor	1912–99	Own entry
32	Patrick O'Daly (Daly)	1888–1957	Own entry
33	(Michael) Kevin O'Doherty	1912–99	Own entry
34	Aodogán John Eoin O'Sullivan O'Rahilly	1904–2000	Own entry
35	John Michael (Sean, Jackie) Ormonde	1905–81	Own entry
36	Cathal O'Shannon	1890–1969	Own entry
37	George Plant	1904–42	Own entry
38	James Plant	Born c. 1903	Mentioned in his brother George Plant's entry.
39	Augustus Percival Harald 'Percy' Reynolds	1895–1983	Own entry
40	Joseph Robinson	1887–1955	Own entry; belonged to Hobson's original Belfast Fianna.
41	Seamus Robinson	1890–1961	Own entry; belonged to Hobson's original Belfast Fianna.
42	Desmond Ryan	1893–1964	Own entry
43	Eugene Sheehan	1903–86	Own entry
44	John Joe Sheehy	1897–1980	Own entry
45	Patrick Joseph Stephenson	1895–1960	Own entry
46	John Walsh	Born c. 1900	Mentioned in the entry for his brother Joseph James Walsh (1905–92).
47	Martin Walton	1901–81	Own entry

Appendix II

Fianna members and leaders who gave witness statements (WS) or contemporary documents (CD) to the BMH

List No.	Name	WS or CD No.	WS date	Location	Notes
1	Richard 'Dick' Balfe	WS 251	19/5/52	Dublin	
2	Seamus Bevan	WS 1,058	7/1/55	Dublin	
3	Liam A. Brady	WS 676	1/5/52	Derry	
4	Michael Brennan	WS 1,068	11/1/55	Limerick	
5	Sean Brennan	CD 316		Dublin	Officer Fianna & IRA Dublin; aide-de-camp to Taoiseach 1933
6	Patrick Burke	WS 1,131	18/3/55	Waterford	
7	James Allan Busby	WS 1,628	6/6/57	Cork	
8	Joseph Byrne	WS 461	16/12/50	Dublin	
9	John Anthony Caffrey	WS 569	14/9/51	Dublin	
10	James Carrigan	WS 613	26/11/51	Dublin	
11	William Christian	WS 646	5/2/52	Dublin	
12	Ina Connolly Heron	WS 919	25/1/54	Belfast	
13	Nora Connolly O'Brien	WS 286	21/7/49	Belfast	
14	Thomas Dargan	WS 1,404	24/4/56	Limerick	
15	Dominic Doherty	WS 846	14/5/53	Derry	
16	John Donnelly	WS 626	14/12/51	Dublin	
17	Stephen Donnelly	WS 1,548	29/11/56	Ballina, Co. Mayo	
18	John Doyle	CD 315		Dublin	Fianna member 1921
19	Patrick Dunlevy (Dunleavy)	WS 1,489	5/9/56	Tuam, Co. Galway	

List No.	Name	WS or CD No.	WS date	Location	Notes
20	Thomas Dwyer	WS 1,198	20/6/55	Enniscorthy	
21	Patrick Egan	WS 327	15/12/49	Dublin	
22	Theobald Wolfe Tone 'Theo' Fitzgerald	WS 218	11/4/49	Dublin	Joint WS with Harry Walpole
23	James Fulham	WS 630	3/1/52	Dublin	
24	Edward Fullerton	WS 890	16/9/53	Newry, Co. Down	
25	Sean Harling	WS 935	30/3/54	Dublin	
26	Sean Healy	WS 47	4/10/47	Cork	Joint WS with Liam O'Callaghan
27	Patrick Hearne	WS 1,742	18/8/58	Waterford	
28	M. [Michael] Hensey	WS 13	19/5/47	Tullamore, Co. Offaly	
29	Archie Heron	WS 577	6/9/51	Belfast	
30	Bulmer Hobson	WS 31	15/10/47	Belfast & Dublin	
31	Robert Holland	WS 280 CD 147	18/7/49	Dublin	
32	Garry Holohan (Géaroid Ua h-Uallacháin)	WS 328 WS 336 CD 135 CD 156	7/12/49 17/1/50	Dublin	
33	Edward Horgan	WS 1,644	26/6/57	Cork	
34	George Hurley	WS 1,630	7/6/57	Cork	
35	Seamus Kavanagh	WS 1,670	9/9/57	Dublin	
36	Sean Kennedy	WS 842	1/5/53	Dublin	
37	Thomas Kettrick	WS 872	27/6/53	Westport, Co. Mayo	
38	Michael Kilmartin	CD 144		Ennistymon, Co. Clare	Fianna member 1920–21
39	Liam Langley	WS 816	19/3/53	Tuam, Co. Galway & Dublin	
40	Michael Lonergan	WS 140	1/8/48	Dublin	
41	William Lynskey	WS 1,749	12/11/51	Dublin	
42	William 'Liam' McCabe	WS 1,212	25/7/55	Ballybunion, Co. Kerry	
43	Seamus Mac Caisin (James Cashen)	WS 8	8/6/47	Dublin	
44	William J. McCarthy	WS 778	22/12/52	Cappoquin, Co. Waterford	
45	Roger McCorley	WS 389	28/5/50	Belfast	
46	David McGuinness	WS 417	28/7/50	Belfast	

List No.	Name	WS or CD No.	WS date	Location	Notes
47	Patrick McHugh	WS 677	15/5/52	Dundalk, Co. Louth	
48	Sean McLoughlin	WS 290	26/8/49	Dublin	
49	Hugo McNeill (Aodh MacNeill)	WS 1,377	20/3/56	Dublin	
50	Niall MacNeill	WS 69	6–7/1/48	Dublin	
51	Tomás Malone (Ó Maoileoin)	WS 845	12/5/53	Athlone, Co. Westmeath	
52	Eamon Martin	WS 591–3 CD 238	1/10/51	Dublin	
53	Charles Meaney	WS 1,631	11/6/57	Cork	
54	Joseph Melinn	WS 168	21/12/48	Tralee, Co. Kerry	Fianna leader rather than boy member
55	William Mullins	WS 123	4/5/48	Tralee, Co. Kerry	
56	Henry J. Mundow	CD 325		Dún Laoghaire, Co. Dublin	Fianna officer 1921–23
57	John C. Murphy	WS 1,217	28/7/55	Mallow, Co. Cork	
58	Kevin Murphy	WS 1,629	7/6/57	Cobh, Co. Cork	
59	P. J. Murphy	WS 869	14/4/53	Cork	
60	Joseph Murray	WS 412	20/7/50	Belfast	
61	Thomas Nohilly	WS 1,437	18/6/56	Tuam, Co. Galway	
62	James Nolan (Séumas Ó Nualláin)	WS 1,369	10/3/56	Waterford	
63	Denis O'Brien	WS 1,353	16/2/56	Kilbrittain, Co. Cork	
64	William 'Liam' O'Brien	WS 323	19/11/49	Dublin	
65	Liam O'Callaghan	WS 47	4/10/47	Cork	Joint WS with Sean Healy
66	Patrick O'Connell	WS 329	15/11/49	Limerick	
67	Thomas O'Connor	WS 1,189	15/6/55	Tralee, Co. Kerry	
68	Patrick O'Daly (P. Daly)	WS 220 WS 387	6/4/49 No date	Tuam, Co. Galway & Dublin	
69	Felix O'Doherty	WS 739	18/10/52	Blarney, Co. Cork	
70	Thomas O'Donoghue	WS 1,666	No date	Dublin	

List No.	Name	WS or CD No.	WS date	Location	Notes
71	William O'Flynn	WS 1,235	29/8/55	Fethard, Co. Tipperary	
72	Charles J. O'Grady	WS 282	21/7/49	Dublin	
73	Donal O'Hannigan	WS 161	2/12/48	Dublin	
74	Michael O'Leary	WS 1,167	17/5/55	Tralee, Co. Kerry	Fianna leader
75	Peadar O'Mara	WS 377	17/4/50	Dublin	
76	Sean O'Neill	WS 1,154	6/5/55	Dublin	Appears to have been a Fianna member
77	Sean O'Neill	WS 1,219	27/7/55	Tuam, Co. Galway	
78	Pádraic Ó Riain	WS 98	5/4/48	Dublin	
79	John O'Riordan	WS 1,117	12/3/55	Boherbee, Tralee, Co. Kerry	
80	James Ormond	WS 1,289	16/11/55	Lismore, Co. Waterford	
81	Joseph O'Shea	WS 21	No date	Cork	
82	Dermot O'Sullivan	WS 508	12/5/51	Dublin	
83	Thomas Pelican	WS 1,109	7/3/55	Listowel, Co. Kerry	
84	Seamus Pounch	WS 267 WS 294	15/6/49 19/9/49	Dublin	
85	Sean Prendergast	WS 755	3/11/52	Dublin	
86	Robert Purcell	WS 573	18/9/51	Dublin	
87	Seamus Reader	WS 627	28/12/51	Glasgow, Scotland	
88	Amos Reidy	WS 1,021	12/10/54	Newcastlewest, Co. Limerick	
89	Joseph Reynolds	WS 191	31/1/49	Dublin	
90	Seamus Robinson	WS 156 WS 1,721	26/10/48 16/12/57	Belfast & Glasgow	
91	James M. Roche	WS 1,225	12/8/55	Rathkeale, Co. Limerick	
92	Moses Roche	WS 1,129	17/3/55	Waterford	
93	James Rowan	WS 871	25/6/53	Dublin	
94	Michael F. Ryan	WS 1,709	9/12/57	Waterford	
95	Sean Saunders	WS 817 WS 854	19/3/53 4/6/53	Dublin	
96	Robert Henry 'Harry' Walpole	WS 218	10/4/49	Dublin	Joint WS with Theo Fitzgerald
97	Patrick Ward	WS 1,140	30/3/55	Dublin	
98	Patrick Whelan	WS 1,420	18/5/56	Limerick	
99	Alfred White (Ailfrid de Faoite)	WS 1,207	12/7/55	Dublin	

Appendix III

Former Fianna members listed in the Pensions Applications and Awards Files of the Military Service Pensions Collection[1]

APA = Army Pensions Acts / MSPA = Military Service Pensions Acts

List No.	Name	Years of birth and death	MSPC file number	Result	Pension grade	Easter Rising service	Treaty stance
1	Cornelius Ahern	1902–26	DP606	Partial dependant's gratuity APA	N/A	No	Anti
2	Richard Balfe	1893–1967	MSP34REF20230	Special allowance APA & service pension MSPA 1934	D	Yes	N/A
3	Patrick Joseph Banks	1904–22	DP654	Dependant's allowance & partial dependant's gratuity APA	N/A	No	Anti
4	William Barrett	Died 24 Mar. 1923	DP668	Unsuccessful claim by mother under APA	N/A	No	Anti
5	Denis Begley	1896–1958	24SP11602	Service pension MSPA 1924	B	No	Pro
6	Michael Bennett	Died 17 Aug. 1923	DP1024	Partial dependant's gratuity APA	N/A	No	Anti
7	William Browne	Born 1902	MSP34REF22	Unsuccessful service pension application MSPA 1934	N/A	No	Anti
8	Frank Burke Jr	Died 1943	MSP34REF23	Unsuccessful service pension application MSPA 1934	N/A	No	Anti
9	John Burke	Died 1946	MSP34REF738	Unsuccessful service pension application MSPA 1934	N/A	No	Anti
10	Joseph Burns	1905–22	DP934	Partial dependant's gratuity APA	N/A	No	N/A
11	Francis Leo Byrne	1903–71	24SP141	Service pension MSPA 1924	A	No	Pro

#	Name	Dates	Reference	Award	Rank	Received	Notes	Stance
12	James Byrne	Died 13 Oct. 1922	2D22	Dependant's allowance & gratuity APA	N/A	No		Pro
13	James Byrne	1899–18 Aug. 1922	DP2434	Partial dependant's gratuity APA	N/A	No evidence for claim he was dispatch carrier		Anti
14	Peter Sylvester Byrne	1899–1959	24SP2562	Wound pension APA & service pension MSPA 1924	A	Yes		Pro
15	John Caffrey	1899–1933	DP510	Dependant's allowance APA	N/A	Yes		N/A possibly Anti
16	Patrick William Cashman	Born 1905	MSP34REF31406	Unsuccessful service pension application MSPA 1934	N/A	No		N/A
17	Philip Cleary	1904–72	MSP34REF52466	Service pension MSPA 1934	E	No		Anti
18	Sean Cole	1902–22	DP3749	Partial dependant's gratuity APA	N/A	No		Anti
19	Roderick Connolly	1901–80	MSP34REF38900	Disability pension APA & service pension MSPA 1934	E	Yes		Anti
20	Martin Considine	1904–23	DP156	Partial dependant's gratuity APA	N/A	No		Anti
21	Joseph Cullen	1900–45	24SP5929	Service pension MSPA 1924	B	Yes		Pro
22	John Joseph Cusack	1903–22	DP3949	Partial dependant's gratuity APA	N/A	No		Anti
23	Patrick Daly	1902–82	MSP34REF5541	Service pension MSPA 1934	E	Yes		Anti

List No.	Name	Years of birth and death	MSPC file number	Result	Pension grade	Easter Rising service	Treaty stance
24	James Delea	No dates on file	MSP34REF29353	Unsuccessful application for service pension MSPA 1934	N/A	No	Anti
25	John Desmond	No dates on file	MSP34REF57269	Unsuccessful application for service pension MSPA 1934 & 1949	N/A	No	Anti
26	John Devoy	1902–22	2D182	Dependant's gratuity APA	N/A	No	Pro
27	Richard James Doherty	1902–23	3D263	Dependant's gratuity APA	N/A	No	Pro
28	Stephen Donnelly	1900–78	1924A22	Service pension MSPA 1924	B	No	Officially Pro, but alleged to have helped anti-Treaty IRA.
29	John Dooley	1901–22	2D259	Dependant's gratuity APA	N/A	No	Pro
30	Michael Doyle	Died 19 Dec. 1923	DP8502	Unsuccessful claim by father under APA	N/A	No	Anti
31	Sylvester Joseph Doyle	1902–68	1924A26	Service pension MSPA 1924	A	Yes	Pro
32	Thomas Doyle	1897–1920	DP1364	Partial dependant's gratuity & dependant's allowance APA	N/A	No evidence to support 1916 service claim	N/A
33	Patrick Joseph Dunne	1902–82	MSP34REF750	Service pension MSPA 1934	E	Yes	Anti
34	Albert Dyas	1899–1960	MSP34REF20529	Service pension MSPA 1934	E	Yes	N/A

35	Michael Edgeworth	Born 1903	MSP34REF1197	Unsuccessful application for service pension MSPA 1934	N/A	No	Anti
36	Christopher Feekery	1899–1993	DP54521	Disability pension APA	N/A	Yes	N/A
37	Michael Finnegan	Died 21 Aug. 1922	2D352	Widow allowance APA	N/A	No	Pro
38	Theobald Wolfe Tone Fitzgerald	1898–1962	24SP3062	Service pension MSPA 1924	C	Yes	Pro
39	James Fleming	1900–61	24SP8655	Service pension MSPA 1924	A	Yes	Pro
40	John Flynn	Died 1 Apr. 1923	3D307	Gratuity APA	N/A	No	Pro
41	Patrick Flynn	Born 1903	4P121	Unsuccessful application for wound pension or gratuity APA	N/A	No	Pro
42	Daniel D. Foley	1902–23	DP3596	Unsuccessful application by father under APA	N/A	No	Anti
43	William Gannon	Born 1902	MSP34REF25776	Disability pension APA & service pension MSPA 1934	D	No	Anti
44	Stephen Gethings	No dates on file	MSP34REF23968	Unsuccessful application for service pension MSPA 1934	N/A	No	N/A
45	Robert Graham	Born 1903	24SP4349	Service pension MSPA 1924	A	No	Pro
46	Thomas Greehy	Died 10 Mar. 1923	DP1837	Unsuccessful application by mother under APA (illegitimate son)	N/A	No	Anti

List No.	Name	Years of birth and death	MSPC file number	Result	Pension grade	Easter Rising service	Treaty stance
47	Patrick Hanley	1904–20	DP4150	Unsuccessful application by mother under APA	N/A	No	N/A
48	Patrick J. Hanlon	1906–23	3D25	Partial dependant's allowance APA	N/A	No	Anti
49	Patrick Hanly	Died 19 July 1922	2D66	Dependant's allowance APA	N/A	No	Pro
50	Patrick John (Percy) Hannafin	Died 27 Jan. 1922	DP4142	Partial dependant's allowance APA	N/A	No	N/A
51	Sean Harbourne	1889–1978	MSP34REF1534	Service pension MSPA 1934	D	Yes	Anti
52	Michael Hayes	1904–22	DP4256	Unsuccessful claim by siblings via aunt under APA	N/A	No	Anti
53	John (Sean) Healy	Fatally wounded on 25 Apr. 1916	1D352	Partial dependant's allowance APA	N/A	Yes	N/A
54	Hugh Hennon	1901–24	DP4364	Partial dependant's allowance APA	N/A	No	N/A Probably Anti
55	Gerard Holohan (Gearóid Ó hUallacháin)	Died 1 Jan. 1967	MSP34REF1385	Disability pension APA & service pension MSPA 1934	E	Yes	Anti
56	Patrick Hugh Holahan	1897–1946	MSP34REF380	Widow allowance APA & service pension MSPA 1934	C	Yes	Anti
57	Walter Leo Holland	1901–57	24SP1402	Wound gratuity APA & service pension MSPA 1924	B	Yes	Pro

58	Arthur Hughes	1903–23	DP4576	Partial dependant's gratuity & dependant's allowance APA	N/A	No	Anti
59	Eamonn (Edwin) Patrick Hughes	Died 7 Oct. 1922	DP4559	Partial dependant's gratuity APA	N/A	No	Anti
60	Joseph Aloysius Hurson	1905–22	2D502	Unsuccessful application by mother under APA	N/A	No	N/A
61	Denis Kavanagh	1901–76	MSP34REF58566	Service pension MSPA 1934	E	Yes	N/A
62	James Keating	1906–28	DP9571	Unsuccessful application by mother under APA	N/A	No	Anti
63	Thomas Patrick Keenan	1904–71	MSP34REF303	Wound pension APA & service pension MSPA 1934	E	Yes	Anti
64	John Kelly	Died 9 Aug. 1922	2D267	Dependant's allowance APA	N/A	No	Pro
65	Gerald Anthony Keogh	1894–1916	DP7628	Dependant's gratuity & allowance APA	N/A	Yes	N/A
66	Gerald Landers	Died 22 Apr. 1927	2RBSD506	Outcome unclear of parents' application under APA	N/A	No	Anti
67	John Lawlor	Born 1901	MSP34REF20940	Unsuccessful applications for wound pension or gratuity under APA & service pension under MSPA 1934	N/A	No	Anti
68	John Lawlor	1903–21	DP23954	Dependant's allowance APA	N/A	No	N/A

List No.	Name	Years of birth and death	MSPC file number	Result	Pension grade	Easter Rising service	Treaty stance
69	Thomas Lennon	1902–23	DP5378	Partial dependant's gratuity & dependant's allowance APA	N/A	No	Anti
70	Thomas Lowe	Born 1903	MSP34REF13187	Service pension MSPA 1934	D	No	Anti
71	Ralph J. Lynch	Died 1934	MSP34REF84	Unsuccessful application for service pension MSPA 1934	N/A	No	Anti
72	Daniel Joseph McArt	Died 15 April 1933	DP6617	Unsuccessful application by widow under APA	N/A	Yes	Anti
73	Christopher McCann	Died 8 Aug. 1922	2D382	Unsuccessful application by mother under APA	N/A	Yes	Pro
74	James Patrick McCann	1901–22	2D208	Dependant's allowance & gratuity APA	N/A	No	Pro
75	Henry McCormack	1900–31	DP8181	Unsuccessful application by mother under APA	N/A	Yes	Anti
76	Micheál Seosaimh MacFochaidh / Michael Joseph Kehoe	1899–1977	MSP34REF23991	Service pension 1934	E	Yes Enniscorthy	N/A
77	Christopher McEvoy	1900–19	DP6950	Unsuccessful application by father under APA	N/A	No	N/A
78	Christopher McGrane	1898–1966	MSP34REF23344	Service pension MSPA 1934	E	Yes	N/A
79	Thomas McGrane	1896–1949	MSP34REF14735	Service pension MSPA 1934	D	Yes	Anti
80	Thomas McGrath	1901–23	DP3164	Partial dependant's allowance APA	N/A	No	Anti

81	Sean McLoughlin	1895–1960	MSP34REF61056	Service pension MSPA 1949	D	Yes	Anti
82	Charles Eugene MacMahon	1904–87	24SP6134	Wound APA & service pension MSPA 1924	A	Yes	Pro
83	James Kevin McNamee	1901–66	MSP34REF59908	Service pension MSPA 1934	E	Yes	Anti
84	Dermot John MacNeill	1902–90	MSP34REF13712	Service pension MSPA 1934	E	Yes	Anti
85	Hugo Hyacinth MacNeill	1900–63	24SP11777	Service pension MSPA 1924	E	Yes (but doesn't claim for it)	Pro
86	James Patrick McShane	c. 1903–76	24SP12471	Service pension MSPA 1924	A	No	Pro
87	John McSweeney	Died 10 Aug. 1922	DP8402	Partial dependant's gratuity & dependant's allowance APA	N/A	No	Anti
88	Joseph Marrinan	1897–1968	DP3018	Wound pension & wound allowance APA	N/A	No	Anti
89	Christopher Martin	1898–1974	24A2015	Service pension MSPA 1924	A	Yes	Pro
90	Eamon Martin	1892–1971	MSP34REF47556	Wound gratuity APA & service pension MSPA 1934	A	Yes	Anti
91	John Martin	Died 23 July 1922	2D108	Dependant's allowance & partial dependant's gratuity APA	N/A	No	Pro
92	Peter Meade	Died 12 May 1921	DP3052	Partial dependant's gratuity APA	N/A	No	N/A
93	James Melia	Died 22 Jan. 1923	DP3083	Partial dependant's gratuity APA	N/A	No	Anti

List No.	Name	Years of birth and death	MSPC file number	Result	Pension grade	Easter Rising service	Treaty stance
94	Herbert (Barney) Charles Mellows	1896–1942	MSP34REF16537	Disability pension APA & service pension MSPA 1934	C	Yes	Anti
95	Michael Moloney	1903–23	DP6108	Partial dependant's gratuity & dependant's allowance APA	N/A	No	Anti
96	James Mooney	1904–23	DP7488	Partial dependant's gratuity APA	N/A	No	Anti
97	Thomas Moriarty	1904–20	DP3424	Dependant's allowance APA	N/A	No	N/A
98	Michael Moynihan	Died 15 July 1922	DP8157	Partial dependant's gratuity & dependant's allowance APA	N/A	No	Anti
99	Michael Mulkerrins	1900–38	24SP906	Service pension MSPA 1924	A	Yes Athenry	Pro
100	Bartholomew Murphy	1905–22	DP8257	Partial dependant's gratuity & dependant's allowance APA	N/A	No	Anti
101	Francis Murphy	Died 1919	DP8365	Unsuccessful application by father under APA	N/A	No	N/A
102	John Leo Murphy	Died 30 Nov. 1922	DP8262	Partial dependant's gratuity APA	N/A	No	Anti
103	Robert Joseph Murphy	Born 1901	24SP9177	Service pension MSPA 1924	B	Yes	Pro
104	William Murphy	1901–65	24SP651	Wound gratuity APA & service pension MSPA 1924	B	Yes	Pro

105	Edward Joseph Murray	1897–1984	MSP34REF12204	Special allowance APA & service pension MSPA 1934	E	Yes	Anti
106	John Murray	1900–20	2RBSD107	Successful application by father under APA	N/A	No	N/A
107	Joseph Murtagh (aka John O'Connor)	1900–64	24SP1583	Wound gratuity APA & service pension MSPA 1924	B	Yes	Pro
108	William Myles	Died 20 Oct. 1922	DP8427	Partial dependant's gratuity & dependant's allowance APA	N/A	No	Anti
109	William Neenan	1903–74	MSP34REF8414	Service pension MSPA 1934	E	No	Anti
110	Richard Noonan	1903–22	DP2685	Partial dependant's gratuity APA	N/A	No	Anti
111	Francis Norton	Died 6 Aug. 1922	DP2693	Dependant's allowance APA	N/A	No	Anti
112	James O'Brien	1899–1962	MSP34REF4836	Service pension MSPA 1934	D	Yes Enniscorthy	Anti
113	Michael O'Brien	1902–21	1D306	Dependant's gratuity & allowance APA	N/A	No	N/A
114	Pádraig Ó Broin (Patrick Byrne)	1900–74	24SP9581	Service pension MSPA 1924	A	Yes	Pro
115	Michael O'Carroll	1901–56	MSP34REF8790	Service pension MSPA 1934	E	Yes	Anti
116	Henry O'Connor	Died 27 Apr. 1922	DP7242	Partial dependant's gratuity APA	N/A	No	Anti
117	James O'Connor	1903–23	DP6680	Partial dependant's gratuity APA	N/A	No	Anti
118	John Thomas O'Connor	1896–1979	MSP34REF21094	Service pension MSPA 1934	D	Yes	Anti

List No.	Name	Years of birth and death	MSPC file number	Result	Pension grade	Easter Rising service	Treaty stance
119	Thomas O'Connor	1904–25	DP6648	Partial dependant's gratuity APA	N/A	No	Anti
120	Patrick O'Daly (Pádraig Ua Dalaigh)	1888–1957	24SP424	Service pension MSPA 1924	D	Yes	Pro
121	Daniel O'Driscoll	1904–21	DP9697	Dependant's allowance APA	N/A	No	N/A
122	Charles O'Hanlon	1904–22	DP6258	Unsuccessful applications by mother & sister under APA	N/A	No	Anti
123	John O'Leary	Died 8 Sept. 1922	1D372	Unsuccessful application by father under APA	N/A	No	N/A Unclear what side he was on
124	Thomas O'Leary	Died 23 Mar. 1923	DP2719	Dependant's allowance APA	N/A	No	Anti
125	Thomas O'Reilly	1900–85	MSP34REF33197	Service pension MSPA 1934	E	Yes	Anti
126	Joseph O'Riordan	Died 26 Oct. 1922	2D203	Dependant's allowance APA	N/A	No	Pro
127	Leo Paul Quinn (Leon O Cuinn)	1903–58	MSP34REF13718	Service Pension MSPA 1934	E	No	Anti
128	Leo Rea	Died 23 June 1922	2D504	Unsuccessful application by mother under APA	N/A	No	N/A
129	Seamus Reader	1898–1969	MSP34REF4300	Service pension MSPA 1934	C	Yes	Anti
130	Joseph Walton Reed (Reid)	Died 29 Nov. 1918	1D103	Dependant's gratuity APA	N/A	No	N/A

	Name	Dates	Reference	Type	Category	Conflict	Side
131	Augustus Percival (Percy) Reynolds	1895–1983	MSP34REF22403	Service pension MSPA 1934	D	Yes	N/A
132	Joseph Francis Reynolds	1897–1966	MSP34REF1151	Service pension MSPA 1934 & wound pension APA	D	Yes (conflict between him & some of his referees about service)	Anti
133	Patrick Joseph Rigney	1900–90	MSP34REF295	Wound pension/gratuity APA & service pension MSPA 1934	C	Yes	Anti
134	Joseph Roche	1900–43	MSP34REF2473	Service pension MSPA 1934	E	Yes	Anti
135	William Charles Roe	1901–76	MSP34REF21737	Service pension MSPA 1934	D	Yes	Anti (left National Army to join Anti-Treaty IRA)
136	Michael J. Ryle	1903–22	DP24836	Unsuccessful application by brother under APA	N/A	No	Anti
137	Michael Sheahan	1904–24	DP24083	Dependant's allowance APA	N/A	No	Anti
138	Thomas Sheehan	1902–c. 1977	24SP794	Service pension MSPA 1924	A	No	Pro
139	Thomas Slattery	1904–22	DP5715	Partial dependant's gratuity	N/A	No	N/A
140	Joseph Spooner	Died 30 Nov. 1922	DP5774	Dependant's allowance APA	N/A	No	Anti
141	Henry Vincent Staines	1901–61	24SP12731	Service pension MSPA 1924	B	Yes	Pro
142	James Staines	1900–29	24SP11475	Service pension MSPA 1924	B	Yes	Pro

List No.	Name	Years of birth and death	MSPC file number	Result	Pension grade	Easter Rising service	Treaty stance
143	William (Liam) F. Staines	Died 2 Nov. 1918	DP5788	Unsuccessful application by mother under APA	N/A	Yes	N/A
144	Patrick Joseph Stephenson	1895–1960	MSP34REF21743	Service pension MSPA 1934	D	Yes	N/A
145	Anthony Swan	Died 9 Nov. 1973	24SP11144	Service pension MSPA 1924	C	Yes	Pro
146	John Timmins	1900–60	MSP34REF25967	Service pension MSPA 1934	E	No	Anti
147	William Toal	1904–22	DP6722	Partial dependant's gratuity APA	N/A	No	N/A
148	Pádraic Toibin	Born 1904	MSP34REF21379	Service pension MSPA 1934	D	Yes Enniscorthy	Anti
149	James A. Torpey	1902–22	DP6753	Partial dependant's gratuity & dependant's allowance APA	N/A	No	Anti
150	Patrick Tubridy	1902–22	DP6554	Dependant's allowance APA	N/A	No	Anti
151	Richard Twohig	1902–22	DP5824	Unsuccessful application by stepmother under APA	N/A	No	Anti
152	Thomas Patrick Wall	1904–22	DP5872	Partial dependant's gratuity APA	N/A	No	Anti
153	Robert Henry Walpole	1895–1964	24SP3669	Service pension MSPA 1924	B	Yes	Pro
154	Stephen White	Died 19 Dec. 1922	DP6027	Unsuccessful application by father under APA	N/A	No	Anti
155	Patrick John Young	1900–90	24SP3765	Service pension MSPA 1924	A	Yes	Pro

NOTE

1   This list was generated through an online search of the files undertaken on 11 July 2018. Only birth and/or death dates noted in the MSPC file are listed in the table. Please see p. 215 for an explanation of the differences in pension grades between the 1924 and 1934 Military Service Pensions Acts.

Appendix IV

Location and strength of Fianna companies in Ireland, c. 1921–22, based on records in the Fianna Éireann Series of the Military Service Pensions Collection

N/A = no applicable record / n/d = no date provided

County	Brigade	Location/Battalion	Members on 11/7/1921	Members on 1/7/1922	Members on another date	MSPC file
Antrim	Belfast Brigade	1st Batt. Belfast	116			FE/34
Armagh	3rd (Armagh) Brigade	-Armagh Batt.	282	311		FE/24
		-Lurgan Batt.				
Carlow		Carlow			At least 5 (n/d)	FE/35
Cavan	3rd Brigade, 5th Northern Division	C Coy, Cavan Town			24 (1921–22)	FE/25
Clare	Mid Clare Brigade	1st Batt.	206	150		FE/19
		-Clooney				
		-Ennis				
		-Doora				
		4th Batt.	122		196 (n/d)	FE/20
		-Miltown Malbay				
		-Ennistymon				
		-Lahinch				
		-Moy				
		-Glandine				
		-Letterkelly				
	West Clare	5th Batt. Kilkee Coy				FE/38
Cork	Cork No. 1 Brigade	1st & 2nd Batt. Cork City & County	895	895		FE/5
		-Youghal				
	Fianna in Cork No. 4 Brigade IRA		36	42		FE/6
Derry	Derry City	Derry City	180			FE/36
Donegal	Sligo Brigade	Bundoran			3 (n/d)	FE/22
Down						N/A
Dublin	Dublin Brigade	6 Battalions (5 in Dublin city & county, 1 in Dublin/Wicklow)	755	788		FE/1
		-F Coy, 7th Batt. IRA, Valleymount, Co. Wicklow	9			FE/3

County	Brigade	Location/Battalion	Members on 11/7/1921	Members on 1/7/1922	Members on another date	MSPC file
Fermanagh						N/A
Galway						N/A
Kerry	Kerry No. 1 Brigade	Brigade total[1]	460	669		FE/10
		-Tralee Batt.	355	328		FE/11
		-Listowel Batt.	21	239		FE/12
		-4th (Castlegregory) Batt.			17/4 (n/d)	FE/13
		-C Coy, 5th (Annascaul) Batt.				
Kildare		Lispole	80	97		FE/14
Kilkenny		Newbridge	37			FE/37
Laois (Queen's Co.)						N/A
Leitrim						N/A
Limerick	-Limerick City Mid Limerick Brigade	Limerick City (Coys A-G)	719 (Coys A-F)	764 (Coys A-G)		FE/17
	-West Limerick Brigade	-4th Batt. Rathkeale Coy	20			FE/18
Longford						N/A
Louth	9th (South Louth) Brigade	-Drogheda Batt.	20	7		FE/29
		-Ardee Batt.	7			
	1st Brigade (North Louth/Dundalk)	-Dundalk Batt.	136	216		FE/23/1
Mayo	South Mayo Brigade	Ballinrobe	65	52		FE/21
Meath	2nd (Meath) Brigade	4th Batt.	19	-		FE/27
	3rd (Meath) Brigade	-Navan Coy			38 (1918–20)	FE/26
		-Mullagh				
		-Moynalty				
		-Kells				
Monaghan						N/A

Offaly (King's Co.)	2nd Brigade	1st Batt. A (Clara) Coy		17 (n/d)	FE/32
Roscommon	Sligo Brigade	-Boyle	49		FE/22
Sligo	Sligo Brigade	-Boyle -Bundoran -Tubbercurry		37	FE/22
Tipperary	No. 3 Brigade (South Tipperary)	1st Batt. -Rosegreen -Fethard -Mortlestown -Clerhian & Newchapel -Coolmoyne 2nd Batt. -Cashel -Dualla 3rd Batt. -Dundrum -Anacarthy 4th Batt. -Tipperary Town -Bansha -Sologhead 5th Batt. -Clonmel 6th Batt. (not listed in file) 7th Batt. -Drangah -Cloneen 8th Batt. -Carrick-on-Suir -Windgap -Clonea		807 (circa 1917–23)	FE/16

County	Brigade	Location/Battalion	Members on 11/7/1921	Members on 1/7/1922	Members on another date	MSPC file
Tyrone						N/A
Waterford	Waterford	-Waterford City -Tramore -Ferrybank -Portlaw -Mount Sion -Dunkett-Sallypark -Ballyduff -Passage	112	320		FE/9
Westmeath	-5th (Mullingar) Brigade -Athlone Brigade	Castlepollard B (Tang) Coy			About 20 (n/d) 8 (n/d)	FE/28 FE/33
Wexford	Wexford	-1st Batt. Enniscorthy -2nd Batt. Wexford -3rd Batt. New Ross -4th Batt. Gorey	192	123		FE/30
Wicklow	Dublin Brigade	-6th Batt. Bray Coy -7th Batt. F Coy, Valleymount, Co. Wicklow			30 (n/d)	FE/31 FE/3
TOTALS			4,437	4,374	1,322	

NOTE

1. Please note that the membership totals for the Kerry No. 1 Brigade include the brigade staff as well as the figures for the Tralee Battalion, the Listowel Battalion and C Company of the 5th (Annascaul) Battalion, which was located at Lispole.

Bibliography

PRIMARY SOURCES

Manuscript sources

National Library of Ireland
Bulmer Hobson Papers
Rosamond Jacob Papers
Joseph McGarrity Papers
J. J. O'Connell Papers

Military Archives, Dublin
Bureau of Military History Witness Statements
Bureau of Military History Contemporary Documents
Collins Collection
Military Service Pensions Collection 1916–23

National Archives, London
Colonial Office files

UCD Archives
Denis McCullough Papers
Richard Mulcahy Papers

Newspapers and periodicals

An Claidheamh Soluis
An Macaomh
Bean na hÉireann
Boys' Friend
Connacht Tribune

Éire
Fianna
Freeman's Journal
Irish Freedom
Irish Independent
Irish News
Irish Press
Irish Volunteer
Meath Chronicle
Nationalist and Leinster Times
Nodlaig na bhFiann
Police Gazette or Hue-and-Cry
Republic
Sinn Féin
Southern Star
United Irishman
Young Ireland

Published primary sources

Baden-Powell, Robert S. S., *Scouting for Boys: A Handbook for Instruction in Good Citizenship* (5th impression, London: C. Arthur Pearson, 1908).

Connolly O'Brien, Nora, *James Connolly: Portrait of a Rebel Father* (Dublin: Four Masters, 1975).

de Markievicz, Constance Georgina Gore-Booth, *Prison Letters of Countess Markievicz* (New York: Kraus Reprint, 1970).

Fianna Éireann Dublin Brigade, *Easter Week 1916–1922 Commemoration Aeridheacht Souvenir Programme, 23 April 1922* (Dublin: Fianna Éireann Dublin Brigade, 1922).

Fianna Éireann Handbook (Dublin: Fianna Éireann, 1988).

Fianna Handbook (2nd edn, Dublin: Central Council of Fianna Éireann, 1924).

Guy's 1921 City and County Almanac and Directory (Cork: Guy, 1921).

Hobson, Bulmer, *Ireland Yesterday and Tomorrow* (Tralee: Anvil Books, 1968).

I gCuimhne (Dublin: Irish Republican Soldiers Memorial Committee, 1926).

Lee, J. J. (ed.), *Kerry's Fighting Story, 1916–21: Told by the Men Who Made It* (Cork: Mercier Press, 2009).

Mac Giolla Choille, Breandán (ed.), *Intelligence Notes 1913–16* (Dublin: Republic of Ireland State Papers Office, 1966).

Martin, F. X. (ed.), *The Irish Volunteers, 1913–1915: Recollections and Documents* (Dublin: James Duffy, 1963).

Martin, F. X. (ed.), *The Howth Gun-Running and the Kilcoole Gun-Running: Recollections and Documents* (2nd edn, Sallins: Merrion, 2014).
Na Fianna Éireann, *The Constitution of Na Fianna Éireann as Amended by the Ard-fheis, 1912* (Dublin: Central Council of Na Fianna Éireann, 1912).
Na Fianna Éireann, *The Young Guard of Erin: Iris-leabhair na bhFiann; the Fianna Handbook* (3rd edn, Dublin: Na Fianna Éireann, 1964).
O'Connell, J. J., 'Memoir of the Irish Volunteers, 1914–16, 1917', ed. Daithí Ó Corráin in *Analecta Hibernica*, 47 (2016), pp. 3–102.
Ó Riain, Pádraic (ed.), *Fianna Handbook* (Dublin: Central Council of Na Fianna Éireann, 1914).
O'Shannon, Cathal (ed.), *Souvenir of the Golden Jubilee of Fianna Éireann, Aug. 16, 1909–Aug. 16, 1959* (Dublin: Na Fianna Éireann, 1959).
Pyle, Hilary (ed.), *Cesca's Diary* (Dublin: Woodfield Press, 2005).
Weekly Irish Times, *Sinn Féin Rebellion Handbook, Easter 1916* (Dublin: Irish Times, 1917).

SECONDARY SOURCES

Books and articles

Augusteijn, Joost, *From Public Defiance to Guerrilla Warfare* (Dublin: Irish Academic Press, 1996).
Augusteijn, Joost (ed.), *The Irish Revolution, 1913–1923* (Houndmills: Palgrave, 2002).
Augusteijn, Joost, 'Accounting for the emergence of violent activism among Irish revolutionaries, 1916–21', *Irish Historical Studies*, 35:139 (May 2007), pp. 327–44.
Blythe, Ernest, *Trasna na Bóinne* (Dublin: Sairséal and Dill, 1957).
Borgonovo, John, 'Politics as leisure: Brass bands in Cork, 1845–1918' in Leeann Lane and William Murphy (eds), *Leisure and the Irish in the Nineteenth-Century* (Liverpool: Liverpool University Press, 2016), pp. 23–40.
Bowman, Timothy, *Carson's Army: The Ulster Volunteer Force, 1910–22* (Manchester: Manchester University Press, 2012).
Boyce, D. George (ed.), *The Revolution in Ireland, 1879–1923* (Basingstoke: Macmillan Education, 1988).
Coldrey, Barry M., *Faith and Fatherland: The Christian Brothers and the Development of Irish Nationalism, 1838–1921* (Dublin: Gill and Macmillan, 1988).
Coleman, Marie, *County Longford and the Irish Revolution* (Dublin: Irish Academic Press, 2003).

Coleman, Marie, *The Irish Sweep: A History of the Irish Hospitals Sweepstake, 1930–87* (Dublin: UCD Press, 2009).
Coleman, Marie, 'Military service pensions for veterans of the Irish Revolution, 1916–1923', *War in History*, 20:2 (2013), pp. 201–21.
Coleman, Marie, *The Irish Revolution, 1916–1923* (London: Routledge, 2014).
Coleman, Marie, 'Compensating Irish female revolutionaries, 1916–1923', *Women's History Review*, 26:6 (2017), pp. 915–34.
Collis, Henry, Fred Hurll and Rex Hazlewood, *B.-P.'s Scouts: An Official History of the Boy Scouts Association* (London: Collins Press, 1961).
Connell, Jr, Joseph E. A., 'Inghinidhe na hÉireann/Daughters of Ireland, Clan na nGaedheal/Girl Scouts of Ireland', *History Ireland*, 19:5 (Sept./Oct. 2011), p. 66.
Davies, Norman, *Vanished Kingdoms: The History of Half-Forgotten Europe* (London: Penguin Books, 2011).
Davis, Natalie Zemon, 'The reasons of misrule: Youth groups and charivaris in sixteenth-century France', *Past and Present*, 50 (Feb. 1971), pp. 41–75.
de Búrca, Marcus, *The GAA: A History* (Dublin: Cumann Lúthchleas Gael, 1980).
Denman, Terence, '"The red livery of shame": The campaign against army recruitment in Ireland, 1899–1914', *Irish Historical Studies*, 29:114 (Nov. 1994), pp. 208–33.
Donson, Andrew, 'Why did German youth become fascists? Nationalist males born 1900 to 1908 in war and revolution', *Social History*, 31:3 (2006), pp. 337–58.
Donson, Andrew, *Youth in the Fatherless Land: War Pedagogy, Nationalism and Authority in Germany, 1914–1918* (Cambridge, MA: Harvard University Press, 2010).
Doyle, Jennifer, Frances Clarke, Eibhlis Connaughton and Orna Somerville, *An Introduction to the Bureau of Military History* (Dublin: Military Archives, 2002).
Duffy, Joe, *Children of the Rising* (Dublin: Hachette Books Ireland, 2015).
Ferriter, Diarmaid, '"Always in danger of finding myself with nothing at all": The military service pensions and the battle for material survival, 1925–55' in Diarmaid Ferriter and Susannah Riordan (eds), *Years of Turbulence: The Irish Revolution and Its Aftermath* (Dublin: UCD Press, 2015), pp. 191–207.
Fitzpatrick, David, *Politics and Irish Life, 1913–21: Provincial Experience of War and Revolution* (Dublin: Gill and Macmillan, 1977).
Fitzpatrick, David, 'The geography of Irish nationalism', *Past and Present*, 78 (Feb. 1978), pp. 113–44.

Fitzpatrick, David, 'Militarism in Ireland, 1900–1922' in Thomas Bartlett and Keith Jeffery (eds), *A Military History of Ireland* (Cambridge: Cambridge University Press, 1996), pp. 379–406.

Flanagan, Michael, '"There is an Isle in the western ocean": The Christian Brothers, *Our Boys* and Catholic/nationalist ideology' in Mary Shine Thompson and Celia Keenan (eds), *Treasure Islands: Studies in Children's Literature* (Dublin: Four Courts Press, 2006), pp. 43–52.

Foy, Michael and Brian Barton, *The Easter Rising* (Stroud: Sutton, 1999).

Gaughan, J. Anthony, *Scouting in Ireland* (Dublin: Kingdom Books, 2006).

Gibney, John, *Sean Heuston* (Dublin: O'Brien Press, 2013).

Gillis, John R., 'Conformity and rebellion: Contrasting styles of English and German youth, 1900–33', *History of Education Quarterly*, 13:3 (1973), pp. 249–60.

Glandon, Virginia E., *Arthur Griffith and the Advanced Nationalist Press: Ireland, 1900–1922* (New York: Lang, 1985).

Greaves, C. Desmond, *Liam Mellows and the Irish Revolution* (London: Lawrence and Wishart, 1988).

Hart, Peter, 'The geography of revolution in Ireland, 1917–1923', *Past and Present*, 155 (May 1997), pp. 142–76.

Hart, Peter, *The IRA and Its Enemies: Violence and Community in Cork, 1916–1923* (Oxford: Clarendon Press, 1998).

Hart, Peter, 'The social structure of the Irish Republican Army, 1916–1923', *Historical Journal*, 42:1 (Mar. 1999), pp. 207–31.

Hatfield, Mary, Jutta Kruse and Ríona Nic Congáil (eds), *Historical Perspectives on Parenthood and Childhood in Ireland* (Dublin: Arlen House, 2017).

Haverty, Anne, *Constance Markievicz: An Independent Life* (London: Pandora Press, 1988).

Hay, Marnie, 'This treasured island: Irish nationalist propaganda aimed at children and youth, 1910–16' in Mary Shine Thompson and Celia Keenan (eds), *Treasure Islands: Studies in Children's Literature* (Dublin: Four Courts Press, 2006), pp. 33–42.

Hay, Marnie, 'The foundation and development of Na Fianna Éireann, 1909–16', *Irish Historical Studies*, 36:141 (May 2008), pp. 53–71.

Hay, Marnie, *Bulmer Hobson and the Nationalist Movement in Twentieth-Century Ireland* (Manchester: Manchester University Press, 2009).

Hay, Marnie, 'Kidnapped: Bulmer Hobson, the IRB and the 1916 Easter Rising', *Canadian Journal of Irish Studies*, 35:1 (2009), pp. 53–60.

Hay, Marnie, 'The mysterious "disappearance" of Bulmer Hobson', *Studies: An Irish Quarterly Review*, 98:390 (2009), pp. 185–95.

Hay, Marnie, 'Moulding the future: Na Fianna Éireann and its members', *Studies: An Irish Quarterly Review*, 100:400 (2011), pp. 441–54.

Hay, Marnie, 'The propaganda of Na Fianna Éireann, 1909–26' in Mary Shine Thompson (ed.), *Young Irelands: Studies in Children's Literature* (Dublin: Four Courts Press, 2011), pp. 47–56.
Hay, Marnie, 'What did advanced nationalists tell Irish children in the early twentieth century?' in Ciara Ní Bhroin and Patricia Kennon (eds), *What Do We Tell the Children? Critical Essays on Children's Literature* (Cambridge: Cambridge Scholars Press, 2012), pp. 148–62.
Hay, Marnie, 'An Irish nationalist adolescence: Na Fianna Éireann, 1909–23' in Catherine Cox and Susannah Riordan (eds), *Adolescence in Modern Irish History* (Basingstoke: Palgrave Macmillan, 2015), pp. 103–28.
Hay, Marnie, 'A "republic of learning": Bulmer Hobson, nationalism and the printed word' in Marnie Hay and Daire Keogh (eds), *Rebellion and Revolution in Dublin: Voices from a Suburb, Rathfarnham, 1913–23* (Dublin: South Dublin Libraries, 2016), pp. 175–94.
Hay, Marnie, 'Scouting for rebels: Na Fianna Éireann and preparation for the coming war, 1909–18' in Rosemary Johnston, Emma Short and Lissa Paul (eds), *Children's Literature and Culture of the First World War* (Oxford: Routledge, 2016), pp. 365–87.
Hay, Marnie, 'Na Fianna Éireann' in John Crowley, Donal Ó Drisceoil and Mike Murphy (eds), *Atlas of the Irish Revolution, 1912–1923* (Cork: Cork University Press, 2017), pp. 173–6.
Hay, Marnie, 'Performing Irish nationalism on and off the stage: Bulmer Hobson and Patrick Pearse' in Eugene McNulty and Róisín Ní Ghairbhí (eds), *Patrick Pearse and the Theatre* (Dublin: Four Courts Press, 2017), pp. 24–36.
Hegarty, Shane and Fintan O'Toole, *The Irish Times Book of the 1916 Rising* (Dublin: Gill and Macmillan, 2006).
Heineman, Elizabeth, 'Gender identity in the Wandervogel movement', *German Studies Review*, 12:2 (May 1989), pp. 249–70.
Heywood, Colin, *A History of Childhood* (Cambridge: Polity Press, 2005).
Honwana, Alcinda, 'Children's involvement in war: Historical and social contexts', *Journal of the History of Childhood and Youth*, 1:1 (2008), pp. 139–49.
Hopkinson, Michael, *Green against Green: The Irish Civil War* (Dublin: Gill and Macmillan, 1988).
Jackson, Alvin, 'Unionist politics and protestant society in Edwardian Ireland', *Historical Journal*, 33:4 (Dec. 1990), pp. 839–66.
Klemm, Alex, 'Witnessing the lockout: Statements gathered by the Bureau of Military History' in Mary Muldowney and Ida Milne (eds), *One Hundred Years Later: The Legacy of the Lockout* (Dublin: Seven Towers, 2013), pp. 16–37.

Laffan, Michael, *The Resurrection of Ireland: The Sinn Féin Party, 1916–1923* (Cambridge: Cambridge University Press, 1999).

Lane, Leeann, *Rosamond Jacob: Third Person Singular* (Dublin: UCD Press, 2010).

Laqueur, Walter, 'Fin-de-siècle: Once more with feeling', *Journal of Contemporary History*, 31:1 (Jan. 1996), pp. 5–47.

Lawlor, Damian, *Na Fianna Éireann and the Irish Revolution, 1909 to 1923* (Rhode, Co. Offaly: Caoillte Books, 2009).

Luddy, Maria and James M. Smith (eds), *Children, Childhood and Irish Society: 1500 to the Present* (Dublin: Four Courts Press, 2014).

Lynch, Robert, *The Northern IRA and the Early Years of Partition, 1920–1922* (Dublin: Irish Academic Press, 2006).

MacKenzie, John M., *Propaganda and Empire: The Manipulation of British Public Opinion, 1880–1960* (Manchester: Manchester University Press, 1984).

Mac Póilin, Aodán, 'Irish language writing in Belfast after 1900' in Nicholas Allen and Aaron Kelly (eds), *The Cities of Belfast* (Dublin: Four Courts Press, 2003), pp. 127–51.

Markey, Anne, 'Patrick Pearse: Literary pioneer and propagandist' in Eugene McNulty and Róisín Ní Ghairbhí (eds), *Patrick Pearse and the Theatre* (Dublin: Four Courts Press, 2017), pp. 37–49.

Marreco, Anne, *The Rebel Countess* (London: Weidenfeld and Nicolson, 1967).

Martin, Peter, *Censorship in the Two Irelands, 1922–1939* (Dublin: Irish Academic Press, 2006).

Matthews, Ann, *Renegades: Irish Republican Women, 1900–1922* (Cork: Mercier Press, 2010).

Matthews, Ann, *Dissidents: Irish Republican Women, 1923–1941* (Cork: Mercier Press, 2012).

Matthews, Ann, *The Irish Citizen Army* (Cork: Mercier Press, 2014).

McCarthy, Cal, *Cumann na mBan and the Irish Revolution* (Cork: The Collins Press, 2007).

McCoole, Sinéad, *No Ordinary Women: Irish Feminist Activists in the Revolutionary Years, 1900–1923* (Dublin: O'Brien Press, 2003).

McElligott, Richard, '"A youth tainted with the deadly poison of Anglicism"? Sport and childhood in the Irish independence period' in Ciara Boylan and Ciara Gallagher (eds), *Constructions of the Irish Child in the Independence Period* (Basingstoke: Palgrave Macmillan, 2018), pp. 279–305.

McGarry, Fearghal, *Rebels: Voices from the Easter Rising* (Dublin: Penguin Ireland, 2011).

McGuire, Charlie, 'Sean McLoughlin: The boy commandant of 1916', *History Ireland*, 14:2 (Mar.–Apr. 2006), pp. 26–30.
McGuire, Charlie, *Roddy Connolly and the Struggle for Socialism in Ireland* (Cork: Cork University Press, 2008).
McGuire, Charlie, *Sean McLoughlin: Ireland's Forgotten Revolutionary* (London: Merlin Press, 2011).
Morris, Brian, 'Ernest Thompson Seton and the origins of the Woodcraft movement', *Journal of Contemporary History*, 5:2 (Apr. 1970), pp. 183–94.
Morrison, Eve, 'The Fr Louis O'Kane interviews in context' in Dónal McAnallen (ed.), *Reflections on the Revolution in Ulster* (Armagh: Cardinal Tomás Ó Fiaich Library and Archive, 2016), pp. 29–39.
Mulvenna, Gareth, *Tartan Gangs and Paramilitaries: The Loyalist Backlash* (Liverpool: Liverpool University Press, 2016).
Naughton, Lindie, *Markievicz: A Most Outrageous Rebel* (Newbridge, Co. Kildare: Merrion Press, 2016).
Nic Congáil, Ríona, 'Young Ireland and *The Nation*: Nationalist children's culture in the late nineteenth century', *Éire-Ireland*, 46:3 & 4 (2011), pp. 37–62.
Nic Dháibhéid, Caoimhe, 'Schooling the national orphans: The education of the children of the Easter Rising leaders', *Journal of the History of Childhood and Youth*, 9:2 (2016), pp. 261–76.
Novick, Ben, *Conceiving Revolution: Irish Nationalist Propaganda during the First World War* (Dublin: Four Courts Press, 2001).
Ó Broin, León, *Protestant Nationalism in Revolutionary Ireland* (Dublin: Gill and Macmillan, 1985).
O'Callaghan, John, *Con Colbert* (Dublin: O'Brien Press, 2015).
Ó Catháin, Máirtín, *Irish Republicanism in Scotland, 1858–1916* (Dublin: Irish Academic Press, 2007).
Ó Catháin, Máirtín, 'A land beyond the sea: Irish and Scottish republicans in Dublin, 1916' in Ruán O'Donnell (ed.), *The Impact of the 1916 Rising: Among the Nations* (Dublin: Irish Academic Press, 2008), pp. 37–48.
O'Doherty, Michael Kevin, *My Parents and Other Rebels* (Dublin: Errigal Press, 1999).
O'Faolain, Sean, *Constance Markievicz* (2nd edn, London: Hutchinson, 1987).
O'Rahilly, Aodogán, *Winding the Clock: O'Rahilly and the 1916 Rising* (Dublin: Lilliput Press, 1991).
Parkinson, Alan F., *Belfast's Unholy War* (Dublin: Four Courts, 2004).
Pašeta, Senia, *Irish Nationalist Women, 1900–1918* (Cambridge: Cambridge University Press, 2013).
Power, Brendan, 'The functions of association football in the Boys' Brigade in Ireland, 1888–1914' in Leeann Lane and William Murphy (eds), *Leisure*

and the Irish in the Nineteenth Century (Liverpool: Liverpool University Press, 2016), pp. 41–58.

Power, Brendan, 'The Boy Scouts in Ireland: Urbanisation, health, education and adolescence, 1908–1914' in Ciara Boylan and Ciara Gallagher (eds), *Constructions of the Irish Child in the Independence Period* (Basingstoke: Palgrave Macmillan, 2018), pp. 257–77.

Power, Brendan, 'Religion and the Boys' Brigade, 1888–1914' in Mary Hatfield, Jutta Kruse and Ríona Nic Congáil (eds), *Historical Perspectives on Parenthood and Childhood in Ireland* (Dublin: Arlen House, 2018), pp. 151–75.

Regan, Nell, 'Helena Molony' in Mary Cullen and Maria Luddy (eds), *Female Activists: Irish Women and Change, 1900–1960* (Dublin: Woodfield Press, 2001), pp. 141–68.

Regan, Nell, *Helena Molony: A Radical Life, 1883–1967* (Dublin: Arlen House, 2017).

Rosenthal, Michael, 'Knights and retainers: The earliest version of Baden-Powell's Boy Scout scheme', *Journal of Contemporary History*, 15:4 (Oct. 1980), pp. 603–17.

Sisson, Elaine, *Pearse's Patriots: St Enda's and the Cult of Boyhood* (Cork: Cork University Press, 2005).

Springhall, John, *Youth, Empire and Society: British Youth Movements, 1883–1940* (London: Croom Helm, 1977).

Springhall, John, *Coming of Age: Adolescence in Britain, 1860–1960* (Dublin: Gill and Macmillan, 1986).

Springhall, John, 'Baden-Powell and the Scout Movement before 1920: Citizen training or soldiers of the future?', *English Historical Review*, 102:405 (Oct. 1987), pp. 934–42.

Summers, Anne, 'Scouts, guides and VADs: A note in reply to Allen Warren', *English Historical Review*, 102:405 (Oct. 1987), pp. 943–47.

Taillon, Ruth, *When History was Made: The Women of 1916* (Belfast: Beyond the Pale Publications, 1996).

Townshend, Charles, 'The Irish Republican Army and the development of guerrilla warfare, 1916–1921', *English Historical Review*, 94:371 (Apr. 1979), pp. 318–45.

Van Voris, Jacqueline, *Constance de Markievicz in the Cause of Ireland* (Amherst, MA: University of Massachusetts Press, 1967).

Voeltz, Richard A., '"…A good Jew and a good Englishman": The Jewish Lads' Brigade, 1894–1922', *Journal of Contemporary History*, 23:1 (Jan. 1988), pp. 119–27.

Voeltz, Richard A., 'The antidote to "Khaki Fever"?: The expansion of the British Girl Guides during the First World War', *Journal of Contemporary History*, 27:4 (Oct. 1992), pp. 627–38.

Walsh, Brendan, *The Pedagogy of Protest: The Educational Thought and Work of Patrick H. Pearse* (Bern: Peter Lang, 2007).

Walsh-McLean, Jason, 'A headstone for Patsy O'Connor: Fianna scout and forgotten Lockout martyr', *Saothar* 41 (2016), pp. 294–7.

Ward, Margaret, *Unmanageable Revolutionaries: Women and Irish Nationalism* (London: Pluto Press, 1995).

Ward, Margaret, 'Fianna Éireann' in Brian Lalor (ed.), *The Encyclopedia of Ireland* (Dublin: Gill and Macmillan, 2003), p. 386.

Warren, Allen, 'Sir Robert Baden-Powell, the Scout movement and citizen training in Great Britain, 1900–1920', *English Historical Review*, 101:399 (Apr. 1986), pp. 376–98.

Warren, Allen, 'Baden-Powell: A final comment', *English Historical Review*, 102:405 (Oct. 1987), pp. 948–50.

Wilkinson, Paul, 'English youth movements, 1908–30', *Journal of Contemporary History*, 4:2 (Apr. 1969), pp. 3–23.

Theses

Hay, Marnie, 'Bulmer Hobson: The rise and fall of an Irish nationalist, 1900–16' (PhD thesis, University College Dublin, 2004).

Power, Brendan, 'Youth movements and Ireland, 1888–1914' (PhD thesis, Trinity College Dublin, 2013).

Watts, John R., 'Na Fianna Éireann: A case study of a political youth organisation' (PhD thesis, University of Glasgow, 1981).

Reference books

Cannon, John (ed.), *The Oxford Companion to British History* (Oxford: Oxford University Press, 1997).

Connolly, S. J. (ed.), *The Oxford Companion to Irish History* (Oxford: Oxford University Press, 1999).

McGuire, James and James Quinn (eds), *Dictionary of Irish Biography* (Cambridge: Cambridge University Press, 2009); also available at http://dib.cambridge.org.

Welch, Robert (ed.), *The Concise Oxford Companion to Irish Literature* (Oxford: Oxford University Press, 2000).

Web sources

1901 and 1911 Irish censuses, available at www.census.nationalarchives.ie.

Hay, Marnie, 'Children and the Irish cultural revival', podcast and script for UCD Scholarcast Series 12, Modalities of Revival, 24 Feb. 2015, available at www.ucd.ie/scholarcast/scholarcast46.html.

Irish Girl Guides, 'History of the Irish Girl Guides', 2009, available at www.irishgirlguides.ie/index.php/history-of-irish-girl-guides (accessed 14 May 2014).

McFarlan, Donald M., *First for Boys: The Story of the Boys' Brigade, 1883–1983*, available at www.boys-brigade.org.uk/first-for-boys.htm (accessed 15 May 2014).

Murphy, Eamon, *The History of Na Fianna Éireann, 1909–1923*, available at https://fiannaeireannhistory.wordpress.com.

Ó Ruaic, Pádraig Óg, 'A short history of the Hibernian Rifless, 1912–1916', 31 Mar. 2013, available at www.theirishstory.com/2013/03/31/a-short-history-of-the-hibernian-rifles-1912–1916/#.UjHVCNKOSuI (accessed 14 Aug. 2013).

Index

active service units (ASU) 77, 80, 194, 200, 213
age 107, 111–12, 193
Ancient Order of Hibernians (AOH) 7, 42–3, 51
   Ladies' Auxiliary 7–8
Anglo-Irish Treaty (1921) 8, 12, 86–8, 104–5, 117, 186, 188, 212
   impact of Treaty split on Fianna 88–9, 228
Anglo-Irish War (1919–21) *see* Irish War of Independence
ard-choisde (Central Council) 31, 39, 43, 45–6, 49, 54, 67, 112, 166
ard-fheis (annual congress) 39, 46–7, 130, 152
   (1910) 39
   (1911) 41
   (1912) 45, 112
   (1913) 36, 46–7, 226
   (1914) 50
   (1915) 53–4
   (1917) 72
   (1919) 78, 81, 171
   (1920) 81, 83, 171
   (1922) 88–90
arms 73, 83–4, 187, 194–5, 196–200, 207, 211, 227
   raids for 76, 83, 85, 144, 198, 211
Army Pensions Act (APA) 104, 211, 216
   dependants' allowances and gratuities 58, 121, 216
arrests 70, 72–3, 82, 89, 192–3, 203, 209, 226, 228
Auxiliaries 187–8, 204

Baden-Powell, Robert 4–6, 10, 20, 162, 176, 224, 226
   Scouting for Boys (1908) 167, 176–7
Balfe, Richard (Dick) 120, 125–6
bands *see* music
Barr, Thomas 52, 66, 179
Barrett, William 127, 209, 221
battalions 78–9, 84
   Belfast 72, 79, 81, 86–7, 92
   Cork 72, 80, 87, 92, 96
   Dublin 49, 51, 53, 57, 66, 72–3, 89, 92–3, 97
Bean na hÉireann (Woman of Ireland) 29, 38, 164–5
Behan, Christina (Chrissie) 12, 18
Belcamp Park 30–1, 35, 137, 162
Belfast Boycott 80, 208
Betsy Gray *sluagh* (girls' troop; Belfast) 40, 45–6, 48–9, 64, 112–13, 153, 191
Bevan, Seamus 44, 109
bicycles 46, 204, 208
Black and Tans 163, 187–8, 193, 204–5, 207, 211
Boys' Brigade 4, 6, 8–11, 24, 138, 148, 153
Boy Scouts (Baden-Powell) 2, 4, 6, 9, 10–11, 20, 24, 26, 52, 90–1, 109, 138, 143–4, 153, 166, 174, 224
Boy Scouts of America 5
Brady, Liam A. 74, 79
Brady, Sean 123, 126, 128–9
Brennan, Michael 118, 120, 122, 125–6, 128
brigades 78–9, 84
   Belfast 79, 85, 89
   Cork 66, 79, 80
   Dublin 73, 76–7, 84, 87, 89
Briscoe, Robert 109, 118, 126, 128–9
Britain 4, 6, 8, 56, 77, 87, 187
British army 4, 6, 11, 29, 45, 51–2, 108, 143, 153, 162–3
British Empire 5–6, 10–11, 37
British government forces 82–3, 86, 187
   see also Auxiliaries; Black and Tans; British army
Bulfin, Eamonn 42, 60, 114

268 Index

Bureau of Military History (BMH) 3, 14, 44, 102–3, 115–16
Busby, James A. 76, 126, 211
Bushell, Ellen (Nellie) 105

Cadet Corps 142, 191
Caffrey, John A. 115, 125–6
Callender, Brian 149, 158–9
camping 7–8, 25–6, 30, 42, 74, 79, 131, 133, 135, 137–8, 165, 196, 224
Carbery, Ethna (pseudonym of Anna Johnston) 21, 40, 151
Carey, Jack 80, 145
Carpenter, Walter 49
Carrigan, James 115, 126
Casement, Roger 43, 161, 163, 167, 170, 176
Catholic Boys' Brigade 4, 6, 16, 22
Catholic Boy Scouts of Ireland 2
céilís 51, 75, 149, 202
censorship 164
Central Council *see ard-choisde*
Chadwick, Mary *see* Kelly, May
Chéad Sluagh, An (The First Troop) 27, 29, 38, 64, 138, 165
child soldiers 188–9
chivalry 161, 176
Christian, William (Billy) 126, 149–50, 159
Christian Brothers
  Our Boys 177–8
  schools 101–2, 110, 123
Church Lads' Brigade 4, 8, 10
Citizen Army Boy Scouts and Girl Guides 76
civil unrest 80
Clann na Gael Girl Scouts (formerly Irish National Girl Scouts) 7–9, 12, 16–17, 44, 75, 113, 116, 202
Clann na Poblachta 118
Clarke, Tom 24, 50, 56
Colbert, Cornelius (Con) 3, 20, 28–9, 47–9, 50, 58, 67, 74, 105, 110, 113, 122–3, 126, 133, 152, 158, 175, 186–7, 190–1, 227
Cole, Sean 127, 213–14, 221
Colley, Alfred (Alf) 97, 213–14, 223
companies *see sluaighte* (troops)/companies
concerts 7, 148–9
Connolly, James 11, 40, 49, 57, 74, 93, 107, 109, 161, 168
Connolly, Joe 49, 106, 115, 192
Connolly, Roddy 11, 40, 49, 93, 109, 118, 120, 122–3, 126, 128
Connolly Heron, Ina 40, 45–6, 48–9, 51, 70, 103, 105, 110, 116, 120, 122, 124, 196

Connolly O'Brien, Nora 40, 46, 49, 105, 110, 116, 118–19, 120, 122, 128, 134, 191, 196
conscription 69, 76–7, 94
Considine, Martin 127, 210, 221
Constitution of Na Fianna Éireann 45, 90
couriers 12, 56, 197–8, 202, 209
Courtney, Seamus 66, 149, 211, 221
courts martial 52, 59, 74
Crimmins, Thomas (Tommy) 121, 140, 149, 159
Cumann na Cailíní (Dungannon Clubs) 40, 61
Cumann na gCailíní (Irish National Girl Scouts) 61, 113
Cumann na mBan 48–9, 55, 61, 74–5, 87, 102, 104–5, 112–13, 116–17, 187, 190–1, 195–6, 202–4, 215–16
Cumann na nGaedheal 104
Curaigh Gaeilge, Na (The Gaelic Warriors) 44
  see also Irish National Guards

Dáil Éireann 78, 80–1, 88, 118
  Dáil Courier Service 78
  Department/Ministry of Defence 83–4, 115, 200
Dalton, Charles 214
Daly, John 42
dancing 75, 101, 174
Darcy, Charles 11
Dargan, Thomas 192, 198, 203–4, 208–9
Davern, Willie 140–1
De Valera, Eamon 72, 93
Derrig, Thomas 118, 123, 126, 128–9
Dictionary of Irish Biography (DIB) 102–3, 107, 120
dispatch carrying 52, 56, 84–5, 105, 195, 202–4, 209
District Councils 39, 45
  Belfast 40, 74, 79–80, 93–4
  Dublin 53
Donelan, Brendan 68
Donnelly, Stephen 117, 120, 126, 129
Dowd, Dan 118, 128
Doyle, Michael 127, 221
drowning 134, 139–41
Dublin Guards *see* Irish National Guards
Dublin Lockout (1913) 1, 8, 49, 55, 67, 115, 139, 167
Dublin Metropolitan Police (DMP) 71, 76, 107, 161
Dungannon Clubs 38, 40, 162
Dunleavy, Patrick 125–6
Dunne, Andy 47, 49, 70, 115, 152, 158–9, 192

Index

Easter Rising (1916) 1, 3, 11–12, 20, 44, 55–7, 59, 69, 71, 77, 186–7, 192–4, 201–5, 208, 215, 224, 227
   Boland's Mill 111
   Co. Galway 59, 203, 215
   Enniscorthy, Co. Wexford 59, 215
   Fianna deaths 68, 115, 175, 202, 213
   Four Courts 57, 59
   General Post Office (GPO) 103
   impact on Fianna 70
   Jacob's Biscuit Factory 59, 152, 201–3, 207
   Magazine Fort 57, 59, 111, 201
   Marrowbone Lane Distillery 58
   Mendicity Institute 57
   Royal College of Surgeons 58, 202
   St Stephen's Green 49, 57–8, 115, 192
equipment 81

Fagan, Margaret (Maggie) 12, 19, 116
Fenians *see* Irish Republican Brotherhood (IRB)
Fianna (mythical band of warriors) 20, 22, 173
Fianna (paper) 50, 90, 145, 164, 169–75, 177–9
Fianna Chief (*Ard fhéinne*) 54–5, 72, 90
Fianna Code of Honour 168, 171, 183
Fianna deaths 68, 83, 115, 139, 167, 175, 179, 209–14
Fianna declaration 81, 90
Fianna Éireann, Na (youth group established in Belfast in 1902) 20–3, 103
Fianna Fáil 102, 104, 118
Fianna Handbook
   1914 edition 49, 77, 133–4, 164, 166–7, 170, 172–7
   1924 edition 172, 186
Fianna president 54–5
Fianna Roll of Honour 139, 167, 175, 220–1, 221
Fine Gael 102
first aid 7–8, 29, 42, 67, 75, 77, 79, 112, 131, 134, 155, 190, 195
First World War 4–5, 9, 11, 50–2, 77, 108, 143–4, 185, 225
Fitzgerald, Theobald (Theo) 70, 91, 93, 103, 120, 126, 158
Foley, Daniel D. 127, 210, 221
Fox, James 3, 57, 68
Fulham, James 116, 126, 135
funding 43, 82, 90
fundraising 43, 74–5, 77, 90, 148

Gaelic Athletic Association (GAA) 21–2, 101
Gaelic League 21–2, 26, 29, 41–2, 101–2, 104, 106, 110, 131, 147, 173

Garda Síochána, An 116–18, 129
gender controversy 27, 45–6, 75, 112–13, 167, 171–2
General Election (1918) 77
Gilmore, George 109, 126, 128
Girl Guides 5–6, 40, 61, 141, 143–4
Gore-Booth, Constance *see* Markievicz, Countess Constance
Great War *see* First World War
Griffith, Arthur 6, 22–4, 29
Groome, Joe 122–3, 126, 128–9
guerrilla warfare 56, 78, 187

halls
   Camden Street (Dublin) 20, 26, 29, 32, 70, 107, 133
   Limerick 41
   Willowbank (Belfast) 23, 38
Hanley, Patrick 127, 212, 221
Hanlon, Patrick J. 127, 221
Hannafin, Dorothy 105
Hannafin, Patrick (Percy) 127, 211, 221
Hannigan, Donald *see* O'Hannigan, Donnchadh
Harding, Robert (Bob) 27–8, 34
Harling, Sean 78, 97, 125
Hayes, Stephen 123, 126, 128
Headquarters (Dublin) 49, 74–5, 79, 82–4, 87, 113, 170, 200
   staff 54–5, 57, 67, 72, 78, 89, 92–3, 97
Healy, Sean (John; Dublin) 3, 68, 127, 202, 221
Healy, Sean (Cork) 53, 66, 126, 138, 149
Hearne, Patrick 52, 69–70, 75, 82, 85, 94, 109, 116, 182, 199, 207
Heron, Archie 109, 114, 120, 125–6, 128
Heuston, Sean 3, 45, 49, 57–8, 67, 114, 123, 126, 152, 175, 179, 186–7, 190, 227
Hibernian Boys' Brigade 7, 16, 43, 109
Hibernian Rifles 7, 187
Hobson, Bulmer 1, 3, 6–7, 10, 21, 23, 26–8, 30–2, 35–6, 39, 41, 43, 45–6, 48, 50, 54–6, 64, 67, 70–1, 112–13, 118, 137, 151–2, 162, 164, 166, 168, 170, 182, 189–90, 196, 224–7
Hogan, Austin 108, 123, 128
Holland, Robert 91–2, 125–6
Holland, Walter Leo 119
Holohan, Garry (Géaroid Ua h-Uallacháin) 45, 47, 50, 59, 67, 69, 72–3, 84, 89, 93, 97, 99, 106, 114, 120, 125–6, 128, 144–5, 151–3, 196, 201
Holohan, Patrick (Paddy) 47, 59, 114, 120, 126, 128–9, 153

home rule 8, 48, 77, 81, 108, 122
Houlihan, Brendan 214
Howard, Sean 63, 68
Howth gunrunning 168, 187, 196
Hughes, Arthur 127, 210, 221
Hughes, Edwin (Eamonn) 214
hunger strikes 2, 12, 18, 210–11
Hurley, George 77, 80, 205, 208
Hurson, Joseph A. 127, 212, 221
Hyde, Douglas 167, 173

inaugural meeting (16 August 1909) 20, 26–7
Inghinidhe na hÉireann (Daughters of Erin) 24, 29–30, 35, 162, 164
intelligence gathering 84, 105, 204–7, 209, 211
Irish Citizen Army (ICA) 8, 49, 102, 105, 115–16, 150, 187, 190, 192, 197, 215–16, 226
   Girls' Ambulance Corps 49
   Scout Corps 8–9, 11–12, 49, 109
Irish Civil War (1922–23) 1, 8, 12, 18, 86–8, 104, 106, 116–17, 179, 186–9, 195, 209–10, 213–15, 227–8
   impact on the Fianna 89–90, 145, 172, 228
Irish Defence Forces 89, 101, 116–18, 129, 135
Irish Freedom 30, 35, 43, 101, 164, 166, 173, 178–9, 190
Irish Free State 1, 12, 88, 90, 117, 175, 188
Irish history 23, 29, 78, 90, 146–7, 172–3
Irish language 6–7, 22–3, 29, 77–8, 90, 145–7, 151, 173
Irish National Girl Scouts *see* Clann na Gael Girl Scouts; Cumann na gCailíní
Irish National Guards 44, 63, 75, 109, 111, 114, 116, 136
Irish Parliamentary Party 48, 50–2, 77, 95, 108
Irish Republican Army (IRA) 12, 48, 80, 86, 88, 90, 97, 101–2, 105, 109, 118, 142, 144, 163, 179, 186–9, 192–6, 199–200, 203–8, 211, 215–16, 227–8
   anti-Treaty IRA 188, 209, 212, 214
   Fianna transfers to the IRA 84–5, 115–17, 126–7, 192
   Provisional IRA 91
   relationship with the Fianna 83–5
Irish Republican Brotherhood (IRB) 21, 24, 30, 32, 44, 46, 48, 50, 54–6, 71, 101, 102, 105, 108, 113–14, 125, 152, 164, 166, 187, 190–1, 197, 226
   Fenians 108, 173
   Fianna circle of 45, 47, 54, 78, 113–14, 190

Irish Volunteer 35, 164, 166, 173, 177–9
Irish Volunteers 2, 41, 48–50, 53, 55–8, 64, 71, 75–6, 79, 82–5, 87, 101–2, 105, 107–8, 112, 114–16, 119, 126, 141–2, 144, 150, 186–7, 189–92, 196, 200–1, 215–16, 226, 228
   split in 50–1
Irish War of Independence (1919–21) 1–2, 12, 76, 78, 80–1, 83, 88, 115, 131–2, 144, 163, 171, 179, 186–9, 193, 195–6, 198, 203–5, 207–9, 211–12, 215, 226–8
   impact on Fianna 81–2, 145

Jacob, Rosamond 11, 75, 136
Jewish Lads' Brigade 4, 10, 150–1
John Mitchel Literary and Debating Society 45, 113–14, 152
   see also Irish Republican Brotherhood (IRB), Fianna circle of
Johnston, Anna *see* Carbery, Ethna

Kavanagh, Seamus 110, 136, 168, 182
Kavanagh, Sean 29, 133
Keenan, Tommy 202
Kelly, Elizabeth 7, 16
Kelly, James 3, 57, 68, 213
Kelly, May (Mary Chadwick) 7, 12, 16, 19, 44, 116
Kennedy, Sean 44, 63, 109, 126, 135
Kenny, John 44, 63, 75
Keogh, Gerald 68
Kettrick, Thomas 125–6
Kilcoole gunrunning 187, 196

Labour Party 117–18
Landers, Gerald 127, 210, 222
Landers, John Joe 'Purty' 118, 123, 126, 128
Langley, Liam 52, 78, 84, 89, 93, 108, 110–11, 122, 145, 183
Lawlor, John 127, 221
Lonergan, Michael 20, 29, 39, 45, 47–8, 114, 126, 133, 152, 190–1
Lynskey, William 111

MacBride, Sean 110, 122, 126, 128
McCabe, William (Liam) 115, 126, 182
Mac Caisin, Seamus (James Cashen) 28–9, 106, 158
McCann, John 118, 123, 128–9
McCarthy, William J. 126
McCorley, Roger 126
MacCurtain, Tomás 41, 150

MacDermott, Sean 50, 56, 74
Mac Eochaidh, Micheál S. (Michael S. Kehoe) 127, 215
McEvoy, Christopher 127, 221
McGarry, Sean 24, 28, 31
MacGonigal, Maurice 118, 123, 126
McGowan, Seamus 7–8, 49
McGuinness, David 38, 40, 48, 52, 125, 126
McHugh, Patrick 111, 114, 126
McKelvey, Joseph (Joe) 79, 92, 126, 128
McLoughlin, Mary 8, 12, 17, 202
McLoughlin, Sean 71–2, 115, 120–3, 125–6, 128
McMahon, Frank 66, 79–80, 92–3, 144–5
MacNeill, Aodh *see* McNeill, Hugo
MacNeill, Brian 103, 108, 120, 126, 128
McNeill, Derry 93
MacNeill, Eoin 57, 59, 105, 107–8, 120
McNeill, Hugo (Aodh) 70, 76, 78–9, 89, 91, 93, 108, 118, 120, 123, 126, 128–9
MacNeill, Niall 59, 67, 72, 92, 105, 108, 126
Madame's boys *see* Surrey House clique
Markievicz, Count Casimir 21, 31
Markievicz, Countess Constance 1, 6–8, 10–11, 17, 20–1, 23–8, 30–2, 39–41, 45–8, 54–5, 58–9, 67, 70, 78, 82, 88, 90, 93, 95, 97, 106, 110, 136–7, 146–8, 152–3, 158, 161–4, 167–8, 171, 174–5, 186, 189–90, 192, 196–7, 224–8
Martin, Eamon 7, 26–7, 29, 45–8, 50, 53, 55–6, 59, 67, 70–2, 81, 83, 89, 93, 97, 106, 110, 114, 117, 120–1, 123, 125–7, 128, 152, 190–2
Meaney, Charles 96, 193–4, 198–9, 203, 205, 207–8, 227
medals 58–9, 214, 216, 228
Mellows, Herbert (Barney) 59, 67, 71, 82, 84–9, 92–3, 97, 106–8, 114, 152, 166, 171, 201, 204
Mellows, Liam 11, 37, 42, 45–6, 48–9, 59, 106–8, 114, 126, 128, 136, 139, 152–3, 164, 171, 175, 191–2
membership figures 73–4, 81, 86, 87, 89, 93–4, 98
military recruitment 51, 77, 162
  campaign against 132, 148, 153, 162–3
military service pensions 58, 104, 116, 118, 195, 214–16, 228
Military Service Pensions Acts (MSPA) 104–5, 195, 215–16
Military Service Pensions Collection (MSPC) 59, 68, 86, 102, 104–5, 210–11, 214–16

military training 7, 10, 48, 79, 84, 90, 132–46, 192, 224, 227
  drill 8, 24, 29, 40, 45, 48, 75–6, 79, 131, 173, 190
  training camps 87, 99, 144–5, 195
  use of weapons 8, 42, 77, 79, 131–2, 135, 176, 190, 192
Molony, Helena 24–9, 30–1, 36, 54, 137, 158, 162–4
Mooney, James 209, 221
moral code 78
  see also Fianna Code of Honour
Moriarty, Thomas 211, 221
Morse code 84, 116
Mount St Benedict 110
Moynihan, Christy 52, 65–6, 179
Moynihan, Michael 210, 221
Mulkerrins, Michael 68, 203, 215
Mullins, Thomas 123, 126, 128
Munster Conventions 41, 53, 89
Murphy, John C. 115, 126
Murphy, Kevin 115, 126
Murphy, P. J. 101–2, 126, 193
Murray, Edward (Eddie, Eamon) 47, 129, 140, 150, 152, 159
Murray, John 80, 221
Murray, Joseph 126
music 39, 118, 137, 148–51, 168, 174
  bands 38, 149–51, 159
Myles, William (Billy) 198

National Army 88–9, 104–5, 116–19, 188–9, 209–10, 213–16
National Guards *see* Irish National Guards
National Volunteers 51
Nelson, John 73, 197
Ní Baoghaoil, Eithne *see* O'Boyle, Annie
Nodlaig na bhFiann (The Fianna Christmas) 49, 164, 167–9, 173, 175
Nohilly, Thomas 125–6
Nolan, Frank 80, 96
Nolan, James 101–2, 125–6, 150, 166, 181
Nolan, J. E. 77
Northern Ireland 1–2, 81, 90, 212

O'Boyle, Annie (Eithne Ní Baoghaoil) 40
O'Brien, Tommy 123, 126, 129
O'Brien, William (Liam) 126, 161–2
O'Callaghan, Liam 53, 109, 126, 138, 149
O'Carroll, Michael 73, 197
O'Connell, J. J. ('Ginger') 142, 157, 191
O'Connor, Henry 211, 221

O'Connor, Patrick (Patsy) 47, 49, 67, 110, 139, 152, 167, 169, 171, 182
O'Connor, Peter 122–3, 126, 128
O'Connor, Thomas 197, 203, 205–6
O'Daly (Daly), Patrick (Pádraig, Paddy) 59, 67, 107, 110, 112, 120, 125–6, 128–9, 201
O'Doherty, Michael Kevin 104, 122–3
O'Donoghue, Thomas 32, 44, 49, 63, 108–9, 114–16, 126, 135–6, 150, 159, 192
O'Driscoll, Daniel 211, 221
O'Flynn, William 186–7, 194, 205
O'Hannigan, Dónal 35, 125–6, 162
O'Hannigan, Donnchadh 30, 35, 162
O'Leary, Michael 73, 80, 126
O'Neill, Sean 125–6
O'Neill, William 24, 106
O'Rahilly, Aodogán 108–10, 126, 128
O'Regan, Martin 44
organisational structure *see* ard-choisde (Central Council); *ard-fheis* (annual congress); battalions; brigades; District Councils; Headquarters; *sluaighte* (troops)/companies
Ó Riain, Pádraic (Pádraig, Patrick Ryan, James 'Jimmy' Toal) 26–8, 34, 39, 41–2, 45, 47–8, 50–2, 55, 71–2, 92, 113–14, 125–6, 133–4, 136, 142–3, 151–2, 164, 166, 168–9, 177, 190–2
Ormond, James 126
Ormonde, John 118, 123, 128–9
O'Shannon, Cathal 126, 128–9
O'Shea, Joseph 126, 138, 150

parades 7–8, 76
partition 81
Pearse, Patrick 2, 39, 56, 74, 110, 167, 169–70, 175, 190–1
Pelican, Thomas 110, 126, 206
Plant, George 109, 118, 126, 128
Plant, James 109, 120, 126, 128
Plunkett, George 90
Plunkett, Joseph Mary 90
poetry 21, 151, 168, 171
postal service 144
Pounch, Seamus (J. J. Puinse) 47, 59, 70, 91, 152, 191, 201–2, 207, 219, 223
Prendergast, Sean 126, 130, 137, 144, 151–3, 166, 181
print propaganda 50, 77, 105, 161, 163–79, 214, 224–5
prison 12, 59, 70, 72, 82, 144, 193, 209–11, 213, 226

raids 207–8, 211–12
see also arms, raids for
Rea, Leo 127, 212, 221
Reader, Seamus 109, 120, 125–6
rebellion (1798) 29, 146–7, 169
Red Branch Knights 24, 28
Redmond, John 50–1, 108
Reed, Joseph Walton 211, 221
Reid, Joseph (Joe) 211, 221
Reidy, Amos 126
religion 9–11, 24, 91, 102, 107, 109–10, 141, 151, 168, 178
    Roman Catholic clergy 42, 111
Reynolds, Frank 151
Reynolds, John Richard 64, 112
Reynolds, Joseph (Joe) 70, 72–3, 77, 81, 89, 97, 120, 125, 204–5
Reynolds, Molly 46, 112
Reynolds, Percy (Augustus Percival) 49, 67, 12, 123, 129, 136, 152, 158–9, 167–71, 182–3
riots 43
Robinson, Joseph 28, 33, 36, 38, 60, 73, 103, 108, 121–3, 126, 128, 197
Robinson, Seamus 23, 33, 103, 108, 120, 122–3, 125–6, 128
Roche, Moses 75, 109, 126
Rogers, Joseph 214
route marches 7, 29, 136–7
Rowan, James 110–11
Rowe (Roe), William (Willie) 97, 117, 129
Royal Irish Constabulary (RIC) 23, 41, 73–4, 108, 110, 153, 162, 187–8, 192, 199, 205–6, 211–12
Ryan, Desmond 42, 45, 60, 123, 126, 128, 129, 152
Ryan, Frederick (Fred) 68, 115, 192
Ryan, Michael F. 52, 108–9, 126
Ryan, Patrick *see* Ó Riain, Pádraic
Ryan, W. P. 107
Ryle, Michael J. 209, 221

St Andrew's National School 24, 106
St Enda's School 39, 42, 60, 72, 110, 137, 141
Saunders, Sean 78, 89, 125
scouting *see* intelligence gathering
scouting skills 24, 29, 79, 90, 131–46, 165, 173, 224
Seton, Ernest Thompson 5
Shallow, John (Jack) 47, 152, 158, 168, 182
Sheehan, Eugene 126, 128
Sheehan, Thomas 209
Sheehy, John Joe 118, 123, 126, 128

signalling 24, 29, 42, 52, 77, 79, 84, 116, 131, 190, 196
Sinn Féin (ourselves) 6, 21, 23–4, 29, 51, 74, 77, 88, 101, 108, 144, 150, 161–2, 174, 188, 228
Slattery, Thomas 211, 221
sluaighte (troops)/companies (by location)
  Co. Antrim 86, 98
    Belfast 38–9, 41, 43, 46, 48–9, 51–2, 64, 70, 74, 81, 85, 148, 212
  Co. Armagh 41, 62, 74, 81, 86, 98
  Co. Carlow 98, 209, 220
  Co. Cavan 98
  Co. Clare 81, 86–7, 98
  Co. Cork 49, 62, 81, 86, 93, 98, 115, 131
    Cork City 39, 41, 43, 51–3, 64, 66, 73, 76–7, 85, 96, 101, 109, 194, 198, 227
  Co. Derry (Derry) 41, 43, 64, 70, 74, 79, 81, 98
  Co. Donegal 79, 98
  Co. Down 86, 93, 98
    Newry 41, 43, 70, 74, 86
  Co. Dublin 41, 49, 62, 64, 86, 98
    Dublin City 38, 45, 49, 72, 77, 81, 85, 91, 138, 148, 165, 227
  Co. Galway 62, 93, 98
    Tuam 46, 52, 62, 112, 148
  Co. Kerry 70, 73, 81, 86, 98
    Ballybunion 49, 109, 115
    Listowel 42–3, 62, 64, 73, 206
    Tralee 62, 73, 105, 114, 205
  Co. Kildare 49, 98
  Co. Kilkenny (Kilkenny) 51, 62, 98
  Co. Laois/Queen's Co. (Portlaoise/Maryboro) 41–2, 62, 93
  Co. Leitrim 98
  Co. Limerick 41, 43, 62, 98
    Limerick City 41, 49, 51, 62, 64, 86, 98, 198, 203
  Co. Louth 86, 98
    Drogheda 86, 98
    Dundalk 43, 83, 85–6, 98, 113
  Co. Mayo 62, 86, 93, 98
  Co. Meath 98
  Co. Monaghan 98
  Co. Offaly/King's Co. 98
    Tullamore 46, 62
  Co. Roscommon 98
  Co. Sligo 86, 98
  Co. Tipperary 49, 81, 98
    Carrick-on-Suir 49, 73
    Clonmel 39, 43, 62
    Fethard 109, 186, 194, 203, 205
    Tipperary Town 49, 62
  Co. Tyrone 98
  Co. Waterford 73, 86, 93, 98
    girls' troop 40, 74, 75, 113
    Waterford City 38, 43, 51–2, 60, 62, 70, 75, 81–2, 85, 101, 116, 150, 199–200, 204
  Co. Westmeath 41, 62, 64, 98
  Co. Wexford 43, 46, 49, 62, 81, 86, 93, 98, 148
    Enniscorthy 41, 62, 64
  Co. Wicklow 98
  Glasgow, Scotland 38, 43, 60, 73, 109, 191
  Liverpool, England 46
Smith, William Alexander 4, 9
social class 107
sport 7, 90, 146, 148, 150–1
  boxing 42, 74
  fencing 112, 136
  football 7, 148
  Gaelic football 23, 38, 118
  Gaelic games 39, 90, 101, 145
  hurling 6, 20–3, 110, 147–8, 151, 158, 174
Staines, Liam 70, 91
Stephenson, Patrick Joseph (P. J.) 72–3, 120–1, 123, 126, 128
Surrey House clique 47, 152

theatre productions 21, 23, 39, 148
Toal, William 212, 221
troops *see sluaighte* (troops)/companies
Truce (11 July 1921) 84, 86–7
Tubridy, Patrick 209, 221

Ulster Volunteer Force (UVF) 2, 9, 48, 190
uniforms 28, 40, 44, 53, 76, 109, 111, 133, 213
unionism 8

Voluntary Aid Detachments (VADs) 143

Walpole, Robert Henry (Harry) 47, 103, 120, 126, 129, 140, 152, 158, 168, 182
Walsh, John 120, 122
Walton, Martin 118, 126, 128, 129
Wandervögel 133, 138, 143
Ward, Patrick (Paddy) 26–7, 48, 110, 114, 125–6, 152, 196
White, Alfred (Alf) 72, 97, 107
Woodcraft movement 5
Woods, William 38

Young Citizen Volunteers (YCV) 8–9

EU authorised representative for GPSR:
Easy Access System Europe, Mustamäe tee 50,
10621 Tallinn, Estonia
gpsr.requests@easproject.com

www.ingramcontent.com/pod-product-compliance
Lightning Source LLC
Chambersburg PA
CBHW070235240426
43673CB00044B/1806